The World Heritage of Gardens

Dušan Ogrin

589 illustrations, 386 in color

Thames and Hudson

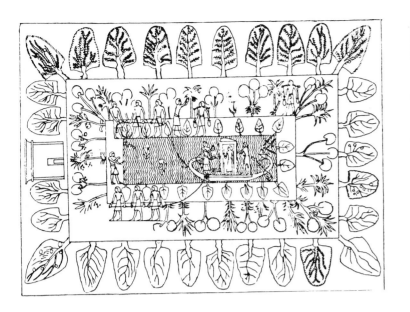

Translated from the Slovenian by Margaret Davies, Maja Bilbija and Milan Mlačnik

First published in Great Britain in 1993
by Thames and Hudson Ltd, London

First published in the United States of America in 1993 by Thames and Hudson Inc.,
500 Fifth Avenue, New York, New York 10110

Original title: Svetovna dediščina vrtne umetnosti
Book produced by EWO Ltd., Ljubljana
Project manager: Barbara Habič Pregl
Production coordinator: Matjaž Zaletel
Copyright © 1993 EWO Ltd., Ljubljana
© text and photos: Dušan Ogrin

British Library Cataloguing-in-Publication Data

A catalogue record for this book is available from the British Library
ISBN 0-500-23666-6
Library of Congress Catalog Card Number: 93-60427

Printed and bound in Slovenia by Gorenjski tisk

Contents

Preface

Both the cultural heritage and the natural environment are attracting increased attention in contemporary society. It is understandable that, within this great complex, a special place should be granted to garden art, as the field of human creativity where cultural efforts are realized within nature or by natural means.

This book has arisen from the desire to present, as far as possible, a comprehensive survey of landscape-architectural heritage as preserved in our own days. It is in no way conceived as a history of garden art. However, since every heritage has to be seen in its historical context, the author thought it fitting to outline the circumstances within which garden art arose in the various regions of the world and in the various periods of historical development.

The material for this book has been gathered over a long period of more than thirty years. At first it was to serve the purpose of research into the theory of landscape design. Gradually it grew into an extensive survey of the garden heritage of the world, so that it seemed appropriate to publish it as a copiously illustrated edition.

The book is, above all, designed to provide as clear a survey of the heritage of garden art as possible. It is divided into self-contained chapters that discuss the various countries, geographical regions, or cultural areas. The introductory part of each chapter outlines general characteristics of garden art and its development; this is followed by a description of selected examples of the heritage of the country in question. The textual part is complemented as fully as possible by - predominantly historical - illustrations and ground-plans showing the gardens either at the time of their origin or later. A second, equally important part of each chapter consists of pictures, presenting the heritage as it has existed during the last three decades. For greater compactness and easier survey, the picture section has been combined into a single unit. The captions do not appear on the plates, so they cannot disturb the visual experience. The reader will find them all gathered in the same place, at the end of the text section, i.e. at the beginning of the plates.

The pictures were specially prepared for this edition, on the basis of the author's visits to and study of the gardens described. Inevitably, the selection of the material for the various chapters is personal, and perhaps to some extent partial. There may be objections to the share accorded to the various national heritages. After all, every author has to make a decision based on his own criteria and knowledge, and to rely on his own judgement. So the legacy of some countries has perhaps been given more coverage than usual and the book also presents numerous objects that have so far been unjustly neglected or wholly ignored.

According to the Commission for Historical Gardens of the International Federation of Landscape Architects, some 2000 gardens that may be counted among the cultural and historical heritage survive. From this treasure, some 250 items have been selected and are presented in this book.

The last chapter gives a short survey of the 20th century. Usually books dealing with the heritage avoid this topic. In spite of the limited space, the author thought it advisable to present at least a short summary of the landscape-architectural endeavours of our time, and to point out some of the more recent phenomena and trends.

In spite of the pains taken by the author, imprecisions and other defects have no doubt crept in, for which the author assumes full responsibility. He is grateful in advance for all observations, corrections and suggestions, and will gladly include them in any future edition.

The vast quantity of material included in this book could never have been collected and processed without the help and understanding of a great number of people, whom I wish to thank here. First of all my family, who patiently bore with my frequent absences, Marian and Alenka also for their help with the manuscript, and especially Maja, who partly translated and did a large part of the editing of the manuscript. Further thanks go to my colleagues at the Department of Landscape Architecture at the University of Ljubljana, who were helpful in many ways, and especially to Mojca Kopač, who made a number of drawings for the book.
Unfortunately I cannot thank by name all the colleagues, friends and institutions around the world for their direct or indirect help but I would like to mention
Professor Makoto Nakamura and his colleagues, University of Kyoto; Professor Hisato Ide, University of Tokyo; the Committee for Capital Construction, Chinese Government in Beijing, who enabled me to get acquainted with the cultural heritage of China; Professor Chuin Tung of the Nanking Institute of Technology, who kindly allowed me to reproduce some illustrations and checked the spelling of the Chinese names; Professor Ravindra Bhan, New Delhi; the late Professor Hermann Mattern, Technical University, Berlin; Professor Gunnar Martinsson, University of Karlsruhe; Professor Hans Luz, Technical University, Stuttgart; Professor Sven-Ingvar Andersson, Royal Academy of Arts, Copenhagen; Professor Jette Abel, Royal Agricultural University, Copenhagen; Jana Zupanc, Stockholm; Jelena and Robert de Belder of the Kalmthout Arboretum; Professor and Mrs. Arnold Weddle, and Professor Anne Beer, University of Sheffield; Professor and Mrs. David Lowenthal, University of London; Professor Edward Bartman, Warsaw Agricultural University; Lawrence Halprin, San Francisco; Professor Peter Walker, Harvard University, Cambridge, Mass.; Professor Reuben Rainey, University of Virginia, Charlottesville; Professor Susan Turner, University of Louisiana, Baton Rouge; and my prematurely deceased friend, Professor Albert Fein of Long Island University, Brooklyn.

Last but not least, special credit must be given to Mr. Slavko Pregl of EWO Ljubljana, who, after many years, did not lose confidence in the book, and also to Mrs Barbara Pregl for her untiring efforts to help this book come into life. Finally, I would like to thank the team of the printing-house of Gorenjski tisk for the excellent collaboration during the production process of the book.

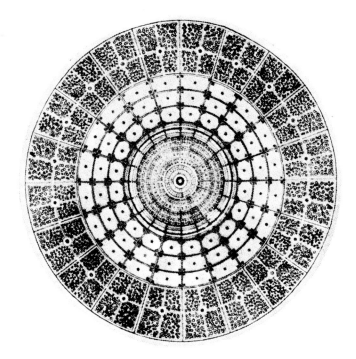

Cosmological images were often an underlying concept for the ideal city or garden as shown by the examples on this page.
Top: a Renaissance plan of the garden on the mythological Isle of Kythera.
One of the few cases where such a symbolic structure was actually built is the 18th-century Baroque city of Karlsruhe in Germany, representing an eloquent layout of the Residence of an 18th-century absolutist ruler with its surrounding garden. Just as clear-cut as the Baroque edifice itself is the message conveyed: this is the centre of the city, of the country, and, in a figurative sense, also of the world (bottom).

Introduction

According to some assumptions the garden was the most ancient form of man's arrangement of space, preceding even the construction of a hut, the beginnings of architecture. In this context, a garden means simply a plot of land fenced in with branches or stones for protection against outside threats. Whatever the truth of such statements, there is no doubt that the very process of enclosure implies certain elements of regular arrangement that gradually led to increasingly varied and perfected structures. This development was slow and gradual, and certainly also connected with the improvement of the cultivation methods for useful plants. It was a long time before the gardens assumed a more developed internal order, a greater complexity and a richer articulation of meaning.

The Social Function of Garden Art

Except for verbal description there is no reliable testimony of the earliest beginnings of gardening art; the paintings in the Egyptian tombs, however, allow us to follow 2000 years of development. They clearly show that the garden was at first a smaller, purposefully designed plot set apart for the cultivation of selected, but always utilitarian, plants. Over time their spatial distribution became more varied and the patterns more inventive. Water was transferred from simple irrigation channels and wells into skilfully constructed ponds. Although these were still partly used as irrigation reservoirs, they gradually acquired new functions. Water was promoted into a gardening motif around which all the other elements could be arranged. The ponds displayed a surprisingly complex form and this was a clear departure from their original, exclusively utilitarian, role. Apparently the tendency was supported by the use of ponds for funeral rites where the dead were symbolically transported into afterlife on a ritual barge.

It is clear that only the higher social classes could own gardens of this type: the Pharaoh, high officials and priests. The arrangement of their residences not only absorbed huge funds, but required expert knowledge of garden design, water management and plant cultivation. So gardens grew into important complements to residential buildings. They transcended their original utilitarian, cultivational role, becoming a setting for open-air living, and at the same time acquiring the characteristics of a harmoniously shaped spatial entity. Their ritual, religious connotations should also be mentioned. In this way a number of meanings combined to increase the residential value of the garden and allowed it to underscore the social importance of its owner, or, in other words, to serve as a status symbol. To have at one's disposal a comparatively large, highly fertile plot of land, chiefly reserved for pleasure, to lay claim to a disproportionate amount of precious irrigation water, to lay out the garden in a way that requires specialized knowledge - all these privileges self-evidently testify to the high social status of the owner. In this way the garden, since early times, encoded the message of its proprietor's social importance. This message was all the more convincing, the more perfect the formal pattern of the garden.

The events at the French court in the second half of the 17th century are an eloquent testimony to this. The young Louis XIV was trying to consolidate his royal authority. Traditionally, state affairs had been handled by prime ministers such as the mighty cardinals Richelieu and Mazarin. After Mazarin's demise, Nicholas Fouquet, Louis' capable and successful Minister of Finance, aimed at the vacant post of premier. He had won the position of Minister at an early age, acquired a considerable fortune, and built himself a splendid residence at Vaux-le-Vicomte near Paris.

This last feat was achieved over a comparatively short period (1655-1661) by three eminent artists, the architect Le Vau, the landscape architect Le Nôtre and the painter Le Brun. Fouquet invited 2000 guests to the solemn opening. All were overwhelmed by the palace and the garden and the young king was amazed at the sight of the residence. Its glamorous design eclipsed his own estates and had no match anywhere in Europe. The message of Fouquet's new creation to the cream of French society on that famous day in August 1661 was unmistakable: the highest position in the state befits the owner of such a residence. The impact was made primarily by the garden. After all, the king's own palace, the Louvre, was more imposing than Fouquet's but it had no garden to give it the splendour of Vaux-le-Vicomte. At that time Versailles was a modest manor with a park of unpretentious design, surrounded by marshes and forests.

No wonder the king had Fouquet arrested three weeks after the feast, charging him with misappropriation of state funds. At the trial that dragged on for three years the magistrates sentenced Fouquet to confiscation of his property without depriving him of his personal freedom. Quite exceptionally, the king reversed the sentence and Fouquet was jailed for life. Vaux-le-Vicomte had indeed demonstrated the minister's excessive ambition.

In this way Louis eliminated Fouquet and consolidated his own absolute power. But as far as building ventures are concerned, the story could not end at that point. To justify and reaffirm his sovereign status in society, the king felt compelled to construct an even more glamorous residence than Vaux-le-Vicomte. The trio that had designed Vaux were now entrusted with the construction of an even larger palace and garden at Versailles. It may reasonably be claimed that without Fouquet there could hardly have been a Versailles - the outsized residence that set the pattern for the embodiment of supreme social power throughout Western civilization. In this context the Baroque garden was more important than the palace, as confirmed by numerous other examples from all parts of Europe.

Even at an earlier time, in the Italian Renaissance, princely residences had developed in the same direction. Here, too, gardens were an important complement to town palaces and rural villas. The most outstanding were the Boboli gardens in Florence, the main part of which was shaped like a large open-air stage. It was used for tournaments, exercises, weddings, solemn processions and other displays of the magnificence of the princes of Tuscany.

Not even the dignitaries of the Church could escape this trend prevalent in Renaissance Italy. The Belvedere courtyard in the Vatican, which Bramante remodelled by papal order, was with its gardens, its large loggias and its daring architectural innovation, the splendid two-flight staircase, clearly intended as a visible sign of social importance. It is no accident that the famous gardens in the surroundings of Rome were mainly commissioned by cardinals and popes. The gardens of the Villa d'Este - impressive even today - were commissioned by Cardinal Ippolito d'Este, an unsuccessful bidder for the Holy See. The glamorous structure of the garden, full of symbolic messages expressed especially through the classical sculpture and the garden motifs, was intended to present the owner as a magnificent, noble and learned man, worthy of occupying the highest post in Church hierarchy. It is interesting to note that Ippolito's chief rival, Cardinal Farnese, was the builder of the famous villa and gardens at Caprarola. Thus the Villa d'Este was erected in a

For humanizing man's early habitat, a high degree of regularity in treatment of structural and landscape elements was needed, as is manifest in this garden in Ancient Egypt (top).
The significance of a regular arrangement is particularly obvious in cases where it was essential to emphasize an individual feature by distinguished layout, as is clearly illustrated by the burial monument of a Swedish king at Drottningholm near Stockholm (centre). The entire large park is conceived in the free landscape style. The only geometrical elements are the radial alleys converging from all directions towards the centrally located mausoleum, the Monument Hill. This is one of the numerous layouts for this structure by F. M. Piper.
A similar confrontation of geometrical and organic forms can be found in the work of the well-known German landscape architect P. J. Lenné. He used it several times in his interesting designs for the royal gardens at Sanssouci near Berlin (bottom).

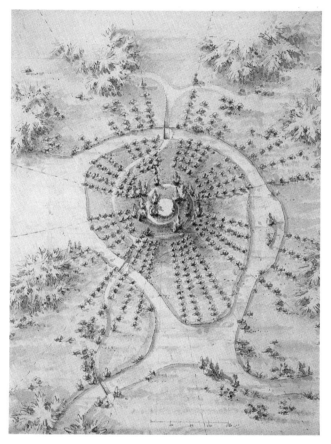

competition for prestige, with the stress on garden design. Similar controversies presided around the creation of the Villa Lante and its unique garden. The Pope several times expressed his dissatisfaction at Gambara's project, which he saw as unfitting to the cardinal's position, and ultimately withdrew his pension for alleged dissipation. In the same spirit the Apostolic Curia, after the cardinal's death, confiscated all his property at Bagnaia.

Any kind of art inevitably reflects social conditions. Even more, art is frequently a powerful impetus to social development. This tendency has often found its confirmation in garden art, and a particularly eloquent example is the English landscape style of the 18th century. Its appearance and compositional structure can be best explained by the social and economic conditions at the turn of the century. Their chief determinant was class rivalry between the court on the one hand, the rising industrial middle classes and the enterprising landed aristocracy on the other. The new layers of society, progressive at the time, found an expression of their ideals in Palladian architecture set in a new kind of designed landscape previously unknown in Europe. It was a free style that declared nature as its design model, and which was in complete contrast to the regimented, trimmed, enslaved nature typical of Baroque gardens. This concept of the garden as a creation of liberal and noble-minded individuals contained a multi-layered message. Above all, the court was denied the role of upholder of progressive social ideals and identified with conservative political absolutism.

This tendency of the movement is clearly shown by the unique fact that it avoided the court altogether. So far new, top-level art had, with few exceptions, always arisen around courtly residences. This was the usual development from ancient Egypt, through ancient or Renaissance Rome and Beijing, to Versailles. In 18th century England, on the other hand, there was not a single creation in the new style intended for the court. Quite the contrary, the new landscape garden arose in the countryside often far from the capital, such as the pioneering Stourhead in Wiltshire or Castle Howard in Yorkshire. This was a clear indication of the new distribution of social power that held sway not only over the economic resources, but also over the development of the arts.

A second message conveyed by the new style concerned the relations between England and the outside world. In competition with France, England had found her own style and managed to associate it with the idea of progressiveness. This was a source of international prestige for England, since the new style was imitated throughout Europe, just as extensively as (or even more than) the Baroque style had been in an earlier period.

In addition to this role, gardens also served as the scene of a rich social life. They offered the setting for other arts, music, ballet, sculpture, theatre, and were therefore an important stimulus to artistic creativity. Garden art was a mirror of the changing times and marked the historic ascendancy of certain countries, particularly during their golden ages. The Renaissance garden was a fruit of 16th century Italy. Nothing could characterize 17th century France in the heyday of political absolutism better than her Baroque gardens. One might justly claim that 18th century imperial England found expression in the landscape style which is perhaps her most unique contribution to the visual arts, as numerous scholars have stated.

When Peter the Great, in the first half of the 18th century, set out to consolidate Russia and weld her into a European power, he was well aware he could achieve this aim only by radical social renewal along the lines of central European countries. In this vogue for Europeanization he availed himself, among other things, of Baroque symbols of monarchical power, which in this case acquired the connotation of social change. Along with splendid buildings, the prime examples of this tendency were large-scale landscape compositions, headed by the magnificent Petrodvorets. Half a century later, Catherine II introduced the English landscape style, in inevitable mimicry of monarchical residences throughout Europe. Thanks to her, Russia's Tsarskoe Selo became an interesting blend of Baroque and the landscape style, such as Germany could boast at the Nymphenburg and Schwetzingen.

In the New World social developments followed a different course from that in Europe, yet they were accompanied by surprisingly similar elements of spatial arrangement. While regular, geometric garden patterns appeared around the colonial governor's palace in Williamsburg and on the plantations of great landholders, the social conflicts brought about a complete reversal of fashion. Here, too, the elements of free landscape design stood for progressive social ideals, such as the overthrow of colonial rule and Abolition. Thomas Jefferson, one of the authors of the Declaration of Human Rights, regarded the English landscape style and Palladian architecture as the most appropriate image of the striving for liberalism and more equal social relations. It is perhaps no accident that he lived and was active in Virginia where the question of equality was particularly acute. Viewed in this light, the erection of Monticello and the establishment of a university campus in Charlottesville represent far more than just the introduction of a new style in architecture and landscape design which happened to be fashionable throughout the world.

Spiritualized Nature

The cultures of the Far East have evolved an entirely different pattern of adaptation of nature for man's residential requirements: a pattern that reflects a primordial concept of the world and of the active forces that govern its course. It proceeds from the assumption that physical nature is an embodiment of supernatural powers that determine the sequence of natural events and influence man's life. Such beliefs in the spiritual powers of trees, rocks, mountains and water are, in fact, typical of the mythologies of the most varied regions of the world. To the present day, trees have remained the object of numerous folk rituals, usually connected with certain seasons of the year. The best example is the Christmas tree, which represents the survival of a tradition dating from pre-Christian times. Ancient Egypt venerated sacred lakes, sacred tree and holy groves. These later reappeared in Ancient Greece and Rome, and then again in the Italian Renaissance, together with the grotto, another dwelling-place of mythical beings.

But only in China and Japan has this mythological outlook persisted through the centuries and decisively marked the character of landscape design. This might be regarded as a quest for security, which only reverence for hidden spiritual powers would ensure, particularly efficacious if the spirits were attracted to the vicinity of human habitations. The central motif of Chinese garden art, *shanshui*, illustrates the structure of the world, with rocks as its chief component. According to Daoism, rocks represent the skeleton and water represents the life-blood of the earth. All matter is composed of tiny particles interlinked and kept in constant motion by hidden energy, the active fluid of life, *qi*. In the visual arts this principle is usually represented by vortices, whirling, wavy, rhythmically agitated strokes. But it is most clearly typified

Power and social pre-eminence were often expressed in spatial terms. A most eloquent example is the rivalry between Louis XIV, the Sun King of France, and his minister Fouquet. The royal palace of the Tuileries in Paris (top) was quite sizable and impressive, certainly more than Fouquet's relatively small new edifice at Vaux (second row).
However, the splendour of gardens at Vaux has outshone the royal residence, for which Fouquet had to pay by being dismissed and imprisoned.
After the victory over the Turks in Vienna, the rising power of the Austrian Empire sought adequate status symbols in the construction of the new residence. This was supposed to surpass Versailles, as is evident from the first design for Schönbrunn by Johann Bernhard Fischer von Erlach (third row).
Even for the court's finances such a layout was too ambitious and Fischer elaborated a new, more modest layout (bottom).

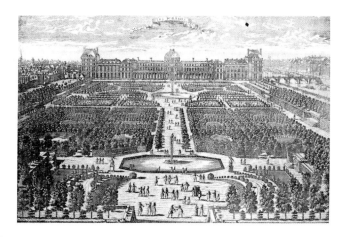

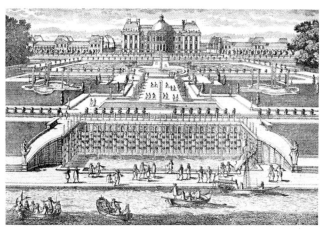

by the furrowed limestone rocks that have predominantly defined the character of the Chinese garden since its early beginnings.

The concept of the presence of supernatural forces in the ground has contributed towards the establishment of the principle of *wu-wei* (noninterference with nature), which in turn requires a maximum adaptation to nature. Above all, this principle has contributed towards a design approach that consequently avoids the transformation of natural features into regular, geometric patterns. Japanese landscape design has been decisively influenced by the Shintoist belief that rocks, trees and mountains are inhabited by *kami*, good spirits. The transposition of selected natural elements into the garden suggests a neighbourhood of supernatural beings and therefore a safer life. This concept predetermines the choice of the chief compositional elements of the garden as well as their formal character, which mainly keeps within the limits of the natural.

Even the architectural concept is attuned to the spiritual orientation of residential space. In opposition to Western civilization, architecture is not a self-contained entity, removed from and dominating the environment. Wherever possible, in Sino-Japanese building tradition, the architectural and garden spaces interpenetrate and fuse into a whole. The building penetrates into the garden, at the same time opening towards it and embracing it. While moving through the garden, man finds himself at every step in the midst of a spiritualized world of which he is an integral part. Therefore this world is not designed for observation from the outside, from a certain viewpoint or along a certain axis, according to the tenets of the European Renaissance and Baroque, but rather represents a microcosm one is supposed to fuse with and experience in one's own self.

In this way, two great civilizations evolved entirely different, opposing patterns of man's arrangement of space. On the one hand is the concept of geometrized and ultimately ordered space born out of the spirit of classical antiquity that imagined the Olympic gods in human shape. Thus man has raised himself above nature, confronted her and tried to dominate her. The result of such an approach is orderly, subdued, humanized nature. The East, on the other hand, has appropriated the concept of subordination to nature, resulting in a pattern of spiritualized, deified nature that, in spite of all transformations and idealizations, still preserves the aspect of primordiality.

Between Emulation of Nature and Original Creation

To be able to fulfil a number of significant social functions, garden art needed an articulated, formal repertory. Through its several thousand years' development, it has created a vocabulary of forms out of various materials: plants, land, water, stone, etc. The materials have remained more or less the same, but their uses have changed over time. This resulted in original forms being expected to describe and express new concepts. Thus, the various historic periods and cultural or national areas acquired their own peculiar features, and thereby an identity of their own. In view of inevitable transformations, natural materials lost their original character, resulting in forms that are non-existent in nature or only partly close to nature.

Depending on the function, two basic approaches have affirmed themselves in landscape design. One is based on regular geometric patterns; the other creates free, organic forms that often at first sight resemble those in nature. Therefore they give the impression of imitating nature, an approach often found in the creations of the East

Asian or English landscape styles. It is precisely this impression that has given rise to the claim that landscape design is based on the imitation of nature. History abounds with theories of this kind and even some champions of geometric styles often claimed their model was nature. One of them was Dézallier d'Argenville, author of a famous Baroque treatise on the theory of garden design, which appeared first in 1709; in later editions he called for more consideration of nature in the design of gardens.

This raises a question fundamental to the art of landscape design and intrinsically linked with the very possibility of its existence as an art. Without insisting on the theory of landscape architecture, it is worthwhile to throw some light on this point, especially since it allows us to grasp the essence of garden art. The concept of art as an imitation of nature was already put forward by Plato and for a long time this interpretation, in various versions, dominated both theory and practice. The claim that art is nothing but emulation of nature (*ars est imitatio naturae*) has infiltrated various arts and so it is no wonder it has also struck a chord in the theory of landscape design. The notion that nature was the ideal model of all design found its widest currency in the English landscape movement of the first half of the 18th century. It was expressed in a number of treatises, one of the most prominent being the writings of Joseph Addison. His aesthetic guideline was that the value of works of art increases proportionately to their similarity to nature. In other words, the utmost perfection was maximum identification with nature. Something similar was expressed in 1783 by the German theoretician of garden art, C.C.L. Hirschfeld, in commenting on L. von Sckell's Schönbusch Gardens: "Art is here so successfully disguised it all looks like nature." A whole century later, the author of *The English Flower Garden*, William Robinson, returned to similar premises with his statement that an artist's work always should carry the mark of his truth to nature.

Similar statements have been made by many a 20th century landscape architect whose works otherwise show pronounced features of regularity. This divergence between the actual character of landscape-architectural works and the natural structure of landscape has been evident practically throughout the history of garden art. It might be helpful and interesting to investigate why such a great number of designers felt the need to stress, again and again, their allegiance to nature. Yet the essential point is that their practice used to be diametrically opposed to their statements. The very fact calls in question the mimetic, or imitative, character of landscape design.

The disputability of such theories is self-evident as soon as the function of the garden - an artificial creation - and of the natural landscape - the result of spontaneous development - is considered. The former serves to satisfy various human requirements. It sets itself a clear purpose and must therefore assume a certain pattern and structure, while the latter is formed under the influence of natural forces. Landscape, in a natural context, is subordinated to ecological laws, which tend towards a maximum variety of plant species, the greatest possible number of organisms and vertical development of plant layers. Therefore it includes ground-level, low, medium and tall plants, from grasses through to shrubs and smaller and larger trees. Landscape design, conversely, reduces the choice of species, sometimes even restricting itself to a single variety. It often makes use of a small number of plant specimens and simplifies the stratification of vegetation, for example, by the use of lawns and ground-cover plants where a single species covers large surfaces. The differences become even greater if we compare the distribution of vegetation, which in a garden follows the principles of compositional structure and is therefore mostly regular, while spontaneous spread is

One of the original ideas of William Kent was regular, almost globular clumps of trees where the characteristics of the species are lost and a new form, unknown in nature, is created: a sketch for Holkham Hall (top).
The same composition technique was used by Sven-Ingvar Andersson in his competition entry for the reshaping of the Karlsplatz, Vienna. Only by combining trees into new recognizable shapes could he realize his concept, which is founded on multiple variations of the ellipse (centre).
Bottom: another example of how important the regular treatment of the natural material in landscape composition is, demonstrates the Tanner Fountain by P. Walker. Only through consistent circular arrangement of natural boulders an effective design control over the entire layout could be achieved (see also p. 384).

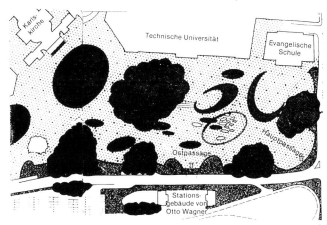

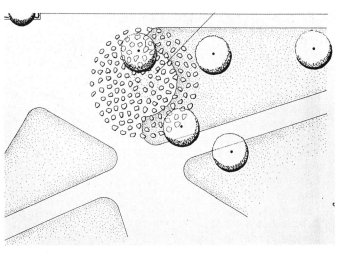

the rule in nature. It is by such methods of formal arrangement of the material that garden art has evolved and enriched its formal language through the ages.

On the basis of preserved evidence it is possible to establish with certainty that the departure from nature began with ancient Egypt, by the regular placing of trees in the form of avenues. The Romans assimilated this principle and developed it further into more complex structures, such as the quincunx, where the trees are regularly placed, not just in a straight line, but also in a spatial grid. Evidently this pattern was taken over by the Arabs, who inventively used it in the Iberian peninsula, as exemplified by the preserved courtyards of the mosques at Seville and Cordoba.

One might say that the ultimate in regular spatial organization of the material is represented by circular tree formations, such as were used to mark Rousseau's tomb at Ermenonville or the intended tomb of the Swedish King at Drottningholm. It is typical that both arrangements were created within a framework which is in the landscape style, and are the only regular motifs within an overall irregular pattern. In both cases, where a special emphasis was required it was found necessary to adopt a pronounced geometrical form, clearly distinguishable from the surroundings which very much suggest natural patterns.

By spatial distribution it is also possible to shape and denaturalize the material with another frequently used method, which was developed in the English landscape style. It consists of combining vegetation into clumps, whereby a tree or a shrub becomes part of a solid mass, loses its original shape and merges into something new. Such clumps show a more or less regular form, with Kent they even become circular. Also their simplified botanical composition departs from nature, being usually reduced to one species only. Lancelot Brown used exclusively trees to make up his clumps and in Germany Sckell, as well as Pückler-Muskau, adopted a similar technique. The principle of agglomeration, or merging of a number of single elements into a new visual whole, also underlies the *shanshui*, or mountain-and-water, motif in a Chinese garden. The same applies to the use of pebbles in Japanese gardens, where the stones are more or less matched in size, shape and colour. This leads to a pronounced visual unity and at the same time emphasizes the impression of man-made, unique scenery. Famous examples of this type are the lake shores of the Sento Gosho villa, or the Ama no Hashidate at Katsura in Kyoto.

Transformation of the Natural

The most radical departure from nature in garden art is the transformation of natural material. In European tradition the trimming of plants to achieve regular forms has been known since Roman times. In this way the plants acquire a new, geometric shape, while the original features are blurred. This amounts to a kind of typification and therefore a certain degree of alienation from the original natural structure. A trimmed pyramid, for instance, does not allow us to judge whether it is made up of lime-tree, hornbeam or yew. Even more, it is impossible to establish with certainty whether the original plant was a shrub or a tree. From a distance it is even impossible to make out whether the pyramid is shaped from a plant or just moulded out of earth and covered with grass. The process of design implies progressive generalization from a single species, with its own individual features, to generalized forms.

To mark the place where his ancestors were buried, primitive man often reshaped his plot of land. This is probably the oldest form of man's transformation of nature. In more developed cultures, burial mounds acquired a regular shape, culminating in the stone-built or earth-shaped pyramids of Egypt and South America. In a later age, artificially shaped tracts of land, with mound like forms such as pyramids or cones, were included in gardens where they became the vehicles for special meanings and messages. It is interesting to observe that this happened not only in the regular styles, but also in the landscape style, most remarkably in the Japanese garden. This is further proof of the importance of artificial forms in conveying various meanings.

One of the most original approaches was the invention of a smooth, plane surface as it does not exist in nature. It is not surprising that it began as a ritual, sacred enclosure in Japan and was also extensively used in Europe for a similar purpose. The same result can also be achieved by another design device. By arranging flowering plants in compact plantings they can be transformed into a flowery carpet. In this way plants lose their natural spatial characteristics and are transformed into a two-dimensional structure. Conversely, the compositional treatment of water must inevitably proceed in the opposite direction if its aim is to transform the liquid material into three-dimensional forms, which can be found in profusion in Renaissance, Baroque and, particularly, modern design.

Without creative transfiguration of natural material it would be impossible to establish a wide range of symbolic connotations in garden art. The appearance of any actual tree is always a reminder of something definite, some reality seen and experienced before. As such it can hardly acquire a new meaning. Only its transmutation into new forms allows a progress in that direction, as exemplified by the Garden of Love at Villandry. An even more refined symbolism of trimmed plants was developed in Japan. Here *o-karikomi*, stack-shaped azalea or camellia shrubs, are used to suggest mountains, or substitute rocks in symbolizing mountains. Outstanding examples of this use of *o-karikomi* can be found in the Konchi-in, Shoden-ji and Shugaku-in.

Even this sketchy survey shows that landscape design inevitably implies the transformation of materials, chiefly by organized spatial distribution and by transmutation of structure. Pure emulation of nature would only result in the replication of the existing, already familiar world. To be able to create a new reality that might help man in times of stress and pave the way towards higher spheres of consciousness, man has had to work out a varied and rich repertory of means of expression. He has adopted the techniques of assimilation, alienation, and generalization - in short, abstraction, and this is what gives garden art its original character and allows it to carry a special message within the context of social development.

The Nature of Garden Art

Garden art belongs to the visual arts, where it holds a specific place. It comprises those creations of landscape architecture that satisfy determined aesthetic criteria and unmistakably and clearly are testaments of their own time, communicating certain messages by their specific means. They become part of the treasury of art, when they demonstrate originality and uniqueness of structure, based on particular formal characteristics.

Garden art is a part of our historic consciousness, a collective embodiment of man's experience. Its productions, too, reflect, with at least the same power as other arts, important social events and aspirations. Nowhere does, for instance, the striving for unlimited power, the need of absolutist rulers for ostentation, the compulsion to

A characteristic intensification of formality, i.e., abstraction, marks the development of the means of expression in the work of the renowned American landscape architect Lawrence Halprin. The sketch at top shows one of his studies of a rock-strewn mountain landscape.
Centre: the design for Lovejoy Plaza, Portland, whose shapes are clearly inspired by natural rocks, yet definitely assert their autonomy as artificial creations. The next and ultimate step on this path of evolution is represented by the concept of Forecourt Fountain, also at Portland (bottom). The spatial context is very much the same as in the highland landscape, but the rocks have changed into abstract geometrical shapes giant cubes of concrete among which the water can play the most varied optical games (all the sketches are by L. Halprin).

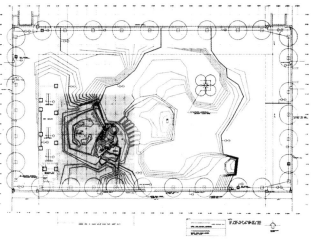

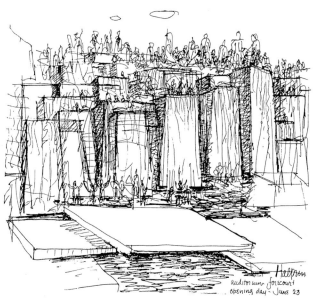

confirm their social status by spatial symbols, show so convincingly as in the Baroque gardens of 17th-century France. The English landscape style, extolled as a symbol of freedom, has been a successful instrument for the promotion of progressive forces in confrontation with the conservative court.

Of course, these creations had more than one meaning. They contributed towards the affirmation of the social forces capable of creating something new, but at the same time helped them to emerge as a ruling class and consolidate their position in society. Thus garden art upheld the social stability of its patrons. At the same time it incarnated man's incessant aspiration to transform and improve the world. By remaking, improving his environment, man could improve himself.

Moreover, garden art allowed man to create the indispensable world of illusions, derived out of the real world with the aid of nature, a world of escapism to which he could resort to find spiritual peace and balance. In short, it helped him to transcend the current level of social consciousness and to raise himself to new spiritual heights. Last but not least, the unique message of garden art is that it enabled man to define his attitude towards often strange and mysterious nature: a relationship that ranges from coexistence to domination.

The material, too, assures garden art its unique position, in a double sense. Firstly, it is the only branch of art that uses natural living material. Secondly, it avails itself of the widest choice of materials, from stone, water, land, vegetation, to brick, wood and concrete. But the material, by itself, could not substantiate garden art, which only arises out of the reshaping of the material by suitable compositional techniques. In this sense, garden art differs radically from the other visual arts and it might be interesting to compare it, from this viewpoint, with painting and architecture:

– painting depicts existing reality by using a shapeless material,

– architecture creates a new reality out of materials that lack shape - at any rate a shape that could induce aesthetic pleasure,

– landscape design creates a new reality mostly out of materials that already possess a determined, autonomous shape; for instance, a tree or a rock represents a self-contained visual organism that functions according to the laws of natural aesthetics and may be beautiful in itself.

In this way, three kinds of new visual reality arise by different methods. Of the three, it is landscape design that has to confront the greatest difficulties while trying to control its nature-derived material. The material cannot be simply adopted, but must be creatively transformed. To this purpose, garden art has developed a number of procedures of abstraction, as described earlier in this chapter.

To Follow Nature or Social Requirements?

What determines form in garden art? This is an old question discussed by numerous authors, both theoreticians and practising landscape architects. At first sight it might appear self-evident that a creativity which is linked to such an extent to natural materials also derives its determinants from the natural environment. Yet historical experience says otherwise.

Throughout Europe, Renaissance and Baroque gardens show common traits. The difference between the various countries, if any, must be ascribed to social, political and cultural circumstances rather than to natural conditions. This is perhaps even more clearly shown in Islamic gardens, distributed in a great arc spanning from the Indian subcontinent to Spain. In spite of the great variations of soil, climate and geographical features, the formal character of gardens in Pakistan, Iran, Turkey and Moorish Spain remains almost the same.

Often the conjecture can be heard that the free styles of landscape design have arisen under the influence of the picturesque nature of China and Japan. This is only a small part of a possible explanation. The roots of Chinese and Japanese landscape design must be seen chiefly in man's need to give the world around him a higher level of meaning. He could achieve this by spiritualizing it and ascribing it supernatural power and significance. Spectacular natural phenomena had an important but by no means decisive share in this development.

Yet natural conditions can trigger off a development in the opposite direction. This has happened in the Islamic countries. The extremely reduced possibilities of survival in the dry desert zones have called forth the image of the best possible world, of paradise as described in the Koran, a garden abounding with water and lush vegetation. The model of the garden, in this case, does not depict existing nature at all, but rather presents an idealized structure that can satisfy man's material and spiritual requirements to the greatest possible degree.

When the landscape style had achieved its definite break-through in England, it was promptly imitated everywhere, from Scandinavia to Russia and Italy, and even in the United States. Irrespective of the vastly differing natural conditions in these countries, the stylistic features were faithfully repeated. This means that the social, political and cultural message was always the most important factor. Ultimately, garden art represents man's attempt to make his mark on the world, to impress the signs of his existence on his surroundings. Therefore it is understandable that natural features could only inspire him while the social and cultural conditions obviously defined the course of the development of landscape architecture, the creativity that produced garden art.

The Heritage of Garden Art

In spite of considerable losses throughout history, the architectural heritage is comparatively well preserved today. Even some buildings that are several thousand years old have survived, though not always in their original integrity. The fate of garden art is quite different. Its historical heritage is, compared to that of architecture proper, much scantier. There are numerous reasons for this situation. First of all, the structure of a garden depends on elements which are subject to growth and changes dictated by the ebb and flow of nature. As soon as gardens are denied the necessary care, the vegetation goes its own way, new plants take over and in a generation the layout of the garden may be radically affected. If neglect lasts even longer, the decay of more solid components sets in, such as fountains, retaining walls, flights of stairs, paths, statues. In regions of humid climate the decay is far quicker than in dry zones, such as the Mediterranean or certain parts of Asia.

Even worse damage than neglect has been caused to garden art by the reconstruction and enlargement of villas or castles and quite particularly by the growth of towns. A great number of precious designs have been swamped by the changing taste of the time, caused by the prevailing social and political ideas, such as in 18th-century England. In that period England irretrievably lost practically all her rich Renaissance and Baroque legacy and this example was followed by numerous European countries. In several instances great historical gardens have been transformed into public grounds, losing their historic authenticity. Such transformed parks include Madrid's

New art movements at the beginning of the 20th century have brought radical changes in our visual thinking. An important step in this development is displacement as a serious break with the traditional order. It was probably Kazimir Malevich who first made this move with his Suprematist paintings, most conspicuous among them being the *Red Square and Black Square* of 1915 (top).
An eloquent example of the composition technique described above can be seen in the competition entry for a cemetery from 1967 by the Swiss landscape architect Ernst Cramer. Two asymmetrical ellipses are placed in an asymmetrical position, each of them in a spatial and functional role of its own, yet both creating a coherent entity (bottom).

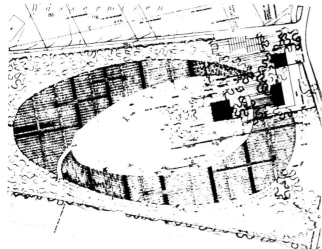

famous Buen Retiro, the gardens of the Villa Borghese in Rome and the Villa Torlonia in Frascati.

According to the Commission for Historic Gardens, which functions as a joint body of the IFLA (International Federation of Landscape Architects) and the ICOMOS (International Committee on Monuments and Sites), some 2000 valuable historic gardens have been preserved around the world. Roughly two-thirds of this number belong to the European heritage. Considering the enormous number of gardens established throughout history in the world's creative periods, this is a rather modest remainder. The importance of the surviving heritage is therefore all the greater. It is not only the embodiment of a unique artistic creativity, but also a complement to the general cultural and historical image of a period or nation. The garden art of certain countries shows a national identity, to at least the same degree as architecture, painting and all the other branches of visual art.

Gardens or landscapes marked by a historical style often supply the indispensable setting for valuable architectural monuments, with which they blend into complexes of unique cultural value. Therefore the heritage of garden art can make a considerable contribution towards general cultural education. It is of quite special importance for professional training since it contains the grammar of landscape design from the earliest beginnings up to modern times.

The above-mentioned points of importance demand the attention of various nature conservation and monument protection services at regional and national level. It is also the responsibility of UNESCO's Department of Cultural Heritage. At international level, a particularly active body is the Commission for Historic Gardens mentioned above, which has collected a vast amount of cataloguing material. By running a number of conferences and summer courses it helps to answer questions concerning the heritage of various parts of the world. An outstanding scientific centre for the study of garden heritage is the Centre for the History of Landscape Architecture at Harvard University, with headquarters at Dumbarton Oaks, USA, where numerous important international conferences on the various national traditions in landscape architecture have been organized.

Thanks to society's increasing awareness of this heritage as well as numerous specialist initiatives, historic gardens are today better maintained than ever and even a number of gardens once considered irretrievably lost have now been restored. An encouraging example of this is the large-scale reconstruction of the Baroque gardens of the royal palace of Het Loo, near Apeldoorn in the Netherlands. Other examples include Painshill and the Renaissance gardens of Ham House in Great Britain, Leonberg near Stuttgart, the gardens of Kroměříž, Moravia, Monticello, Virginia, Petrodvorets and Tsarskoe Selo near St. Petersburg, Kuskovo near Moscow, several old gardens in Japan, and above all, the numerous gardens of Suzhou and other sites in China. However, there are still countless gardens awaiting restoration, especially in Iran, India, Korea, Vietnam and in several European countries.

There is an increased interest in cultural heritage everywhere. This is shown by, among other things, numerous book publications casting light on the so far unstudied regions or periods. In spite of this encouraging development there are some national traditions that are still too little known, such as those of Korea and Vietnam. We can say with pleasure that the last few years have seen the appearance of some reputable magazines concerned exclusively with the subject of historic gardens, such as *Journal of Garden History*, published in London, and *Gartenkunst* in Germany. Another journal, *Garden History*, is published by the Garden History Society in Great Britain, active since 1965. Material on historical heritage is also periodically included in magazines such as *Landscape Architecture Journal* and *Landscape Journal* in the USA, *Landscape Design* and *Apollo* in Great Britain, *Gartenarchitektur* and *Garten und Landschaft* in Germany, and *Landskap* in Scandinavia.

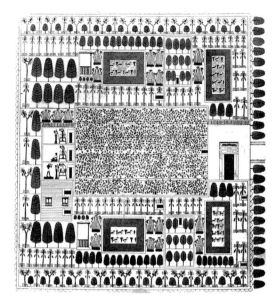

Egypt and the antique world
in the Mediterranean basin

Egypt

Greece

Imperium Romanum

The heritage of ancient Rome

The House of the Vettii

The House of Octavius Quartio

The House of the Tragic Poet

The House of Venus

Hadrian's Villa

Piazza Armerina

Little is known about the gardens of ancient civilizations, though they have had a far-reaching effect on subsequent developments in landscape architecture in Europe and the Middle East. Egypt, which left plentiful records of its garden art in the form of sepulchral wall-paintings, represents a rare exception. Regretfully, no such legacy was left by the Sumerians nor by the Assyrians though their garden culture, according to the written accounts, was similarly well developed.

Since the flow of the Euphrates River could be kept under control in ancient times only by the efforts of large communities, the city-states populating the fertile plains of Mesopotamia rose as early as 3000 B.C. It was here that agriculture - the tilling of soil and the cultivation of crops by irrigation - began, concurrent with the advent of civilization. With abundant water for irrigation, green oases appeared between the Euphrates and Tigris Rivers while the desert, in vivid contrast to the fertile fields and gardens, surrounded the agricultural belt along the banks. As in Egypt, Persia and wherever life depended on similar contradictory circumstances, the garden became an idealized symbol of fertility, comfort, and well-being.

The Sumerians may have been the first to give such cultural importance to gardens. Their famous hanging gardens were originally described prior to 2000 B.C. Since more complex construction methods were then unknown, these are likely to have been terrace or roof gardens situated on top of single-storey buildings. The terraces of the great Ziggurat of the 21st century B.C. were planted with vegetation overflowing the roof tops creating the appearance of a "hanging" garden. However, no reliable information on the structure or composition of these gardens is available. According to a few reliefs - the only surviving records - one can assume that their design was relatively regular.

Egypt

Only a few ruins remain of the landscape architectural legacy of ancient Egypt. Many murals survive in Egyptian tombs, however, and they give a clear image of the oldest known gardening art on Earth. For this we can thank the cult of the dead, a belief based on a perception of earthly life as only a single stage in human existence. Life continues after death and one's possessions are transportable. Consequently, valuables and household goods were placed in the tombs. Since the garden, an item of particular value, could not be taken, an image was substituted. Reduced-scale clay models of gardens were also found as sepulchral offerings.

The ebb and flow of life in ancient Egypt was determined by the flooding of the Nile, which would rise each year as much as 6 metres. In addition to an abundance of fertile silt, it contributed water, the essential commodity of life. The Egyptians developed an ingenious technique for pumping and land-irrigation and through it an effective agriculture. All land cultivation was originally for production of crops. It is impossible to determine specifically when and how the amenity garden emerged as a separate spatial structure in which production became of secondary or negligible importance. While references to the gardens date from the 3rd Dynasty (2600 years B.C.), their development was gradual. Many centuries passed before the garden became an independent, multipurpose structure that could function as a residence, for recreation or retreat, as a status symbol and for the cultivation of plants.

All surviving records of early garden design portray it and its elements as transition from simple to more complex design. As a rule the inherent water motif in these plans is consistently of a regular pattern. This formal scheme is undoubtedly based on the

The rudiments of garden design already appear in Assyrian times. Particularly striking is the avenue of trees flanking the temple in the right half of the picture. It shows the regular arrangement of trees in the alley on the principle of repetition (top).

The emancipation of the pool as a nonutilitarian component of the garden was an important stage of development: the drawing on the left (centre) shows a simpler version, with an accompanying double alley, reminiscent of the rows of trees flanking an irrigation canal; alleys hemming in the pool on all four sides form a compact structural whole with the body of water (centre, right).

In time the pool became the point of departure for the composition structure of the garden, especially when further lines of trees were added. A T-shaped layout represents a more developed and articulated form of the pool, and indicates the development towards symmetry (bottom).

The garden of a high official of Amenhotep III at Thebes shows an extremely perfected design. The symmetry is not merely developed in the longitudinal sense, but also transversally. The centre of the garden is, surprisingly, not a water motif, but a large pergola, in relation to which the four pools, the building, the alleys and the plantations are regularly arranged (previous page).

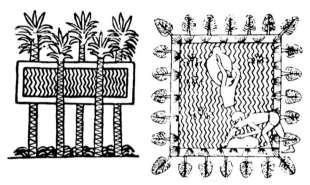

importance of water. In order to use the water efficiently, it had to be supplied in the shortest way, through straight ditches, which eventually led to the planting of trees alongside. In time the tree plantation acquired a formal alignment and the first formal landscape formation, the alley, emerged.

Subsequent addition of vegetation and other elements resulted in an ever more complex structure and thus the garden adopted the principles of spatial organization from that of agricultural land cultivation. This is an important way in which the origins of Mediterranean-European gardens differ from those of East Asia, which were based on mythology and natural scenery .

Since the basin served for water storage, it occupied the central position in the garden. In addition, it provided coolness and visual pleasure and defined the symmetrical structure of the garden. It was also frequently used in the funeral rite of passage of the deceased into the Underworld. Given these important functions, it is understandable why the water basin appeared often and in considerable dimensions. Sources cite as many as 11 basins in the so-called water-court of the royal palace Maru-Aton in Akhenaton's capital, Amarna. Its northern garden, measuring 200 by 100 metres, boasted a water basin of 120 by 60 metres. This type of water motif, designated as sacred, was also part of religious premises such as the lakes by the Temple of Amon in Karnak.

The water elements play a fundamental role in design even in the most fully developed garden plan of the 14th century B.C. The water is no longer situated on the axis: four water basins surround a central pergola and in this way determine the axial structure. This already represents a highly developed formal articulation of the garden space, in which other elements appear along the axis.

Two other examples of such high achievement in landscape design of ancient Egypt deserve a mention. One is the large, 3 kilometre-long avenue that connects the Temple of Amon in Karnak with the Temple of Queen Hatshepsut. Sphinxes, preserved to this day, are situated along the alley, and in the old times, as recorded by one of the Pharaohs of the XVIIIth Dynasty, it had been lined with trees and flowers. The Temple of Hatshepsut is of particular interest as a terraced structure of axial design built on a slope. Following the "orders of the god Amon", Queen Hatshepsut had formal gardens built on the terraces.

The Egyptian contribution to the evolution of garden art is invaluable. It developed regular forms and patterns, axial plans based on mirror symmetry, various kinds of water motif and plant formations such as alleys. These achievements have been largely taken over by subsequent periods of European landscape architecture.

Greece

Ancient Greece knew long periods of considerable social equality. Consequently, the lack of an aristocratic social stratum was reflected in a corresponding absence of magnificent buildings and fine gardens. Priority was given instead to public spaces and facilities such as plazas, gymnasiums, temples, and academies. A well-known example is the circular plaza in Sparta which was surrounded by plane trees and therefore called *platanistas*. Aristophanes described the academy of Athens (originally a private garden) as being abundantly planted with trees.

The mythology of Ancient Greece portrayed the gods in human form and situated them in an earthly, though idealized, environment. The immediate expression of this image was the sacred grove with sacred trees, familiar already to the Egyptians. Conceptually close to the sacred grove was the grotto, usually a natural rocky cave, covered with trees and accompanied by statues of Pan and nymphs. This motif became a standard feature of Renaissance, Baroque and later European garden art either as a nymphaeum or a grotto.

The Spartan, restrained mentality of classical Greece hampered the development of more splendid, pleasure-oriented gardens. These arrived with the Hellenistic Age through contacts with Eastern cultures, particularly Persian. During the time of Alexander of Macedonia, garden culture blossomed throughout Greece and the Middle East, particularly in Alexandria and Antioch. Both large parks and private residential gardens flourished. The peristyle, an internal court surrounded by columns and enclosed on four sides by the house, pre-dated the time of Alexander, though modern excavations reveal that these courts were paved. As garden courts they are described by contemporary writers as sometimes even luxurious.

The design of ancient Greek gardens was clearly rather restrained and followed patterns found in nature. The garden described in the pastoral romance *Daphnis and Chloe* is a noted exception that points to some formal elements, such as the central position of the altar to Dionysus and trees aligned formally in rows. Evidence of highly developed Greek gardening is also furnished by the abundance of cultivated garden plants, including a large collection of large flowering roses.

Imperium Romanum

The civilization of the Romans, who were possibly the greatest builders in history, also created a highly developed garden culture. The empire extended over three continents - Europe, Asia and Africa - and could build on the accomplishments of other civilizations due to the prosperity of Roman society. It is not of minor importance that the Romans were skilled at farming and developed sophisticated techniques of plan cultivation. All this led to strong attachment to the earth and countryside. Ownership of rural property, *Villa Rustica*, conveyed status to those belonging to higher social strata. It is here, on the farms of the Roman aristocracy, that the first pleasure gardens on European soil originated. Among the renowned Roman gardeners was Cicero, to whose accounts we owe much of our knowledge about the gardens of that era.

In the last century B.C., Rome witnessed a great rise in garden culture. Greek models and Oriental garden design encountered in the Middle East inspired Roman endeavours. During this period, a number of famous villas with large gardens sprung up in Rome: *Horti Pompeiani, Horti Luculliani, Horti Salustani*, and others. The basic design for the dwelling, which developed from the Italic and Greek courtyard house, was already established. However, this century witnessed a new addition - the peristyle and its extension into the *xystus*, a formal garden at the edge of the house. The *xystus* and most other gardens were based on a formal design and included the standard symmetrical water motif and a geometrical arrangement of trees called a quincunx. Water is the central feature of a peristyle garden. This is particularly visible in the case of Pompeii, where the garden design was greatly enhanced by the construction of an aqueduct. In addition, the garden was generally adorned by other elements such as portico-terraces, pergolas, benches, mosaic pavings, statues (mostly of mythological figures) and small temples, niches in the walls or small objects, *lararia*, dedicated to the souls of their ancestors.

Roman emperors contributed large-scale and brilliant layouts around their residences. Nero's Golden House, *Domus Aurea*, is a prominent example. This was a complex

The Temple of Peace, *Templum Pacis*, also called the Forum of Vespasian, in Rome was one of the city's characteristic open spaces, with a large formal garden (top).
The House of the Vettii at Pompeii displays a characteristic ground-plan. The peristyle with the garden is surrounded on all four sides by the rooms of the house or by walls (bottom).
A - entrance
B - atrium
C - peristyle
D - garden

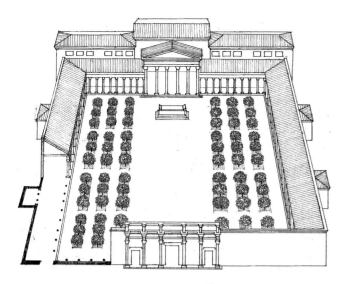

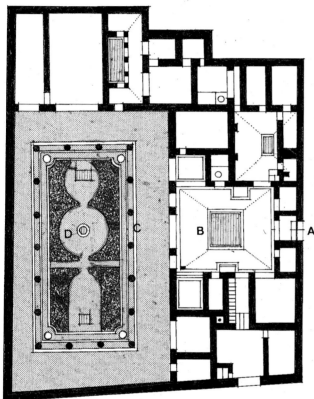

of residences and temples with gardens, groves, and fields situated by an artificial lake. In this way Nero unified urban and rural life and realized the ideal of the period, *rus in urbe*. The highest accomplishment of this concept was achieved by the Emperor Hadrian with his Villa in Tibur (Tivoli) near Rome. Remnants of the enormous complex of palaces, temples, theatres, baths, and numerous gardens are still visible today.

In spite of a strong tendency towards the amenity private garden, Ancient Rome also devoted considerable attention to public parks. The first such public facility was the promenade at the Theatre of Pompeii. This was equipped with groves and fountains dating from the year 55 B.C. Agrippa built a large park next to the baths, for public use after his death, and the public gardens on the Field of Mars, *Campus Martius*, were popular.

The gardens of Ancient Rome demonstrated sophisticated garden design for the first time on European soil. This is reflected in the further perfection of the formal and even axial design, the inventive use of water elements, basins and fountains, the accomplishment of the nymphaeum, the regular spatial arrangement of trees in the quincunx, the topiary, shaping of trees and shrubs, *opus topiarium*, and the adequate use of sculpture in the composition of gardens. Although hardly anything was left of the Roman landscape architecture a millennium later, the Renaissance creators found great inspiration from and emulated the Roman style. The Villa of Hadrian is a prime example. Echoes of its motifs can be found in the Isolotto in the Boboli Gardens and in the water parterre of the Villa Lante. Presumably, the Canopus was the model for the design of the large canal on the axis of the gardens at Versailles.

The Heritage of Ancient Rome

The fullest testimony of the gardens of the Roman period has been preserved owing to the catastrophic eruption of Vesuvius, which buried Pompeii in 79 A.D. Under the layer of lava, buildings, pavements, statues and even carbonized plants have survived intact. From these remains, can be formed a good idea of the private residence of the time, in particular in the following instances.

The *House of the Vettii, Domus Vettiorum*, is the best preserved example of a peristyle garden, with statues and other features. The *House of Loreius Tiburtinus (or Octavius Quartio)* is an extraordinary case of a rich garden; behind an atrium (the central hall of the house) which includes flower tubs, there is a peristyle opening onto a covered terrace. From there a symmetrically placed double pergola runs all along the garden, and down the centre the water falls in steps towards a nymphaeum surmounted by a small temple. The *House of the Faun* and the *House of the Tragic Poet* (p. 32) are famous for their mosaic pavements. The *House of Venus* (p. 31) and the *House of the Golden Cupids* contain interesting murals on the garden side. The *House of Julia Felix* has an exceptionally large garden with a huge pergola and four interconnected basins. Nearby Herculaneum, similarly affected by the catastrophe of 79 A.D., includes two houses with interesting gardens: the *House of the Mosaic Atrium* and the *House of the Stags*.

Hadrian's Villa at Tivoli near Rome stands out as an extensive and complex arrangement with a number of interesting elements. It was constructed in 118-134 A.D., on the basis of the emperor's own ambitious designs, and covers an area of 300 hectares, with a number of outstanding buildings and a profusion of gardens. Hadrian's Villa must have adopted numerous traits from Greek and Egyptian art. A famous feature is the so-called Canopus (p. 29), a 119 by 18 metre basin surrounded by caryatids modelled on the antique Erechtheon. A second remarkable item is the so-called Maritime Theatre, consisting of a circular island surrounded by a moat and still showing remains of a colonnaded court and a garden. Hadrian used it as a retreat.

Piazza Armerina, Sicily, is another imperial residence, preserving among other things the remains of a peristyle garden and a profusion of mosaic pavements (p. 30). Outside Italy the Roman settlement of Conimbriga - near today's Coimbra, Portugal - sports a well-preserved peristyle with splendid mosaics and a garden which is, in fact, a richly articulated parterre d'eau. It is certainly one of the most interesting designs for a peristyle garden found anywhere. A comparatively clear formal design is evident also in a large garden (100 by 70 metres) adjoining a villa excavated at Fishbourne, near Chichester, England, and dating from the first century A.D.

p. 29
One of the best preserved parts of Hadrian's Villa at Tivoli near Rome: the Canopus, a longitudinal basin, once skirted along its entire length by statues and cariatids.

p. 30
Pavements in sophisticated design, executed with great skill at Hadrian's Villa (top) and at Piazza Armerina, Sicily (bottom).

p. 31
The peristyle garden of the House of the Vettii at Pompeii (top). The House of Venus at Pompeii shows widely spread illusionist painting on the walls of the peristyle aiming at extending the visual scenery of the garden or enriching it with new motifs (bottom).

p. 32
The pavements of interiors or open spaces often display a highly varied repertory of motifs. The illustration shows the entrance and the pavement of the House of the Tragic Poet at Pompeii.

Cloister gardens and medieval court gardens

The Secluded Garden

The Garden of Delight

The Middle Ages in Europe are period in which change was slow and conventions rigidly followed. With regard to garden art, this statement is valid only for the early Middle Ages. Later garden architecture not only becomes stronger but is enriched with a greater variety of gardens. And it should not be forgotten that at the end of the Middle Ages, from the 14th to 15th centuries, those features of garden style which were the starting point for the birth of the unique Italian Renaissance were formed.

The Secluded Garden

After the decline of Rome in the 5th century and, with it, ancient civilization, there was no longer a suitable social environment for garden culture. As is often the case in history, the new ideology rejected the old values. Until the end of the millennium (with rare exceptions) no gardens are mentioned. These exceptions are monastery gardens which were, especially at the beginning, intended exclusively for utilitarian purposes, for the cultivation of medicinal herbs and vegetables. As institutions in which existing knowledge was gathered and new knowledge discovered, monasteries were able to develop expertise with regard to plant cultivation, along with which design skills also evolved. The design of the cloister was undoubtedly derived from the antique peristyle garden. In both there is an inner courtyard which is, as a rule, enclosed on all four sides by walkways with colonnades. The courtyard was also used for garden cultivation. An early and reliably documented record of a monastery garden dating from the 10th century is the famous plan (a sort of blue print, not the record of a real garden) preserved in the monastery library at St. Gallen in Switzerland. From this it is possible to make out quite a variety of garden types: a herb garden, *herbularius*, a vegetable garden, an orchard, which was also used as a cemetery, and several cloisters. The characteristic cross-like division of the garden into four parts, usually four quadrants, can already be seen here. Where the paths cross, at the exact centre of the garden, stands a fountain. This is a widely found pattern which can be traced back partly to the ancient *chahar bagh* motif of Persian origin. This became what might be called the basic design formula of the Islamic garden which, through Moorish culture in Spain and partly through Sicily, easily permeated to other parts of Europe. This is especially likely because these designs are accompanied by a centrally placed fountain, which is an established element in Islamic layouts. Such a division of a garden which is rather small and enclosed on all four sides also gives an impression of greater spaciousness. Add to this the symbolism of water as the source of life and also, perhaps, that of the cross itself, and a four-part division proves to be an ideal ground-plan for a cloister.

Although the cloister is, in a sense, perhaps the most typical, it is not the only type of medieval garden. Gardens with different purposes appeared, especially in the castles and halls of the nobility, and later at the houses of the wealthier bourgeoisie. One thing they all have in common, even the castle gardens, is their small size, which was due to the necessary economical use of space within the fortified towns and castles. This is one of the reasons why secular gardens, as well as those in monasteries, were enclosed with walls, as can be seen in a number of pictorial representations and book illustrations. Hence the impression of enclosure in the medieval garden which is conveyed by the frequently used expression *hortus conclusus*, or enclosed garden.

The medieval cloister at the Cistercian monastery of Mogyła in Poland, as it was still in 1838 (top).
The garden shown in this pictorial representation (centre) comes from the school of Hans Memling (second half of the 15th century) and contains raised, rectangular beds and regularly shaped trees .
A scene in a court garden from the 16th century: at the front, a simple division into rectangular units and, at the back of the picture, a gallery of clipped trees (bottom).

A painting from the 15th-century romance Le Roman de la Rose *(previous page).*

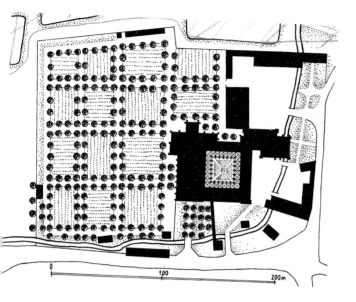

The Garden of Delight

The size as well as the design of the medieval garden did not encourage development towards representation. Therefore it was more inward-oriented, adapted to the basic needs of men who lived a more spiritually and spatially restricted life. The garden served as a dwelling place, a place for pleasure, for feasting, for love, and even for communal bathing, for which it fully merited the name pleasure garden, or *Lustgarten* as it was known in Germany. For this the garden needed more surface space, which was created by a lawn covered with flowers. At the edge of this lawn were turf benches, which are unique to the medieval garden. A number of surviving pictures bear witness to the considerable use of pergolas and arbours which were covered over by different plants, including roses. The garden beds were regularly shaped and raised above the surrounding ground, which remained a characteristic of the Middle Ages.

The French literary work *Roman de la Rose*, with its rich illustrations, is a eulogy to this kind of garden. In it can be found orchards and herb and pleasure gardens, separated by walls or hedges. This is the highest expression of the medieval symbolism of the garden as a space intended for love and amenity; an image also conveyed by individual elements in the garden, especially plants such as colourful roses and other flowers. These different meanings were in embarrassing contradiction to the role of the garden in the monastery where the structure of the garden was supposed to represent paradise, or at least a place of ascetic purity intended for religious contemplation. Of course, flowers also had symbolic meanings in the religious world: the lily, for example, and the rose were symbols of purity, and of the Virgin Mary.

The well-known medieval scholar Albertus Magnus (1200-1280) left an exceptionally clear description of the nature of secular enjoyment of the garden. In his book *On Plants (De Vegetabilibus)* there is a special chapter describing the non-utilitarian garden ("Guide to the Garden of Delight"). This was, according to Albertus, designed to provide visual delight and pleasing scents. The flowers on the lawn should enliven the garden whilst various herbs were to provide scents. At the centre should be a fountain of pure water and the garden should also contain pergolas and trees to give shade in the summer.

In the High Middle Ages, when there were already powerful ruling courts and a wealthy bourgeoisie, increasing prosperity contributed to the appearance of more richly designed gardens. In 1305 Pietro de Crescenzi from Bologna published his highly informative work on agriculture *Opus ruralium commodorum*. In it the Italian variant of the medieval garden is described. According to Crescenzi the non-utilitarian part of the garden comprised beds and areas of lawn adjacent to the house, so as to be connected with it and easily seen. The orchard was situated at the rear and thus formed a spatial frame for the garden. The garden surface was effectively divided into a greater number of elements, creating a richer articulation of its structure, which began to show itself in the movement from simple rectangular placement to more developed, ornamental patterns. These were later developed by the Renaissance, which also took over other design principles, such as the spatial frame formed by trees and the use of fountains.

Although, except for some cloisters, no medieval gardens have been preserved, different sources give an image of quite varied activity which had something to pass on to the succeeding, flourishing era. It is scarcely possible to talk about the heritage of medieval gardens for usually only the frameworks of buildings which used to contain cloister gardens have survived. What can be seen today among the cruciform pathways in the monasteries of Europe seems to adhere closely to the spirit of the medieval cloister, which is the reason for including a limited number of examples in this book.

p.37
The cloister garden of the Gothic cathedral of Utrecht in Holland has been restored in the medieval spirit. This involves both the regular arrangement of numerous rectangular beds and the selection of different medicinal and other herbs.

p.38
Instead of a fountain, a plant of a striking shape sometimes stood at the centre of the cloister, as can be seen at the 15th-century church of San Lorenzo in Florence (top). A small cloister full of medieval spirit next to the Gothic church St. Just at Narbonne in Southern France (bottom).

p.39
The Romanesque-Gothic cloister of the monastery of St. Trophime in Arles from the 12th-14th century retains a typical division into four parts (top). Similar features, especially the cruciform pathway, mark the Romanesque cloister of the cathedral St. Sauveur in Aix-en-Provence from the 12th century (bottom).

p.40
Portuguese cloisters from the Late Gothic are notorious for their decor. Particularly flamboyant is the ornamentation of the arches at the Hieronymite monastery in Belem, near Lisbon, which is matched by a richly ornamented cloister garden (top). "Paradise" is the name given to a porch on the west side of the church of the Benedictine abbey of Maria Laach. Such porches had been known since the early Christian basilicas and served as gathering places for the faithful. The inner courtyard was partly planted or paved. The name paradise, Greek *paradisos*, indicates that it used to be primarily a garden and, at the same time, conveys a symbolic meaning (bottom).

p.41
The splendid Claustro Real, King's Cloister, in the monastery of Santa Maria da Vitoria in Batalha, Portugal. The flourishing Manueline style of late Gothic provides a perfect frame, especially in the grill-like ornamentation of arches, for the strict geometry of the shaped dwarf box in the parterre.

p.42
The cloister garden of the Franciscan friary in Dubrovnik, from the first half of the 14th century (top). Beside the double colonnettes with capitals which show transitional Romanesque-Gothic stylistic features, there is an especially interesting arrangement of stone benches in the central part of the cloister. At the far end of the picture stands a fountain which, exceptionally, is not situated symmetrically in the centre. Another masterpiece in Dubrovnik is the cloister of the Dominican monastery from the 15th century (bottom). Both cloisters were heavily damaged during the Serbian bombardment of Dubrovnik in 1992.

p.43
The Certosa di Pavia near Milan (top) boasts two cloisters. The smaller one is surrounded by arcades which are lined with terracotta from the 15th century and the parterre is embroidered with trimmed box. The garden of the Basilica of St. Paul *(Sao Paolo fuori le mura)*, in Rome, dates from the 12th century; its design has been changed frequently in the present century to conform to changing tastes (bottom).

p.44
The nunnery garden at the monastery of Santa Chiara, Naples. The interior of the Gothic church was redecorated in the middle of the 18th century in Baroque style and at that time the garden was also largely changed. A pergola was added to the cruciform paths; it was originally arched, but today its upper part is flat. It is supported by 64 pillars which are connected at the bottom with benches and are all covered with tiles of majolica (hence the name *Chiostro delle majoliche*). The atmosphere of this unique garden is, in accordance with the period of its creation, more effusively Baroque inspired than monastically restrained.

The Italian Renaissance
New horizons

A new world

Man and nature: harmony and subordination

Capital of the world - cradle of the arts

The garden as a theatre of waterworks

The birth of Baroque

The universal garden

Gardens today

A remarkable but often overlooked feature of Italian garden art as a whole is its stylistic unity. In this branch of art Italy has remained faithful to her Renaissance tradition. She was immune from the striving for magnificence typical of French Baroque, and even less affected by the English landscape style, which could never strike roots on the peninsula. As a consequence, Italy's heritage of landscape architecture consists mainly of gardens laid out in the period of the Renaissance and its transition into Baroque.

A New World

A survey of any aspect of the Italian Renaissance will reveal an abundance of amazing creativity. It looks as if a charge of immense cultural energy, long restrained, suddenly erupted into creative action, unmatched by any earlier or later era of European history. This also applies to garden art, which reached its peak in this period. The rise of the "Italianate" garden is logically connected with the age of Renaissance, when all the arts and other cultural activities could thrive in a new atmosphere based on an unprecedented prosperity. One must not, however, overlook the fact that the new art was erected on foundations laid by the preceding age. The cultural explosion known as the Renaissance was triggered by changing economic and social conditions. From the 12th century onwards, a monetary economy grew, manufacture flourished, commerce and banking developed. The cities were growing and had developed into strong and complex economic and political organisms, setting the stage for a productive cultural life.

Cultural life was mainly patronized by the great aristocratic families; the princes of the Church also contributed their share, especially in Rome. The prosperous middle classes followed their lead. There is no doubt that tensions between the social classes, and the competition waged between individuals, families and cities, favoured the spread of art. At the same time one must not underestimate the encouragement offered by the new intellectual climate of openness and freedom and by the comparatively well-preserved heritage of classical antiquity.

The classical world was not only present in the remains of ancient cities, temples and villas, but also inspired the spirit of Renaissance intellectuals through its literary legacy. Scholars ordered copies of the writings of Roman and Greek poets, writers and thinkers, and often invested their entire savings in libraries. Latin was the common language of the humanists. The achievements and values of the classical age were congenial to the new era of intellectual curiosity, this generation rediscovering and desiring a joyful life, full of diversity, the charms of an idyllic countryside, and striving for a deeper insight into this world, to be achieved by way of reason and by artistic experience.

The grounds for this had been largely prepared by the writings of various authors, chiefly Boccaccio and Petrarch. Their work pioneered a new interpretation of nature as a world friendly to man, where one can move without fear and feel at home. Boccaccio's companies of friends and his lovers meet outdoors, in gardens and grottoes. Petrarch, who climbed mountains to enjoy the spectacular views, can be regarded as the first European artist to foreshadow the new approach to nature. His was the most penetrating, inventive contribution and he also rightly enjoys the reputation of greatest poet of the Renaissance. It is not widely known, however, that he was also a geographer, cartographer, travel writer, possibly a garden designer, and above all, the first European intellectual to experience nature to the full. His

Top: Giovanni Bellini, *Allegory of Souls*. The painting is highly illustrative of the new presentation of the world. For the first time in European painting, the Renaissance places an orderly, geometrical, man-designed world into primary nature. The clear polarity of the pictorial motifs seems to announce the concept of the Italian garden, which is placed in a natural setting with which it establishes a dialogue: design co-existing with spontaneous growth. This means a complete break with the medieval interpretation of man's world, withdrawn into itself and shut off from nature.
A decisive contribution towards the high degree of visual order in the plastic arts was made by the rediscovery of perspective in Renaissance Italy: a perspective study by Leonardo da Vinci from 1481 (bottom).

A scene in the garden from the influential Renaissance work by Francesco Colonna, Hypnerotomachia Poliphili, *1583 (previous page).*

description of his own mountaineering experience is a mixture of exaltation, bewilderment and zest for exploration - in short, it reflects a genuinely Renaissance attitude to nature. Natural scenery was increasingly appreciated, and even Pope Pius II, when immobilized by illness, arranged to have himself transported into the mountains on a litter, to enjoy the panoramic vistas. This openness to the charms of the landscape suggested the location of houses on hill-sides. The new consciousness of nature, in both her affable and savage aspects, was bound to be reflected in the arts and sciences.

This shift of attitude is particularly noticeable in painting. Since this art implies a visual interpretation of the world, its influence is all the more important. Changed outlooks show in both subjects and manner. Medieval painting used nature - or rather, elements taken from nature - largely for their symbolic value. For instance, the lily was a symbol of the Virgin Mary, and its white colour stood for purity. Mountains were distorted and presented in false proportions. The choice of natural features was limited, and their role within the composition was rather modest. They crowd the picture as unrelated details, each suggestive in its own right, but without fusing into a unified image. Renaissance painting also uses a wide repertory of landscape motifs, including rocks, waves, ravines, waterfalls, rivers, clouds, as well as all kinds of vegetation, groves, woods, etc., but what is striking in this wide usage of natural elements is the new visual treatment. The landscape included in the painting is no longer chosen for its symbolic implications, but is simply a fruit of the artist's experience and attempts to render the real world. A further decisive innovation of Renaissance painting is the rigorous composition. All the components of the picture are organized into an integrated whole, on the principle of hierarchy, and the single parts cannot live independently. This coherence is assured, above all, by central perspective, rediscovered by Renaissance artists and equivalent to an attempt at scientific, objective portrayal of reality. These approaches pioneered by the art of painting the wealth of natural elements, the integration of man with the open landscape, and the creation of a unified, hierarchically structured and geometrically organized scenery, were also taken up, with some delay, by landscape architecture.

Man and Nature: Harmony and Subordination

The first Renaissance gardens continue and develop the trends foreshadowed in the Middle Ages. The most telling record of this creativity are not preserved gardens but a curious book from 1467, compiled by the Dominican friar Francesco Colonna, entitled *Hypnerotomachia Poliphili*. Though disguised as a story, this is, among other things, a treatise on architecture and garden design. It describes various types of gardens: the vegetable garden, the botanical garden, the fruit garden, the rose garden, the peristyle garden, gardens with geometrical parterres, flower beds and other elements. The precious illustrations accompanying the text indicate a fairly high level of designing skill.

The book was to exert a long-term influence on Early Renaissance gardening. The same applies to the writings of Leone Battista Alberti (1404-1472), one of the most universal minds of the age, art theoretician, architect, writer, composer, lawyer, physicist and mathematician. His most celebrated publication, *De Re Aedificatoria* (1440), outlines the chief principles of architecture, modelled on the achievements of classical antiquity. He defines the typical Renaissance catchword of harmony as "consonance of all components of a work of art". Alberti's outlook found an echo, and

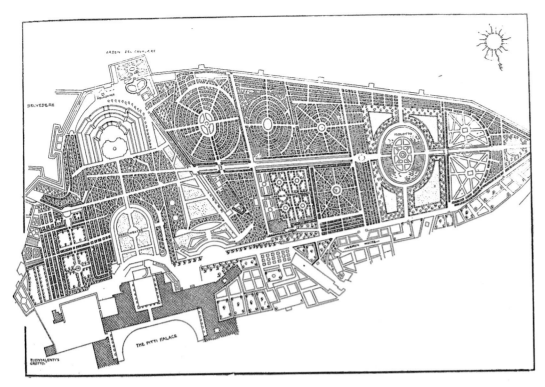

At the end of the 16th century the Flemish artist Utens produced a series of lunettes illustrating Medicean palaces and villas with gardens; they preserve a unique historical testimony. The lunette of Pratolino (top) shows a characteristic design based on numerous inventive water motifs. They began at the top, near the villa, and extended downhill through a number of cascades. The water also served as a formal accompaniment of the grottoes featuring various hydraulic automata.

Centre: Castello near Florence on a Utens lunette. The garden shows a far more complex structure and covers a larger area than its present-day remains. But the current state allows an almost complete restoration, which would be a big step towards the revival of the brilliant activities of the Medici in Tuscany.

One of the most radical steps in Renaissance garden design was taken by Bramante when he built the stairs in the Belvedere Courtyard, between the Vatican Palace and the Belvedere (bottom). The difference in height was bridged by an ingenious twin double stairway. This was to become a standard formula, capable of innumerable variations, in later Renaissance and Baroque garden design.

The Boboli gardens (this page on the left) represent an extensive landscape structure. The main part is seen at the bottom of the plan, where first an amphitheatrical parterre opens up behind the Pitti Palace; then the layout ascends, to end in a terrace-like semicircular termination, rising around the Neptune basin. Transversally, the great axis starts on the slope and leads past a number of bosquets to the Isolotto.

influenced contemporary garden designs. One of his most persuasive principles, adopted from classical antiquity, was the preference for a villa built on a hillside, with a sweeping panoramic view. Another important development was the unity of house and garden, established by links such as loggias and colonnades. The book also contains detailed instructions for the layout of grottoes, pergolas and fountains, as well as recommendations - largely inspired by Pliny - for garden plantations.

Alberti was able to put his ideas into practice in 1446, when he built the Rucellai Palace in Florence, and again in 1459, when (as some scholars believe) he designed the Villa Quaracchi, which also included a garden, partitioned by a pergola arranged along an axis, and framed by a hedge of trimmed box. There was also a privy garden, *giardino segreto*, an enclosed compartment set apart for privacy, which was to become an indispensable ingredient of Italian Renaissance gardens. Unfortunately none of these influential gardens is preserved. Hardly anything survives of another renowned Early Renaissance garden, adjoining the Villa Careggi and laid out by Michelozzo Michelozzi for Cosimo, one of the Medici of Florence. It owes its fame to the fact that it was the meeting-place of Cosimo's Platonic Academy, which gathered artists such as Brunelleschi, Donatello, Michelangelo, Michelozzo and others.

In 1458-61 a remarkable concept of a garden and house was carried out in Fiesole, near Florence, on a daringly terraced steep slope. In this Villa Medici Alberti's ideal of a villa set on a hillside with a wide view was realized in its purest form, designed also by Michelozzo (p. 74). One of the terraces connected with the house still preserves a *giardino segreto*. In spite of subsequent changes, the original layout of the garden remains, as the first terraced garden structure. This milestone of Renaissance garden design was an exception in Tuscany where gardens were, as a rule, laid out on flatter ground. Such radical reshaping of hilly sites did not reappear until half a century later, in the vicinity of Rome, for example the Villa Madama, the Villa d'Este, and several others. The 15th century gardens of Tuscany, though partly reverting to the features of medieval layouts, may be considered as a first step towards the glories of 16th century High Renaissance.

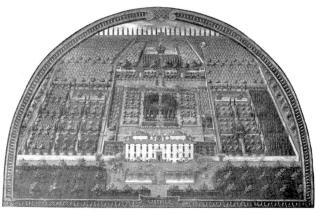

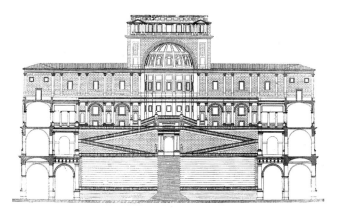

Capital of the World - Cradle of the Arts

If the artistic bloom of Tuscany was based on the economic prosperity of Florence and growing political power of the Medici - who commissioned an impressive array of garden villas - the flowering of Rome was founded on the return of the popes from Avignon and reaffirmation of ecclesiastical authority. While Tuscany achieved its Golden Age already in the 15th century, Rome only recovered in the 16th century, when the papal court had assumed certain traits of a secular court. It became a gathering-place not only for the high ecclesiastic, but also for artists such as Bramante, Raphael, and Michelangelo. Though Roman 16th century art was predominantly religious in content, its manner was close to that of secular art. It aimed at splendour, monumentality and even power. This applies to all genres of art, including landscape architecture. All the important 16th century gardens in Rome and her surroundings were commissioned by popes or cardinals. They mark a new era, the most brilliant in the entire history of Italian, and possibly European, garden art.

The development was started in 1503 by Bramante, who redesigned the Belvedere Courtyard between the Vatican Palace and the Villa Belvedere for Pope Julius II, a great patron of architecture. Bramante's plan included a miniature private garden for the pope, *atrio di piacere*, a tilt-yard for tournaments and festival processions, and a monumental stairway to bridge the grade. The two-ramp garden stairway, symmetrically placed in the axis of the buildings, was one of the most ingenious and revolutionary novelties in the history of landscape architecture. Its importance cannot be exaggerated, for it was to become one of the standard models for gardens laid out on uneven ground. Another important new aspect was that as a central design it favoured axial composition. It ushered in the age of axial garden layouts, which culminated in the Early Baroque gardens of the turn of the next century as demonstrated by the gardens at the Villa Aldobrandini at Frascati. Bramante's courtyard survives in essentials, though it was bisected in the early 19th century by a wing of the Vatican Library.

A second revolutionary contribution was made by Raphael, who designed the Villa Madama on the outskirts of the city, in 1516, for Cardinal Giulio de' Medici. Both the villa and the multi-terraced garden are boldly cut in the hillside, in a way that was to become the standard for later layouts (p. 64). Though the garden was never finished, due to Raphael's death in 1520, the basic outlines of the design are still recognizable after almost 500 years. The terraced structure divides the space into a number of levels, each remarkable in itself. The most attractive, even today, is the one on which stands the Casino. The building opens in the north onto a small *giardino segreto*, but in a new way - directly, not through a porticoed loggia. Thus Raphael's plan introduced two radical innovations: the inventively varied terrace structure of the garden, and the perfect solution of its integration with the villa.

When Pirro Ligorio was asked to design a garden with a Casino for Pope Pius IV at the Vatican in 1560, he tackled his task in the same spirit. The result was a dramatically articulated layout on a slope, with a main terrace, comprising the Casino, an oval garden court, and an open loggia which reaches down to the Nymphaeum on the lower terrace, linking the two levels. Originally the upper section of the garden was surrounded on three sides by a thicket, *bosco*, which served to emphasize the privacy of the garden, where the pope used to retire alone or with a company of friends.

After a sequence of outstandingly successful terraced layouts, the new concept set a fashion, and hillside locations became more popular than arrangements on level ground. Nevertheless, Vignola conceived a remarkably structured garden on flat land in 1550, the Villa Giulia outdoing any terraced layout in drama. He proceeded from the same guideline as the hillside designers, aiming at a maximum of spatial development and articulation. He fully achieved this aim in the villa built for Pope Julius III on the outskirts of Rome. The design develops in a longitudinal direction. It sets out from a semicircular courtyard framed by the house and, on the other three sides, by a double colonnade. At the bottom the colonnade opens up, to allow passage into a second small court, called the Nymphaeum. This consists of a sunken terrace and, even lower down, a grotto with a fountain and a set of caryatids, creating the illusion of dramatically structured ground. The layout continues and concludes with a *giardino segreto*.

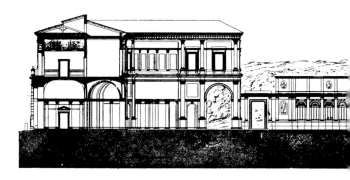

There are no strict boundaries between building and garden; exterior and interior are only part of a single spatial continuum. The Villa Giulia is an unsurpassed *tour de force* on two accounts: by its spatial articulation and by its perfect fusion of exterior and interior, unheard of even in oriental garden art.

Vignola produced another thrilling instance of structured space at Caprarola, where he was invited to build a Casino for Cardinal Farnese. The access to the Casino leads uphill over a *cordonata*, a gently rising double stairway with a chain cascade down the middle. When the top of the steps is reached, a surprise view opens on a small, harmoniously proportioned *giardino segreto*, one of the finest ever laid out in the age of the Renaissance. On the other side of the Casino, the garden continues in a geometrical arrangement, dramatically contrasted with the exuberant natural forest that surrounds it. None of Vignola's creations is cut deep into the slope, his terraced structure is, as far as possible, adapted to the grade. The most eloquent example of this is the garden of Villa Lante, in Bagnaia. Here the arrangement gradually rises uphill from ground level in a number of smaller terraces, almost casually embedded in the *bosco*. This is the last stage in Italian Renaissance garden design, ranging from the Villa Medici at Fiesole, Belvedere Courtyard, Villa Madama, Villa Giulia, Villa d'Este to Caprarola and the Villa Lante, whereby the vertical articulation of sloping gardens was developed to unsurpassed perfection.

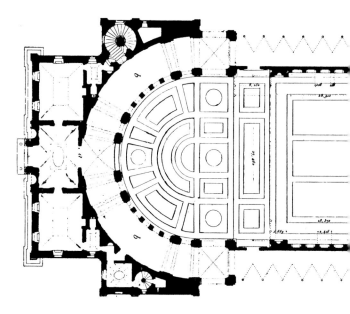

The Garden as a Theatre of Waterworks

Italy's most famous garden, created around the villa of Cardinal d'Este in the most glorious period of Roman Renaissance, deserves a chapter by itself. Here Ligorio has not only inventively conceived one of the most demanding hillside arrangements, but has also created a unique panorama of water motifs which is in no way limited to the usual fountains also known to the Middle Ages and Early Renaissance. Water is now treated as a versatile, plastic material, which can be shaped in an infinite number of forms, in various types of waterworks, either independently or connected with statues. In addition to its role as sculptural medium, the acoustic characteristics of water are also exploited. The hydraulic feat known as a water organ, already used by the ancient Romans and described by Vitruvius in the ninth book of his work on architecture, was revived at this time. The repertory of water patterns was complemented by mirroring surfaces of running or standing water. The Villa d'Este gardens are filled out to the last nook and cranny with hundreds of water motifs. Simultaneously a second celebrated waterworks arrangement was being laid out around the Villa Pratolino, near Florence. The wealth of its water motifs is preserved on a lunette by Utens. It was also described by M. de Montaigne in his notes on his travels to Italy. The

The Villa di Papa Giulio, the suburban villa of Pope Julius III in Rome. The ground-plan and the cross-section reveal the highly composite structure of this architectural and scenic entity, perhaps the most inventive and integrated design ever bequeathed by the Italian Renaissance. In spite of the symmetric arrangement of the ground-plan, the movement of the visitor within this richly articulated space is multi-directional and multi-layered, and produces a thrilling sequence of contrasting spatial experiences.

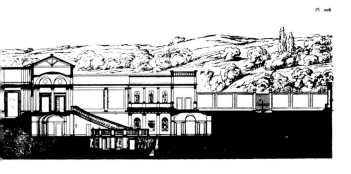

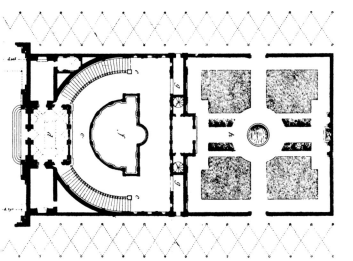

philosopher was deeply impressed by the grotto with sound effects, the statues moved by the action of water and the various waterworks machinery. The classic example of compositional use of water is the Villa Lante, with its subtly designed water parterre, and a whole axis of water motifs, along which the iconographic programme of the garden develops. At a later age Italian Early Baroque produced two extraordinary instances of shaped water at Frascati: the Villa Aldobrandini and the Villa Torlonia, with its famous theatre of waterworks.

The age of High Renaissance, in the 16th century, also launched a third interesting regional development, after Tuscany and Rome - in the Republic of Venice, whose art was profoundly influenced by Andrea Palladio. He preferred to locate his buildings on sites with a splendid view. He seems to have created only a few gardens, of which that of Villa Maser is partly preserved. It shows typical Venetian features, a more subdued structure, gradual blending into nature, harmonious proportions, and reliance on the thematic programme rather than on outside effects.

The Birth of Baroque

It is no accident that the characteristics of Baroque were foreshadowed in Rome. The secular power of the Church was increasingly reflected in the designs of gardens and buildings, particularly in the second half of the 16th century, so that a new style had taken shape by the turn of the century. It was rooted in the striving for glamour, grandeur and glitter. The chief stylistic features of the new approach were already developing in the productions of the High Renaissance. Centric layout was already announced by Bramante's garden stairway, axial division was introduced in the Este, Lante and Caprarola gardens.

The forerunner of the new style was the Villa Aldobrandini at Frascati. The building was now placed at the end, not at the beginning of the layout. From the entrance, which is located on the compositional axis, the programme develops along a sequence of trimmed palisades. It gradually intensifies towards the monumental two-ramp stairway fronting the palace. The axis continues behind the building, through a symmetrically placed Nymphaeum and a stepped cascade, and leads into the open landscape behind (p. 79). From now on the palace, by its central position and size, dominates the space and defines the axis, which runs out into the space beyond the confines of the garden. The design is becoming longitudinal, everything is subordinated to the main axis and the auxiliary axes. The components of the garden are given gentler, smoother shapes, to integrate into the fluent rhythm of the overall concept. Therefore the former private gardens, *giardini segreti*, are replaced by interconnected parterres, with lower ornamental patterns. The more representational character of those gardens calls for large-scale details, especially water motifs. This is a feature particularly noticeable in the gardens of the Villa Torlonia, also situated at Frascati, Villa Marlia and others. These early Baroque works are in many respects still typically Italian in style with features such as the terraced structure and moderate proportions. The large-scale splendidly representational Baroque layouts were yet a long way ahead in the era of French absolutism in the second part of the 17th century.

The Universal Garden

To carry out a thematically complex and formally diverse programme, Renaissance art developed a varied vocabulary of garden features, derived from several sources. The use of water patterns described above is an instance of this abundant store of forms. Another example is the repertory of sculpture employed in the composition of the garden.

The thematic programme relies heavily on themes and motifs from ancient mythology. The gardens are often converted into veritable sculpture galleries and the statues often play a key role in the spatial design, like the caryatids in the *giardino segreto* at Caprarola (p. 63). This pre-eminent role of the sculpture is chiefly based on its allegoric or symbolic implications. A particular example is Bomarzo, with its collection of unusual, often macabre statues in a wooded terrain. This repeats, in a grotesque, partly caricatured form, the motif of the holy grove, *sacro bosco*, already known to classical antiquity. The iconographic programme was similar in Pratolino, where only a larger-than-life statue of the Apennines is preserved, related to a smaller figure at Castello. These, too, are an expression of the exuberant Italian humour verging on the macabre. The grotto motif also belongs to this thematic programme. The first grottoes were of regular design; later on, irregularity was increasingly preferred, as a more suitable backdrop to the scenes from classical mythology or pastoral poetry.

Geometry supplied another vocabulary of form. In this field the Renaissance not only logically continues the historic evolution, but also creates its own unmistakable language. In comparison to the preceding periods, the repertory of geometric patterns is significantly widened and perfected. A fully developed, complex and purposefully organized geometric ground-plan, to which all details are strictly subordinated, appears for the first time. Unique contributions in this respect are the terraced articulation of the garden space and Bramante's two-ramp staircase. The vegetation, too, must be subordinated to geometry, and appears almost exclusively in clipped forms, which are one of the dominating design features. Since evergreen woody plants are preferred (box, laurel, *Quercus ilex*, *Viburnum tinus*), the *chiaroscuro* effect of the garden, with its alternating elements of light and shadow, is striking. This development also accounts for the prevailing monochrome character of the Renaissance garden, where colourful flowers are used with restraint and are allowed to play only a limited role in composition.

Gardens Today

This section can indicate only a selection from the rich garden heritage preserved in Italy. Some of the more important gardens not illustrated in the plate section of the book are listed at the end of the chapter.

Rome and Environs

The most splendid gardens of Italy are concentrated in and around the city that has at long times been the focal point of the civilizations of the Peninsula. The vast material, intellectual and political resources gathered in this area for centuries have inevitably left their mark on cultural activities, and particularly on gardening art.

Villa Madama. This is one of the oldest Renaissance garden villas, and is situated on the slopes of Monte Mario. It was built for Cardinal Giulio de' Medici, from 1516 onwards. The original plan was drawn by Raphael, but Giulio Romano, Antonio Sangallo the Younger and Giovanni da Udine also worked on this project. Both the garden and the villa are laid out on terraces cutting deep into the hillside (p. 64). The villa is a classical example of an open building, linked with the garden through terraces and courts. To the north the house opens on a *giardino segreto*, enclosed by a barrier of greenery, which sets off two giants by Bandinelli, which are the only remains of the

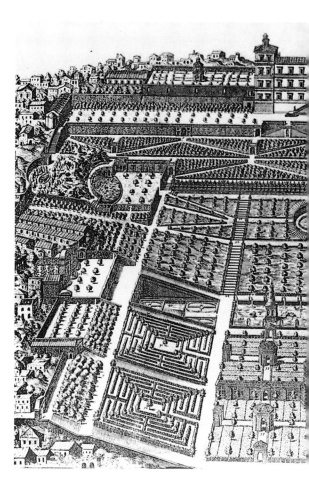

The exceptional position occupied by the gardens of the Villa d'Este in the Italian Renaissance is justified not only by its unique repertory of water motifs, but even more by its rich design. While the Villa Giulia achieved its vertical articulation with great effort, Ligorio, by means of terracing, carried out a demanding programme with surprising ease on the steep slope of Tivoli. Today the garden is in many respects mutilated; in particular, most of the sculpture is missing. Yet the main features are preserved in a form comparatively close to the etching dating from 1573 (top). The structure of the garden shows a symmetrical grid, with a pronounced main axis rising from the garden portal towards the entrance to the villa. According to the original plan, the garden was supposed to have nine longitudinal and thirteen transversal paths, complemented with a few diagonal links in the steeper upper section of the garden. Such a number of pathways implies, of course, a certain lack of unity and clarity; at the same time it prevents the various elements from assuming a leading role in the total composition.

The first principal motif noticed by the visitor as he enters the garden is a cross-shaped pergola; according to the original design, it should be flanked on each side by mazes, which were never laid out. The exit from the pergola marks the beginning of the first transverse axis, designed as a symbolic sequence of motifs. It began at the left, on the hill, with the Fountain of Nature, or Organ Fountain, where once used to stand Diana of Ephesus, symbol of fertility. From here the water flows into a sequence of ponds; it was supposed to end up in the Sea Fountain at the extreme right, another feature that was never built. This transverse water course was intended as a glorification of nature.

Higher up on the longitudinal axis is the Fountain of the Dragons, where the central place was reserved for a Hercules statue. The owner, Cardinal Ippolito d'Este,

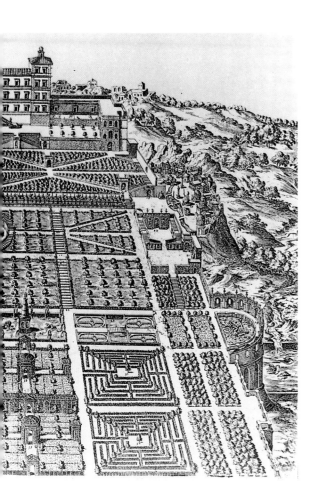

rich collection of garden sculpture. Because of its daring graded layout and its inventive interlacing of house and garden the complex was an inspiration to generations of landscape architects, both in Italy and abroad.

Villa di Papa Giulio in Rome. This was constructed in 1550-1555 as a suburban villa. The idea was conceived by the pope himself but the actual designs are by Vasari, Michelangelo, and, above all, Vignola and Ammanati. In its present-day state the garden shows only traces of the original arrangements, but the unique ground-plan is still discernible. No other Renaissance garden in Italy, and hardly any elsewhere in Europe, shows such a perfect blend of house and garden. The architectural elements encircle and create the garden space, which in turn invades the building (p. 65).
The complex begins with a semicircular courtyard embraced by the colonnaded side-wings of the palace, its parterre today simplified and overgrown with grass. Its backdrop is formed by a straight wall, with a portal located on the axis of the complex. Through the portal the path leads down a semicircular stairway into a sunken plateau, also semicircular. It houses, on an even lower level, the famous Nymphaeum, a classical motif with caryatids and a basin. Two levels above the Nymphaeum another portal leads into the *giardino segreto*. All along the longitudinal axis, over a comparatively small distance, the space widens and narrows, opens and closes, rises and falls. It would be difficult to find another instance of such convincing logic, such natural structuring of space, where garden concept and architecture define and complement one another to such an extreme degree. Understandably and inevitably, the residential entity in this case - quite exceptionally in Italian Renaissance design - does not open outwards and so consequently lacks any links with the surroundings.

Villa Medici. Situated on Mount Pincio, in the immediate vicinity of the Spanish Steps, it presumably marks the site of the ancient garden villa of Lucullus. The garden is laid out on a plateau rising above the city. While the entrance façade of the building is rather plain, the garden façade is intensely articulated, and opens onto the garden by a profusely decorated terrace, a typically Italian link-up of exterior and interior (p. 61). In front of the high building there is a wide parterre, enclosed on one side by a wall with a terrace and several niches, and on the other side by the *bosco*, a dense grove with shady alleys skirting the paths. The villa was commissioned by Cardinal Ricci in 1554 and designed by Giovanni Lippi (not by his son Annibale, as sometimes stated). The residence later passed into the hands of Cardinal Ferdinando de' Medici. The garden has, on the whole, preserved its original layout, though the parterre is greatly simplified. The grounds can only be visited exceptionally, by permission from the French Academy, owners of the villa.

Villa Pia, Vatican Gardens. Laid out in 1560 after a plan by Pirro Ligorio, it is, like so many other residences in Rome, a masterpiece of vertical articulation, with the design programme arranged on two separate levels. In the upper section, in front of the Casino, there is a courtyard, surrounded by a wall and backdrop of trees. The lower level includes the classical Nymphaeum (p. 62), a grand arrangement in a rather restricted space. Visits are only possible by permission from the Vatican administration.

Villa d'Este, Tivoli, is the most famous example of Italian gardening art. It would be hard to find a more ideal site for this, so typically Renaissance creation. It sprawls on a steep slope in classical Tivoli, near Hadrian's Villa and offers a beautiful view of the city. Cardinal Ippolito d'Este commissioned Pirro Ligorio to design a garden villa to replace a small building on the site. While the new palace turned out to be a

identified himself with this ancient mythological hero, which explains the key position of the fountain. Immediately behind the fountain, a second transverse axis crosses the main avenue; it has the same length and the same termination as the lower. Its beginning at the extreme left is marked by the Tivoli Fountain, today called *Ovato*, Oval Fountain. It is set off by statues of the Sibyl and of the divinities of two local rivers, Aniene and Erculaneo.
Even higher up rises the figure of Pegasus, symbolically marking the spot as Mount Parnassus. The axis continues towards what is probably the most famous motif of the garden, the Pathway of the Hundred Fountains, characterized not only by the innumerable jets of falling and splashing water, but also by symbols from the Este coat-of-arms. The path ends at the *Rometta*, a diminutive model of Rome, with a figure of the goddess of the city and a number of famous ancient buildings. At a slightly lower level there is the Fountain of the Emperors, today called the Fountain of Persephone; close by is the Fountain of the Owl, once notorious for its hydraulic automata. The pressure of water triggered off the twitter of bronze birds, which suddenly stopped with the appearance of the figure of an owl. Today the fountain shows only the remains of the Apples of the Hesperides; above them the eagle from the Este coat-of-arms can be seen.
The upper section of the garden is thus a glorification of art, and at the same time an attempt to interpret the garden as an image of the ancient Garden of the Hesperides. The owner and creator of the garden is therefore singled out as a man of exceptional virtues. In other words, this garden is just another version of the known theme: the owner presents himself to the world as a man of special merit - an important consideration in the competition of cardinal families for the highest post in the Vatican hierarchy.

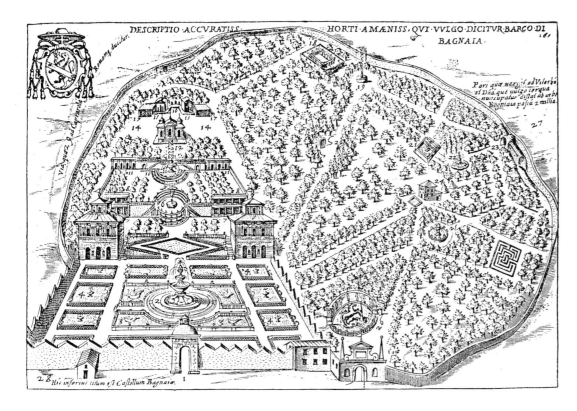

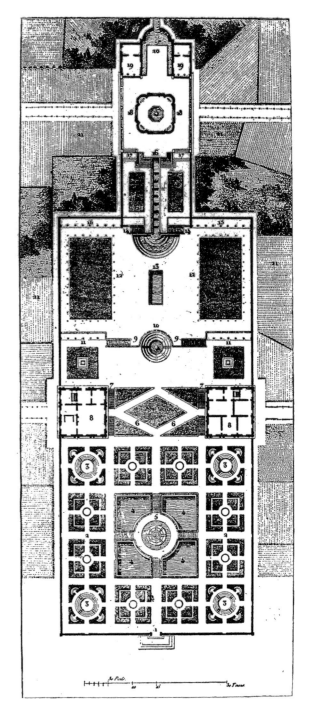

comparatively mediocre product, the garden is, from any viewpoint, an exemplary achievement. Its arrangement began in the mid 16th century and was probably not concluded before the 17th century. The garden is laid out on the slope beneath the palace, in the form of a network of rectangles on several terraces. The original access was from below, along the axis of approach to the villa. This main axis is crossed by an important transversal line, the Terrace of the Hundred Fountains, ending on one side in a model of ancient Rome, and on the opposite side in the famous oval fountain (p. 76). The abrupt terrain is structured into a sequence of terraces linked lengthwise and crosswise by flights of steps, fountains and grottoes.

But the most brilliant feature of the garden is its water system. The abundance and variety of water motifs is unmatched anywhere. Ligorio has diverted the water of the nearby Aniene river through a 600 metre tunnel that carries 1200 litres per second. This huge quantity of water is used to feed the unbelievable profusion of water motifs: 50 fountains, 250 sprinklers, 53 fans, 290 spouts, 60 sources, 50 gargoyles, 250 waterfalls, 100 basins, 20 stepped cascades. It is a triumph of Italian hydraulic engineering, by then already highly developed. The garden is calculated both to dazzle by its close-range visual effects and long-range views, and to charm by its acoustic impressions. It has also been appreciated by visitors because of its refreshing atmosphere, contributed to by the splashing water and the air currents on the slope.

Villa Lante, Bagnaia, near Viterbo, 60 kilometres northeast of Rome. If the Villa d'Este is the most renowned example of Italian landscape architecture, the Villa Lante certainly deserves to be called its most perfect achievement. It was conceived by Vignola for Cardinal Gambara, probably from 1566 onwards. The next owner, Cardinal Montalto, added a few valuable improvements, especially the central fountain. The garden has preserved the chief features of its layout. It is built symmetrically. The longitudinal axis, starting from the entrance, bisects the parterre and leads, over a double stairway, uphill where it continues over four terraces with fountains, a chain cascade, an octagonal basin and other elements, all framed in by a

The Villa Lante at Bagnaia (above) shows an interesting division of the grounds into two. The larger right-hand side on the engraving above, left, is covered by a park, in the Renaissance period usually intended for hunting. This part had a special entrance and was open to the public. Just beyond the entrance is the large, oval Pegasus Fountain; more fountains were arranged along the avenue, so the visitor could follow, step by step, a thematic programme.

This part is today practically unrecognizable. At the passage to the more rigorously arranged formal garden (the plan above) a new program begins to unfold. Its elements are arranged along the water axis, descending over three terraces. The highest terrace features first, in the background, the Fountain of the Deluge, and subsequently, at the passage to the lower terrace, the

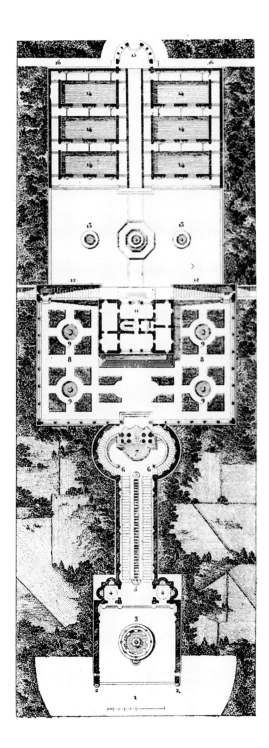

Fountain of the Dolphins, from where the water, mainspring of fertility, runs downhill over a cascade. The cascade is dominated by the sign of Cancer, emblem of Cardinal Gambara. The middle terrace begins with the Fountain of Giants, featuring the fluvial divinities of the Tiber and the Arno, the two rivers fertilizing the cardinal's estates. The symbolism is completed by the figures of Pomona and Flora. The terraced section is concluded by the Fountain of Lights, flanked by the grottos of Neptune and Venus, who stand for fertility. The counterpart to this terraced section is the flat lower garden with its prominent water parterre crowned by the Fountain of the Moors.

Above: as a whole the scheme of the garden of Villa Farnese at Caprarola displays great similarity to the layout of Villa Lante's garden.

dense thicket. The square-shaped lower parterre is richly articulated, consisting of two rows of smaller squares. The outer ring of squares, marked by patterns of trimmed box, encloses the four inner squares, comprising a water parterre with the circular Fountain of the Moors, surmounted by the figures of four putti carrying the Montalto coat-of-arms. From there the geometrical arrangement follows the axis up the wooded slope, running out into an extensive *bosco*, which stands out from the formal arrangement by its natural exuberance. It is a convincing confrontation of man-made geometry with spontaneous, unsubdued nature. As in all his designs, Vignola displays a marked preference for terraced structure but here the appearance is less dramatic than usual, and the gentler transitions allow a more compact arrangement of the components. Seldom is the garden so emphatically independent, as the two symmetrically arranged Casinos are discreetly relegated to the second plane.

Villa Farnese, Caprarola, near Viterbo. This is another creation by Vignola. He erected the imposing villa, commissioned by Cardinal Farnese, on the foundations of a never-finished pentagonal fortress. The splendid gardens, intimately connected with the villa, have not been preserved. But the garden adjoining the Casino, conceived from 1584 onwards, at some distance from the villa, is in a good state of preservation. It is reached by an alley walk. The access is indicated by a circular basin, situated on the axis of the stairway, which is accompanied by two large rustic grottoes. The flight of steps is surmounted by a fountain, with a sculpture of a river god. Here a surprise view opens up into the *giardino segreto*, a narrow parterre of trimmed box framed by a low wall surmounted by vase-bearing figures, *canephori*. This part of the garden is overlooked by the Casino, around which the path leads into the last section of the grounds, surrounded by a setting of dense natural vegetation. The Casino garden is one of Italy's most celebrated arrangements. It fully deserves its fame, subtly nestled into the slope, it offers spatial surprises at every turn, successfully combines geometrical and natural features and particularly impresses by its fine proportions.

Bomarzo, near Viterbo, north of Rome, is one of the most peculiar gardens ever created. In a valley, deep beneath the Orsini castle, the visitor is stunned by an irregular arrangement of grotesque beasts and buildings, monsters and mythologicial figures. They are hewn out of the local rock outcrop, and include a giant, a seated woman, a sleeping nymph, a river god, Fortune, a siren, a dragon and a lion fighting a snake. In addition to this jumble of figures, the park includes constructions like a distorted house, a temple, a chapel, theatres and grottoes. Everything about this garden remains puzzling. Neither its origins and purpose, nor the meaning of the various components can be satisfactorily explained. It was laid out by members of the Orsini family, Gian Carlo and his son Vicino, in the mid 16th century. Recent research suggests that Vicino, the chief creator, was inspired partly by personal experiences such as the death of his wife, military campaigns and confinement as a prisoner-of-war, and partly by literary works, chiefly Torquato Tasso's *Gerusalemme Liberata*.

Villa Aldobrandini, Frascati, 17 kilometres east of Rome. This was constructed on a fairly steep slope for the nephew of Pope Clement III, from a plan by Giacomo della Porta at the end of the 16th century. The garden clearly foreshadows the Baroque ground-plan, with an emphasized axis starting out from the entrance, at the bottom, and running as a trimmed alley towards the castle, which tops a wide two-ramp stairway. The axis continues on the other side of the palace with a Nymphaeum and ends by a cascade. In summer the waterfall serves to cool the space between the

Nymphaeum and the villa. By a number of compositional features, in particular the consequent axial design and firm formal links with the building, this complex represents Italy's purest Early Baroque design.

Villa Torlonia, formerly called Villa Ludovisi, also at Frascati. The garden was damaged by bombing in World War II, and has suffered further ravages by its conversion into a public park after the war. Nevertheless, the visitor is still overwhelmed by the magnificent flight of stairs at the entrance, and by the giant cascade surmounting the open-air theatre (p. 79), which allows one to imagine the vanished splendour of the famous theatre of waterworks.

Villa Doria Pamphili, or Villa Belrespiro, from the middle of the 17th century. It was built on Monte Gianicolo, Rome, from a design by Alessandro Algardi of Bologna. The garden is arranged on three terraces. The only comparatively well preserved feature is the parterre on the second terrace, beneath the Casino. The third, lowest, terrace was originally the most impressive and included a large amphitheatre, an open-air theatre, fountains and an array of sculptures. Later interventions, especially the rearrangement in the English style, have suppressed most of the motifs of this terrace. Belrespiro once competed in size with the Villa Borghese gardens. The area covered by the formal garden has shrunk, but the characteristic three-terrace layout remains, as do the numerous picturesque umbrella pines *(Pinus pinea)*, for which this garden and its surroundings have always been famous.

Tuscany

Tuscany was the cradle of Italian Renaissance garden art, whose characteristic features first appeared in Florence and the surrounding area.

Villa Medici, Fiesole, near Florence. This was the first harbinger of the new concept of a rural residence. By embedding his terraced structure in a steep slope, Michelozzo put into practice, in 1458-1461, Alberti's principle of locating the building on an elevated spot commanding a good view (p. 74). The highest terrace is directly connected with the house, while a lower terrace is accessible from the basement. Both the villa and the garden have been later reshaped, but the distinctive structural features, which have made this Medici residence a model for innumerable later gardens, have survived practically intact.

Castello, another Medici villa, on the outskirts of Florence, was designed in 1540 by Il Tribolo for Cosimo I. In spite of later transformations, the main part has preserved its original character of a closed garden, or *hortus conclusus*. Its cloistered character is emphasized by the fringe of trees, which merges into a bosco on the edges of the upper terrace. This terrace includes a pond with a small island surmounted by the mythological figure of January by Bartolomeo Ammanati.

Boboli Gardens, Florence. This is the largest of all the Medici gardens, covering an area of 35 hectares. It was also laid out for Cosimo I, mainly from a design by Il Tribolo. When the artist died in 1550, the works were unfinished, and some changes were carried out in the 17th century. The basic structure of the garden consists of a huge semicircular amphitheatre opening behind the Pitti Palace (p. 72). At the upper end it tapers off towards the slope, where it runs out in a small oval space centred on a basin with a Neptune statue. The terraced flanks of the amphitheatre are crowned by a row of statues. Here the public used to gather for the famous Medici banquets which celebrated weddings and similar occasions. A particularly precious feature of the garden is the Isolotto, an oval islet in a basin of the same shape (p. 73). The islet

By its pure and consistently executed axial layout, the Villa Aldobrandini at Frascati opens the Baroque period of landscape architecture (top). The defining axis is prominent both in the ground-plan (bottom) and quite particularly in the perspective view (middle); behind the villa it runs out into a semicircular nymphaeum, surmounted by a cascade. Especially striking is the formal fusion of building and garden, based on the central axis and the symmetrically arranged elements; it is vividly illustrated by the view shown in the central picture.

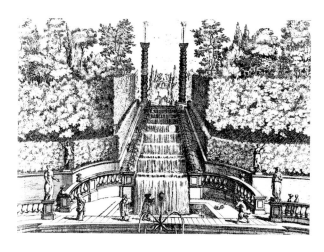

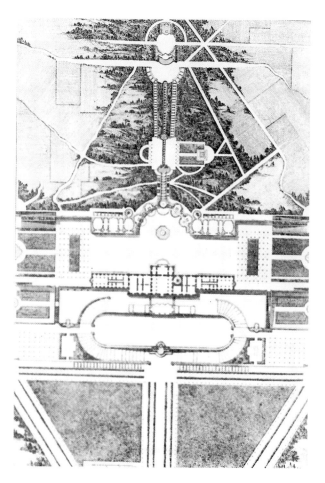

supports a giant fountain, with the figure of Oceanus overlooking the allegoric representations of the rivers Euphrates, Nile and Ganges.

Villa Gamberaia, Settignano, a few kilometres east of Florence. This commands a splendid hill-crest site, with a fine view of the valley. The present-day version of the garden presumably dates from the 18th century, when it passed in to the hands of the Capponi family. Some important modifications have also been introduced in this century. But in spite of all these changes, it not only preserves a number of outstanding formal features, but even the character of a Tuscan garden. Its most salient section is the *parterre d'eau* which faces the villa and is concluded by an arched wall of clipped greenery. In the vicinity of the villa there is also a remarkably preserved grotto with a terrace.

Villa Celsa, 10 kilometres west of Siena. The current appearance of the garden largely differs from its original form conceived by the architect Peruzzi in the early 16th century. The most valuable existing section is a survival of the 17th century Baroque version, consisting of a semicircular basin surrounded by a characteristic *bosco*. The approach to this motif originally led under a pergola, and is today flanked by an undulating clipped hedge.

Villa Marlia, Fraga, near the city of Lucca. After its Renaissance beginnings the garden was given its present shape at the end of the 17th century. Starting from the entrance, the various motifs are arranged as openings in a dense *bosco*. The most remarkable feature is a rectangular basin, 40 metres long by 20 metres wide, enclosed by a balustrade and a multi-layered clipped hedge. Further on, there is another interesting detail, an open-air theatre decorated with the statues of Harlequin, Columbine and Pulcinella. Here, too, the *chiaroscuro* atmosphere and measured proportions suggest the refinements of chamber music. Another attractive motif is located behind the villa: a small parterre garden set off by a semicircular basin and several fountains. Though the grounds, as a whole, lack a unified plan, some of the details are among the masterpieces of landscape design.

Villa Garzoni, Collodi, 15 kilometres east of Lucca. Here Count Garzoni laid out a curious garden in the mid 17th century, probably after his own design. The first view the visitor sees at the entrance shows a feature rather unexpected in the Baroque period: the garden is not linked to the palace. The centrepiece of the layout is a magnificent symmetrical stairway of unusual dimensions, which dominates the composition by its three terraces. The axis continues over a simple flight of steps, passes a cascade, and ends in a giant statue of Fame holding a horn of plenty overbrimming with water. The thematic weight of the stairway is underscored by the accessory motifs which consist of a theatre embedded in greenery, a Nymphaeum and several walks lined with statues representing Neptune, Apollo, Daphne, Chloe, Diana and others. In spite of the bold conception of the stairway on a steep grade, one cannot help feeling a certain disproportion between its monumental size and the modest parterre arranged on the plain beneath.

Villa Torrigiani, Camigliano, near Collodi. The garden was remodelled in the 19th century. Only a small Baroque section near the villa survives from the original version. It is an interesting spatial ensemble, whose initial stage consists of a rectangular basin bordered by trees and, closer to the ground, several rows of lemon trees, which have earned this section the name of Lemon Garden. From there a double flight of stairs leads down into a sunken garden with a flower parterre. This unique *giardino segreto*, called the Garden of Flora, hides a feature once frequent in

Italian gardens, a system of humorous waterworks *giochi d'aqua*. The host could obstruct the stairway to a company of visitors by a barrage of jets of water. Further surprises followed all along the route, until the guests took refuge in the Temple of Flora, where they were drenched by a final shower. The Garden of Flora, together with the Lemon Garden, forms a design of harmonious proportions and a perfectly unified composition.

Gardens in other regions

Villa Barbaro, Maser, near Treviso, Veneto. The garden adjoining the villa is Palladio's masterpiece in this genre, which accounts for the detailed description given in his treatise *Quattro Libri di Architettura*. The villa was designed about 1560 for the Barbaro brothers, and reflects the experiences of the architect's visit to Rome. It is located, in classical Renaissance fashion, on a hillside commanding a fine view. The upper floor of the villa, which houses numerous frescos by Veronese, runs nonchalantly into the back garden. This includes another fine instance of a *giardino segreto*, surrounded by a semicircular Nymphaeum. This classical motif is clearly connected with the subjects of Veronese's murals. Both point to the passion for classical culture cherished by the two brothers Barbaro.

Isola Bella, island garden on Lago Maggiore. What was originally a desolate cliff was reshaped from 1630 onwards by Count Borromeo, who called it Isola Isabella, after his wife. The consecutive designers were Angelo Crivelli, Francesco Castelli and Carlo Fontana. The symmetrical Baroque ground-plan runs all the length of the island, underlined by a sequence of ten terraces all helping to overcome the gradient. Today the terraced structure is less in evidence because the island is overrun by vegetation. The numerous exotic plants and other later additions have, to a considerable extent, obliterated the original stylistic traits; but some valuable details remain, notably a large grotto, decorated with statues and rocaille patterns, which overlooks a parterre.

Caserta, Naples. This Late Baroque garden is the last triumph of Italian garden art. Charles III, king of Naples, entrusted the plans for his new residence to Luigi Vanvitelli in 1751. The design rivalled Versailles in grandeur and brilliance, but was, not surprisingly, destined to remain unfinished. The concept is in the purest Baroque manner. The longitudinal axis was to start with a 25 kilometre avenue of plane trees leading all the way from Naples to Caserta. While this part of the design has not been carried out, the 3 kilometre extension of the axis on the garden site, ending in a water-staircase on the slope, has been brought to a successful conclusion. It features a rich programme of stairways, basins, fountains and sculptured areas. From the circular Fountain of Margherita the prospect leads to a large basin with the Fountain of Dolphins, then over a long lawn terminated by the Fountain of Aeolus, a vast architectural and sculptural composition surmounted by a lengthy terrace with a cascade basin, continuing in a further wide cascade-agitated water surface which is perhaps Caserta's finest motif. The flat section of the axis finds its conclusion in the Fountain of Venus. From there a flight of stairs leads onto the platform fronting the Fountain of Diana, picturesquely located under the water-staircase, from where an overwhelming view opens towards the palace (p. 82).

Caserta is more than the final chord in Italian garden art, it is the most ambitious attempt to glorify the power of an absolute ruler - so ambitious, indeed, that it was doomed to failure, the classical example of how the realities of space will curtail schemes which do not take into account the actual scale of the landscape.

The water theatre with a cascade is the central feature of the garden of Villa Torlonia at Frascati (top).
The Farnese gardens of the Roman Palatine were also designed on a number of terraces. In the 16th century they were famous for their rich decorative features, and in the 17th century they formed a large botanical collection (centre).
Caserta, as monumentally conceived and presented by Luigi Vanvitelli in a sketch from his *Dichiarazione*, a collection of designs, dedicated to his patron Charles III. Only the central section along the main axis was translated into practice (bottom).

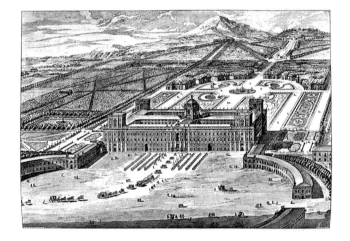

In addition to the examples described, the heritage of Italian garden art also includes other remarkable gardens, of which we can only list a few. At Frascati there are three more fine complexes: *Villa Muti*, with its extraordinary trimmed parterre, *Villa Mondragone*, and *Villa Piccolomini*. In Vignanello near Rome, the *Villa Ruspoli* is famous for its parterre of clipped box. The *Villa Capponi*, in the environs of Florence, boasts a 16th century garden. Also in this area, at Sesto, is the *Villa Corsi Salviati*. *Pratolino*, north of Florence, was one of the most celebrated Renaissance gardens, of which only Giambologna's giant statue of the Apennine survives. On the Brenta Canal is situated *Villa Pisani*, Stra, with an interesting placement of the long pool between the villa and the stables. Two interesting gardens of Genoa adjoin the *Pamphili* and *Podesta* palaces, and the third one, *Durazzo Pallavicini,* is situated on the outskirts. The North of Italy has a number of further examples: *Villa Crivelli Sormani-Verri*, in Castellazzo; *Villa Il Bozzolo* in Casalzuigno near Varese, with a sequence of terraces and an impressive stairway, *Castello Balduino*, in Montalto di Pavia, with a curious trimmed parterre, *Villa Cuzzano*, dating from the 17th century, on the outskirts of Padua, with a parterre and a grotto, and *Villa Cicogna*, in nearby Bisuschio, with a 16th century sunken garden.

The importance of the Italian Renaissance as a milestone in the development of landscape architecture, both by ideas that it has generated and by its compositional techniques, can never be overemphasized. European man, long confined in the enclosed medieval garden, suddenly stepped out into the open landscape. After centuries of retreat from nature into a sheltered, cloistered space, Renaissance architecture opened the building towards the garden, and linked both into a single residential complex. It was an isolated moment in European history, since the next period, the Baroque, broke the link and kept it at a purely formal level. The Renaissance garden opened a new, infinitely varied world to man. It allowed him to define himself within nature, exploring, sampling and enjoying his spatial setting. In short, it was a theatre of the world itself, mirroring all its meanings and contents, delights and anxieties, ranging between ostentatious pride and a search for the deepest truths, careless playfulness and serious contemplations, satisfying all the spiritual and physical needs of Renaissance man. At the same time it developed a unique vocabulary of artistic forms, expressed with such aesthetic perfection that later ages could hardly improve on it.

p.61
View from the terrace towards the garden parterre of the Villa Medici, Rome. The unique location atop Mount Pincio offers a splendid panorama of the city: in the background looms the dome of St. Peter's.

p.62
Villa Pia in the Vatican gardens. The oval courtyard, with the patterned pavement, is surrounded by a low wall, once bordered by thick planting (top). At the right there is a loggia, and beneath it, on the outside, the intimate nymphaeum (bottom).

p.63
As the visitors approaches the casino at Caprarola along the flight of stairs, the intimate *giardino segreto*, flanked by *canephori*, suddenly comes in sight.

p.64
Villa Madama, Raphael's ingenious use of a steep slope. On the left, set into the hedge, Bandinelli's two statues of Giants in the *giardino segreto* are visible.

p.65
Villa di Papa Giulio. A horseshoe-shaped garden courtyard; in the background, behind the stairs, the passage leading to the nymphaeum (top). The nymphaeum is situated far below the level of the garden, so it optically deepens and enlarges the space (bottom). The double flight of stairs, divided in the centre by a *catena d'aqua*, or "water chain", is an element of transition from the lower to the upper garden at Villa Lante (right).

p.66–67
The garden of Villa Lante with the water parterre in the middle, topped by the Fountain of the Moors which culminates in Cardinal Montalto's Coat of Arms.

p.68
Villa Celsa: oval Baroque basin in the background with the access pathway emphasized by the wavy clipped hedge (top). Isola Bella. One of the most interesting views is offered by the spacious Baroque grotto, which satisfactorily concludes the upper five terraces (bottom).

p.69
Teatro verde, Green Theatre, at Villa Marlia, with the figures of Columbina, Harlequin and Pulcinella (top). Parterre fronting the Casino of the Villa Doria Pamphili, Rome (bottom).

p.70
Villa Gamberaia. In the foreground, the water parterre made in our century; in the background, the arched green wall behind which a fine view opens over the surrounding landscape (top). The Giardino Giusti in Verona: a view of the recently restored parterre with the villa in the background (bottom).

p.71
The imposing flight of steps along the main axis of the layout completely dominates the garden scenery of the Villa Garzoni. At the top of the central motif, a soaring statue of Glory pours water into a stepped cascade.

p.72
Boboli Gardens. The amphitheatre-shaped parterre flanked by stairs at the two ends was intended, and actually used, as a setting for festivals. In the background, the axis of the design extends to the higher terrace and culminates at the Neptune fountain.

p.73
The Isolotto is perhaps the most attractive part of the Boboli Gardens (top). Castello: though created in 1540, the simple geometrical parterre, surrounded by a wall, displays the features of Early Renaissance (bottom).

p.74
As early as the 15th century, the Villa Medici at Fiesole exemplified the villa situated on a hillside with a fine view as the most satisfactory mode of residence. It is not surprising that Cosimo de' Medici should gather in this choice spot the luminaries of his Platonic academy (top). Palladio's villas, too, are located at select sites dominating the landscape, for instance the famous Villa Capra just outside Vicenza (bottom).

p.75
The Villa Barbaro at Maser near Treviso is another work by Palladio, though his garden design is preserved only in part. A view from the villa towards the valley (top). The *giardino segreto* with the nymphaeum is accessible directly from the first floor of the villa (bottom). Only the Villa Madama shows a similar close contact between the interior and the garden.

p.76
The garden of the Villa d'Este is, in fact, a waterworks theatre. The copious *Ovato* fountain, with an imposing statue of the Sibyl in the centre (top, right), and the Pathway of the Hundred Fountains (bottom, right). The Fountain of the Dragons, with the palace in the background (top, left), and the d'Este Eagles Fountain (bottom, left).

p.77
The mightiest water motif in the garden of Villa d'Este is the Neptune Fountain. Above it, somewhat recessed, stands the famous Fountain of the Organ, which could produce genuine music.

p.78
Bomarzo. The sitting woman with a basket on her head is one of the numerous mystifying figures hewn out of solid rock in the garden.

p.79
This is what remains of the once magnificent waterworks theatre, with a cascade, at the Villa Torlonia, Frascati (top). Bottom: the nymphaeum of the Villa Aldobrandini at Frascati; above the nymphaeum there is a cascade that fills the space fronting the villa with stimulating murmurs and refreshes the air.

p.80–81
Villa Pisani, Stra. The garden is firmly anchored by the long reflecting pool linking the main villa (top, right) and the stables (top, left). A romantic scene from the gardens to Villa Durazzo Pallavicini on the outskirts of Genoa (bottom, left). Sculptured figure of January by Bartolomeo Ammanati on an island at the upper terrace of the garden of the Villa Reale in Castello near Florence (bottom, right).

p.82
Caserta. View along the Baroque axis towards the huge palace; in the foreground, the Venus group (top). The Diana Fountain at the bottom of the cascade that terminates the axis (bottom).

p.83
Upper section of the axis. In the foreground, the Little Cascades; in the background, the Grand Cascade, which concludes the whole ambitiously designed layout of Caserta.

p.84
The sunken intimate garden of Villa Torrigiani with numerous *giochi d'aqua*; in the background well- proportioned double stairways leading up to the lemon garden.

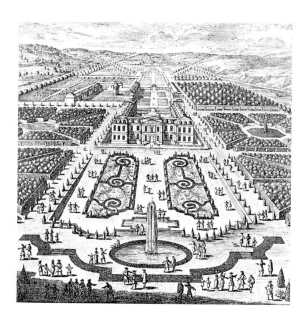

France
Nature made symmetrical

Feudal court gardens
Garden designers and theoreticians
The great illusion as reality
Back to nature

Gardens today

In 17th century France, the High Baroque produced an original version of garden art which became a characteristic element of the national tradition in this field. Moreover, the French garden is also the purest expression of the mature Baroque style. Having said this, the fact should not be overlooked that garden design had already flourished in France in the Middle Ages, developed further during the Renaissance and, after the successful Baroque, formed part of the wave with which the Romantic movement stirred Europe.

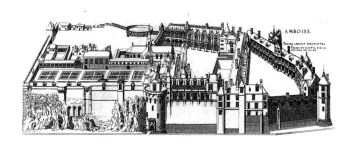

Feudal court gardens

It is known from literary sources and from pictorial evidence that gardens of pleasure appeared quite regularly as an element of the residences of the medieval nobility in France. Their structure is simple, showing a division into geometric, mainly rectangular forms furnished with fountains, pergolas and galleries. The ground-plan of these gardens probably did not change much until the first contacts with Italian culture, brought in by the armed expeditions of Charles VIII, Louis XII and François I. When, in 1494, Charles VIII marched into Naples, he could not avoid comparing his own modest residence with the glamorous palaces and gardens of the Neapolitan court. From that moment on, French creative work was richly influenced by Italian art for more than a century. This influence is also clearly visible in the design of gardens. Because of the great demand, many Italian masters settled in France and thanks to their work, French garden design prospered. Here we come across a few well-known names such as Pacello de Mercogliano, Guido Mazzoni, Fra Giocondo and others. Mercogliano was especially productive, being responsible for a large number of the garden arrangements at the châteaux along the Loire.

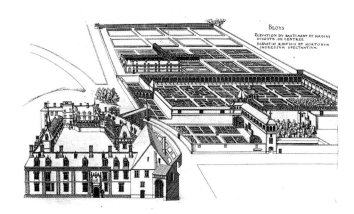

The first among them was Amboise, a fortress in which it was only just possible to find enough space for a series of parterres which, in accordance with the medieval tradition, have no contact with the buildings. At approximately the same time, at the end of the 15th century, Mercogliano arranged the garden of another royal châteaux, Blois, beside the Loire. As shown by the illustration on this page, the construction here is more complex and involves more terraces. Mercogliano's arrangement of the garden for Cardinal d'Amboise in Gaillon is of slightly later date, from the beginning of the 16th century. Here, the garden is still separate from the residential building and is divided by means of terraces into a number of unconnected units, programmed in accordance with medieval symbolism (garden of love, garden of salvation, etc.). Most striking here is the obvious axis, which is even connected to the pavilion at the entrance to the garden. Gaillon was famous for its fountains, the main one, *grande fontaine de marbre blanc*, was more than six metres high. Similarly planned were the gardens at Bury, with the exactly symmetrical structure of its main garden in relation to the forest and the castle, and at Anet, which was the work of royal architect Philibert de l'Orme. Similar basic arrangements from this period can also be found at some other châteaux, such as Chantilly, Fontainebleau and Montargis. As with the châteaux along the Loire, here too, in spite of the active presence of the Italian masters, characteristic features of the French medieval garden were retained: enclosure, separation from the building, division into units by means of terraces which are not connected among themselves, colourful parterre designs and the furnishing of gardens with fountains, pergolas, trellises, galleries and other features. In the middle of the century there appeared a few gardens which can, at least in their ground-plan, be compared with their Italian models, even though they were designed by French masters. Verneuil and especially Charleval

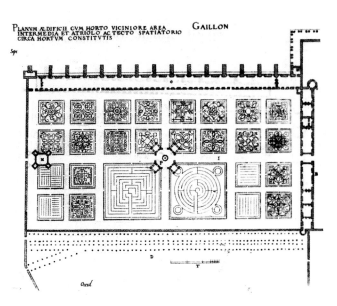

The Château of Amboise, with a simple garden parterre which, for lack of space, had to be placed in one of the side courtyards by the cemetery (top).
A considerable step forward in size and design can be seen in the layout of the gardens at Blois (centre).
The garden at the Château de Gaillon is the work of a Neapolitan gardener Pacello de Mercogliano. The inventively developed parterre from the beginning of the 16th century displays a symmetrical structure, yet with basic features of the medieval closed garden (bottom).

Louvois, a typically symmetrical Baroque layout shown in an engraving by Perelle (previous page).

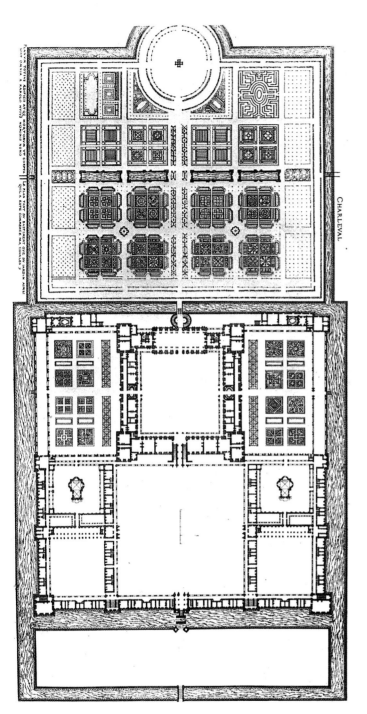

Charleval is perhaps the most perfect of the French Renaissance gardens. The consistency of symmetrical structure, the imaginative organization of the parterre sections, especially with the oval ending of the axis, and the new use of water in which moats have an important articulating role, are the outstanding features here. Especially interesting is the combination of four longitudinal pools, which divide the parterre laterally. Unfortunately, nothing remains of this interesting structure but the plan by Du Cerceau (above).

belong here. Both have a distinctive axial plan, which in Charleval is stressed by two side wings of parterres and by the circular ending to the axis. At Charleval, one's eyes are especially drawn to the network of moats which, even if they still have a defensive role, also undoubtedly serve as a means of spatial arrangement. Not only do they surround the area of the château and its garden, but they also divide it laterally. Even though they were never completely realized, it is important that in the mind of society ideas matured about complex, much more perfected arrangements than were expressed at Charleval. The plans for Charleval were made by Jacques-Androuet Du Cerceau (1520-1584), who became famous with his *Les Plus Excellents Bastiments de France* (1576-9) in which he published engravings of contemporary châteaux and their gardens. He is to be given credit for this unique documentation of a range of châteaux from the 15th and 16th centuries.

From the reigns of Louis XII and François II onward, the concentration of power in the king's hands increased, after much dynastic discord and religious struggle the monarchy became stronger. Thus the foundations of the unified, absolutist state, as it appeared a century later, were gradually laid down. The status symbols were important instruments in the consolidation of his power, being a reflection of his social worth and acknowledged strength. Here, an important role was also played by gardens which, along with the châteaux themselves, were becoming more and more complex, perfected in structure and increasing in size.

The next important period is the second half of the 16th century, when Italian influences are very noticeable, partly because of the royal family's connections with the Medicis and partly because of the Italian tours of the French masters. This influence is especially marked at the château of Saint-Germain-en-Laye, which was designed by Du Pérac after his return from Italy. The garden descends from the château towards the Seine on a steep slope in six terraces. These are linked by magnificent staircases, which are joined into an axis and thus connect the structure of the whole in a longitudinal direction. Nowhere else did French garden design adopt the Italian spirit to such an extent as in this garden, whose structure is strongly reminiscent of the Villa d'Este. The reconstructions at Fontainebleau, which were also carried out by Henri IV, were of a similar character. The area around the château took on a strictly regular form, even though the individual gardens and parterres were still separate. Especially striking is the large parterre consisting of four sections with fountains in the middle made by Tommaso Francini, who came from a great Italian family of fountain and garden designers.

By the beginning of the 17th century, the Renaissance style of garden design had exhausted itself and the new features which would lead to a new era began to appear. A harbinger of this development is the design for the garden of the Palais du Luxembourg by Jacques Boyceau, who was also a well-known theoretician of landscape architecture. In contrast to previous parterres, which were built up of minor details and were often naively patterned, but in such a way that each individual section was separate and independent, Boyceau introduced a unified overall design. The parterre is organized along an axis and all its sections are linked together into a recognizable whole by their form and pattern. A completely new conception of the parterre is revealed here and it is justifiable to see in the design of the Luxembourg garden a clear forecast of the French Baroque style. One more arrangement of this kind appeared before the start of the Le Nôtre period, the residence of the ambitious Cardinal Richelieu. The architect Lemercier planned the Château de Rueil for him, whilst the garden was designed by Thiriot; it seems that the young Le Nôtre collaborated. The design is clearly Baroque, with an axis which defines the whole space in front of the château, as well as that on the garden side, in which a uniformly shaped parterre can also be seen.

Garden designers and theoreticians

Thus, by the middle of the century, all the prerequisites for a great new style were in place. A great deal of knowledge had been amassed and a great number of competent masters had emerged. The great care and attention which, for understandable reasons of prestige, had been lavished on the building and gardens at the French court, began to bear fruit. French masters developed alongside their numerous Italian counterparts, soon taking all the important work into their own hands. Thus in the 17th century, when French landscape architecture began to develop and reached its peak, this work was carried out mainly by members of two families, the Mollets and the Le Nôtres. Among the Mollets, the most outstanding is Claude, who was not only the king's main garden designer but also the author of the well-known theoretical work *Le Théâtre des Plans et Jardinages*. According to the author, this was the first introduction to the *parterre de broderie* in France. His son André worked at many European courts and became famous with his *Jardins de Plaisir*. It was published in 1651 in Stockholm, in several languages, and contributed much to the assertion of French style elsewhere. The other great family were the Le Nôtres, who served royal families for three generations. The first was Pierre Le Nôtre who was Catherine de Médicis' gardener at Les Tuileries. The most important member of the family was his grandson André who should be counted as one of the greatest landscape architects of all times.

As well as excellent practitioners there were also influential theoreticians. Jacques Boyceau, already mentioned, with his *Traité du Jardinage selon les Raisons de la Nature et de l'Art* (1638) was very important, also Olivier de Serres, with *Le Théâtre d'Agriculture et Mesnage des Champs* (1651), then both the Mollets, and a little later, A. J. Dézallier d'Argenville, with his *La Théorie et la Pratique du Jardinage* (1709). Apart from the usual technical descriptions and instructions these books all contained weighty reflections on design and aesthetics which encouraged the progress of garden art.

The great illusion as reality

The strength of the French state increased under the leadership of the two influential statesmen, Richelieu and Mazarin. Centralization of power increased after Mazarin's death in 1661, when the young Louis XIV did not want to name a prime minister and took all the power into his own hands. Thus he established an absolute monarchy, which rested on exceptional class opposition and exploitation. From then on, the state controlled every aspect of social life, including art, which was taken care of by the Academy of Fine Arts, headed by the royal painter Le Brun. The glorification of the king became the arts' main duty. The king, who named himself "the Sun King" and identified the state with his own person (*l'état c'est moi*), said to the members of the Academy: "I entrust to you the greatest treasure - my fame". The court became the main client for artistic works and the most important commissioner in the country, employing all the important masters. The extremely heavy taxation, which drove a great many into poverty, was used to provide the absolutist court with the vast funds it required for the creation of its status symbols.

Saint-Germain-en-Laye was one of the few French structures where great unity of the whole was achieved on a steep site with terraces. A vital role was played by the large staircases, which reveal the Italian spirit either of the Queen Marie de Médicis or the architect Du Pérac, who had been in Italy before this, or the garden designer Francini (top).
Fontainebleau: the more developed layout from the end of the 16th century also represents a more mature form of the French Renaissance garden, which consistently introduces formal discipline in the arrangement of individual elements, especially the parterres (bottom).

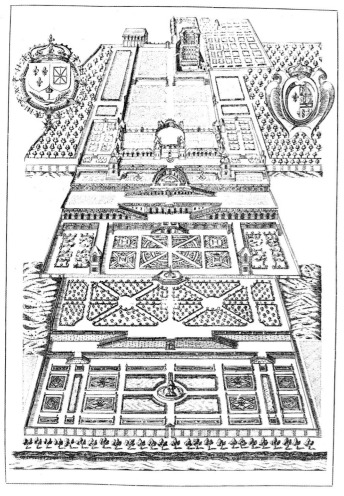

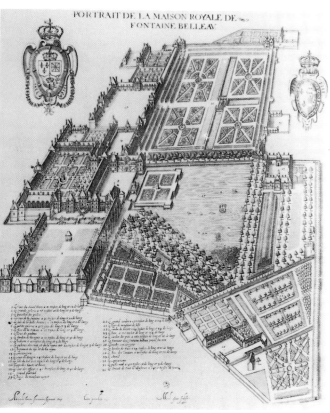

In this cult, more than ever before, garden art played an important role, vividly illustrated by the destiny of Louis' Finance Minister, Fouquet. He built himself a château and garden at Vaux all designed by three great artists, the architect Le Vau, the painter Le Brun and the landscape architect Le Nôtre. This trio fulfilled their assignment extremely well. Le Vau made a tripartite layout for the château, with the central section of the garden façade standing out from the edifice, accentuating the axis and thus becoming formally incorporated into the garden space. Even more brilliant and fresh was Le Nôtre's garden composition, which immediately threw every other design achievement in the country into the shade. The new creation was widely admired, both as a formal accomplishment and because of the new possibilities it offered for public performances. This was demonstrated by a great inaugural festivity organized by Fouquet, on the 17th August 1661, in which the court, with the king at its head, also participated. Several thousand invited guests dined off gold and silver plates and watched a play written especially for the occasion by Molière, as well as a ballet, fireworks and other performances, all of which made a great impression on everyone, most of all the king.

In a little over two weeks, the king had Fouquet arrested. The background to this event has never been fully explained. Fouquet may have dug too deeply into the state purse to finance the building of his château, although recent research does not prove this assumption. On the other hand it is quite certain that the king had been deeply offended by the splendour of Vaux, especially the garden. At this time, the king had his official palace in the Louvre, but Fouquet's garden far exceeded anything the king possessed and this was certainly not in accordance with the position an absolute ruler should enjoy. Immediately after Fouquet's fall, the king employed the trio from Vaux to build a residence worthy of the Sun King, at Versailles.

From a modest hunting lodge with only partly a formal garden, they built, during the following decades, the most majestic royal residence in Europe, comparable only with the Forbidden City of the Chinese emperor in Beijing. It was a residence of immense dimensions, embodying all ruling thought and strength, filled with all the available splendour of the world.

Only a personality such as André le Nôtre could have coped with the task of mastering a space with such dimensions (2.5 x 3.5 kilometres) and visually present a world dominated by a single will and, at the same time, create a scene suitable for splendid public performances. Le Nôtre had been educated in painting, geometry, architecture and also, by his father, in garden art. He received the order for his new life's work at just the right time, after his experience at Vaux, and he carried it out with Michelangelo-like grandeur and strength. Of course a great number of builders, sculptors, fountain designers, gardeners and others worked on Versailles, but the plan was completely Le Nôtre's work. Here, he improved the axial design with ingeniously conceived lateral interruptions. He bridged the differences in altitude with gentle banking, to enable the smooth transition and flow of motifs. The axis represents the monistic social order on the basis of complete subordination to one power, as well as assuring formal control of the immense repertoire of water, parterres, bosquets, vistas and so on. Water is irreplaceable here, the most noticeable material of this *Cité des Eaux*, where the large water surfaces reflect the palaces, trees and sculptures, giving them new dimensions. Water introduces both optical variety and movement, thus strengthening the sense of agitation and fluctuation, characteristic of this world. To describe it a statement from Descartes' *Treatise on Method* can be used: "a space which is unlimitedly and unlimitably extensive in length, breadth, and height or depth...". What astonishing dimensions were created here: not long before this, timid medieval man had shut himself between four walls into his enclosed garden, then the Renaissance opened itself up to nature, but the Baroque placed itself above it, building a magnificent illusion - the garden as an image of a world which is arranged, finally, according to a single will.

This was a great moment in the development of garden art, and, at the same time, an important contribution by French Baroque classicism to the liberation of the human mind. Its stylistic features are: a consistently implemented axial plan, a tripartite development of the programme in a longitudinal direction (the entrance with the *cour d'honneur* - the château - the garden), an illusionist perspective which, along the axis, extends the image of the garden's inner order onto a universal level; large, reflecting water surfaces and an abundance of moving water; various kinds of parterre with elegantly flowing patterns, which run from section to section; the contrasting masses of bosquets with clipped edges; a profusion of symbolic, mainly mythological, sculptural works; a number of precisely calculated views and the rhythmical movement of the whole in a longitudinal direction. Here, it is worth mentioning that the Baroque style created an exceptional formal symbiosis of building and garden, unknown to any other period. This was, of course, made possible only by such a high level of abstraction in the structure of the garden.

Parallel to Versailles, other great compositions emerged from Le Nôtre's hands, Chantilly, Saint-Cloud, Sceaux and Fontainebleau. Many others have been ascribed to him but without any real evidence.

Back to nature

With Le Nôtre's death, the great century of French garden art came to a close. For large projects such as Versailles and Marly, sufficient funds for maintenance no longer existed. Already, at the end of the century, but even more at the beginning of the new one, with the Rococo, a certain softness of features and natural picturesqueness started to penetrate the plastic arts. The new conception and definition of the world which was, in its naturalness and sensitivity, a counter-balance to the cold and monumental regularity of Baroque classicism, was founded on social contradictions. It arose as part of the mode of thinking of the bourgeoisie in their struggle with the nobility and so should not be simply equated with the change of taste of the period.

Rousseau's philosophy that triggered a call for a return to nature struck a popular chord in France, though it left relatively few traces in the country's garden design. The Romantic unrest of 18th century France was probably embodied most directly in Ermenonville, the garden of the Marquis de Girardin (p. 120), which in its structure and usage of classical elements and monuments is similar to English gardens dating from this period. An influential designer at the end of this century and the beginning of the next was Gabriel Thouin, who proposed a plan for the arrangement of an immense country park at Versailles with idyllic country scenes, hamlets etc. Méréville, with its numerous antique ruins and unusual buildings, became famous as an ambitious attempt in this new style at the end of the century. A similar search for the unusual and the remote is expressed also by the frequent inclusion of rustic elements into the garden, such as the well-known hamlet of Marie-Antoinette in Versailles' Petit Trianon, Le Hameau.

The garden of the Palais du Luxembourg with a new type of parterre, claims attention by its complete subordination to the axis plan. The constituent parts of the parterre are based on a single pattern, which ensures formal coherence along the axis. Here, development into the later French Baroque garden is indicated (top).

The Château de Richelieu not only strengthened Boyceau's incorporation of the parterre into the structure of the garden but, moreover, emphasized the axis as the backbone of the whole spatial composition (centre).

The plan for Vaux-le-Vicomte shows the exceptional maturity of Le Nôtre's first large independent work. Its perfection is confirmed by his later design for Versailles which was built according to an almost identical scheme. A great deal was contributed to the coherence of the axial composition by the architect Le Vau, who developed an innovatory concept of the château. This improved upon the earlier Renaissance form of the rectangular unified block, transforming it into a tripartite structure whose central part extends into the garden. On the entrance side the visitor faces the *cour d'honneur;* this creates a concave-convex articulation of the edifice which firmly anchors the longitudinal axial alignment of the composition. Other characteristics of Le Nôtre's design technique are also apparent, such as the marginal use of bosquets and, especially obvious, the development of the total layout across the main axis with lateral axes and views (bottom).

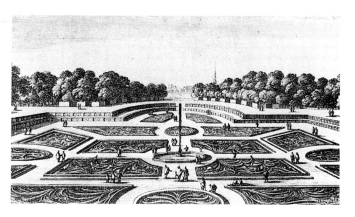

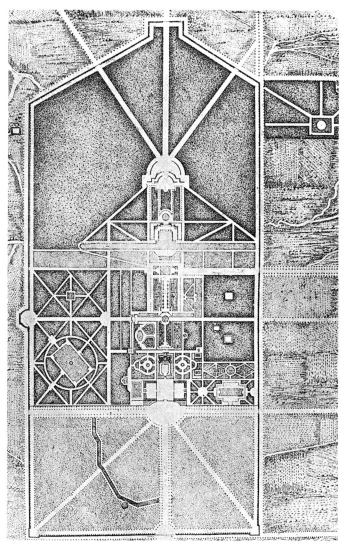

The formal features of this movement strongly influenced the designers of larger city parks, especially in 19th century Paris at the time when Haussmann was active. This is well illustrated by outstanding examples such as the Bois de Boulogne, Buttes-Chaumont and Parc Monceau.

Gardens today

In spite of the fact that time has erased many famous gardens, the French heritage boasts numerous characteristic examples. From them, it is possible to get quite a good overview of the wide range of landscape-architectural creativity from the Renaissance onwards. Some exemplary renovations from the 19th and 20th centuries have contributed a great deal here.

Bois de Boulogne, Paris. This well-known park covers a large area of about 900 hectares. Originally royal forest, it was given to the city of Paris in 1852 by Napoleon III. The size and present layout are mainly due to the work of Haussmann and Alphand in the second part of the 19th century who brought into the park numerous features, such as wide avenues, lakes, cascades, various gardens, racecourse, etc. It is a successful large-scale attempt to create an urban park in English fashion on French grounds (p.118).

Buttes-Chaumont, Paris. This unusual park was developed from old quarries in an irregular layout, by G. E. Haussmann and J.-C.-A. Alphand in the 1860s. The whole scenery is arranged as a sequence of surprising views, especially around the 50m high rock, crowned by a pillared temple. Many artificial features were made out of concrete to imitate nature which provides for a bizarre, yet charming impression (p. 119).

Champs-sur-Marne, 34 kilometres east of Paris, on the left bank of the River Marne. The château was begun in 1720 and one of its owners was Madame de Pompadour. The original regular structure was, in the 19th century, changed into the English style. In the 20th century, the garden was renovated according to H. Duchêne's original 18th century plan, as a symmetrical arrangement. The axis starts with a long trimmed allée of pleached trees and ends in a *cour d'honneur*. It is continued on the other side of the château with a *parterre de broderie*, flanked by two rows of palisades made of limes, and completed by a round pool with a sculpture and a fountain (p. 116).

Chantilly, the garden of what is now the Condé museum, approximately 30 kilometres north of Paris. The oldest parts of the château date from the beginning of the 16th century, with additions from around 1600. Gardens of simple rectangular form appeared around it but the château itself is surrounded by large water surfaces which were originally defensive moats. Louis II de Bourbon, the Prince of Condé, hired Le Nôtre in 1662 for the rearrangement of Chantilly. Obviously he, like his royal cousin Louis XIV, was fascinated by the splendour of Vaux-le-Vicomte. Le Nôtre dedicated the whole of the next twenty years to this new task, which resulted in one of his most full-blooded works (p. 112).

In it is perhaps the most unusually designed garden axis. The château, with its irregular structure and its lateral position, made the usual development along the axis impossible; therefore, Le Nôtre directed it towards the Great Terrace. At the entrance the visitor is faced first with the *patte d'oie*, paths patterned in the shape of a goose's foot; from here a diagonal access to the château is possible. On the continuation of the axis stands an equestrian statue of the first owner, the famous warrior Connetable, which visually dominates the area. Beneath the statue, the axis descends the great staircase to the magnificent water parterre. It begins with a large, pool-like water surface, called the Manche, and ends in a crescent-shaped grass motif which, together with the allée, disappears into the distance. Laterally, the Manche is connected to the Grand Canal, which is 80 metres wide and 1800 metres long. The richness of water motifs is complemented by the two parterre sections on both sides of the Manche, each of which contains five pools.

At Chantilly, Le Nôtre developed a new variant of his ambitious cruciform water designs and splendidly executed the arrangement of the park as a practically independent composition, not influenced by the château in any sense.

Chenonceaux, situated 32 kilometres north of Tours. The château was built by Thomas Bohier on the foundations of a mill which had previously stood on the river Cher, between 1515 and 1522. Later, it came into the possession of Diane de Poitiers, who ordered a bridge to be built across the river, above which two more storeys were later added. The château itself is uniquely situated on the riverside. In 1558, Diane des Poitiers had large gardens arranged there. They were surrounded by buildings and a wall built above the moats. Apart from the moats and the wall, nothing of the original garden was preserved. They were partly renovated in the 19th century in a rather free way, which aroused opposition even then. Today Diane's large parterre and the smaller parterre of Catherine de Médicis remain (p. 104). The château and the gardens with the riverside form a uniquely harmonious whole, which vividly illustrates the Renaissance spirit.

Courances in Milly-la-Forêt, 18 kilometres west of Fontainebleau. The château and the original garden date from the first half of the 17th century, and it has numerous water motifs based on an abundance of water sources. At the beginning of the 20th century, Achille Duchêne renovated the garden with a symmetrical *parterre de broderie* beside the château. Further along the axis there is a large water mirror, a rectangular pool surrounded by lawn, groups of trees and sculptures. Near the pool, among the frames of greenery, runs a cascade-like water-course. This garden, in its current carefully maintained condition, represents an interesting mixture of the formal and the natural.

Ermenonville, an area of 50 hectares, through which runs the small river Launette; it is an implementation of the ideas of the great Romantic Jean-Jacques Rousseau. The garden is the work of the Marquis de Girardin, who had travelled widely in England and had come to know many important works in the landscape style, which he used in his layout of Ermenonville. The garden consists of two parts, separated by the château. The southern one is more important, its centre represented by a lake surrounded by paths which direct the visitor to different views. The arrangement is full of symbolism: the sparkling waterfall, the cliff of the Naiads, monuments, the temple of philosophy on the slope, the Poplar Island with Rousseau's tombstone (p. 120).

Fontainebleau, a royal château from the beginning of the 16th century, situated 70 kilometres south of Paris. The original gardens were of simple design, geometrical sections with borders, parterres, bosquets and canals from the reign of François I. Important improvements were contributed by King Henri IV at the beginning of the 17th century, with the collaboration of Jacques Mollet. Then, more regularly arranged parterre sections were added. The large (1,200 metres long by 40 metres wide) canal also appeared at this time and, parallel to it, allées consisting of several rows of trees. The large pond, which dates from the time of François I, also took on a new, more regular shape.

The most important changes were carried out by Le Nôtre, who was probably working on the plans for Fontainebleau as early as 1645, and certainly in 1662. He rearranged

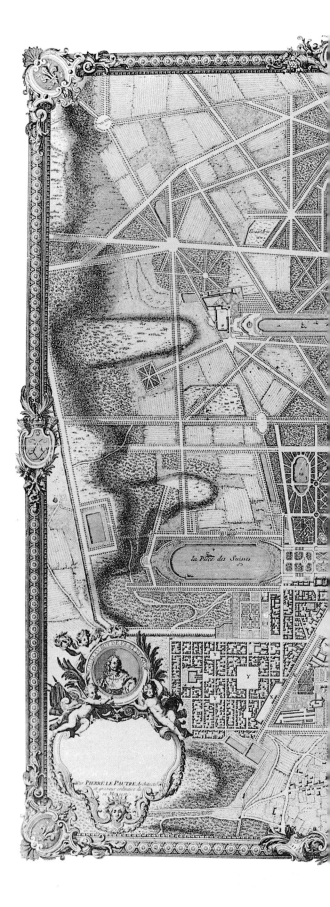

Because of its size, the overall structure of the garden at Versailles can be fully comprehended only from the ground-plan which reveals all its enormously ambitious complexity. Here can be seen the three-part access to the *cour d'honneur*, the château building

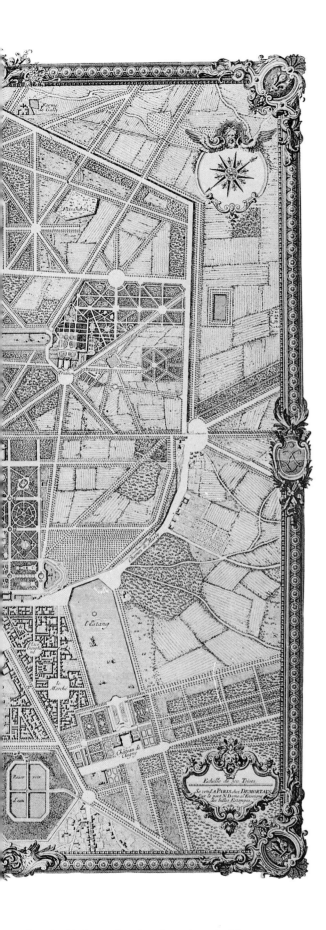

aligned with the garden, then the main part of the garden with parterres and bosquets, and finally the cross-shaped water axis which, with its longest, upper arm, crosses the frontiers of the garden into the outside world.

the large 310 by 395 metres Parterre du Roi (the King's Parterre or Parterre de Tibre), which consists of four parts and a central square pool with a fountain in the middle. He separated the parterre from the carp-pool with many-rowed allées, which can still be seen. But Le Nôtre's *parterres de broderie* no longer exist, because they are covered over with grass. Le Nôtre also directed the axis of the parterre towards the Grand Canal and the château, thus attaining a higher level of order of the whole and a greater formal condensation. Between the parterre and the beginning of the Grand Canal, extensive cascades are arranged, stretching the full width of the canal (40 metres). Their structure resembles the water motif at Vaux-le-Vicomte. The arrangement of the cascades not only enriches the garden, but also acts as a link between the two large motifs and brings in a new spatial tension. Between 1809 and 1812, at Napoleon I's behest, the former garden of pine trees beside the carp-pool was reconstructed into an informal landscape structure (p. 102). The rearrangement of the Garden of Diana in the English style belongs to the same campaign. The charming sculpture of the goddess of hunting, set in a round pool, is outstanding. Thus, in Fontainebleau, one finds remnants of various periods, from the Renaissance onwards, which makes it a unique residence - and not only in France.

Jardin de la Fontaine, Nîmes. This garden was made on an old Roman site with a temple, baths and a theatre, which was discovered in 1735, arousing considerable interest in the Antique. Between 1740 and 1760 an arrangement, symmetrically linked with a street in the town, was carried out. The central point is a square island surrounded by water, on which stands a sculpture of a nymph. An abundance of flowing water, which gave the arrangement its name, also conveys to it an interesting character (p. 117).

The *Jardins du Luxembourg* go back to 1612, when Marie de Médicis ordered gardens to be arranged even before the palace was built. They were planned mainly by Boyceau. One of their special attractions was the Medici fountain, a work by the famous fountain designer Francini. The fountain is the only element preserved from the original design. At the time of the revolution a forest was planted in the gardens. Today they display a colourful Baroque structure together with the elements of later park design.

Marly is a remnant of a once magnificent royal garden in Marly-le-Roi on the western edge of Paris. It is not yet clear who planned it. It seems that Louis XIV himself chose the site as well as the form of the garden, with the help of the royal architect Hardouin-Mansart. The rather uninteresting, simplified geometrical structure lacks Le Nôtre's imaginative flair. The arrangement of the garden was begun in 1678 and the king gave his last instructions in 1714. The main axis of the garden ran along a valley, beginning at the top of a slope, and descending in a great cascade of 53 stages. Beneath the huge cascade stood a château, and behind it began the parterre, consisting of many large pools, beside which stood six pavilions. Here the king entertained his chosen guests during visits to his "peaceful retreat". After the king's death it was neglected. During the Revolution the furniture was sold and the château and pavilions were demolished. Today, the main axis, with the pools in the parterre, can still be seen.

Menars, northeast of Blois, in the Loire valley. Still a modest residence in the 16th century, it became a château in the 17th and then famous as the residence of Madame de Pompadour. At her behest, the château, and probably the garden partly too, were rearranged by the royal architect Gabriel. Even greater improvements were carried out by the Marquis de Martigny. The château was rearranged for him by the architect

Jacques-Germain Soufflot, who also built the famous rotunda, *Temple d'Amour*, orangery and grotto and designed the structure of the large parterre. It received new supporting walls and ramparts against the Loire. The main gardener, Jean-François Neufforge, contributed a detailed parterre arrangement. A rich collection of sculptures, for which Menars became famous, has been almost completely sold off. Remaining from this once famous garden are the interesting parterre, with its eight sections between the chateau and the Loire, and the entrance *cour d'honneur*, which begins with a magnificent gate of wrought iron, and is surrounded by a box-like, clipped hedge, and two pavilions.

Parc Monceau, Paris, was arranged towards the end of the 18th century for the Duc de Chartres. In the original layout the park boasted numerous *folies* of antique, oriental, medieval and other inspirations, such as a naval battle, *naumachia*, a minaret, windmill, colonnade, temples etc. During the Revolution the grounds were made a public park; since then many of these features have disappeared. In 1861 Alphand restored the garden in the romantic taste of the period.

Rambouillet, a château 52 kilometres southeast of Paris, dates from the 14th century. The first gardens were laid out in the 15th and the 16th centuries. More important interventions occurred only at the end of the 17th century, when d'Armenonville created, among other things, one of the largest water surfaces in any French garden with three canals in the shape of a goose's foot, *patte d'oie*. In the second half of the 18th century, English-style arrangements were introduced, including a grotto, a farm cottage and, upon the orders of Louis XVI, a garden for Marie-Antoinette next to the dairy. In its present state, the garden impresses most with extensive canals, which run from the parterre in front of the castle. Another interesting feature is the quincunx, approximately 100 x 80 metres large, a regular plantation of trimmed limes, one of the biggest of its kind surviving in modern Europe.

Rosny, 50 kilometres northeast of Paris. The Duc de Sully's château, built in 1595, with a garden with parterres, bosquets, grottoes and a large terrace along the Seine. In 1718, Count Senozan designed the large front court with an access allée of trimmed limes, accompanied at the sides by box-tree parterres with pools and sculptures. This part is now covered with grass and surrounded by a magnificent backdrop of trees (p. 113). At the beginning of the 19th century, part of the garden was rearranged in the landscape style and from then dates also the interesting Temple of Love. Plans for this were made by Isabey, the Duchess de Berry's drawing teacher. Between the château and the Seine, Duchêne rearranged the parterre with trimmed box-trees, which calls to mind the formal arrangement of Count Senozan.

Saint-Cloud, Paris. The original building and the gardens on the steep slope above the Seine were built by the Florentine archbishop Gondi at the end of the 16th century. Archbishop Gondi added a few arrangements but the garden lacked a unified structure. When Philippe d'Orleans, Louis XIV's brother, took possession in 1658, building activity on the château and the garden began again. Philippe's architect, Le Pautre, and after him, to some extent, Hardouin-Mansart, enlarged the château so that it was possible to connect it formally with the garden. This task was mainly achieved by Le Nôtre who, together with Le Pautre, built a network of allées running west-east and north-south. This was not an easy task because of the steep slope above the Seine, so they had to introduce arrangements on different levels, connected by ramps and staircases. Most of the château fell into decay, especially during the war of 1870. The best preserved remnant of the building complex is the Pavilion de Valois. On the terrace

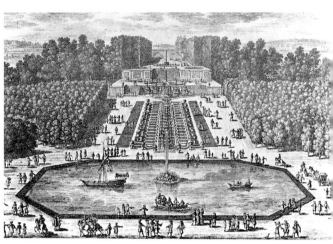

The Fountain of Latona at Versailles with the Apollo group and the Grand Canal further in the background (top, left).
Trianon de Porcelaine at Versailles, no longer extant, was one of the first introductions of *chinoiserie* into the country. The interior and the exterior of the tea pavilion were covered with china and majolica plates and the gardens were richly decorated with flowers (top, right).
The *Grandes Cascades* fronted by the octagonal *pièce d'eau* at Sceaux is another great work of Le Nôtre (bottom left).
Chantilly. The complete ingenuity of Le Nôtre's solution can be appreciated only from the plan or from an air view: an exceptional arrangement of Baroque garden with an axis which is entirely independent of the building. The château is linked to the axis at the side, in a diagonal direction, a very exceptional arrangement for a Baroque scheme (bottom right).

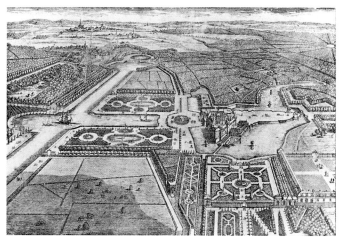

beneath it begins the main axis of the garden, running towards the west. In fact, this is a narrow longitudinal parterre, formed by avenues of trees. The axis gradually ascends across a large staircase, reaching first of all a round pool, Petite Gerbe, situated in the middle of the orangery parterre. The next large motif is of the two canals, with 24 fountains, surrounding a pool in the shape of a four-leaf clover. This is followed by a narrow strip of the lawn, *tapis vert*, which leads on to the next surprise, the large fountain of Grande Gerbe.

The south axis starts at the same point as the west one and descends first to the semicircular pool, continuing across a great horseshoe and a circle of balustrades. Near the main terrace, the large 90 metre long cascade descends towards the Seine. It is the most remarkable feature of Saint Cloud and the most immense structure of its kind in European garden art. Most probably, Le Pautre built it on the site of the original cascade from Gondi's time; it was later enlarged by Hardouin-Mansart (p. 110).

Saint-Cloud holds a special place among French gardens of the 17th century because of its structure, which was supposed to be in harmony with the steep slope and with the Italian origins of its first owners as it was designed in the Italian spirit. Attempts therefore to transform it into a Baroque structure could not be wholly successful, not even for such a strong personality as Le Nôtre.

Saint-Germain-en-Laye is one of the oldest gardens of the French royal house. François I had built a château here and arranged some gardens. The more important gardens appeared under Henry IV, around 1600, in the style of André Mollet. During the reign of Louis XIII they were replaced by Boyceau's parterres. In the middle of the 17th century, Le Nôtre began a thorough rearrangement of them. One of his most ambitious arrangements was the great terrace along the Seine. This is 2.4 kilometres-long and rises 60 metres above the river. The promenade on the terrace had originally not been covered by grass, giving it a grander appearance. Le Nôtre tried to moderate the terrace's considerable length by making the promenade concave, thus shortening it optically. The huge series of terraces descending to the river have mostly disappeared.

Sceaux, situated 15 kilometres south of Paris. The first residence was built as early as 1597. It became significant only after it had been bought by Colbert, Louis XIV's finance minister, who entrusted the garden design to Le Nôtre. At the enlarged château, Le Nôtre installed two allées, to form the longitudinal and the larger lateral axis. On the latter, Le Nôtre introduced the Grandes Cascades, running down the slope and surrounded by mythological sculptures. Further down the cascades an octagonal pool was built. Both structures can still be seen (p. 111).

Colbert toyed with the idea of building a Grand Canal, following Le Nôtre's plan, but he found it too ambitious. He was probably also being cautious after Fouquet's fall. The plan was carried out finally by his son, the Marquis de Seignelay. Only then did Sceaux become the magnificent structure which can still be seen today, in spite of the disappearance of a number of features. The Grand Canal was conceived with a boldness typical of Le Nôtre, its cross-like structure forming the compositional backbone of the garden. The main arm of the cross runs parallel with Diana's allée and the cascades, and is connected laterally to the octagonal pool. The canal is approximately half the length of the one in Versailles, but it completely dominates the whole structure of the garden and it is possible to experience it visually from various perspectives.

Tuileries, Paris. These gardens have a long history, starting with Catherine de Médicis in 1576. The first gardens were simple sections with parterres and regular plantations of trees. In the middle of the 17th century, the central allée and two symmetrical *parterres de broderie* were added. This more tidy structure shows the hands of Mollet and Le Nôtre at work. A great change occurred during the reign of Louis XIV, when Le Vau finished the palace and André Le Nôtre rearranged the garden. The new structure depends on a strongly emphasized axis with various parterres, bosquets, regular plantations of trees and pools. Among the pools, the most visible is the octagonal one at the end of the axis, which retains its basic form, up to the present day. Currently, the Tuileries gardens are under reconstruction. They are a notable survival of the garden art of the 17th century and later periods.

Vaux-le-Vicomte, situated 5 kilometres east of Melun. The garden was laid out at the same time as the château, on the orders of Nicolas Fouquet, the Finance Minister. The work took place between 1656 and 1661; the work on the gardens was guided by Le Nôtre, whilst the architect Le Vau was responsible for the building. Judging by the harmony of the building and the garden, the two men collaborated fruitfully during the creation of one of the most perfect Baroque ensembles ever. The château and the garden were neglected until 1875, when both became the property of A. Sommier, who had them renovated. The whole structure rests on the axis, which begins with a series of courts in front of the château. It is marked by a low colonnaded fence which accompanies the approach to a portal with a high wrought-iron fence. The path continues across a quartered grassy court and across a moat to a new *cour d'honneur* in front of the château. The succession of visual effects and surprises already begins to develop in this front part of the garden. This is especially the case with the water, which cannot yet be seen from the portal. And above all, from here it is impossible to see what is behind the château, because it blocks the view. Therefore the visitor is even more surprised when he arrives at the garden façade of the château and a rich scene of parterres, water motifs and sculptures, framed by masses of greenery, opens up before him. Here, Le Nôtre and Le Vau formed a new tripartite pattern for an aristocratic residence. First, a magnificent approach to the château, then the château itself, followed by the rich, glorifying image of the garden.

The axis of the structure is continued so that it emerges symmetrically from the château, descending across a staircase and a few smaller terraces to a sunken *parterre de broderie*. On its right side is a *parterre des fleurs* and on the opposite, left-hand side the *parterre de la couronne*, which is named after a pool in the shape of a royal crown. At the end of the parterre the axis is interrupted by a round pool. This interruption is stressed by two longitudinal pools which, at the same time, form the first large side axis. With it, the spectator experiences a surprise and at the same time also becomes aware of a new lateral dimension to the garden. In its continuation, the axis is accompanied by two grass parterres, *parterres de gazon*, with two pools in the shape of a four-leaf clover. This section is followed by a square pool, which simultaneously ends the parterre and announces a new programme. Here, everything changes immediately. A kilometre-long canal forms a new, large, lateral feature, with a rich programme developing at the intersection with the longitudinal axis. The next surprise is the water motif of the Grandes Cascades, which is cut into the ground at the end of the parterre and is therefore not visible from it. Approaching the canal, the roaring of water can be heard more and more strongly and, eventually, the mood intensifies with the simultaneous visual and aural experience of the cascades. On the opposite side of

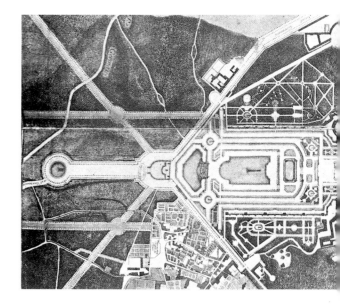

Ground-plan of the garden at Marly-le-Roy lacks the dynamics and rich complexity typical of Le Nôtre's work; there is, for instance, no development across the main axis (top).
Parterre and bosquet patterns as suggested by André Mollet in his book *Jardin de Plaisir*, dedicated to the Queen of Sweden and published in Stockholm in 1651 (bottom, left).
Parterres of a later development, especially by Le Nôtre, were more articulate and complex. They were also designed on a larger scale (bottom, right).

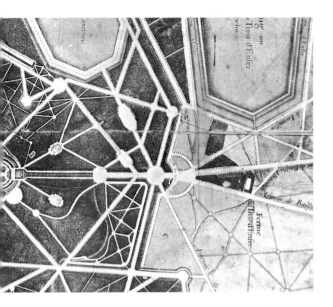

the canal, the scene is dominated by a large grotto with numerous sculptures. Above it opens a grassy surface, *tapis vert*, which ends in a huge sculpture of Hercules. The structure does not end here, but continues into the area where there are allées in the shape of a *patte d'oie*.

The view from the end of the axis also offers a rich scene (p. 106). From here, it is possible to see the true vertical dynamics of the garden and the slightly raised position of the château, reflected in numerous water surfaces. In spite of many changes to the site, the differences in height, which were sensitively mastered by Le Nôtre with terraces, remained. It is interesting to note that the structure develops symmetrically only immediately along the axis, whereas at the edges more varied elements usually appear, which still fuse completely into the harmonious whole. An outstanding characteristic of Vaux is also the firm discipline of the axial layout, intensified not only by the imaginative location of the different parterres, water elements and sculptures, but also by the effective setting of the green framework. This is tapering towards the lowest part of the garden and, with vertical planes, leads one's eyes to the climax of the axis - a sculpture of Hercules.

Versailles, the site of a royal residence from the 17th century, covering approximately 1000 hectares. Firstly, from 1623 onwards, a hunting lodge stood here. This was replaced by a larger château, built by Philibert Le Roy for Louis XIII in 1631. This building of brick and stone could not compete with the splendid residence of the Finance Minister Fouquet in Vaux-le-Vicomte. After Fouquet was dismissed in 1661, the king entrusted the renovation and enlargement of Versailles to the trio from Vaux, the landscape architect Le Nôtre, the architect Le Vau and the painter-decorator Le Brun. When Le Nôtre arrived, only part of the present garden, from the château as far as the Pool of Apollo, had been laid out. The structure, which was most probably the work of Boyceau's nephew Jacques de Menours, consisted of an axis with parterres, ending with a pool on the lower terrace. Le Nôtre started work in 1663 and dedicated most of his creative energy to Versailles. The château gradually became larger, in accordance at first with Le Vau's and later with Hardouin-Mansart's plans, and parallel to this the gardens also became enlarged. To this latter project Louis XIV dedicated a great deal of attention personally. Just how much the garden meant to the king's fame at that time is shown not only by the grandeur of its structure, but also by the fact that Louis himself put together guides for the viewing of Versailles, *Manière de Montrer les Jardins de Versailles*. He also used to take his guests personally round the gardens.

The site is not easy to view; it is not possible to take in the whole garden from one point, as it is at Vaux-le-Vicomte. Also, because of its exceptional size, the links between the individual sections are weak and thus the whole is sometimes over-extended and rather wearying. However, it should not be forgotten that the present state of the garden is, in a number of respects, but a pale reflection of its former splendid arrangement, which was rich with water displays, clipped hedges, sculptures, open-air theatres and so on. Some of this can be recaptured on those Sunday afternoons when, for an hour, all the water machinery of the garden of the *Grandes Eaux* is put into action, showing this great landscape spectacle in its true light. Up to five million litres of water are needed to produce one hour of water displays, which explains the rarity of their occurrence. It is not hard to imagine the volume of water which the 1,400 fountains functioning in the royal gardens for Louis XIV must have used. Versailles is the most majestic monument to authoritarian rule, not so much for its size as for its perfectly executed and consistent structure.

The layout as a whole shows the tripartite pattern, already worked out in Vaux: an ambitious entrance in the shape of a *patte d'oie*, ending in a *cour d'honneur*, the large building complex of the château and the garden itself. From beginning to end, the structure adheres strictly to an axis (p. 107). The axis in the park is 3 kilometres-long, but gives the optical impression of becoming lost on the horizon. It starts at the exit from the château with symmetrically placed pools forming a water parterre. From here, the ground descends to the next terrace on which there is the parterre of Latona. This is a key point in the composition. The garden at Versailles is also an allegorical representation of the Sun King by means of ancient mythology. The ruler is identified with Apollo, whose mother was Latona. Therefore, the main programme of the park is displayed between the Pool of Latona and the lower-placed Pool of Apollo, and is rich with mythological symbols, representing the world and its events. The sculpture in the pool shows a scene from Ovid's Metamorphoses, when the peasants of Lycia refused to show any hospitality towards the fleeing Latona and her children, Diana and Apollo. As punishment, they were changed into half frogs, half men - which of course hints at the contemporary political conflicts in France and the victory of the crown. From here, the axis goes to a lower *tapis vert*, which runs in the narrow corridor formed by two high green walls of clipped limes, bordered by two rows of sculptures and urns. At the end of these green walls, the space opens out and at this turning point stands the statue of the sun god Apollo, ready to bring the light of day to mankind (p. 107). At this point, the axis becomes the Grand Canal, which is 1,560 metres long and 120 metres wide. The axis is lost on the horizon, leaving one with the impression that everything is subordinated to the laws of geometrical order which rule in this glamorous theatre of the world whose only director is the Sun King.

Across the main axis, Le Nôtre set a number of lateral axes, which carry weighty programme elements. The most important is probably the first, which crosses the water parterre in front of the chateau and, on the northern side, runs across the south parterre and the orangery to the Lake of the Swiss Guard. To the south, it crosses the north parterre, passes a sculpture of bathing Nymphs, and runs along a water allée to the Fountain of the Dragon and Neptune's Pool. The subsequent lateral axes lead to the bosquets, in which there are many important elements, especially mythological representations. At the four key points are the pools of Winter, Spring, Summer and Autumn, represented by sculptures of Saturn, Flora, Ceres and Bacchus. In the bosquet south of the Pool of Latona there is an interesting addition from the end of the 18th century, when Louis XVI ordered the rearrangement of the Apollo Bathing group. It is set in romantic manner in the cave of a large rock. During the *Grandes Eaux*, water surrounds the rock, and the motif is open to the visitor. The final large lateral axis is formed by a canal, one arm of which runs from the Pool of Apollo to the north and the other to the south, to Le Grand Trianon.

Trianon was originally created to be a personal residence, away from the noise of the Court. Firstly, Le Vau built the so-called Porcelain Trianon, which was later rebuilt by Mansart. The garden structure at Trianon is the work of Le Nôtre's nephew Le Bouteux. The arrangement consists of a formal floral parterre, descending in steps in an axis indicated by a peristyle, and is complemented by many interesting elements, especially water motifs such as pools and fountains.

Not far from here is Le Petit Trianon, with the hamlet, Le Hameau, which was designed for Queen Marie Antoinette. Thus it can be seen that Jean Jacques Rousseau's Romantic ideal of the return to nature and to a simple life reached even the Court. The fairy-tale

The *Bains d'Apollon* at Versailles, in a new setting that provides a more romantic atmosphere in the cavern of a huge artificial rock.

hamlet, dating from 1783-1785, is quite well preserved, with its mill, stable, dovecot and cottages set in a natural garden environment (p. 109).

Villandry, 17 kilometres from Tours. The château was built in 1532 for Jean Le Breton, secretary of state to François I. During the course of the centuries, the original structure has been completely lost. In 1906 it was bought by Joachim Carvallo who, in the twenties, renovated the gardens on the basis of drawings by Du Cerceau dating from 1570.

The gardens are located on different terraces. On the lowest terrace is situated Villandry's celebrated feature, the *jardin potager*, a vegetable garden covering an area of 100 square metres. It is divided into 9 squares, each of which is further divided, and contains an urn on a stand. Various kinds of vegetables are grown in the beds, the first planting occurring in March, the second in June. The garden is at its most picturesque in September (p. 101). The next terrace is a parterre garden with trimmed box-trees and yews, surrounded by limes clipped into cubic shapes. Close to the terrace of the castle is the *jardin d'amour*, the garden of love, which consists of four squares with symbolic figures, representing gentle love (hearts with orange-coloured flowers), unhappy love (borders in the shape of a sword's blade and with red flowers), fickle love (shapes of butterflies and horns with yellow flowers) and passionate love (12 broken hearts with flowers of various colours). On the highest terrace is a formal parterre with a larger pool, from which water is used to irrigate the gardens. In this successful reconstruction of a Renaissance garden, not only can the 16th century be felt but even a slight hint of the medieval garden style.

In a selection of French gardens the following might also be included: *Dampierre*, in the vicinity of Paris, is probably the work of Le Nôtre, with extensive parterres and large water area; *Compiègne*, 75 kilometres northeast of Paris, was at first a formal arrangement based on Jacques-Ange Gabriel's plan with parterres and quincunx plantations but, in the 19th century, was rearranged in the landscape style; *Raray*, 45 kilometres northeast of Paris, boasts an unusual garden court which, on its south and north sides, is surrounded by two arcades, with sculptures representing hunting scenes in the Italian style; *Mortefontaine*, Vallières, is one of the few purely landscape structures in France, the original arrangement dating from the 18th century and, subsequently, often rearranged. It is not open to the public.

The French garden has, in its historical development, gone through many phases, from medieval, Renaissance and Baroque through to romantic arrangements. It reached its peak with Le Nôtre, and his ambitious Baroque structures created an unsurpassable example of a garden as a status symbol, which embodied a human desire for absolute power and at the same time final perfection in the arrangement of the world. It is therefore not surprising that it has been so vigorously imitated throughout Europe and that the French have never been able to renounce it. After all, in it an evolution of the symmetrical design, the most perfect form of spatial order, has been brought to a culmination; an evolution started in ancient Egypt and continued throughout practically all important cultures of later periods. Hence it is not difficult to understand why efforts to pursue the landscape style in France had such a modest success, although serious attempts were made.

p.101
Villandry. The garden is divided into terraces with characteristic parterres. At the front of the picture is the parterre of love with its four sections: unhappy love (sword blades - bottom, left), gentle love (hearts - top, left), passionate love (broken hearts - top, right) and fickle love (butterflies and horns - bottom, right). In the background, on the lower terrace, is the famous *jardin potager*, patterned with vegetables.

p.102
Fontainebleau. Large *parterre de Tibre* (top); Grand Canal, as seen from a spot above the Great Cascade (centre); carp-pond, with English garden in the background (bottom).

p.103
Rambouillet. The tripartite *patte d'oie* of the canal (top); the large geometrical plantation, quincunx (bottom).

p.104
Chenonceaux reflects traces of the characters of two women in the structure of the garden: in the top picture is the parterre of Diane de Poitiers, in the bottom picture is that of her rival, Cathérine de Médicis.

p.105
The gardens of the Tuileries: view from the axis across the round pool towards the octagonal pool and obelisk, which can be seen in the background of the picture (top). In the Jardins de Luxembourg (bottom), one is seeing a design made later than the original, with green walls and sculpture leading towards the château in the Baroque manner.

p.106
Vaux-le-Vicomte. The main parterre in the axis of the château. At the bottom of the picture a wide grotto can be seen and behind it a *tapis vert*, with a statue of Hercules as a *point de vue*, opens to visitors. The longitudinal course of the axis is firmly anchored through the whole composition by the convex-concave articulation of the building. Small differences in level between the terraces are interesting, ensuring the smooth transition and linking of spatial units (top). The château viewed from the opposite side, in a reflection in the water - one of the characteristic features of French Baroque landscape architectural composition (bottom).

p.107
In the main axis of the gardens of Versailles, two water motifs carry the basic symbolic message. The first is the Pool and the Fountain of Latona, Apollo's mother (top). The second feature, lower on the axis, is the group of Apollo, depicting the sun god in his golden chariot, rising from the water and bringing the light of day to mankind (bottom).

p.108
The *Bains d'Apollon* at Versailles are placed in the large artificial grove with three groups of Sun Horses and Apollo tended by Nymphs, after the long ride. Whereas the former scene in the Pool of Apollo represents the sunrise, here the sunset is symbolized; it is particularly impressive during the *Grandes Eaux* (top, left). A delicate exedra with busts on pedestals integrated into the hedge at the Grand Trianon (top, right). The Mirror Pool (bottom left). Only when the huge water supply system at Versailles is running can some arrangements come to full expression, like the intimate *Salle de Bal* (bottom, right).

p.109
The south part of the first lateral axis, with the *Bassin des Dracons*, at which the water allée starts, ending in the south parterre in front of the château (top). The parterre of Le Grand Trianon, at the bottom of the picture is the end of the southern arm of the Grand Canal (centre). The hamlet, Le Hameau, in Le Petit Trianon, with rustic buildings on a romantic lake (bottom).

p.110
Saint-Cloud, the large cascade, is the most impressive surviving structure of its kind.

p.111
Sceaux is a magnificent water composition with a quite well-preserved cascade (top). A view of the Grand Canal and the extensive octagonal pool (bottom).

p.112
Chantilly: a view from the Great Terrace to the parterre with its circular pools (top). The château of Chantilly on the water, with the *parterre de la volière* in the foreground (bottom).

p.113
Rosny: renovated parterre, with the Seine in the background (top). A remnant of the lateral axis of the once famous royal gardens of Marly-le-Roy (bottom).

p.114
Menars: the parterre on the upper terrace of the garden; the orangery with a rotunda, or temple of love, can be seen at the rear (top). Saint-Germain-en-Laye: the almost two and a half kilometre long terrace by the Seine is the most authentically preserved remnant of this once large complex of gardens (bottom).

p.115
Courances: the parterre, renovated in the 20th century, with a water mirror in the background (top). The remains of the original garden are today covered over with grass. A water cascade between a lawn and a back-drop of trees (bottom).

p.116
Champs-sur-Marne: view of the axis of the garden and, in the opposite direction, from the circular pool towards the château.

p.117
Nîmes, the Jardin de la Fontaine, a garden on water with numerous islands, passages, sculptures and a Baroque axial structure, which connects with an urban avenue in the background. In the centre of the picture is a statue of a Nymph on a square island.

p.118
Large cascade, a typical neo-sentimental detail from the Bois de Boulogne park in Paris, which was romanticized from 1852 onwards, as a late echo of the movements of the 18th century.

p.119
The most outstanding feature of Buttes-Chaumont is the high rock with belvedere (left). View of the *naumachia* in Park Monceau, Paris (right).

p.120
Ermenonville: the famous *Isle des Peupliers*, on which Rousseau was buried. Today, there is only a sarcophagus, made to a design by Hubert Robert.

114

England
The new landscape

European inspirations
The landscape movement
Poetic vision
The picturesque landscape
The pure landscape style
Gardens today

The meteoric rise of the landscape style in the 18th century has eclipsed all other periods of English gardening art. But even before its general spread, the British Isles could boast a varied and lively tradition of garden design. Unfortunately, most of the gardens created before the turn of the 18th century were swept away by the tide of the new movement. Even after the decline of the landscape style, some interesting trends sprung up in Britain, especially about the turn of the century. Therefore the British Isles preserve an exceptionally rich and diverse heritage of garden art, difficult to present with a limited selection in a single chapter. Since the times of the Renaissance, a large number of fine gardens have accumulated in England, reflecting the country's high level of garden culture and centuries of unimpeded prosperity.

The garden art of the British Isles can be divided into several distinct periods. Evolving from medieval gardens, the first formal layouts appeared in the age of Early Renaissance, cut short by the Civil War in 1642. With the Restoration, in 1660, the development resumed, from more complex Renaissance plans to Baroque solutions. About 1720, conditions were ripe for a complete reversal of the philosophic and aesthetic approach to landscape design, resulting in the new landscape style. This fashion faded out by the end of the century, after which horticultural aspects prevailed over formal innovations for about a century. In the late 19th and early 20th centuries, several interesting trends arose, towards a search for more regular patterns.

The earlier periods of English garden art, before the break-through of the landscape movement, have been unjustly underestimated. As in all other countries of Western Europe, the orderly pattern of medieval gardens was the starting point for all further developments, gradually leading towards the Renaissance. In the second half of the 15th century the gardens of the higher nobility began to assume a more complex plan and a richer repertory of motifs. The pre-conditions for a proper artistic bloom that was to place the fine arts and garden design on a new footing were present as soon as the Tudor dynasty came into power. This point can be illustrated by the surviving description of the royal gardens of Richmond Palace at the time of the wedding of Catherine of Aragon. The guests were able to admire a knotted parterre, pergolas, game courts, and various plantations.

European Inspirations

Henry VIII, a typical Renaissance potentate, liked to surround his court with glamour, which included the construction of showy gardens. His penchant for strong rule and luxurious life favoured the arts. It was in his reign that the sophisticated Cardinal Wolsey laid out the extensive gardens adjoining Hampton Court Palace. This was the first grand-scale design in England, reflecting not only the need for a representative setting, but also the competition for prestige with the French King François I. This spirit of defiance showed in a peculiar feature of garden design, the use of heraldic devices, emblematic colours and animal motifs symbolizing the house of Tudor. The palace garden was dominated by these patterns, but it also included a large, walled private garden, *giardino segreto,* with pergolas and an artificial observation hill.

The reign of Elizabeth I in the second half of the 16th century shifted the emphasis to plants symbolizing the virtues of the queen. She was most frequently equated with the Tudor rose and awarded the flattering name of Rosa Electa. The most famous garden of the Elizabethan age was that commissioned by Lord Burghley at Theobalds. It consisted of a sequence of enclosed courtyards with gardens, displaying the hallmark of the early English gardens, the knotted (as opposed to embroidered) parterre. The

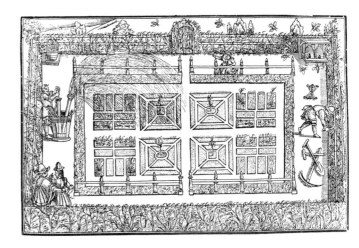

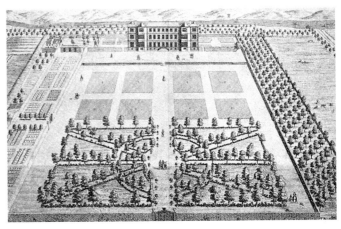

The simple geometry of a 16th-century garden (top, left).
Ham House is one of the first 17th-century layouts in England trying to develop a more clearly formulated formal link between the house and the garden (top, right).
Chatsworth, from the same period, after an etching by Kip, a Dutch printmaker specializing in town views and country houses. The Baroque design extends far from the house, over the slope of a hill; it follows the large-scale, orderly pattern of French examples, especially Versailles (bottom, left).
Hampton Court in its Baroque version by London and Wise, as recorded around 1700. Particularly striking are the characteristic semicircular end of the parterre, and the *patte d'oie*, with the emphatic axis marked by the central canal and double alley. This prominent feature has survived to the present day (bottom, right).

The Temple of Ancient Virtue at Stowe (previous page)

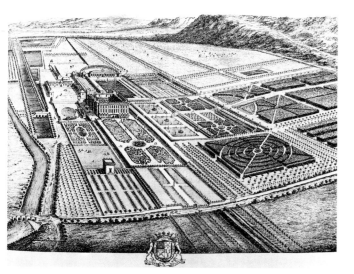

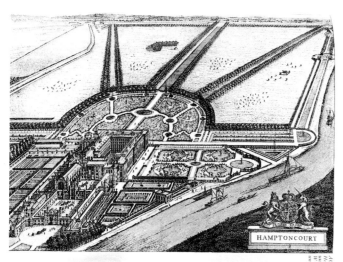

HAMPTONCOURT

knots were either open or closed. The basic pattern was formed by rosemary, thyme and, somewhat later, box. The intermediate spaces were filled with multi-coloured gravel and flowers.

In the early 17th century, Renaissance innovations swept the country, arriving either via France or via Holland. An important contribution in this sense was made by the Frenchman Salomon de Caus, who was a hydraulic engineer, architect and garden designer. He had a thorough knowledge of Italy, and had worked in a number of countries on the continent. He introduced a profusion of Italian motifs, grottoes, water machines, fountains, sculptures, etc., into the gardens laid out for the Danish-born Queen Anne at Somerset House and in Greenwich, and later into the gardens of Richmond and Hatfield House. No less important was his brother Isaac de Caus, whose English career began in the 1620s. His most celebrated and influential design was the garden created for Lord Pembroke at Wilton. It was an outstanding Mannerist work, adjoining the Palladian house designed by Inigo Jones. The approach was centred straight onto the porch of the villa, faced by a four-sectioned parterre with a central fountain. A further attraction was a large, profusely designed grotto, a *parterre d'eau* in the spirit of the Villa Lante, and a terraced amphitheatre cut into a slope. This pronounced Italianate character of the garden seems to indicate that the guidelines were laid down by Inigo Jones, who had returned from his tour of Italy soaked in Italian traditions and conversant with the latest fashions. He exerted a profound influence on his contemporaries, and in many respects foreshadowed the landscape gardens of the 18th century.

A more immediate impact was made by André Mollet, the boldest of a famous family of French garden designers. He made two visits to England, both times invited by the court. During his first visit he laid out the gardens of St. James's Palace, and during his second sojourn, those of Wimbledon House, in 1641-1642. Here Inigo Jones re-shaped the building, while Mollet remodelled the gardens, introducing Baroque parterres, alleys, bosquets and terraces. The new Wimbledon complex was also distinguished by the perfect integration of house and garden. Before the ravages of the Civil War, which broke out in 1642, Mollet's English creations were a link between Renaissance and Baroque.

In the following two decades, the Civil War not only suspended all development, but also laid waste to a number of gardens. After the death of Mollet, John Rose was appointed royal gardener in 1666. His disciples, George London and Henry Wise, were England's most distinguished garden designers in the formal style. They jointly redesigned the gardens of Hampton Court for William III, introducing a new Baroque ground-plan with an emphasized central axis and radial alleys. The rivalry with the French court was resumed, to lead eventually into the emergence of a native style in the 18th century.

Towards the end of the century, London and Wise designed two more Baroque gardens, Melbourne Hall and Chatsworth. The latter is particularly renowned, as a happy blend of heterogeneous elements. Originally it was an extensive Baroque layout, with a characteristic embroidered parterre, *parterre de broderie*, on the axis of the building, and a profusion of accompanying motifs on a slope. The most famous of these features is the surviving stepped cascade. By the turn of the 18th century, English Baroque gardening had reached its mature stage, both in its repertory of features and its formal patterns. But it was an imported style, unable to fulfill the needs of a new society, which was one of the reasons for its demise.

The Landscape Movement

The rise of English landscape gardening in the 18th century is one of the most complex chapters in the history of garden art, and is still insufficiently explored. Most of the attempts to explain this unique movement stress various secondary causes such as the influence of painting, the insular climate, or the reaction to French Baroque. A phenomenon that reorientated the outlook of an entire nation and radically affected the landscape of the country must, clearly, have arisen from a whole set of complex circumstances. But the underlying motive must be sought in the social, political and economic conditions. It was an age when the English countryside changed its appearance because of the modernization of farming. The growing demand for food and, above all, wool for the expanding manufacturing industry called for a land reform that involved the enclosure of pastures. There were various views on how this reform should be carried out. A vast percentage of the English rural landscape was involved. A total area of 1.2 million hectares was enclosed in the course of the 18th century. Forestry faced a similar dilemma. Britain's forests were exhausted and could not supply the shipyards with the amounts of timber required by a country that had become the world's major maritime and colonial power. Therefore a national afforestation movement was launched by Parliament and the question of how to tackle the problem was widely discussed. An influential publication on the topic was written by the gardener John Evelyn, under the title *Sylva* in 16§

The new-fledged world power found herself compelled to underline her vast military and economic power by a corresponding pre-eminence in the spatial arts - architecture and landscape design. Understandably, the reigning Baroque fashion, imported from her greatest rival, France, was little suited to display British grandeur. Therefore a new, original style was needed. It was sought in a direction suggested by the political differences between the new social power, the influential middle class, and part of the nobility on the one hand, and the court on the other. After the Whigs had seized power in the Glorious Revolution at the end of the 17th century, free thinking and political liberty were the order of the day.

The rebellion against autocracy affected views of nature and landscape design and the concept of natural versus a rigidly designed landscape. In his essay *The Moralist* (1710) Lord Shaftesbury, the influential humanist, expressed his preference for natural forms over artificial gardens associated with princely courts. Joseph Addison, in his contributions to *The Spectator*, lost no opportunity of emphasizing the superiority of the natural landscape found in the countryside. He also launched an idea that won enthusiastic acclaim: the transformation of an entire estate into a kind of garden complex. The notion that natural forms were, both aesthetically and morally, preferable to artificial ones gained wide currency in many treatises of the period. It was often given a political turn, since nature was equated with freedom. In his poem *Liberty* (1735) Thompson extols the irregular English garden as an image of freedom, as compared to the French garden, where "nature is enslaved". William Mason regarded a winding path as a symbol of freedom, as opposed to the rigid, straight alleys favoured by the Baroque era.

Poetic Vision

The leading role in the promotion of the new movement was certainly played by the men of letters, who gave wide publicity to the topic. The literature of the time did not merely discuss the merits of natural versus artificial landscapes, but also ventured into

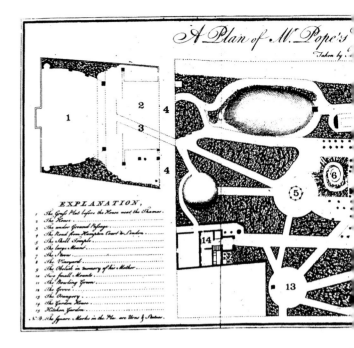

The famous garden that Pope designed for himself at Twickenham in 1720 was the first departure from regular design in England. To link the two parts of his garden, which were separated by a road, he made an underground passage which was given the character of a grotto. The skirting pathways are laid out in wavy Rococo lines, typical of the early beginnings of landscape gardening. This comparatively modest design was to give a decisive impulse towards the formation of a new style (top).

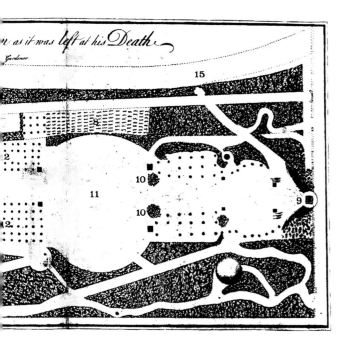

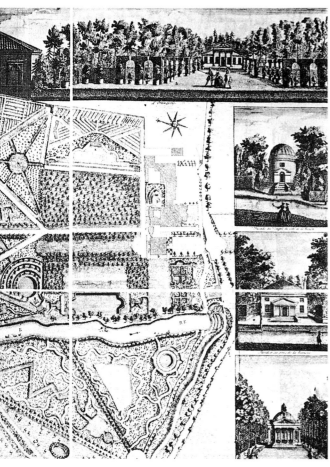

Chiswick, the garden of Lord Burlington, situated between Twickenham and London. It was laid out from 1725 onwards, when Burlington erected his Neo-Palladian house, modelled on the Villa Rotonda and soon famous throughout the country. The deviation from formal geometry is even clearer than in Pope's case. The axis of the garden leads past the building; most of the pathways are traced in wavy lines; and the garden contains a sprinkling of smaller buildings (bottom).

programmatic discussions. It searched for new approaches and reacted to all contemporary events. The cultural history of the world probably knows no other period when garden art attracted such wholesale attention from the leading creative minds of a whole nation. In fact, poetry foretold all the chief features of the coming landscape gardens. It found its inspiration mainly in the works of Horace and Virgil, from whom it borrowed pastoral landscapes and mythological settings, sacred groves and grottoes. The ancient idea of a rural retreat, Arcadia, was revived and became a reality.

The central figure of this poetic movement was Alexander Pope. He found his model in Horace. In one of his poems, the *Epistle to Lord Burlington*, he points out that architecture and design must take account of nature and follow the genius of the place. He, too, identified natural forms with liberty. He put his ideas into practice in his own widely copied garden at Twickenham, the first ever to deviate from a rigid formal pattern (plan at top). A member of the same circle of Whig intellectuals and artists, Lord Burlington was an amateur Palladian architect. He designed his own villa at Chiswick. This shows, on the whole, a regular ground-plan, but numerous details are deliberately erratic, an idea developed by Bridgeman and by Kent.

The corresponding revolution in garden design was started by Charles Bridgeman (1738). He emerged from the Baroque school of Wise and Vanbrugh. This is apparent in all his ground-plans, though he tends to relax the rigidity of the pattern. He moved towards the new style and this was a venture of historic significance. A showpiece of his art is Stowe, where he has created a magnificent central vista, surrounded by masses of trees. A similar fringed layout can be discerned at Rousham, where Kent's later remodelling has softened the outlines. Bridgeman was probably the first to use the ha-ha, a dry ditch separating the garden from the rest of the estate and keeping the cattle out, thus dispensing with the need for a fence (p. 151). In this way the view from the house and garden could range freely over the surrounding landscape. These two worlds, so far kept rigidly separate, could now blend into one.

The Picturesque Landscape

The loosening of Baroque geometry was only the first stage. The new approach continued to develop within the framework of the old pattern. The most telling example is Stowe, where Kent introduced new compositions within Bridgeman's original layout. William Kent (1685-1748) had lived in Italy for a long time, training to become a painter, for which he showed no particular aptitude. Instead, he devoted himself to interior decoration, architecture, and, rather late in his life, garden design, the activity that was to win him fame. Lord Burlington called him back from Italy and employed him at Chiswick and then Lord Cobham invited him to Stowe. Here he thoroughly broke up the original formal structure, especially the straight lines of vegetation and regular shapes of pools. Some of his details were major breakthroughs in English garden design, in particular the Elysian Fields. This is a narrow valley skirted by trees, crossed by a winding stream and by two smaller buildings, the Temple of Ancient Virtue and the Temple of British Worthies (p. 148). The prevailing atmosphere is classical, with echoes from antiquity, but the underlying ideals, such as the praise of selflessness, are modern. By the end of the century, Stowe contained a collection of motifs in the new style, with a profusion of architectural, mostly classical elements. It was widely visited and copied by admirers from the whole country, and even from the continent.

The first integral creation in the new style was Rousham. The original design was drawn up by Bridgeman, but the actual layout was conceived by Kent, who arranged a sequence

125

of classical scenes. Though these motifs are not fused into a firm whole, Kent's mastery of detail is indisputable. He has sprinkled the slope between the Cherwell river and the villa with a number of stage-sets. Clearly, he must have found his inspiration in the stage designs of Inigo Jones and the Italian masters. Like Stowe and other complexes of the picturesque style, Rousham points rather to compositional links with Italian and English stage design than to the influence of landscape painters, such as Claude Lorraine, Poussin and Salvator Rosa.

In the footsteps of professional designers, a multitude of rich land-owners arranged their own gardens. Perhaps the most brilliant of them was the banker Henry Hoare, creator of Stourhead, the unsurpassed masterpiece of the picturesque movement. It is an ideal Arcadian landscape, organized around a lake, with a number of skilfully chosen and placed programmatic features of classical inspiration. The complex is not only one of the most perfect garden allegories in existence, but also remarkably designed, with a superbly aligned circular path that captures all the principal views. Another typical example of a layout where the garden scenery must be viewed from various points along the periphery was The Leasowes, also dating from the middle of the century and conceived by the poet William Shenstone. This arrangement implies the abandonment of the Baroque principle of a single static viewpoint, usually located near the building. In fact, The Leasowes put into practice Addison's idea of the beautiful farm, the *ferme ornée*.

The Pure Landscape Style

About the middle of the century, Lancelot Brown, nicknamed Capability Brown (1715-1783), became the central figure of the landscape movement. Unlike Kent, he combined a profound classical education with practical expertise in gardening. His spectacular career spanned from designer of Stowe to royal inspector of gardens and waterworks.

He developed an extremely simple style of composition. Indeed, he might be called (with the possible exception of the designers of Zen gardens) the greatest purist in the history of landscape architecture. His formal language consists of gently rolling lawns, curving lakes melting into the background, mighty masses of tree clumps and fringes of tall vegetation. Brown's compositions are based on soft, rhythmically undulating lines and on contrasts between bright surfaces of lawn or water and dark masses of trees.

This is the ultimate stage of the landscape style, almost abstract and quite as remote from virgin nature as the old-fashioned regular patterns. While Kent and his contemporaries had made extensive use of architectural elements, though subordinating them to the landscape, they had often merely added them as an afterthought. Brown practically dispensed with architecture and built up his compositions out of pure landscape elements. He had a delicate sense of scale, which allowed him also to manage designs on sites of large dimensions, such as Blenheim, his most impressive creation. Unfortunately, his immense fertility (more than 200 gardens are ascribed to him), and his zeal for what he proudly called "improvements" led him to destroy a number of valuable formal gardens.

At this point it is interesting to note an oddity. Castle Howard, dating back to 1713, is a precocious forerunner of both versions of landscape, Kent's picturesque and Brown's purist gardens. By its articulation of space through symbolic architectural features, placed at key points in the landscape, it foreshadows Kent's style. But the delicate choice of the site, shrewd appreciation of its natural elements and restrained use of landscaped elements rather anticipate Brown's spirit. A synthesis of both styles before they even existed, Castle Howard stands at the very beginning of the English landscape movement.

Bridgeman's contemporary Stephen Switzer (1682-1745) was active rather as a writer on gardens than a designer. He published a number of influential books in which he argued for a new taste in landscape design where "Art would not spoil the beauties of Nature". As a pupil of the Baroque school of London and Wise he could not quite escape from regularity, which he preserved around the building and along the axis, as exemplified by a ground-plan from his *Ichnographia Rustica* (1718). The design represents a "Wooded or Rural Garden", as he called his layouts that gain a natural look especially by soft lateral features. He emphasized that the architect and the gardener had to work hand in hand, in consultation, if the garden was to form a harmonious whole with the buildings (top).

Just like Switzer's, Batty Langley's designs try to break away from Baroque regularity towards wavy Rococo lines; this ground-plan comes from his book *The New Principles of Gardening*, published in 1728 (centre).

The high-water mark of the aesthetic of soft, wavy lines is represented by the sketches of the painter William Hogarth, published in his *Analysis of Beauty* in 1754 (bottom).

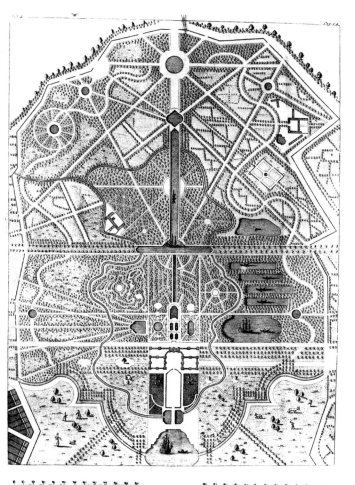

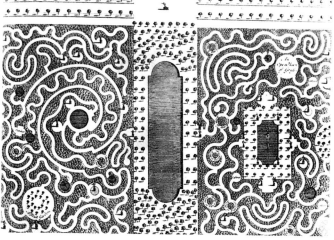

Brown's tradition was continued, with certain modifications, by Humphry Repton (1752–1818). Under the influence of the contemporary fashion for exotic plants, he began introducing flower motifs into his designs. He even fell back on certain formal elements, in order to achieve a more efficient integration of house and garden. In one of his treatises he claims that symmetry is admissible, and even necessary, in front of a façade of regular design. Repton, writer of several authoritative books on the theory of landscape design, often engaged in polemics with the critics of Brown's works. These included, in the second half of the 18th century, Uvedale Price, Richard Payne Knight and William Gilpin, who attacked the monotony of Brown's layouts and championed picturesque wild landscapes. They shaped the philosophy of the Romantic untamed landscape, soon to spill over to the European continent.

The 19th century only exaggerated what had been laid down by the 18th century and allowed the horticultural aspect to overshadow the design. This inevitably led to attempts at a return to order and revival of more regular patterns, convincingly championed by Reginald Blomfield, crusading against William Robinson, creator of the English flower garden. At the turn of this century, the two trends were reconciled by the architect Edwin Lutyens and the garden designer Gertrude Jekyll (p. 138). Their joint achievements stand out because of the intimate connection between house and garden, clear geometric ground-plans, with regularly placed terraces, stairways and pergolas, but, within this formal framework, freely arranged plantings of varied composition. Lutyens' and Jekyll's creations have opened up a new era of garden culture.

In the 20th century, some interesting new gardens have arisen, combining outstanding formal aspects with amateur horticulture. They are eclectic by character, and draw on England's wide repertory of historic styles. Typical examples are well-known gardens at Bodnant, Hidcote, Nymans and Sissinghurst.

Gardens Today

The English gardening heritage lends itself less than that of any other country to a selection of a few characteristic and valuable works. The British Isles can look back on an amazing gardening tradition that includes both a bewildering number of productions in the native landscape style and a fair number of distinguished formal gardens. Therefore our survey is necessarily limited and omits numerous remarkable examples.

Blenheim, Woodstock, near Oxford. The palace was presented to the Duke of Marlborough as a reward for his victories against the French. Construction started in 1705, from a plan by Vanbrugh. At the same time Henry Wise began laying out the gardens on the southern side of the palace, in a formal style. The complex, centred on the Baroque palace, was arranged along a north-south axis, running for a distance of some four kilometres, and outlined in the northern section by a wide multiple alley. Striving for a monumental total effect, Vanbrugh built a grand-scale bridge over the Glyme river, to underscore the access to the palace. But the bridge only came into its own when the total area was redesigned by Capability Brown. He abolished the parterre and extended the lawn right up to the palace. His great creative contribution was the addition of an extensive lake landscape. By damming up the little river, he raised the water level and increased the areas of both lakes, which now reach all the way to the bridge, providing it with a scenic background. The lake shores, reshaped with extreme refinement, provide the finishing touch to Brown's achievement (p. 152–153).

In this century the formal patterns have been restored, from designs by Achille Duchêne, eastwards with an Italianate garden, and westwards with a *parterre d'eau*.

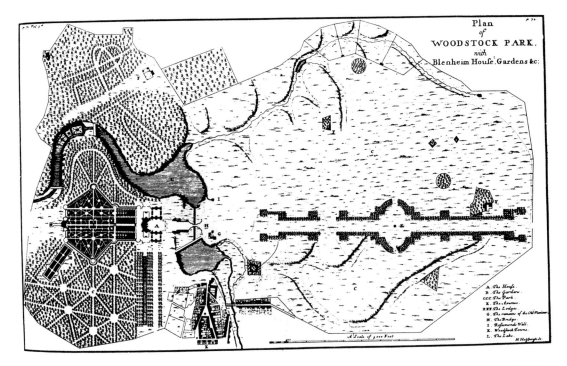

Plan
of
WOODSTOCK PARK,
with
Blenheim House, Gardens &c.

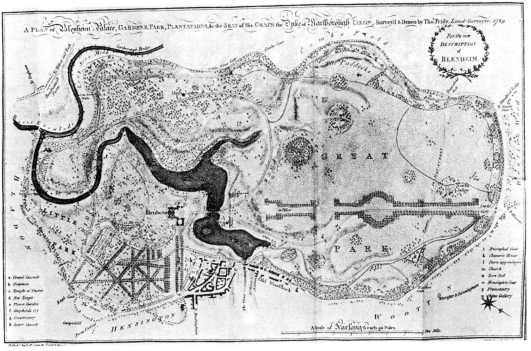

A PLAN of Blenheim Palace, Gardens, Park, Plantations, &c the Seat of His Grace the Duke of Marlborough OXON, Surveyd & Drawn by Tho. Pride, Land-Surveyor, 1789.

For the new
DESCRIPTION
of
BLENHEIM.

The large-scale Baroque layout by Henry Wise and John Vanbrugh at Blenheim. The mighty alley, which is supposed to represent the arrangement of the Duke of Marlborough's troops at the battle of Blenheim, is linked as an axis, via the Victory Column, to the Palace designed by Vanbrugh. In front of the Palace there was an extensive, formal Baroque parterre, from which numerous bosquets departed in all directions (this page, top).

Brown's rearrangement preserved the alley of access, but eliminated the original parterre, and thereby caused one of the most regrettable losses among the Baroque gardens of England. But at the same time it introduced perhaps the most magnificent landscape arrangement in the country. Brown reshaped the lakes with special ingenuity, purposefully integrating them within the scenery (this page, bottom).

Opposite page:
Rousham, the first integral creation in the landscape style, faithfully follows Kent's basic principle that "Nature rejects straight lines". Yet the execution of certain parts betrays Bridgeman's sense of formal order, e.g., the vista in front of the house and the straight alley of elms in the lower part of the illustration. The layout was created on the basis of Bridgeman's design after Kent's preliminary sketches and modifications in the course of execution (top).

Kent's sketch for the cascades in Venus Vale, which is one of the central motifs of Rousham. His gardens were composed of scenes of this kind, which he designed to perfection. He was substantially aided by his knowledge of Italian Renaissance gardens and by his study of modern stage design. It is not difficult to imagine how close to the landscape style of the period were such mythological and rustic paintings where beings from classical antiquity populated idealized scenery derived from the domestic landscape (bottom).

Bramham, 12 kilometres southwest of York. The first design originates from the first half of the 18th century. The original layout, known from a plan by John Wood from about 1782, is preserved almost intact. An extensive wooded area is criss-crossed by a network of straight paths. The house is located on the periphery, in the northern sector. Since there is no room for depth effects in front of it, the main axis leads along the building, in a southerly direction, where it finds its visual termination in a tall obelisk. Approximately one-third of the way, before the terrain drops abruptly, is the most powerful formal motif of the garden, the so-called Obelisk Fountain. From this point a fine view ranges back towards the palace, southwards towards the Rotunda and the

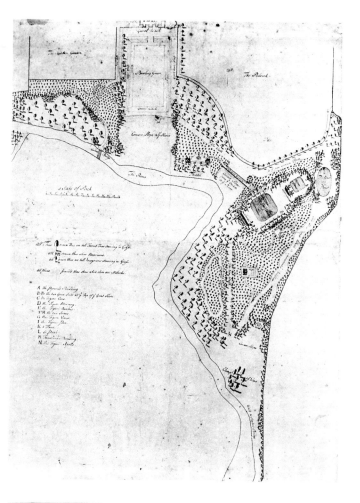

obelisk, and along an additional transverse axis, eastwards into the open landscape and westwards to a Gothic temple. This line at the same time marks the limit of the first, more abundantly furnished part of the garden, which also includes a T canal, further temples and some sculptures.

Castle Howard, some 20 kilometres northeast of York. The Howard family began arranging the palace and the garden at the beginning of the 18th century. The layout is highly unusual and in many respects revolutionary. Even the location of the Baroque building in the centre of the complex, without any formal links to the approach, is a departure from tradition. What is more, some other elements of the design prefigure the coming landscape style.

The bulk of the landscape features are concentrated in the eastern section of the complex. Here, on typically English rolling ground, one of the most original landscape compositions of the 18th century strikes the eye. At the end of the path leading eastwards from the castle, through a wood, the view suddenly opens, marked by Vanbrugh's Temple of the Four Winds. At the same time, a bridge which is a copy of one of Palladio's bridges, appears at the foot of the slope, and the Rotunda Mausoleum, where members of the Howard family are buried, looms in the background (p. 145). These three architectural elements, each a masterpiece in itself, make up a triangular grid, and, with the water, the softly modelled lawn and the tectonic masses of woodlands, fuse into a unique landscape scene. If, as Christopher Hussey claims, this is an embodiment of poetic reality, then it is certainly heroic poetry. A designed landscape as dramatic in concept, as gigantic in scale and as effective in its linking of remote elements can be found nowhere else. Surprisingly, the designer of the layout was not recorded but it was probably guided by Charles Howard in person. To the south of the castle the parterre was restored in the mid 19th century, from a design by W. A. Nesfield, and the symmetrical, three-sectioned, typically Baroque building could today hardly be imagined without it.

Chatsworth, some 25 kilometres southwest of Sheffield. It has undergone a number of changes since its beginnings at the end of the 17th century. First George London and Henry Wise designed a formal garden for the first Duke of Devonshire. An engraving by Kip shows that the garden was consequently designed in the regular style and organized in several terraces, but lacked a guiding concept expressed in a main axis. The abundance of natural water (the Derwent river skirts the garden) has allowed the inclusion of numerous water motifs. The most famous of them, a remarkable cascade probably designed by Grillet, a disciple of Le Nôtre, survives today (p. 141). Half a century later, in the heyday of the landscape style, the new fashion stripped Chatsworth of practically all its formal elements. Capability Brown, among others, contributed to the redesigning of the garden, organically blending it with the surroundings.

In the 19th century Joseph Paxton was employed as head gardener. He erected, among other constructions, a huge glasshouse that became famous throughout the country, a forerunner of his Crystal Palace built for the Great Exhibition. Paxton's improvements also include an impressive water-jet in the so-called Long Canal, in front of the house. It was finished by 1844, when a visit from the Russian Tsar Nicholas was expected. Chatsworth is an example of the stylistic changes in English landscape architecture, and is also one of the country's most attractive landscape structures, with its formal arrangement surrounded by splendid pastoral settings.

Chiswick House. The garden adjoining this famous villa is a joint work by Kent and Bridgeman for Lord Burlington, Kent's patron and promoter of Palladian architecture.

It displays a combination of formal and irregular elements, the majority of them reminiscent of Italian gardens with temples, sculpture, columns, trimmed hedges, etc. Outstanding surviving elements are the exedra and the domed temple with a circular pool, obelisk and orange trees in tubs (p.144). With its irregular components, the layout of this garden is regarded as one of the pioneering works paving the way for the oncoming landscape style.

Folly Farm, Sulhamstead, Berkshire. This is a joint creation by Edwin Lutyens and Gertrude Jekyll, dating from 1906. The garden, with its straight and circular lines of terraces, paths, stairways and trimmed hedges, produces a clear-cut effect. This formal purity is matched by the consistent use of materials, mostly brown brick, for the building and all the architectural elements of the garden. The ground is gently undulating which creates an illusion of spaciousness in this rather small garden, and at the same time underlines the privacy of the various sections (p. 138).

Ham House, Petersham, on the western fringe of London. The original building was built in 1609, when a geometric garden was laid out nearby. A preserved drawing from this year shows an axial, symmetrical garden design, with parterres centred on the house. The garden has recently been restored, and represents one of the rare integral Renaissance entities in Britain. The entrance is symmetrically placed opposite the house front. Immediately behind there is a courtyard with a circular pavement, flanked on both sides by brick walls rhythmically broken up by niches with busts and bordered by a sequence of cylinder-shaped clipped shrubs. A second key-note of the garden is the strictly geometric, simple parterre, planted with low ground-cover plants punctuated with cones of evergreen shrubs (p. 140).

Hampton Court, a royal palace near London. The nucleus of the building was erected by Cardinal Wolsey, who presented it to the King in 1525. Soon afterwards the palace was expanded and the gardens redesigned, to mark the increasing power of Henry VIII. Behind the original sequence of simpler enclosed gardens with knotted parterres, more complex designs were added: the Pond Garden, the Privy Garden, etc. (p.139). A typical feature of the age was the omnipresent heraldry, both in the buildings and in the gardens. A second glorious age of Hampton Court followed in the second half of the 17th century, when Wren built extensive additions with Baroque stylistic features rivalling Versailles. The usual open space in front of the palace was shaped into the symmetrical *parterre de broderie*, with a rounded extension from which three long avenues set out. The central avenue is emphasized by a long canal, which marks the axis of the ground-plan.

Of the formal arrangements described, the long canal and the *patte d'oie* pattern of the three alleys are well in evidence today. The sunken Pond Garden and the larger Privy Garden rank among the country's oldest preserved formal gardens. Particularly interesting features are the fence panels and the wrought-iron gates, produced at the end of the 17th century by the Frenchman Jean Tijou (p. 142). They were for some time removed to a museum, but have been replaced since. The maze, now of clipped yew and privet, originally of hornbeam, also dates from the 17th century. The one-time Wilderness, arranged as an English counterpart of French bosquets by Wise and London, is today mostly overgrown with grass and flowering bulbs.

Hidcote Manor, some 15 kilometres south of Stratford-on-Avon. This is one of the famous 20th century gardens reflecting the influences of earlier formal styles, an enviable level of gardening technique and exceptional horticultural devotion. It has been created since 1907, chiefly by an amateur enthusiast, Major L. Johnston. The area covers 4.5 hectares, and is divided into a number of independent sections and gardens. The key-

Woburn Farm (top) was, together with Shenston's Leasowes, the most famous *ferme ornée*, or embellished estate. It was arranged by Philip Southcote in the mid 18th century. According to Whateley's description in *Observations on Modern Gardening* (1770), the entire estate covered 60 hectares. Of this area, about a quarter was arranged as a garden, while the rest was occupied by cultivated ground. A winding path skirted the grounds, along a broad belt of trees and shrubbery, which separated the farm from the surrounding space and provided a unity. Along the paths, picturesque views opened out and the scenery changed continuously. Nothing remains today of Woburn Farm. As a historical example it testifies to the spirit of the age, which was so obsessed with the picturesque that gardens began to obtrude on farming lands. Such impulses have helped to shape the basic features of the so much admired English landscape (top).

One of Brown's most critical opponents was Richard Payne Knight (1750-1824), who developed his own version of the theory of the picturesque landscape. He disliked Brown's simplicity of layout: in Brown's empty and purified scenery, nymphs and driads could find no shelter. According to Knight, the picturesque landscape should be based on the wide variety encountered in wild natural scenery. His views are expressed in *Landscape. A Didactical Poem* (1794), where he also published these two illustrations. The first shows Brown's "empty" type of landscape (centre), and the second, the true picturesque landscape according to Knight (bottom).

note of the gardens is the structural element of clipped trees or shrubbery, appearing in the form of partition walls, bordering hedges, abstract shapes, and animal figures. A second characteristic is the exemplary use of various garden plants, including a collection of rare species. Some of the most interesting sections are the Long Walk, the White Garden (p. 160), the Red Borders and the Stilts Garden.

Kew Gardens, London. The Royal Botanic Gardens not only boast unique plant collections but also contain sections of remarkable design value. The gardens were developed from the royal estates where the first layouts were contributed by Charles Bridgeman and William Kent, and later radically remodelled by Capability Brown. Beginning in 1757, Sir William Chambers made several important additions, among them the Chinese Pagoda (p. 158), ever since then one of the most notable features of Kew Gardens. Since the middle of the 18th century it has developed into a botanical and horticultural institution of world importance.

Levens Hall, near Kendal, is one of England's most curious formal gardens. The original design, from 1692, was probably prepared by Guillaume Beaumont, a master of the French Baroque school. It displays superb examples of the English school of topiary work. Though the garden has undergone certain changes and expansions during the three centuries of its existence, the arrangement preserves the regular division into rectangular flowerbeds. The varied patterns of clipped box, yew or arbor vitae create a lively interplay of green masses with the undergrowth of grass or flowerbeds, resulting in a composition of pronounced tectonic structure (p. 137).

Melbourne Hall, 20 kilometres southwest of Nottingham. The garden covers an area of about 6 hectares. The arrangement was begun by Thomas Coke, aided by Wise and London, in the late 17th century. Coke had returned from a tour of France fascinated by Le Nôtre's gardens. After the breakthrough of the landscape movement Melbourne was neglected. It was partly restored early in this century. The ground-plan is symmetrical. From the house the garden falls in gentle terraces (today without parterres) towards the basin, whose curved ending is surmounted by the main curiosity of the garden, a "Birdcage" arbour of wrought iron (p. 143), produced by R. Bakewell in 1706. Behind the basin there is an extensive bosquet, in which a circular basin is preserved. The bosquet also contains the most famous sculpture of the garden, a huge lead urn representing the Four Seasons, by the Dutch Baroque sculptor Jan van Nost, who also created several interesting statues for other sections of the complex. The urn of the Four Seasons is located in a vantage point where alleys of clipped trees converge from all directions.

Nymans, Handcross, 7 kilometres south of Crawley. Both its structure and its furnishings remind one of Hidcote. It was created roughly at the same time, from the end of the 19th century onwards, and similarly combines elements of the classical formal style with horticultural showpieces. It is divided into several thematic sections, such as a sunken garden, a heather garden with a rich collection of heather species and other plants difficult to cultivate, a pinetum and an elevated garden with a rose plantation. A particularly interesting motif is a four-sectioned walled garden, with a fountain in the centre, surrounded by four ornamentally clipped yew-trees. The flower borders along the paths were laid out at the suggestion of William Robinson and Gertrude Jekyll. Perhaps the most attractive section skirts the remains of the house, which was burnt down in the 1940s and now gives the impression of an artificial ruin. The original façade is overgrown with climbers and blends perfectly with the surrounding vegetation (p. 159). Nymans is a creation of its owner, L. C. R. Messel, and his gardener J. Comber.

Painshill, near Cobham, is another great amateur work in English garden art. It was created by its owner Charles Hamilton during the period from 1738 to 1774 on a rolling site of almost 100 hectares. Developed around the 6 hectare-large serpentine lake, it boasts a sequence of classical and natural features including a Gothic temple, mausoleum, Temple of Bacchus, hermitage and many others. Of particular interest is a grotto, quite unusual in European landscape design. Made out of hollow and twisted limestone, it comes in its appearance very close to Chinese water and mountain, *shanshui*, rockeries (p. 150).

All these features are carefully sited around the lake and can be enjoyed during the walk as a constantly changing vista according to the Japanese "hidden and seen" principle. Painshill was one of the famous picturesque gardens and used to attract visitors from all over the country. After World War II it fell into decline and was largely overgrown by forest vegetation. Since the 1980s the Painshill Park Trust has undertaken large-scale restoration works which will hopefully lead to a successful revival of this unique creation in the picturesque style.

Petworth, 9 kilometres east of Midhurst, Sussex. This is one of the most authentic and most integrally preserved creations of Capability Brown. The original Elizabethan garden was established in the last decades of the 16th century. When the existing mansion was built in 1688-1693, the Duke of Somerset began reshaping the gardens in the reigning Baroque fashion, presumably on the basis of a project by London. Brown was first commissioned in 1751, and drew his design in 1752. In the following years he abolished the Baroque parterres along the western façade of the building, replacing them with a gently rolling lawn. Here is Petworth's most impressive feature, a serpentine lake, which Brown created by damming up a stream and shaping the banks into wavy hills. On the slope and ridges he had planted clumps of trees, chestnuts, oaks and beeches (p. 156). The most overwhelming view of this scenery opens from the house. The winding outlines of the sheet of water recede into the distance and fade into the background, merging with the undulating lines of the rounded hills and tree clumps.

To the north of the house, the outlines of the formal arrangements of pre-Brown times survive. Originally this section contained the Pleasure Grounds. Brown added a ha-ha and two classical temples, one Doric, the other Ionic. In 1872 grilles of wrought iron, imitating Tijou's masterpiece in the Hampton Court gardens, were placed along the western front and at the entrance of the park.

Powerscourt, on the outskirts of Dublin, Ireland. The palace was built in 1743, on a slope where an Italianate formal garden was laid out a century later. The bulk of the garden consists of an axial design facing the southern front of the building, from where the arrangement descends in terraces towards the Triton Basin. The first terrace is framed by two sculptures and two clipped trees. The next terrace is profusely decorated by a railing of wrought iron, flanked on both sides by statues and paved in multi-coloured geometric patterns. There are five more terraces, the last one ending in a basin set off by a wrought-iron grille and two Pegasus figures. The optical axis of the garden finds its termination in the sculpture rising out of the centre of the basin.

Prior Park, Widcombe near Bath. The setting reminds one of Italian, especially Palladian arrangements on a slope. A concave clearing rises to a mighty Palladian villa, erected by John Wood about 1730. The open, grassy clearing is hemmed in on both sides by contrasting masses of trees (p. 157). At the bottom the area runs out into a small lake, whose dam is hidden by a Palladian-style bridge. Both the garden and the bridge are attributed to Capability Brown.

To demonstrate his designs, Humphry Repton produced sketches showing the state before and after his alterations; so he could convincingly bring his concepts home to the customer. Several of his so-called Red Books are preserved, from which these two drawings are shown.

Rousham, 20 kilometres north of Oxford, is one of the most perfectly preserved creations of William Kent, and at the same time one of the most influential models of English 18th century garden design. Some vestiges of the original design by Charles Bridgeman survive, but largely overshadowed by a new concept introduced by Kent, who championed winding lines which was a radical departure from formality. He used elements from the classical world, but placed them in a natural setting, more suited to the new outlook. This backdrop set into relief the vision of an idealized world of antiquity, represented by statues and temples.

The complex was created in the 1730s. The regular features are restricted to the bowling green in front of the house, from which a view can be seen of open landscape of fields and meadows, which seem to be part of the garden scenery (p.151). A restored mill looms on the horizon. A kilometre and a half behind there is a fake vaulted façade, deliberately erected as an eye catcher. The chief programme of the garden develops on the western side. The path setting out from the lawn in front of the house leads first through a thicket and then to an open terrace concluded by a colonnade with the statue of a dying gladiator. From there the view of the open landscape is repeated. Continuing along the path, the visitor discovers a new feature beneath the terrace, the seven-arched Praeneste Terrace. Another surprise comes soon after in the shape of the Venus Vale; in a crescendo sequence, one passes the upper cascade, with a Venus statue, an octagonal basin, and finally the lower cascade. Lower down, the Long Walk begins, a grassy avenue crossing a forest and ending with an Apollo statue. Further on, a smaller temple is hidden in the corner of a clearing. The entire arrangement is spread out on a slope overlooking the Cherwell river and is reminiscent of a stage-set.

Sheffield Park, 8 kilometres northwest of Uckfield, Sussex. The first memorable project on this 40 hectare garden was completed by Capability Brown for Lord Sheffield about 1775. Today's third and fourth lakes should probably be ascribed to him but the plantations of the entire garden were reshaped in 1909-1934. At that time the owner, A. G. Soames, extended and enriched the stands of picturesque exotic species and introduced and improved park stock. The complex is most remarkable for its rich collection of conifers and for its deciduous trees with their lively autumn colours, splendidly reflected in the four lakes. In this way Sheffield Park combines the character of an arboretum with valuable features of garden design.

Sissinghurst, near Cranbrook, represents perhaps the purest example of an English 20th century garden whose ground-plan combines formal principles and free naturalist design. It is one of a series of magnificent creations, including Hidcote, Nymans and Great Dixter. The garden was laid out by Vita Sackville-West and her husband Harold Nicolson on an abandoned lot near an ancient Elizabethan tower. The complex is organized around a sequence of longitudinal or transverse axes and vistas, firmly marked by formal elements, such as hedges or walls of greenery. Within this formal framework, the exuberance of multi-coloured blossoming vegetation reigns uncurbed. The flowers also determine the thematic keynote of the various subsections of the garden, such as Spring Garden, Summer Garden, White Garden (p.158) and Rose Garden.

Stourhead, near Mere, Wiltshire (p. 146–147). If any English 18th century garden can be said to be the perfect embodiment of the ideal of picturesque landscape, then it is certainly Stourhead. The core of the complex is the lake created by a dam on the Stour river. The programme develops along the shores of the lake, and can be fully grasped in the course of a walk on the circuit path. This arrangement is a parallel to Chinese and Japanese designs centred on a lake (e.g. Zhuo Zheng Yuan, Katsura).

The scenery unravels gradually, in a calculated sequence of motifs. First a partial view opens on a grass-grown bridge and a stretch of lake behind. Then the curtain seems to fall back and the main scenery is unveiled: the lake with the Pantheon. One seems to be contemplating one of the heroic landscapes of Claude Lorraine. Further along the path is the Temple of Flora, from where another attractive view opens on the lake. After a longer walk the circular route leads to a grotto, from where the view ranges back to the Temple of Flora and the bridge. The thematic complement of the grotto is a statuary group consisting of a sleeping nymph and a river god. It is the best preserved construction of its type in England. The path continues to a rural cottage in the Gothic style and finally reaches the Pantheon, erected by Flitcroft who was an enthusiastic follower of the fashion for Palladian architecture. The last stage along the circular route is the Temple of Apollo or the Sun, rising above the southern shore of the lake.

Stourhead thus represents a compendium of the ideal picturesque landscape, given a deeper meaning by allegorical architectural and sculptural elements from antiquity. The concept was a sensational novelty and was widely imitated. Typically for its age, it was designed by an amateur, the cultured banker Henry Hoare. He evidently found his inspiration in classical antiquity, and the layout can be interpreted as an ascent from the underground world of the grotto, through the worldly glamour of the Pantheon, to the sublime heights of the Apollo Temple. The garden is integrally preserved and splendidly maintained. The only jarring note is the partly unsuitable vegetation: recent planting has brought in an exaggerated quantity of exotic varieties.

Stowe, 5 kilometres north of Buckingham. More than any other famous garden, Stowe carries on the historical developments of English garden art from the early formal designs to the mature picturesque style. The original concept dates back to the late 17th century, when the chief formal components of the garden were created, the great avenue, the terraces and the lake. But the great age of the park dawned in the next century when the complex was owned by Richard Temple, later known as Lord Cobham, a leading politician of the period.

From 1713 onwards, Charles Bridgeman was in charge of the works. He considerably expanded the original ground-plan, basically retaining the formal style, though modified by new, gentler features. These are most in evidence in the areas beyond the range of the main avenue, where natural outlines increasingly prevail, both in the freer arrangement of vegetation and in the winding pattern of paths, characteristics further accentuated by Stephen Switzer. A decisive contribution to the definite image of Stowe was made by Kent, who was active here from 1730. He made the most out of the natural, relaxed flow of the outlines and developed picturesque components. His masterpiece is the Elysian Fields, situated on the eastern fringe of the original avenue. Here Kent has effectively placed several architectural features, of which the two outstanding ones are the Temple of Ancient Virtue and the Temple of British Worthies (p. 148). A second important area that shows Kent's hand is the Grecian Valley, with the temples of Concord and Victory. As at Rousham, Kent has organized his composition as a sequence of typical landscape stage-sets, made of landforms, water, vegetation and architectural elements. Capability Brown, too, worked at Stowe for nine years as a young beginner. Some of the more grandiose features might be ascribed to his hand, such as the impressive tree masses hemming in the wide clearings, for example in Kent's Grecian Valley.

A sketch for Stowe, after Bridgeman's design, still predominantly regular, whose formal backbone is the north-to-south axis. The emphatic termination of the view down the axis is an octagonal lake, called the Octagon (top).
Stowe in the second half of the 18th century, after the rearrangements contributed by Brown. The layout acquired more of Brown's spirit: it became more tectonic, constructed out of formal contrasts between the large masses of vegetation and the lawns or water surfaces; even more important is the firmer compositional integration of the whole. In its present state, Stowe has preserved the main structural features and elements of design (bottom).

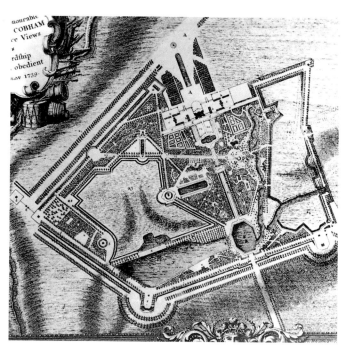

The star features of Stowe, which made it famous in the 18th century, are its symbolic buildings, temples, arches, obelisks and 38 bridges. They cover the entire repertory of architecture of the time, from Greek and Roman to Neo-Gothic and Palladian elements. The area of the park, which comprises some 160 hectares, also has a ha-ha designed by Bridgeman, possibly the first of its kind in the country.

Studley Royal, 3 kilometres southeast of Ripon, North Yorkshire. This exceptional creation was conceived by the well-known financier John Aislabie in the early 18th century. Aided by his gardeners and architects he has produced one of England's most original landscape arrangements, skilfully exploiting the natural potentials of the winding valley of the little stream called Skell. By damming up and dredging, a sequence of lakes and basins of regular forms has been achieved, whose curving outlines suggest a meandering river. This magnificent *parterre d'eau* is surrounded by masses of trees and punctuated by temples and inventively placed classical statues (p. 154). At a later date Aislabie integrated nearby Fountains Abbey, an abandoned 12th century Cistercian monastery picturesquely sited beside the Skell river, into his park complex. The result is one of the most attractive examples of a landscape with "ruins", a never-failing inspiration to the following Romantic generation. Studley Royal, as a whole, is an unsurpassed tour de force: a formal water arrangement that manages to merge unobtrusively with the natural setting.

Temple Newsam, 8 kilometres east of Leeds. The Tudor and Jacobean building tops a rolling incline with effectively arranged clumps of trees, a typical production by Capability Brown from 1765-1770, recently restored. The 360 hectare area is today owned by the city council. A few recent innovations have unfortunately affected the historical integrity of the park.

West Wycombe, about 12 kilometres north of Reading. The arrangement of the garden was tackled by Sir Francis Dashwood in 1735. A few years later he entrusted the construction works to Thomas Cook. By damming up the Wye river, a lake with two islands was created. After 1770, a Temple of Music was built on one of the islands (p. 154). Before the end of the century, Humphry Repton carried out a few alterations. The most notable feature of the garden is the blending of the Palladian villa with the open lawn in front and the adjacent lake.

The numerous stylistic turns in gardening and the exceptionally high standard of horticulture have bequeathed England what is probably the world's richest national heritage of garden art. The dominant feature of this legacy is the landscape garden, perhaps England's most original contribution to the world treasury of visual art. Its historical importance was equally epoch-making at home and abroad. It was the last brilliant reflection of the ancient dream of rural Arcadia, an earthly abode of classical gods, a world superior to the world of day-to-day reality. Its re-creation comes even closer to the ideal envisaged by the poetry of Horace and Virgil than the settings created by Italian Renaissance and French Baroque. So the English landscape garden, the last of the three great historical styles in the Occidental civilization, crowns Europe's almost 2000 years long search for an earthly paradise. By its forceful illusionist suggestivity, it also played a part in the conflict of old and new, of the outdated court aristocracy and the prosperous middleclass and a symbol of progressive ideas and outlooks. In its advance, the new style developed a number of universally acceptable structural features, destined to later become the standard for public parks all around the world. It is a fortunate circumstance that a large part of this heritage survives in a comparatively good state of preservation today.

p.137
Levens Hall is certainly different today from what it was at the time of its origins, in the late 17th century. Though it is impossible to recognize a clear design, the whole makes an impact by the interplay of various tonally shaded, trimmed masses.

p.138
Folly Farm is a work by Edwin Lutyens and Gertrude Jekyll. Among the formal elements - trimmed hedge walls, the semicircular flight of stairs, the straight supporting wall - they freely disposed various, mainly flowering plants (top). An Elizabethan knot garden has been recreated at Hampton Court, though a consistent use of contemporary rather than modern plants would enhance a true historical sense of the layout (bottom).

p.139
The gardens of the Royal Palace of Hampton Court show a sequence of varied architectural styles. The Pond garden is a reconstruction on the original site.

p.140
Restored parterre at Ham House (top) and the wall with busts and trimmed elements in the eastern section, in front of the house (bottom).

p.141
The cascade at Chatsworth, dating from the end of the 17th century, one of the few remnants of the once large-scale formal layout (top). Bramham Park is well-known for its inventive use of water and for beech hedges of outstanding height (bottom).

p.142
Famous Baroque panels of wrought iron by Jean Tijou form the garden enclosure along the Thames at Hampton Court.

p.143
At Melbourne Hall many features from the period preceding the landscape movement survive. Particularly well preserved is Bakewell's cage pergola of finely wrought iron; it is situated precisely on the axis of the garden, as is apparent from the photograph.

p.144
The exedra at Chiswick House, with statues of Caesar, Pompey and Cicero, is situated next to the patte d'oie (top). The Orange-Tree Garden with the Obelisk Pond and the Temple recall the classical inspiration more than any other feature at Chiswick (middle). View of the Palladian villa designed by Lord Burlington (bottom).

p.145
The setting of Castle Howard is an excellent synthesis of rolling landscape and structural elements disposed on the key triangulation points. In the foreground stands Vanbrugh's Temple of the Four Winds, on the right, a bridge, and in the background, Hawksmoor's Mausoleum. Perhaps more than anywhere else, here the germs of the nascent landscape style are obvious. The genius loci demanded by Pope fully comes alive in this layout (top). A formal parterre with a fountain by W.A. Nesfield fronts the palace of Castle Howard (bottom).

p.146
The first and most characteristic view of Stourhead. During a walk along the winding path skirting the lake, the single architectural elements, such as the Turf Bridge, the Pantheon, the Grotto and the other features, appear and disappear as a succession of picturesque scenes.

p.147
Stourhead. View from the grotto across the lake.

p.148
Stowe boasts a great number of architectural elements. They include the Temple of Ancient Virtue in the Elysian Fields (top, right), Cobham's Pillar (top, left), a Palladian Bridge, erected at the end of the Octagon, as a conclusion of the lake panorama (bottom, right), and the Temple of British Worthies devoted to merit,

virtue and honesty; the niches of the semicircular building carry busts of famous Englishmen: Bacon, Newton, Shakespeare, and others (bottom, left).

p.149
View from the Octagon towards the great house at Stowe. The Grand Avenue - formerly a Baroque-style straight line - was subsequently given softer, broken edges, but still supplies a monumental frame to the view towards or from the house (top). A view in the opposite direction, from the great Portico (bottom).

p.150
The grotto of Painshill is unique in Western garden history (top). A view of The Gothick Tent, Hamilton's well-known folly, at Painshill (bottom).

p.151
Rousham: the main vista from the house across the Bowling Green and further to the Eye-Catcher on a distant hill in the background (top). The Venus Vale, probably Rousham's most powerful motif (centre). The ha-ha, or ditch with a fence in the bottom, originally a military feature adapted for use around country mansions in order to prevent animals straying into gardens without an unsightly barrier (bottom).

p.152–153
The damming of the Glyme river and the remodelling of the shores at Blenheim has resulted in a mighty lake landscape that is certainly Brown's grandest work. At the same time he has ingeniously used the potentials of the original landscape.

p.154
View of the Temple of Reverence, across the Moon Ponds at Studley Royal (top). West Wycombe, the picturesque area around the lake, with the island on which stands the classical Temple of Music (bottom).

p.155
Sheffield Park, created by Brown and later perfected by Repton, is today chiefly notable for its varied plant collections.

p.156
Petworth, an early work of Capability Brown, is a model example of the application of the serpentine line, so much praised by the painter Hogarth (top). Clumps of trees were an indispensable element of Brown's composition. He used them to create thrilling contrasts between the dark clumps of trees and bright surfaces of lawns and water, seen at both Petworth (centre) and Temple Newsam (bottom).

p.157
The large, convex lawn in front of the semicircular terrace erected by John Wood the Younger at the Royal Crescent, Bath. The new elements of open spaces in the cities received their first formal impulses from the English landscape style (top). Bottom: Prior Park is another masterpiece of contrasting volumes and planes, making skilful use of an existing valley which is dramatically topped by the Palladian mansion. The role of the Palladian bridge is to divert attention from the visually less interesting artificial lake.

p.158
The White Garden at Sissinghurst (left). The main remains of William Chambers' work at Kew are architectural features, most impressive among them being the Chinese pagoda (right).

p.159
Nymans is a blend of formal and free elements. In the background, the remains of the façade of the burnt-out house (top). The perennial flower border represents one of the outstanding design elements of British landscape gardening: here at Hidcote (bottom).

p.160
The White Garden at Hidcote Manor is built, like many related English gardens, on the contrast between regular framework and varied planting. At the same time it is an example of a successfully designed thematic garden, sometimes concentrating on a single colour or restricted to a single plant species.

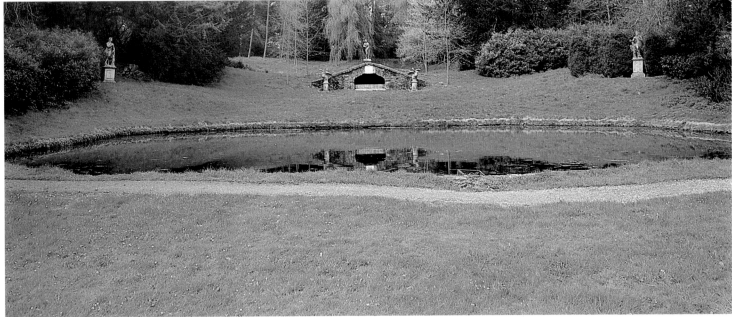

The Gardens of China
Between the square and the circle

The beginnings

Mountains, islands and immortals

Philosophy, painting and poetry

The garden as a place of refuge

A big world in a small place

Yian qi

Structural features

Development

Gardens today

The oldest preserved garden art in man's civilization, with almost 3000 years of uninterrupted development, is scarcely known outside its own country. It is remote not only to the consciousness of the greater part of the cultured world but also, to a large extent, to its scientific and technical literature - with a few exceptions. How to explain this circumstance? The first and probably the main reason for it lies in the unusual design and composition of Chinese gardens, constituting a truly exceptional phenomenon, so singular that it can scarcely be compared with any others in the history of garden art. Garden structures in which rocks of unusual shape and form so obviously predominate, whether in great piles, in water or beside it, in front of windows and walls, on pedestals outside or in buildings, undoubtedly astonish the foreign visitor. He will also have difficulty not knowing how to explain the absence of lawns, the abundance of varied pavements, the relatively limited use of plants, the winding or zig-zag paths rising and dropping, the unusual bridges, pavilions which float above the water, and on top of all this, rocks, everywhere... Only a deeper penetration into this unusual world of shapes, a recognition of the social background, of the philosophical starting-points and of the cultural currents can make it possible to understand the Chinese garden as a harmonious and exceptionally meaningful whole, to whose centuries-long formation a multitude of the nation's chosen spirits devoted their creative efforts, from rulers, politicians, scholars, poets, painters and professional designers to a throng of unknown cultivators.

A further problem lies in information and study, since difficulties of language and script render the rich classical Chinese sources barely accessible. Moreover, reasons of ownership, the frequent wars of the 19th and 20th centuries and obstacles to travelling made the gardens themselves relatively inaccessible until recently. Chinese garden art has proved a fertile influence on the development of Japanese gardens. It is interesting that there were powerful echoes in Europe too, without this art really being known here. Marco Polo in the 13th century sent back enthusiastic reports about the gardens in Kingdom of the Middle, while Abbé Attiret's descriptions of the imperial Yuan Ming Yuan are especially famous and also represent precious documentary evidence. An interest in Chinese gardens among the pioneers of the landscape movement in England, launched by William Chambers' powerfully influential study *On Oriental Gardening*, acted more as a support than as an inspiration.

The Beginnings

From the evidence preserved in old descriptions, literature, handbooks and pictorial representations, it is possible to create a fairly faithful picture of the way the Chinese garden came into being and to understand the heritage preserved today. Naturally such inventive and richly articulated creations which made their appearance in the Song or Ming period as well as later have behind them a lengthy development of philosophical thought, aesthetic theories, design technique and general culture.

The beginnings of this development reach far back, according to the scant sources, even to the 15th century B.C. A simple note has been found on stone drums dating from this period, including an ideogram composed from the character *mu*, a tree, with four such signs having the meaning "garden" or "park". *Shi Jing,* the *Book of Odes*, from the 10th century B.C., mentions gardens with terrace plantations. Probably these were still structures of a more utilitarian nature, planted mainly with fruit trees. Only in the collection of *Chu Ci*, 'Songs of Chu', do we find descriptions which point to the construction of gardens with pavilions, terraces, galleries and water motifs. Later, for

At the time when European Renaissance painting still treated nature as of subsidiary importance, and when Petrarch was just beginning to look at nature, wild mountain scenery had already been an inalienable part of Chinese cultural history for a millennium and a half, especially in poetry and painting. Confucianism shows how deeply rooted is the concept of the mountain in Chinese civilization. As the philosophy of an ordered society this otherwise has a superior attitude to nature, but attributes positive values to mountains: "A wise man finds delight in water, but a good man in mountains" (Confucius, *Analects* VI&21).
Searching for Dao in autumnal mountains, 10th century. Even more than the motif itself, it is the characteristic yin–yang aspect of painting that attracts attention, with its bright-dark features (top).
An early ideogram for the garden. It is composed from four characters of *mu*, which stands for a tree (bottom).

A Chinese garden in perspective view, displaying great structural richness and variety (previous page)

the Han dynasties, from the 3rd century B.C., extensive imperial parks began to come into being.

As was common in other societies too, it were the centres of social power that played a leading role in the development of art in China. Only much later did non-utilitarian gardens intended for spiritual enjoyment and recreation, spread to other social classes, especially the bourgeoisie. The history of Chinese gardens shows a more or less straightforward development, without such stylistic twists and turns as can be observed in Europe. This is true of imperial parks and bourgeois gardens alike. Both were designed on a common basis, evident from the numerous common elements in their construction. The difference lies mostly in the abundance and richness of their essential elements and in their scale.

Mountains, Islands and Immortals

Apart from the buildings, there is nothing straight or geometrical in the Chinese garden. Its decidedly natural character poses the question how far this is due to the rich and varied nature of the country. It is not difficult to imagine that this diverse countryside, with its at times wildly picturesque landscapes, must inevitably have roused the Chinese spirit from the earliest times. The first mythological notions were mostly connected with natural phenomena, which, in the vicinity of mountain ranges such as the Himalayas, is not surprising. Not only mythological notions but creeds and philosophy in China too are linked with natural phenomena. Even before gardens were created, there was a belief in China that the immortals live in the western mountains or on islands in the Eastern Sea. Very close to such ideas was the Indian Buddhist concept of the holy mountain, dwelling place of Buddha (in Japan, Mount Sumeru), also similar to the mythical mountain Kailas in the Himalayas where the God Shiva dwells.

However, it was Daoism in both its religious and the philosophical forms that most developed and established the concept of the mountain in the spiritual life of Chinese society. As faith, Dao Jiao, it teaches that it is necessary to subdue nature, and encouraged turning away from the natural course of life and searching for immortality. Many distinguished people, including emperors, were inspired by this notion and endeavoured by means of spiritual exercises and eating specially chosen food, herbs and the life-prolonging mushroom to attain the state of immortality. Above all they sought contact with the immortals themselves in their dwelling-places. Here is to be found the origin of the islands of the immortals, which the emperor Wudi had arranged in the second century B.C. in order to attract and associate with them. There is a similar inspiration for the second great motif mountains-water, *shanshui,* which was very widely adopted in painting and garden design and became the Chinese term for landscape.

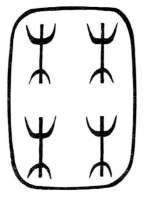

Philosophy, Painting and Poetry

In traditional China, philosophy from the very beginning played an essential role in a person's education, especially moral education, and was thus highly influential. For many spheres of spiritual activity, in particular painting and literature, but still more for garden design, Dao Jia, the philosophical aspect of Daoism, is of fundamental significance. In contrast to the religious aspect, this above all taught the necessity of following nature, and that everything good comes from it. It is impossible to describe briefly this complex teaching, so only those characteristics that are significant for our purposes will be mentioned. Dao represents a way, a searching, a process. One of its fundamental starting-points is the notion of the space-time connection between the world and phenomena in it, of their indivisibility. The world is not split into individual parts, but everything is linked together interdependently. This whole, composed of vortices, veins and currents, unceasingly moves and alters. Man, too, is a part of it, and must recognize it, be involved in it and harmonize with it. Since one of the main principles is naturalness, non-activity against nature, *wu-wei*, harmonizing means allowing the natural order of things to remain, changing it as little as possible. This refers especially to the dragon veins, the currents of water in the ground, and to the placing and constructing of human dwelling-places in such a way as to ward off ill-luck. This could be achieved by geomantics with its system of *fengshui* (wind and water) practices, consisting partly of the knowledge of natural science and partly of superstitions. Accordingly, houses were placed near water, orientated towards the south, and adapted to the site, avoiding any need for excavation. In general, respect was shown for what already existed in nature.

In this connection, the dialectically opposed conceptual pair yin-yang occupies its own unique place. Originally yang signified light, the bright side of the mountains, and yin its absence - darkness. Later this conceptual sphere was broadened, so that yang also came to mean hard, active, warm, dry, erect, high up, while yin meant soft, passive, cool, damp, prostrate, deep down. Yang predominates in the mountains, in summer and the south, while yin predominates in the valleys, in the vortices of clouds and water, in the winter and the north. The main aim of Dao is to create harmony and this it achieves by combining the opposing elements yin-yang. This searching for harmony, actually the reconciling of dichotomies, manifests itself in various ways in Chinese civilization. The imperial throne in the Forbidden City in Beijing is situated in the Hall of Supreme Harmony, the biggest preserved imperial park is called Yi He Yuan, the Park of Peace and Harmony, while one of the best-known gardens in Suzhou is Yi Yuan, the Garden of Harmony. All this conceptual world of course found a powerful echo in painting too. It was expressed especially in the portrayal of landscapes, the painting of dark-light features in the mountains, of vortices, veins and furrows in rocks. The artist had to understand the course of "dragon veins" so as to know how to place them properly in the picture, so that they flow and discharge themselves into each other. In judging a picture's artistic merit it was important to assess to what degree the painter had succeeded in creating harmony, in determining the intermingling of the veins, and in calling forth the secret fluid, the world-permeating vital spirit or *qi*. This aspect of painting is also tremendously significant for the design and understanding of Chinese gardens.

One of the tasks of painting was to enable those who could not themselves go into the countryside to enjoy the mountains. The great landscape painter Guo Xi (11th century) in his study on landscape painting says it is in human nature to wish to get away from the noise of urban society so as to catch "sight of the immortals, hidden in the clouds". Moreover, he believed it was possible to transfer mountains and water into every house, if the observer trained his spirit appropriately. The technique of painting was adapted to this end. Landscapes were painted on long scrolls, so that as they were unrolled and the motif thus gradually unfolded, the observer might experience the scene in the same kind of sequence as if he were actually walking in the country. This principle of the time-space development of the scene is also characteristic of Chinese gardens and is entirely in the spirit of the Daoist concept of movement and of ceaseless

In the course of the centuries, the ability to observe nature was highly cultivated. A dialogue between the emperor and one of his ministers bears eloquent witness to this. The emperor's question as to how he compared himself with the prime minister evoked the characteristic answer: "I am not his equal in politics, but I surpass him in appreciating scenery".
A large number of pictures shows a Daoist hermit traveller or dweller in a mountain hut, who with enraptured gaze immerses himself in magnificent natural scenery.
A solitary dwelling-place beneath a tall tree by Sheng Mao-yeh, 1630 (top).
The poet in the mountains, Shen Zhou, 427-509 (bottom).
Graphic representation of the yin-yang (this page)

I built my hut in a quarter inhabited by man,
Yet nowhere can be heard the rumble of horse or cart,
Perhaps you know how that is possible?
A heart withdrawn creates a wilderness around itself.
I pluck chrysanthemums under the eastern hedge.
Then gaze long at the distant southern hills.
At dusk the mountain air is fresh.
The birds wing their way back in pairs.
In these things a deep thought lies hidden.
But when we want to express it, words
all of a sudden forsake us.
(Tao Qian)

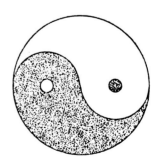

change in the world. This unusually widespread style of painting also developed a talent for a penetrating observation of the landscape, which was reflected in a more suitable presentation of its structure and characteristics, in a feeling for its inner construction, and in its lines and tonal relations.

An important step forward in this direction was achieved with the development of monochrome painting, in pictures executed with brush and ink. This is referred to in the fundamental Daoist work *Dao De Jing* with the warning that "five colours confuse the eye, five flavours confuse the tongue". There is also the well-known phrase, "black is for ten colours". To a great extent these notions were transferred into the composition of gardens, where colour had practically no role in either constructional or plantation elements. This was a perfectly natural outcome, for many distinguished painters were at the same time garden designers and could win for themselves an equal reputation whether in designing gardens or in painting.

A parallel is to be found among poets, who with the creative artistry of words recorded their impressions of nature, which then became a stimulus to garden design. Many poets were famous for their own garden, like Tao Qian (378-427), whose poetic impression of evening from his garden is an exquisite example of the Daoist experience of natural scenery. Similarly active was one of the greatest of Chinese poets, Bai Ju-yi (772-864), who was also a high-ranking official. Several times he fell into disfavour at court and in such periods he sought equilibrium and satisfaction in gardens which he himself had arranged. Particularly famous is his garden with a hut, which was situated in a lonely spot near the Lu-shan mountain and which exemplifies the designing of a garden as a place to withdraw from a hostile society. This fugitive fate was similarly experienced by Si-Ma Guang, a former prime minister who fell into disgrace and removed to his city garden in Luoyang, where he lived in seclusion, becoming one of the greatest historians of China.

The Garden as a Place of Refuge

Beyond the determining factors already described, namely, the unique countryside, the philosophy, painting and poetry which together shaped the Chinese garden, special stress must also be given to the social background as an essential element in its formation. Throughout the centuries, life in China was full of uncertainty, of invasions, of wartime devastations, of social conflicts and of battles for power. The victims of such conditions were very often artists, scholars or high-ranking officials, for example the poet-official Bai Ju-yi. And it was precisely these people who withdrew into the solitude of the mountains, spiritually sustained by the Daoist philosophy of non-interference, avoidance of conflict and searching for the meaning of life in harmony with nature. Their retreat into solitude was in essence a consequence of social, class conflicts. The satisfaction they customarily expressed at being away from the city, removed from noise, actually meant that they had turned aside from problems of social life. At first it was in this way that abodes of hermits came into being in the mountains beside chosen beauty-spots as a kind of return to nature. Later, partly under the influence of painting, and with the transference of mountain motifs, it was gardens that took over this role, having the particular advantage of accessibility at any time, and unlike paintings they represented real nature, though on a smaller scale. Urban gardens could not mean of course a physical retreat from the city, but they developed into a refuge for spiritual withdrawal where generations sought peace, inner balance and renewal of spirit.

A Big World in a Small Space

The Chinese garden, which down through the centuries has proved to be the source of lasting inspiration, represents a unique design of space. Its construction is very striking in its abundance of constantly changing motifs as the space opens out or is closed in, moving from light to dark and back again, paths winding with unusual switches of direction or rising and descending. Everywhere, on the ground, in the vertical planes of the walls or the windows, in the rocky piles and among the plants, the observer can decipher a whole series of direct or abstract visual messages. Everything is arranged in such a way that in every spot the garden has something to say. In this profusion it is not possible to embrace everything with a single glance, from one vantage point. The concept here is the opposite of the European Baroque, which demonstrates a superior attitude towards nature by its particular geometrical design, placed along the axis of the palace from which this layout can be completely perceived. In the Chinese concept, on the other hand, man is placed in a garden which in order to experience and understand he must move through. Hence the abundance of images which shower him with impressions and constantly command his attention. This is made possible by the garden's exceptional articulation, for it is so inventively divided by walls, galleries and buildings that it creates the impression of being much more extensive than it actually is. Consequently it could most suitably be described as a time-space sequence of various motifs which together create a picturesque and highly-charged visual entity. It is characteristic that in this diverse whole, no one individual element has a dominant role, which is true even of the rock arrangements which present themselves at almost every step.

Yian qi

Alongside all this abundance of the natural in the Chinese garden it was, however, essential to have elements created by man. A garden was never a mere addition to a house, neither was it an independent creation, but an integration of both into a residential whole, garden - house, *yian qi*. This provides the clue to understanding the saying that a place containing a pavilion deserves to be called a garden, for only the possibility of human residence gives to a garden its true content. This viewpoint explains why there are so many buildings scattered throughout a garden or even surrounding it. The garden should be present as much as possible in the interior of the house and outside contact with the house should be felt as strongly as possible. The constructional looseness of the building's shell makes it possible for exterior and interior space to flow into each other. The walls do not function as support, this role is assigned to pillars, between which there can be any kind of openings, windows, doors. Through these man experiences the surroundings and through them the garden enters the house. Two worlds move into each other and combine in a unique organization of exterior and interior living spaces. The windows and doors are partially or entirely filled in with lattice work of immensely varied design, contributing to the optically enhanced view of the outside world. There is an interesting feature here: the doorways in pavilions are generally rectangular whereas in garden walls they are mainly circular.

What especially strikes the eye in the house-garden relation is the contrasting character of their form. Chinese architecture is without exception strictly geometrical, while the garden is of free, organic shapes. According to traditional Chinese cosmology a square signifies the earth and human social organization, while a circle denotes heaven and at the same time the riotousness and the infiniteness of nature *Tian-yuan, di-fang* or

Top: in a solitary hut, a Daoist hermit dreams how his soul journeys to immortality. It is characteristic that the scene takes place high in mountains with imposing rock formations and dramatically shaped pines. The design of the picture is built on expressive contrasts. The right hand side, representing reality, is concrete, solid, dark and heavy; but the left, which belongs to the other world, is ethereal, floats in airiness and luminescence. It is an example of the type of painting which, with its symbolism as well as with its realistic morphology, actively influenced Chinese garden design (*A Dream of Immortality in a Mountain Hut,* attributed to Zhou Ch'en, 16th century).

Bottom: beside the emperor Huizong, probably the greatest admirer of rocks was the poet and calligrapher Mi Fei. In his garden there was a large rock which he greeted every day, and called it "his elder brother" (From the handbook *Yuan Ye*, 17th century)

heaven-circle, earth-square. Between the two, as the well known expert N. Wu puts it, stands the Chinese garden. This mandala-like construction, an attempt at uniting the human and the heavenly, the rational and the emotional, the man-made and the natural, was worked out as early as in the first century A.D., but the peak was reached with the design of the Temple of Heaven in Beijing. A similar concept of the architecture - landscape relation is also found in Japanese gardens, while in Europe it was promoted in this century by Le Corbusier's doctrine of pure constructivist architecture in the midst of freely developing greenery.

Structural Features

Walls. The openness of residential architecture in the Chinese garden was made possible by enclosure, for the garden was always surrounded by a wall several metres high. Within, other walls and galleries break up the garden and link the pavilions, following the natural contours of the site. Covered galleries make it possible also to walk about in heat or in rain. The walls were constructed of clay, bamboo or stone and, to achieve a smooth surface, were plastered with lime mortar or papier-mâché and, in the final stage, waxed and polished to a gloss. In this way there came into being the so-called mirror wall, a perfect background against which picturesque rocks or plants are silhouetted (as seen on page 180). Their top is often terminated by a wavy line to suggest floating clouds, hence the name *yun qiang,* cloudy wall. A famous example of this kind can be seen in Yu Yuan, Shanghai, where the wall is topped by a dragon tail and therefore called dragon wall.

Paths and Bridges. Like the walls and galleries, the paths also do not run straight. Their function is not to link two points in the garden by the shortest possible alignment but to so lead the visitor that he will see and experience as much as possible. Thus they constantly change direction or sometimes turn sharply at right angles. Some explain the latter feature by the belief that this prevents evil spirits from gaining access, because they can only move in a straight direction. This is certainly superstition and in essence the path is meant to prepare the observer so that several times he catches within his field of vision more views than he would by walking straight ahead. This is a unique design technique which, with its richness of visual impressions, creates a big world out of a small one. This same idea lies behind the arched bridges or the rising and falling galleries, where the observer as he walks along is afforded a shifting perspective and thus sees the same motif in a variety of ways.

Pavements. Apart from water, rocks and plantations, there are not many free areas in the Chinese garden, and in particular there are no lawns. These are replaced by pavements executed in different ways, which also carry various visual messages. Occasionally they are of sand, but more often of stone or mosaic with geometrical patterns in many cases designs featuring flowers, leaves, animals and even utilitarian objects are used.

Shanshui. Rock arrangements are a permanent element of the Chinese garden and have powerfully dominated its image for more than two thousand years. The Daoist cosmological concept that rocks are the skeleton and waters the veins and arteries of the world also placed them in high esteem. It was on this basis that the most powerful garden motif of all - mountains and water, *shanshui* - was formed. It is impossible to conceive of a garden without rocks, they are its most definitive material and the most original Chinese invention in garden design. The way they were used changed with time, from huge piles, *jia shan*, to selected smaller groups or even individual rocks. Tradition and written sources have preserved the memory of some exceptionally grand designs, but three are well-known among those preserved. The first is the voluminous group on the water in Shi Zi Lin, Suzhou, with paths and tunnels leading over and through them. Similar is the gigantic rock construction with tunnels and galleries in Yu Yuan in Shanghai. Then there is the pyramidal group, Piling up of Beauty, in the garden of the Imperial Palace in Beijing.

Alongside the usual symbolism of the mountain, rocks were often used to represent animals and not infrequently as an image of clouds. One layout, for example, bears the name Barrier of Clouds, or Pavilion above the Clouds (p. 177), while an individual rock is called Cloud-crowned Peak. Far above everything else, of course, is the arrangement of mountains and water. Here the island of the immortals motif is linked with mountains and at the same time a series of yin-yang contrasting relationships are realized: damp-dry, cool-warm, soft-hard, profound-elevated as well as the visual polarities: light-dark, smooth-rough, etc. The finest written testimony to the expressive value attributed to rocks is Tu Wan's 12th century *Catalogue of Rocks and the Forest of Clouds*: "All things which are the core, the summation of heaven and earth, are linked together in rocks". The most sought-after rocks came from the Great Lake, Taihu, near Suzhou, the city of gardens. These so-called flower rocks, furrowed by water, were the most picturesque. In fact, the more hollowed-out and furrowed they were, the greater their value. During the later evolution four criteria for aesthetic appreciation of rocks were formulated: *lou*, perforated, *shou*, slender, *tou*, transparent, and *zhou*, corrugated. They were taken far and wide, and for this the cultured emperor and painter Huizong (Zhao Ji, 12th century) gained special fame, as he initiated a similar craze to the Dutch tulipomania of the 16th century. He laid out the enormous rock garden *Gen Yue*,

Chinese gardens boast highly sophisticated pavements built in technically demanding patterns (top and centre).
Window lattices in garden walls are one of the outstanding features in the Chinese garden design. They appear in an endless variety of forms (bottom).

Impregnable Mountain, to safeguard him from the evil powers of fate. For this garden the emperor ordered rocks to be collected throughout the whole country, but his insatiable petromania weakened the economy and cost him his throne.

Ji Cheng's classic handbook of the seventeenth century *Yuan Ye, On Landscape Gardening,* describes how rocks should be arranged. It particularly stresses that they are best situated in the middle of water and linked with a flying bridge, and that there should be tunnels and grottoes in the layout: "here the moon will peep in and one can bid a welcome to the clouds". Apart from these groups, the second most frequent use of rocks was along the water's edge. In both cases it was important to arrange the rocks so as to harmonize the course of their strata, grooves and furrows and thus give the impression of an amalgamated whole. An individual rock should have its narrower part below and broaden out towards the top or, as *Yuan Ye* says, "the rock should make the impression of floating like a cloud".

Plants. Rocks thus predominate in Chinese gardens, their prominence providing virtually the main feature, and plants are more in the background. They are certainly much less common than is the custom in European garden design. At first glance this seems contrary to nature. In garden culture, which is so close to nature, one would expect plants to play a richer part, both in quantity and in the way they are used. This would be especially understandable in a country with such an exceptionally rich and varied vegetation. It is the habitat of over 3,000 species of trees, more than in the entire northern hemisphere outside the borders of China. A multitude of plant species were introduced into Europe from China in the 18th and 19th centuries, especially England and France. These scarcely surveyed assortments of coniferous and deciduous trees, evergreen or flowering shrubs and various flowers first inundated botanical gardens and arboretums. Then they triggered off the rise of a particular garden form - the collector's garden, which is still very common today in the British Isles.

Despite the attractiveness of the indigenous flora, comparatively few species have found their way into Chinese gardens. Probably the main reason is that in China a symbolic significance is ascribed to individual species. There should be embodied in them a hidden beauty of a special kind, which is revealed by meditation and observation. Chinese poetry abounds in lyrical descriptions of plants, as probably no other literature has. The same is true of painting, where flowers and birds figure as a specially frequent theme.

The plum tree, for example, speaks most eloquently for this symbolism ascribed towards plants. Its tiny white blossoms clustered on dark, bare, gnarled branches in the early spring announce new life, successfully defying frost, bringing hope. That such a modest plant should arouse delight in the observer it is necessary, beyond the symbolism mentioned, to have a trained eye, and to this end Chinese landscape painting, ink sketches and calligraphy made a considerable contribution.

Observing the blossom of the plum, the peach (a symbol of spring and immortality for the Daoist), the tree peony (moutan, *Paeonia arborea*) and others was frequently a social event with invited guests. Flowers were the subject of observation at different times of the day and also at night, by moonlight. Pre-eminent among plants is the lotus flower (*Nelumbo nucifera),* which certainly is owing to the influence of Buddhism, for Buddha is often pictured sitting on a lotus. It was also the sign of one of the eight mythological immortals. Above all, the lotus illustrates aspirations to purity, to nobility, as it grows from the mud, rises through the water and climbs up towards the sun, into the light, where it unfolds its tender, rose-flushed petals. In this it is a picture of man's spiritual growth, of his ascent from the material and earthly into the pure world of the spirit. The most appropriate place for observing the lotus is the pavilion on the water which was sometimes built specially for this purpose.

With the picturesque structure of its leaves and stems, the bamboo is, of course, not only a favourite motif among painters, but also widespread in gardens as a symbol of a firm and noble person, whom the wind bends but does not break. The pine with its picturesque, sometimes gnarled growth and evergreen needles suggests permanence and is thus a symbol of eternal life. For a garden it is, one might say, indispensable. Among deciduous trees the Indian bean (*Catalpa)*, whose wood is valued for making furniture and musical instruments, is very common. Of equal significance is the big-leaved *wu-tong* tree (*Sterculia platanifolia*), which is less known in Europe and is hardy only in the Mediterranean. Both species are frequently grown beside pavilions in a garden. In addition to peonies there is the traditionally well known chrysanthemum, cultivated for a long time and originally used as a herb.

As a rule the Chinese arrange their plants individually and only rarely in groups (with the exception of peonies and chrysanthemums). In such a way their essential characteristics find clearer expression. It is also worth mentioning that in China they have long practised cultivating dwarf trees in pots: they go by the name *peng jing*, the same as the Japanese *bonsai*, which is better known outside Asia.

Development

Following the early beginnings mentioned in the *Book of Odes* and *Songs of Chu*, the development of Chinese gardens continued primarily alongside imperial residences. Throughout history the emperor as son of heaven held unlimited power in his hands. This was reflected as well in the construction of parks. The first great park representing the ruler's power was Shang-liu built by the emperor Qin Shih Huang of the Han dynasty (3rd century B.C.). Eight rivers from all four corners of the globe flowed through this enormously extensive park, full of trees and animals gathered from the entire empire. It functioned as a hunting-ground and at the same time as an image of the world.

Symbolic, mythological elements were introduced into the court park by the emperor Han Wudi (141-46 B.C.). Here he arranged three islands on a lake, hoping to attract the immortals to come and settle on them. Moreover the park was rich in pavilions, mountains of rock and many species of plants. The islands of the immortals recur as a motif later in Chinese garden design, and also became popular in Japan, where they have been preserved to this day (the Silver and the Golden Pavilion).

The Chinese court often stressed its greatness extravagantly, but never more so than in the great Western Park in the capital city Luoyang, made for the emperor Sui Yangdi at the end of the 6th century. Within the almost 100 kilometres-long perimeter of the park they dug out a 10 kilometres-long lake with three islands of the immortals, and beside them built numerous pavilions. Altogether five lakes, four seas and a host of other arrangements were meant to represent an organized world, which almost a million people had created. This park remained the archetypal image of a residence fit for an emperor. In the following Tang period (7th to 10th centuries) there developed a more subtle taste for arrangement: layouts were not on such a grand scale but were smaller, though inventively designed.

The most renowned for his passion for constructing gardens, especially rock motifs, was the Emperor Huizong of the Song dynasty (1100-1126), who built a veritable mountain range of rocks in his park, 70 metres high and 5 kilometres in circumference.

In China all religions availed themselves of similar spatial designs for their buildings: this is a Buddhist site for cremation in Paohuachan. On a terrace with two circular motifs the well-known square-circle composition occurs within the smaller one (top). Spatial designs of ceremonial structures were defined already several centuries before Christ as compositions of concentric, geometrical form. Records from the time of the Hsu dynasty refer to ceremonial buildings composed of circular and square elements. Such a temple, dating from the first century, was found near the walls of the ancient Han capital city, Chang'an, which could be one of the Halls of Light, *Mingtang piyung,* with a circular moat surrounding it. This has a square elevated terrace made of earth, bordered by a wall with corner buildings and four axially placed entrance halls. In the middle of the area is another circular, earthen terrace on which stands the main ceremonial building. The whole is encircled by a moat, with access across it from all four directions, while along the moat are stretched dense plantings of trees (bottom).

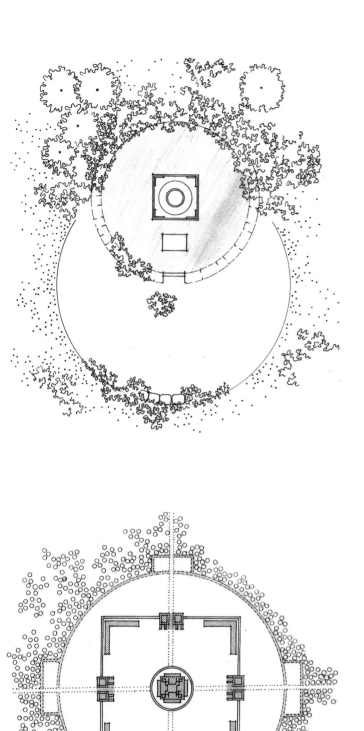

He gave names to individual rocks which he then had engraved in golden letters. It was in his time that rocks from the Tai lake became famous. Like Sui Yang-ti, he lost his throne and ended up poverty-stricken.

The next significant period in this development began with Khubilai Khan, who arranged a park with three lakes in Beijing that remains to this day. Qiong Hua, the island of the immortals from this period, can still be seen on Beihai. Later, a magnificent park was created for the emperor Qian Long (1710-1795). In the surroundings of Beijing he had the most famous park of all laid out: Yuan Ming Yuan (Garden of Gardens or Garden of Perfect Brightness). This majestic achievement with 3,000 pavilions, lakes, canals, numerous rock motifs, and pagodas, gathered together the most exclusive motifs that the empire could afford and justifiably roused the admiration of European diplomats and visitors. The missionary Castiglione even set some Baroque designs there, which on account of their geometrical nature and symmetry were not well received by the Chinese. In 1860 the park was brutally burnt by British and French troops. The last great imperial park was Yi He Yuan (the Park of Peace and Harmony or the Summer Palace) in the immediate vicinity of Yuan Ming Yuan which the empress Dowager Ci Xi arranged at the end of the 19th century. This signalled the end of the great landscape-architectural designs illustrating the ruler's might and representing the world in miniature while also giving an opportunity for recreation and "refreshing of the heart", as Quan Long put it in his explanation of why the emperor needs a garden.

Outside the court, gardens followed a different line of development. On the one hand, they originally came into being as secluded Daoist dwelling-places in the mountains, where in particular a deep feeling for understanding nature matured. On the other hand, the need grew in urban centres for a daily withdrawal from the anxieties of life - a need that could be met by the garden as a secluded oasis in the middle of the city where, as the poet Tao Qian says, "the heart creates a wilderness around itself". Examples of this were certainly not lacking from the ranks of scholars, artists and politicians, such as Bai Ju-yi, Li Bai, Si-Ma Guang and others. The cities Hangzhou and especially Suzhou contributed greatly to the development of the city garden, from c. 100 A.D. onwards. It was here that "garden art south of the Yangtze" developed. The pavilions here were monochrome and not so picturesquely ornamented as in the imperial gardens in Beijing. The scale was smaller, but the gardens were richly articulate, inventively designed and full of a variety of motifs, carefully wrought. As a generalization it can be said that landscape-architectural creativity in China gave rise to three basic types of garden: the big imperial park, the secluded, modestly laid-out abode in the countryside, with its interesting scene or natural elements, and the enclosed, small-scale city garden with a compositionally rich structure.

Gardens Today

It is at present still not possible to completely define China's garden art heritage. The presentation in this book does not give a true quantitative survey although it embraces a good part of the accessible gardens or those described in the recent literature. Though the ravages of war and damage of other kinds have, over the centuries, caused the ruin of many gardens, nevertheless we can suppose there are numerous valuable places sufficiently preserved for it to be possible to restore them and so list them as part of a living cultural heritage. This may be particularly true of gardens in remote places or

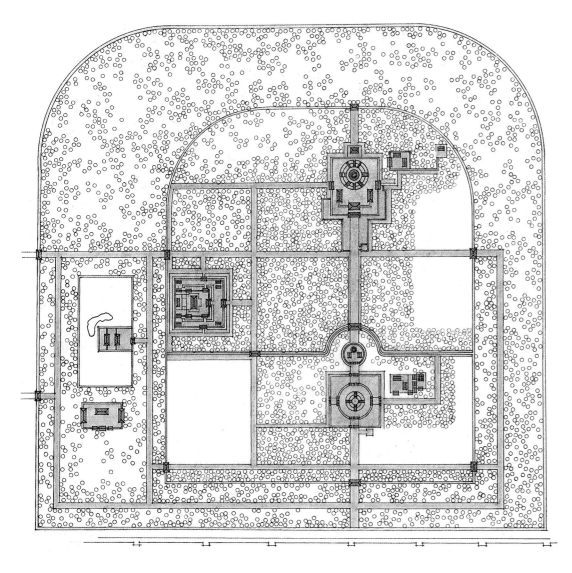

Tiantan, the Temple of Heaven area, lies within a large park. Its inner construction represents an extremely accomplished realization of the notion of how to unite the human and earthly with the heavenly in the same spatial layout (left).

The content is articulated symmetrically along the longitudinal axis, which is oriented in a north-south direction, the same as the axis of the Forbidden City. This magnificent ceremonial scenery was designed for the emperor to offer gifts and prayers for a good harvest. The main element is the Altar of Heaven, *Yuanqiu*, at the southern end of the axis. Formally this is a highly accomplished archaic ceremonial burial mound. The terrace is composed of nine concentric circles, the first containing nine stone plates, and each additional one a multiple of the number, so that the last one has 9 x 9 = 81. Odd numbers are heavenly, so the highest, nine, belongs to the emperor, who is the son of heaven. A triple stairway, each containing nine steps, leads to the Altar of Heaven.

At the opposite, northern end of the axis, the Hall of Prayers for Good Harvest, *Qiniandian,* with its triple roof and circular ground-plan is set on a three-tiered circular terrace: the symbolism of circle and square recurs in its ceiling as the logic of roof construction. Access to the hall is also by a triple stairway with nine steps. Between these two extreme points lies The Imperial Heavenly Vault, *Huangqiongyu,* in which among other things ceremonial tablets were deposited; characteristically, it opens only toward the south.

Set along a 30m wide path, which at the same time represents the spatial axis, numerous pillars and portals with engraved cloud motifs underline the idea of the veneration of heaven, a similar role being fulfilled by the roof-tiles on the buildings and walls, which are normally blue.

In addition, imprinted on this spatial image is the symbolism of the direction of heaven, of colours, of the yin-yang concepts, of the seasons, etc. Thus the south is red, signifying summer and the zenith of yang, while the north is black, representing winter and is dominated by yin.

1. *Yuanqiu*
   Altar of Heaven
2. *Huangqiongyu*
   The Imperial Heavenly Vault
3. *Qiniandian*
   Hall of Prayers for a good Harvest

those belonging to temples and monasteries. In this sphere, China's art history still awaits much rewarding work. It is also to be hoped that the restoration works, such as those in the Forbidden City, the Temple of Heaven, the Summer Palace, and the gardens of Suzhou and Shanghai, will be continued to preserve the country's magnificent heritage of garden art. They can serve as an example to many countries that materially are much more developed.

Gardens in the Beijing area

Yi He Yuan, the Garden of Peace and Harmony, generally known as the Summer Palace (p.181). The only example still preserved of a 2,000 year long tradition of great imperial parks, it was started by the emperor Qian Long in 1750, who gave it the name *Qing Yi Yuan*, the Garden of Clear Ripples. The central elements of the park are the Kunming lake, which takes up three quarters of the whole area, and the Imperial Longevity Hill, lying to the north. It was so named by the emperor when he had built Wan Fo Dian, the Temple of 10,000 Buddhas, a reference to the façade, which is covered with tiles bearing the Buddha's image. Like Yuan Ming Yuan, the park was destroyed by fire in 1860 and restored in 1880-1890 by the Empress Dowager Ci Xi, using money intended for the national navy. At that time it acquired its present name. In 1900 and during the last war it was again damaged, but was restored to its present state after the Revolution. Today it is open to the public and represents one of the most popular excursions in the surroundings of Beijing.

The posthumous imperial Ming residences at Beijing, *Ming Shisan ling*, are built in an original way and with a unique arrangement of forms. The two-part composition contrasts two meaningful fundamental elements. The first comprises portals, a hall, sacrificial altar, etc., which in their rectangular forms belong to human organization, the earthly world. Over against this stands a tumulus, a circular burial mound, belonging to eternity; the symbolism is further underlined by a plantation of pines, representing eternal life. Thus the spatial design takes up the pattern, according to which man steps from his geometrically and symmetrically arranged abode into eternity, symbolized by a circle and constantly present nature (the tomb of the Emperor Wanli, above).

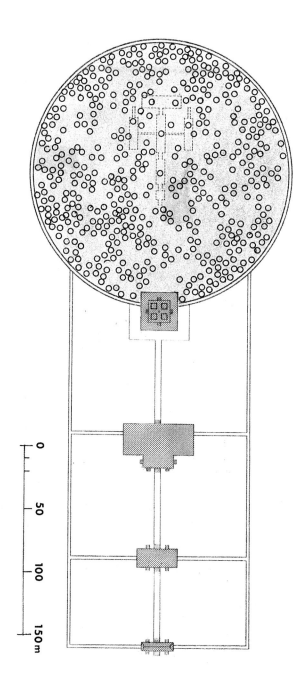

The area as a whole covers 290 hectares and is embellished in the imperial style with hundreds of pavilions, halls, galleries, promenades, towers, pagodas, terraces, bridges and other features. The slopes of the hill afford fine views of the lake, and are dotted with numerous well-known buildings, the Hall Dispelling the Cloud, the bronze Pavilion of Precious Clouds, the Hall of Incense for Buddha, and a pagoda. Interesting structures also include the almost one kilometre-long covered gallery *Zhang Lang*, the Long Corridor, which runs beside the lake, the Marble Ship (a tea pavilion on the lake) and the Jade Belt Bridge.

Xie Qu Yuan, the Garden of Harmonious Interest, or the Garden-within-a-garden (p. 195). This belongs to the Yi He Yuan group and lies in the extreme eastern part by the entrance. Qian Long had it laid out on the model of the famous Ji Chang Yuan from Wuxi. On all sides airy pavilions, covered passage-ways and bridges encircle a small lake, dotted with lotus flowers, creating a pleasing sense of scale and a secluded, intimate atmosphere.

Jianxinzhai, The Garden of Mental Discovery (p. 195), lies not far from the Summer Palace, towards the west, on Fragrance Hills (Xiangshan). Created in the years 1522-1526, it is very small and consists of a tiny lake, surrounded by a pavilion and covered gallery, both with a horseshoe-shaped ground-plan. Screened in by tall trees, it is a unique example of an enclosed garden, fitting for a retreat into solitude and meditation.

Wofosi, the Temple of the Sleeping Buddha. Its layout was begun in 1331 in an area somewhat more to the north than Jianxinzhai. A pavilion was created for the huge statue of the recumbent Buddha (53 tons) and later a symmetrical park layout was added with an entrance gate, pavilions, fountains, bridges and remarkable old trees, especially junipers.

Yu Hua Yuan, the Garden of the Imperial Palace, is situated in the northern part of the Forbidden City, alongside the centrally placed Hall of Imperial Peace. It comprises several interesting pavilions, formal flower beds, mostly planted with peonies, as well as fountains, rockeries and ancient trees. Precious examples of rock on pedestals are scattered throughout the garden; of special interest is *Dui Xiu*, Piling up of Beauty, a large heap of rocks, on top of which is the Pavilion of the Imperial View (p. 179).

Tiantan, the Temple of Heaven. It lies on the southern margin of the Forbidden City and is linked with it in plan by the celestial north-south meridian. An extraordinary cult layout in an open space, it is almost without parallel in our civilization, especially in the consistency and perfection with which the basic idea is executed. In traditional China it was the most important sacred place. It began to be laid out in 1420, when *Qiniandian* (Hall of Prayers for a Good Harvest) was built.

The Park of Three Seas in Beijing. It extends parallel with the main axis of the Imperial Palace, to which it directly belongs. Lying in a north-south direction are three separate lakes, the Southern, *Nanhai*, the Central, *Zhonghai*, and the Northern, *Beihai*, whose origin probably dates back to the 12th century. Apart from their size, all three exemplify an imperial park on a grand scale. They are rich in design and interesting constructions, especially Beihai with its famed white dagoba. Until recently they were closed to the public.

Suzhou, the City of Gardens

The city with its mild, humid climate and abundant water dates from the 3rd century B.C. It is criss-crossed by numerous canals, and has over 300 bridges, a feature which earned it the name of the Chinese Venice. The city was already flourishing at the time of the Song dynasty and became an important cultural centre in southern China, especially because of its painting and garden art, which here developed side by side. Today it is renowned for its many cultural monuments, temples, pagodas, pavilions and especially for its gardens.

Shi Zi Lin, the Lion Grove (p.178, 183). It was arranged around 1336. With the passing of time, the original layout has been considerably altered, yet without losing its main feature of the famous rock motifs. Among them the most impressive is the big rockery on the water, *jia shan*, with grottoes and paths. Outstanding also is the group of rocks resembling animals, which alongside the old trees with their twisted trunks creates a truly unusual atmosphere.

Cang Lang Ting, Pavilion of the Blue Waves. Covering about 0.8 hectares, it was built in the 11th century by the poet Su Zimei. It has been remodelled several times, especially following its destruction during the Taipin insurrection in 1870. The layout beside a canal (hence its name) is preserved in its original form, but the garden and its pavilions have been partly rearranged. It features a high artificial hill and numerous covered galleries. A characteristic example of a house and garden as one whole, *yian qi*.

Zhuo Zheng Yuan, The Garden of the Stupid Officials (p. 191, 192, 196). Probably it served as a residence during the Tang dynasty, later it was a temple, and in the 16th century a garden was built here with a house. The well-known painter Wen Cheng Ming, who also lived in it and painted it, contributed much to its plan. The reason for the garden's name is not completely clear, it may stem from the owner's having lost his state position on account of stupid officials: or possibly the city council did not know how to care for the garden properly when it took it over in the 17th century. It covers about 5 hectares and is now under the protection of the central government in Beijing, as this excellent place deserves. The garden has a very richly articulated design, with a central lake, beside which are the famous Hall of Distant Fragrance, a tea pavilion, a ship with a terrace and a specially characteristic small pavilion Quiet Retreat among Bamboos and Wu-tong Trees (p. 185). There is an interesting spatial division made by pavilions, galleries and walls, and among them are arranged attractive motifs with rocks, hills, trees, pavements and winding pathways.

Wang Shi Yuan, the Garden of the Master of the Fishing Nets (p. 177, 188–189). It covers only half a hectare, but nevertheless represents a small world in itself. Pavilions and galleries surround a small lake, creating among them numerous tiny courtyards with interesting motifs. The house is magnificently designed with richly decorated walls, windows and doors. Among the effective arrangements on the shores of the lake is the typical Barrier of Clouds, a bank composed of rocks giving window-framed views from the pavilion. The garden is tiny, yet a brilliant masterpiece of landscape architecture.

Liu Yuan, the Garden to Linger In. Dating from the 16th century, it covers approximately 2 hectares and is under the protection of the central government in Beijing. The garden is dotted with many pavilions and galleries, surrounding a central lake and offering intriguing views through picturesque windows and doorways (p. 179, 182), in particular the view from the Hall of the Mandarin Ducks revealing the courtyard with the famous rock Cloud-crowned Peak (p. 179). Adjoining it in a small courtyard is Eagle Rock, which has its double on the other side of the wall, a window providing visual contact between them and thus creating the impression of a mirror image. The northern part of the garden contains an extensive collection of dwarf trees, *peng jing* .

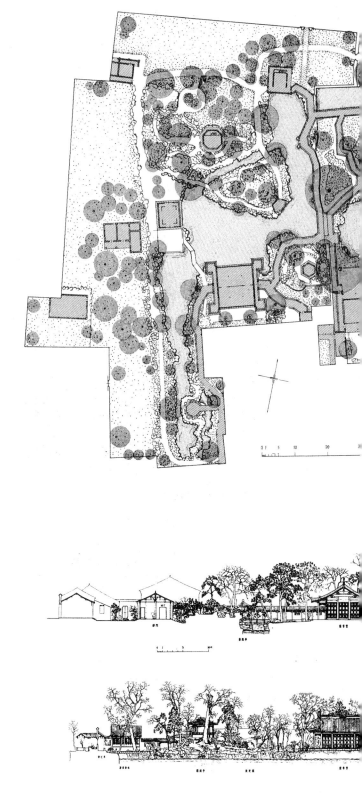

Zhuo Zheng Yuan in Suzhou. The plan and sections show the unique structural complexity of the Chinese garden. This is evident both in the horizontal and vertical articulation, and in the way the buildings and the garden merge one into another creating an integrated residential entity.

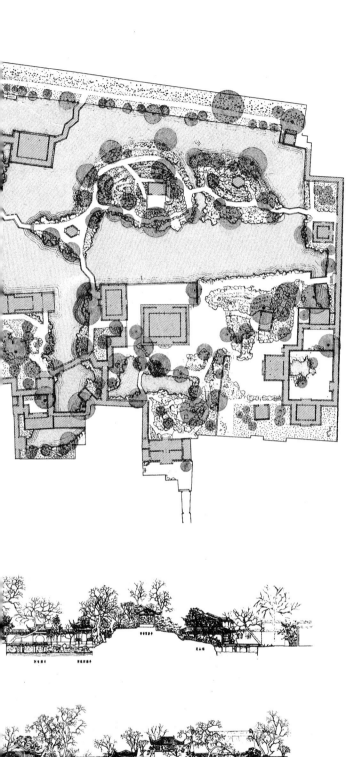

Xi Yuan, the Western Garden. It lies directly beside Liu Yuan to the west, hence its name, and is about one hectare in extent. Originally it was a residence, later a monastery, containing the famous statue of Buddha with a thousand hands. Its interest lies especially in the picturesque double-roofed pavilion on the water (p.193).

Yi Yuan, the Garden of Harmony. A smaller garden, laid out in the 19th century, with many classical motifs. Of particular interest is the ship-pavilion, rock groups and pavements (p. 193).

Hu qiu, Tiger Hill. This lies 3 kilometres from the city, and is widely known for its 10th century pagoda. It gives to the area the character of a large rock and a natural rocky platform. It has an interesting bridge, a moon gate in the living rock and pavilions on the hillside.

Ji Chang Yuan in the city of Wuxi near Suzhou. This 16th century garden is picturesquely arranged beside the water with rockeries and galleries. Of great renown in its time, it inspired the emperor Qian Long in laying out the Garden of Harmonious Interest in the Summer Palace.

Shanghai

Yu Yuan, the Garden of Ease. It lies in the northern part of the old city and covers about 2 hectares. It was laid out by the official Pan Yun Duan in the years 1559-1577, but was badly affected by the mid 19th century wars. It was extensively restored after 1956. It comprises two main parts, the older and bigger being *Yu Yuan*, or the West Garden, while the later, *Nei Yuan*, the Inner Garden, dates from 1709. At the entrance is carved a typical inscription *Zhien Zhia* (Beauty penetrates gradually). There are exceptionally large rock arrangements with a tunnel running through them. The southern part has one of the biggest rocks in the empire, which was meant for the emperor Huizong from the 12th century and is called Exquisite Jade Rock. A special feature of the garden is its white walls undulating like the back of a dragon and terminating in a dragon's head or tail. There are several interesting pavilions with original windows and mirrors providing optical effects. It is one of the most richly designed gardens of all.

Gu Yi Yuan. A relatively large garden about 7 hectares in extent but less rich in interesting motifs than Yu Yuan.

Hangzhou

For some time the capital, it was famed even in the time of Marco Polo, illustrated by the saying, "Heaven above - Hangzhou below". Several times it was plagued by famine, the worst occurring in the 19th century. Some of the park layouts beside the lake with pavilions and monasteries are still preserved. The lake features the famous island shaped like a three-leaved clover, with the name Three Lanterns Reflect the Moon.

The Chinese gardens represent the result of a millenia-long creative search. They have embodied a philosophical tradition and the relevant spiritual, sociopolitical and cultural currents which have marked the life of the Chinese nation during its long history. The monumentality of the garden art of China can thus only be properly understood if it is seen in relation to all these aspects. Only then will these gardens, often strange to the foreign observer, reveal their deeply human content and message.

p.177
Shanshui, mountain and water, is a universal motif appearing in endless variety in Chinese gardens. Here this archetype of Chinese landscape design takes on a particular metaphorical role as an arrangement entitled "Barrier of Clouds" which also forms the background to the view through the window as seen from the pavilion of Wang Shi Yuan garden in Suzhou.

p.178
The largest preserved motif *shanshui*, "Mountain and Water", in the Lion's Grove (Shi Zi Lin), Suzhou.

p.179
A monumental group of rocks in the garden of the Forbidden City in Beijing, called "Piling up of beauty" (top, left). Sitting on water near rocks is an ideal position for observation and contemplation in Shi Zi Lin, Suzhou (bottom, left). Garden scene with the title "Pavilion above the Clouds" in Yu Yuan, Shanghai. An understanding for this kind of allegory, for the conceptual transformation of hard, heavy, earthly masses into transparent and weightless heavenly substance, developed early under the influence of philosophy. It belongs to the same category as the ability to see a whole mountain range in one rock, the world in a grain of sand or, as Dung Zhun says, to see "in voids solids and in solids voids" (top, right). Conspicuous rocks are often situated as a central motif of the garden to be easily seen and enjoyed from the house. A view of one of the largest garden rocks in China, the 6.5m high Cloud-crowned Peak as seen from the Hall of Mandarin Ducks in Liu Yuan (bottom, right).

p.180
Garden walls divide and articulate the space and at the same time serve as a projecting background for rock and plant arrangements. For this purpose, shining whitewashed wall surfaces are specially appropriate (Cang Lang Ting, Suzhou).

p.181
Rocks are allotted an eminent position not only in garden design; they were often placed as chosen sculptural works, *shi feng*, on specially prepared pedestals as here in the garden of the Summer Palace, near Beijing (top). A monumental Rock of Jade Delicacy, *Yu Ling Lung*, in Yu Yuan, Shanghai (bottom).

p.182
Open contact between house and garden to the furthest extent possible in the Cedar Hall of Liu Yuan, Suzhou.

p.183
A distinguished group of rocks, visible from the house. Such groups were often placed by the entrance as rocks of welcome (Shi Zi Lin, Suzhou).

p.184–185
Not only is the content of the garden important, but also the way of seeing it. In this respect the symbolism of various doorways, *di xue*, can have a special significance. This refers particularly to round openings, or moongates, for the circle in China is a celestial form and stands for heaven. Left: moongate in the garden wall in Zhuo Zheng Yuan. Centre: a picturesque wooden moongate frames an important garden scene in Liu Yuan, Suzhou. A view through moongates of the pavilion "Silent Refuge among Bamboos and Wutong Trees" in Zhuo Zheng Yuan (right).

p.186
The visual quality of a window scene is sometimes enhanced by the addition of colour inserts: a window in the Hall of 36 Mandarin Ducks in Zhuo Zheng Yuan (top); a window seen through a moongate in Liu Yuan (bottom).

p.187
The oneness of house and garden, *yian zhi*, depends also on the optical link between them. So the concept of the exterior world sometimes dictates the appropriate design of the window plane. A good illustration to this is the Wang Shi Yuan garden (top). Another window in Wang Shi Yuan represents quite an exceptional example: the lattice work in a "cracked ice" pattern creates the cinemascopic effect of a moving picture when looked at by a moving observer with the rock composition "Barrier of Clouds" (see also page 151) in the background (bottom).

p.188–189
Windows frequently offer extremely attractive scenes and so replace wall pictures. Here, at Wang Shi Yuan in Suzhou, the structural elements of the window and those from the outside scenery merge into an integrated image changing in the course of the day, the season and the year.

p.190
The illusionist world of the Chinese garden is richly supplemented by various pavements executed in a careful technique (top, right: in Zhuo Zheng Yuan; top, left: in Wang Shi Yuan; bottom, right: in Liu Yuan; bottom, left: in Shi Zi Lin).

p.191
The Courtyard of Flowering Crab-apples in Zhuo Zheng Yuan takes its name from the stylized flowers in the pavement.

p.192
The garden offers the possibility of retreat from society; the culmination of this sentiment is the ship-pavilion, which can bear a person to the distant ocean of visions. In this way alienation as a way to inner peace increases to extremes: the lotus scene called "Stand and Listen" in front of the ship-pavilion in Zhuo Zheng Yuan, Suzhou (top). The lotus is a symbol of man's desire to ascend in the heights of light and pure spirituality (bottom).

p.193
A pavilion on the water is the most appropriate place for meditation. With its double upward-curving roof, the pavilion floats above the water in Xi Yuan, Suzhou, (left). Ship-pavilion from the Garden of Harmony in Yi Yuan, Suzhou (right).

p.194
Garden walls and galleries run in such a way that they accommodate themselves to the unevenness of the ground and do not affect the "dragon veins" beneath it, as in this example from Yu Yuan in Shanghai (top). The windows with their variety of forms reflect the Daoist concept of ceaseless change. At night, lighted candles are placed in them, thus stressing even more the diversity of their forms (Yi He Yuan, bottom).

p.195
As a rule, paths in the Chinese garden are never straight. With their zig-zag alignment they make a visitor encompass a wide field of vision (top, right). A covered gallery is a frequent element of the Chinese garden, making walks, and thus enjoyment of the garden, possible in all weathers: the Garden of Harmonious Interest, Beijing (top, left). The secluded Garden of Mental Discovery is an enclosed, peaceful layout with gallery, pavilion and tall backdrop of trees (bottom).

p.196
An arched bridge that leads the observer up then down as he walks, increases his field of vision. The light-weight construction justifies the name "Flying Rainbow Bridge" (Zhuo Zheng Yuan, Suzhou).

178

188

196

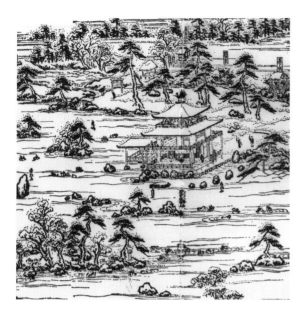

Japan
Gardens as nature and as symbols

Nature and early beliefs

The Sacred Mountain
and the Isles of the Immortals

Gardens of excellence and
the Pure Land

Zen Buddhism as a garden ideology

Garden as an environment
for the tea ceremony

Compositional characteristics

Materials

Gardens today

Japan's geographical isolation as an island also brought about a fairly independent cultural development. In its past it was susceptible to external stimuli and influences, but at the same time was able, in its art, to express itself in its own way. This rather general statement also applies to Japanese garden art, which is, both in volume and in stylistic qualities, a unique contribution to the world treasury of landscape architecture. Almost one-and-a-half thousand years of continuous development gave Japan those particular stylistic variants which express the unmistakable features of the country. At the same time, these reveal a wide formal span: from naturalistic layouts, closely resembling natural scenery, to formally abstract, extremely purified arrangements as, for instance, the dry sand gardens of Zen Buddhist temples.

Nature and early beliefs

Unlike the garden in Mediterranean and neighbouring civilizations, which began to develop out of the utilitarian cultivation of plants for economic purposes, the roots of the Japanese garden reach into the mythology and early beliefs of this island country. Here, Japanese development is similar to the Chinese, where the abundance of symbolic elements in the design-structure of gardens can undoubtedly be ascribed to this mythological aspect.

Nature in Japan presents a rich and colourful variety of plant species and vegetation. The chain of islands which forms the country arches from north to south, as does the volcanic chain which in places falls steeply towards the plains and the sea. On its slopes run the multitude of water-courses which colour the relief and create a picturesque scene with waterfalls, rapids and other phenomena. The vegetation, too, is colourful and appealing. Thus the Japanese landscape - rich as it is with relief forms, numerous water-motifs, picturesque rock formations and varied vegetation - offers attractive opportunities for transformation into mythological scenes, creating images of their special, exclusive worth and their function in life.

In Japan, as in many other countries' mythology, the idea arose that individual natural phenomena held supernatural power. The Shinto faith teaches that they are the dwelling-places of benign spirits, *kami*. These spirits inhabited a mass of natural elements, especially mountain peaks, rocks, rivers, rapids and trees. The homes of the spirits, *ivakura*, were marked by ropes of worship, *shimenawa*, which are still to be seen today, usually on rocks or trees, especially at Shinto shrines. Particularly for this purpose outstanding examples were chosen, developing a sense of selection - of discrimination and evaluation by appearance - which shows the origins of the later ordering of natural materials. One theory ascribes this high evaluation of nature in Japan to the fact that the tribes from the bleak, infertile Korean, Siberian and northern Chinese plains who settled it saw, under the influence of its luxuriance and fertility, supernatural powers at work within it. Thus early attempts to make sense of the world around them, discerning in it creative forces above both man and nature which create and control order in the world, made an indelible impression on men's consciousness and decisively influenced the shaping of gardens. The meaning of material in design doctrine is particularly relevant in garden creation, tactfully accepting its original, natural characteristics, and only exceptionally transforming them. This extreme respect for material of any kind is reflected in other creative areas, which points to the long tradition of this phenomenon and bears witness to its influence in Japanese culture.

The ascription of special meaning to individual elements in nature was the first step on the way to the creation of more worthy natural structures, which would be of

The imperial residence at Kyoto represents a reconstruction of a palace from the Heian period. The characteristic design is in the *shinden zukuri* style. The garden is a pure sand surface with a few bamboo shrubs (top).
The Ninomaru Garden at the citadel of Nijo. The centre of the arrangement is a lake garden, *chitei*, with a large island, *horai* (bottom).

Ginkakuji, Silver Pavilion in Kyoto (previous page)

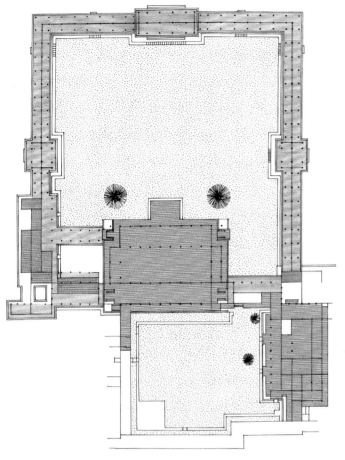

relevance to man. The active arrangement of space with these elements represents the next development. One of the characteristic and important developments of arrangement is connected with Shinto ritual. A piece of land was cleared in the forest, covered with white gravel and enclosed with rope or fencing. The thus "purified" land, rectangular in form, was bare except for a single, sacred tree through which spirits descended to the earth. Such ceremonial preparation of land still takes place in Japan at the most famous shrine, in the Ise region, where, at 20 year intervals, a new temple is built in the heart of the forest on a gravelled, rectangular plot.

The early form of garden took shape as a pure, level and regular plane and this is illustrated by the terminology. In Japanese *niwa* means garden and presumably comes from *haniwa*, which is an expression used to describe land with a special purpose. The related term *yuniwa* (cleared land) occurs in the oldest Japanese chronicle *Nihon Shoki*, as a description of the space beside a 5th century palace. When space was used for secular purposes it was called *oniwa*. Gradually more and more elements - rocks, water, plants - were brought into the *oniwa* which lay beside the homes of the nobility. Members of the higher social classes travelled extensively and returned from their journeys with impressions of the picturesque scenery which abounded in Japan, especially along its coasts. Thus garden motifs came to be enriched, and along artificially made lakes stylized imitations of interesting coastlines started to appear, usually as pebbled, *suhama*, or rocky, *ariso*, shores. This kind of layout is mentioned by the chronicle *Nihon Shoki* and has been confirmed by archeological finds, dating from the 8th century, on the site of the former capital Nara, where a meandering water arrangement with pebbled and rocky shores was discovered.

The Sacred Mountain and the Isles of the Immortals

It can be reliably stated that in the days before the arrival of Buddhism from China at the end of the 6th century, various forms of garden arrangement existed which can be classified as originally Japanese. Later, in the era of Asuka and Nara (6th to 8th centuries), two important garden motifs appeared.

The first was based on the Buddhist notion of the Sacred Mountain, Sumeru (Japanese *Shumi-sen*), which is the highest peak and the centre of the world. This was expressed in the garden by an ascending arrangement of rocks. That this motif came from outside is confirmed not only by its religious origins, but also by a description in *Nihon Shoki* which mentions a certain Takumiya, a newcomer from Korea and an expert in erecting such structures. In the period mentioned above they were quite common, which is attested by excavations in Nara, where they were found in several places. The other motif of mythological origin is the Isle of the Immortals, usually called *horai* and identical to the Chinese *P'eng lai*. This came from Daoism and played an important role in China's early development, but later disappeared. In Japan, development followed a different pattern. Islands had been an integral part of garden design even before they acquired and maintained a secure place as one of the obligatory garden motifs as symbolic habitation of the immortals. Basically, islands were stone constructions, raised above their surroundings. At first it was a uniform motif, in time it diversified and finally appeared as *horai*-island, *horai*-mountain, *horai*-rock, all striving to represent immortality. A special derivative of this motif developed later, in the 14th century, taking on the direct yet highly abstracted form of two animals. The tortoise was chosen for its long life, and the crane on whose wings the immortals travelled across the sky.

So in this development, in which different views and beliefs came together and "cross-fertilized", one of the characteristic features of Japanese garden art appeared. The new did not actually replace the old here, but rather developed alongside it, the two often existing in fruitful symbiosis. This was true at the time of the official proclamation of Buddhism in the 7th centuty, during which Shinto elements were still present in gardens. Similarly, Buddhist and Daoist motifs were used side by side and even amalgamated into new ones. This is strikingly different from development in Europe, where changes of style and taste led to rapid and complete revolutions, as clearly occurred with the landscape movement in England. Here, formal gardens were transformed on a massive scale, as also happened elsewhere in Europe.

Gardens of excellence and the Pure Land

At the beginning of the 8th century the capital moved from Nara to Heian-Kyo, today's Kyoto. Increasing prosperity accompanied the emergence of the nobility, who built splendid residences set in rich gardens. Each residence consisted of a symmetrically ordered complex of buildings and pavilions, of which the most important, *shinden,* was situated in the centre and to the north. Those at the side were connected to it by covered passageways and at the southern end were a lake pavilion and a spring pavilion. These were all placed around a lake garden. Between the *shinden* and the lake lay the south garden, *nantei,* intended for ritual purposes. The only surviving example of this design is Byodo-in at Kyoto, whose lake lies in front of a Phoenix Hall. Lake gardens cannot exist without islands and access to them was by means of arched bridges which allow boats to pass beneath them. One of the fundamental characteristics of gardens in the *shinden zukuri* style is that they were designed for the enjoyment and diversion of the nobility, especially for lake journeys. At the same time they possess a profusion of elements, not only islands, but shore-lined rock and stone compositions, artificial hills, *tsukiyama,* and rock groups in the form of waterfalls. Often there is also a water-course, *yarimizu,* which as a rule runs from north to south, determined by geomantic rules. These rules were also applied to other elements, especially buildings. This is actually the only kind of garden in Japanese history, designed solely for enjoyment and as a symbol of social status, and is the first to free itself from religious themes, serving only secular purposes, even though it employed the same formative elements.

Towards the end of the Heian period (11th to 12th centuries), garden style began to change under the influence of Esoteric Buddhism. Uncertain social conditions, civil wars and destruction formed the basis of this change. This state of uncertainty suited this particular branch of Buddhism, which offered escapism with its ideas of flight from this miserable world and the search for paradise, *gongu jodo.* Whoever lived modestly would benefit from rebirth in the Pure Land of the West. With time, this idea took on an earthly form as the paradise garden. Its spatial design was based on the complex circular form of the mandala and took in different buildings and garden elements, such as the hall of treasures, the lotus-lake and its island and the symbolical bridge which the chosen would cross to salvation. A partly preserved example of such a layout is the temple of Byodo-in (11th century) in Kyoto, whose ground-plan takes the form of a bird (from which the name Phoenix Hall derives) in front of which is a lake. It is also preserved to a greater extent in the temple of Joruri-ji, from the 12th century, which was renovated after the last war.

Saiho-ji. The ground-plan clearly shows how the lake garden predominates within the total structure. The motifs of the dry garden are concentrated in the northern section of the area.

A - Dry garden with cascade
B - Upper garden
C - Ogonchi lake
D - Lower garden

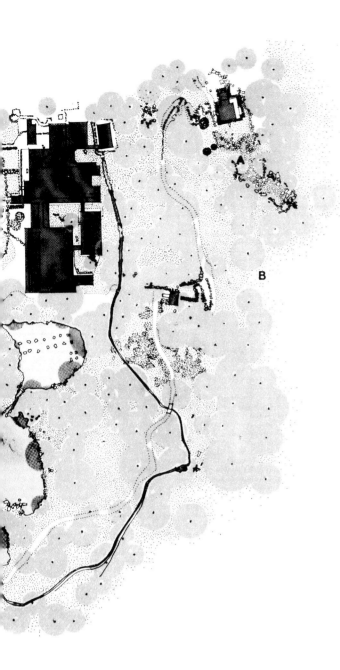

Zen Buddhism as a garden ideology

The next few centuries continued to be unstable and militaristic forms of government predominated, as in the Kamakura period (12th to 14th centuries). The Zen Buddhist sect, which came from China in the 13th century, found fruitful ground in such conditions. As a distinctively contemplative doctrine, which turned upon profound questions of human existence, it did not partake of wealth or splendour. It stood for modesty and simplicity, which was in tune with the spirit of the time and close to the attitudes of the military castes.

The first important reflection of these views is the work of the famous monk and creator of gardens Muso Soseki - known also as Kokushi (teacher of the nation) - at the temple of Saihoji in Kyoto. He designed the garden so as to integrate the classical lake garden, *chitei*, with the dry garden, *kare-sanzui*. The design is in a sense a dual one both spatially, and in terms of contents. On the lower level is a lake-garden in the paradise style. On the upper level, on the hill slope, are dry-garden motifs, which consist only of rocks and extend partly towards the lake shore. A central position is occupied by the motif of the waterfall or cascade, *kare-taki*, which continues down the slope in other compositions, one of which takes the form of a tortoise. The whole layout can be interpreted as a confrontation between two different designs - the splendid lake image of the paradise garden and a modest, abstract rock composition. Muso gave priority to the latter as a more worthy expression of reality. Apart from the dry garden, Muso introduced another innovation into garden design, creating the lake garden so that it could be appreciated from without, rather than through journeys across it. Formally, this is a significant movement away from the *shinden* style and at the same time a shift in the notion of the garden as an environment for spiritual experience. Contemplation from the outside took the place of a more relaxed enjoyment within it. With this the garden's role was extended. It increasingly became a place of retreat, of escape from reality, the seeds of which had already been sown in the paradise garden.

A number of gardens have been ascribed to Kokushi, but Tenryuji is one of the few which are indisputably his. Into it, he brought a number of innovations. The garden in front of the abbot's hall, *hojo*, is also a lake garden. The lake is small and is adapted not for boats, but for viewing from afar. This is emphasized by the central landscape feature, which is a waterfall constructed of rocks. This was an expression of a different concept of architecture provided by a new style, *shoin*, in which the garden would be designed above all for viewing from one particular point.

Saihoji was widely imitated, especially in the Muromachi period (14th to 16th centuries), when garden art in Japan achieved its greatest flowering. The most famous examples are the Golden Pavilion and the Silver Pavilion. The latter had a dual design, with a lake section and a dry garden, which is only partly preserved.

Kare-sanzui can be seen as the finest achievement of the Japanese garden tradition. Its features can be traced back over centuries, from *ivakura* - a rocky dwelling-place for spirits - to sandy "purified space", and appear in the shoreline arrangements of rocks and stones in the Heian period. But only in the Muromachi period did these features find a common focus. Its spiritual base and aesthetic point of departure were derived from Zen, while an appropriate social patronage stemmed from the ascetic atmosphere of military government.

A famous garden manual from the 11th century, *Sakutei-ki*, written by Tachibana-no Tashitsuna, gives, in its short second chapter, instructions for the design of "dry landscape". But at that time, and in the whole Heian period, *kare-sanzui* was only a constituent part of the garden and not an independent composition. It was Muso Kokushi who brought it this status. Just as one needs to know the philosophical background before one can understand the Chinese motifs of mountain and water, *shanshui*, one also needs at least a partial insight into Zen philosophy and aesthetics to understand the particular rock formations influenced by it.

Zen is a philosophy which strives for knowledge and awareness through direct experience, on the basis of meditation. To achieve enlightenment one must think more deeply and more extensively and search for the higher truth even in simple things such as bushes or rocks. So, the environment in which the Zen adept lives is very important. Among the buildings of the large temple precincts were a number of open spaces suitable for Zen gardens which would provide settings for spiritual exercises, *zazen*. To be suitable, the garden would have to conform to the aesthetic rules of Zen art, asymmetry, simplicity, naturalness, freedom from earthly materialism, profundity, tranquillity, and so on. These also called for a great degree of moderation in the selection of materials and modes of expression. So the key concepts in Zen garden creation became simplification, condensation, limitation and abstraction, which gradually led to the exclusion of all elements which might remind the viewer of some already-known reality.

This development can be clearly seen in the span from early to mature forms of Zen garden. Whilst *kare-sanzui* in Saiho-ji still represents a waterfall (page 220), Ryoan-ji reveals an ultimately simple design which does not represent anything from nature and symbolizes nothing. This design is a purified, plastic scheme which does not hinder contemplation by any associations with reality. With this was achieved the great leap from naturalism to abstraction - liberation from the materialism of the natural world.

The difference in topography is of a similar character. The waterfall in Saiho-ji is set on the slope of the hill. In Daizen-in and Taizo-in it is set on a plain, but arranged as an artificial mountain (page 216). Both Ryoan-ji and Shoden-ji, meanwhile, are purely level compositions which show a clear tendency to diverge from the natural. An increasing simplification of plastic expression can also be found here. These two are the clearest examples of *kare-sanzui*, being designed solely on the basis of the relation between planes and volumes (rocks or shaped bushes, *karikomi*), forming dramatically stressed contrasts. It is clear that a garden with such formal characteristics and such a philosophical foundation could not be very extensive and, above all, had to be seen from one particular place. All *kare-sanzui* are small projects and are divorced from the outside world to provide an atmosphere conducive to contemplation.

Garden as an environment for the tea ceremony

Before the brilliant Muromachi period came to an end it provided the next major variety of Japanese garden art, the tea garden. This also arose from Zen thought and was formed on the basis of Zen's austere aesthetic. Its existence and meaning are closely connected with the tea pavilion, which is used for the ceremonial preparation and drinking of tea, *cha-no-yu*, for which an atmosphere of peace and concentration is needed. The garden is supposed to lead the guest to the tea pavilion and prepare him spiritually for the ceremonial. Thus the garden and pavilion form, in terms of purpose and the meaning of their constituent elements, an indivisible whole. The tea garden, *chaniwa*, unlike *kare-sanzui*, does not guide towards contemplation, but only creates

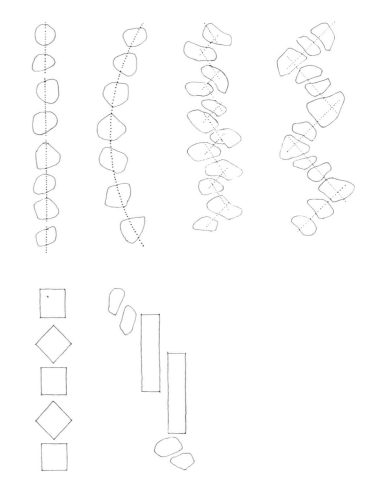

The backbone of the *roji* is a paved path. The basic form is composed of stepstones, *tobi-ishi*. There are a number of formulas for the various versions, depending on the size of the slabs, their mutual distances, and the position of the intial and terminal stones.

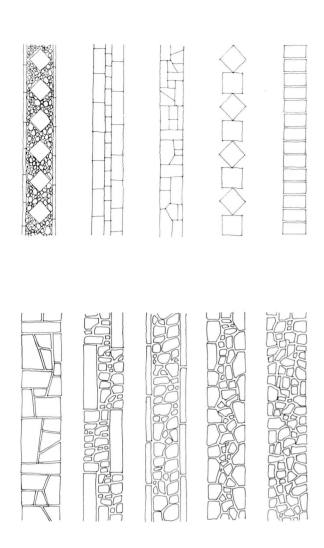

a strong atmosphere of simplicity - a lonely wilderness in which one can take refuge in pure spirituality. This also is an example of characteristic Buddhist withdrawal into a better, fictitious world. This striving is underlined by the development of the tea pavilion itself, which at first had windows and a verandah. But the great master Sen no Rikyu dispensed with these in order to achieve a greater concentration during ceremonials. The main creators of the tea garden were acknowledged masters of the tea ceremony such as Sen no Rikyu, Kobori Enshu and Furuta Oribe.

The design of *chaniwa* involves a rather narrow space alongside the pathway which leads to the tea pavilion known as *roji* (which can mean dewy path, dewy ground, on the way, a narrow plantation of trees). The design is as simple as possible, employing simple materials. The garden unfolds longitudinally, in a straight line in one direction, rising from its entrance to the pavilion. In places it opens out, so that spatial tension and relief alternate. In front of the tea pavilion there is a simple stone water basin which symbolically indicates purity and intensifies the mood. Beside the paved pathway are stone lanterns but otherwise nothing is present which might disturb the guest's concentration. Hence there is an avoidance of flowering plants and a use, wherever possible, of evergreens. Low, dense shrubs close the space beside the path in order to create the impression of being isolated in a forest, which can be emphasized by low-growing plants, moss, ferns and scattered pine needles. The paths are of natural stone, the wood is untreated, the roofs are of straw, in short, materials are used in such a way as to give an air of rustic simplicity.

Eloquent examples of *chaniwa* are the two gardens at the schools of Ura-senke and Omote-senke in Kyoto. Katsura, the Emperor's villa in Kyoto, also shows many elements of the tea garden.

In the 17th century (the beginning of the Edo period), the development of garden art in Japan produced further interesting variations, among them the samurai garden and the rotating garden. The latter was designed to be experienced from the curving pathway from which all the main motifs could be seen (for example, Ritsurin park in Okayama, Suizen-ji, to a certain extent, and Katsura). One specially famous samurai garden is Shizen-do belonging to the highly educated samurai Ishikava Yozan, which presents an unusual integration of house-space with the surrounding environment and a skilful use of Zen elements from the dry garden as well as the tea garden.

Compositional characteristics

In the whole course of its development the Japanese garden did not adopt geometric form. A partial exception is the *shinden zukuri* style, in which a symmetrical arrangement of the complex of buildings and a regular position for certain garden elements were established. Otherwise gardens were consistently designed so as to be irregular, organic, and based on a compositional order close to the natural. Here the main role is played by a contrasting arrangement of elements which gives the Japanese garden a tectonic character and creates its main visual impact. This contrast is formed between the planes constituted of sand, plants or water and the volumes of rocks or trees and shrubs. There are also many tonal contrasts, between light and dark elements and among shades of green and no bright splashes of floral colour disturb this visual balance. In general, the Japanese garden is distinctly monochromatic, giving a very graphic impression of a range of textures through leaves, sand and pebbles (typical examples are found beside Shokin-tei in Katsura, and the Silver Pavilion). Its

Slabs placed in contact form the *shiki-ishi* pavement, and are always of dressed stone. A second version of compact pavement is called nobedan, and consists of slabs of various form arranged in a straight line (lower row).

sculptural character, which is shown in its plastic use of planes and masses, is fully expressed within this simplicity of colour.

On this basis were formed the early gardens in which archetypal elements such as the Isle of the Immortals and the mountain Shumi-sen, as well as mimetic scenic elements (shorelines, waterfalls and watercourses), were employed. It is these particular elements which were bearers of tectonics and their spatial organization always exhibits contrasting which bring a plastic tension into the design. Here the compositional development of the Japanese garden shows an intensification with a purification and simplification of expression which led to such pure designs as Ryoan-ji and Shoden-ji, in which smooth planes of sand and the masses of rocks or pruned shrubs are placed in opposition. Perhaps nowhere and at no other time in the world of garden art has there been such a pure, simple but expressive design, which could be so strongly compared with the abstract modes of painting of the 20th century. It is interesting that the Japanese also showed here a skill which was otherwise foreign to them, namely the remodelling of plants. It was normal to prune plants - especially pine trees - in order to make them grow more picturesquely with, for instance, twisted branches and gnarled trunks. It was expected that the true nature of the plant would thus be better expressed. It is a completely different thing to "depersonify" a plant and transform it into an anonymous mass, as is the case with the pruned shrubs or *karikomi* and in the European formal style. Such a transformation creates a neutral "building material", and *karikomi* is used not as a plant, but as a volumetric unit, as an element of mass in composition (p. 224). Thus in *kare-sanzui* and similar designs the priciples of *wabi*, a little from nothing, and *sashai*, a little means more, are realized.

Putting together and spatial allocation of rocks is a special chapter in design and not easy to describe briefly. The most important motif is a pyramid structure representing the holy mountain, *Shumi-sen-seki*, which can be constructed on a sandy plane, on moss (p. 226), or on an island. The Buddhist trinity motif, *sanzon ishigumi*, which is a highly developed structure of three elements (*shu-seki* - the central, *fuku-sek*i - the first subordinate, and *kia-seki* - the second subordinate stone), has a similar formal character. All three are of different size and are arranged in an irregular triangle (p. 219). This asymmetrical triangle is also characteristic of the basic structure of *ikebana*. The design of water motifs, lakes, shores and waterfalls also shows a large degree of variation which is emphasized in the Japanese garden and contributes to its strong impression of rhythmical movement. The imaginative arrangement of elements and alternation between open and closed space also gives a sense of rhythm to the garden. This is especially noticeable in the tea garden. Here motifs are ordered in considered succession and are gradually perceived in accordance with the principle of *mie-gakure* (seen and hidden). An even more developed form of succession is rotation, in which motifs are ordered around a larger garden unit, usually beside a lake, and enter the viewer's field of vision as he walks.

The technique of "borrowed landscape", *shakkei*, is also quite common. It incorporates distant landscapes into the visual scenery of the garden (page 233). This phenomenon is often seen in the Zen garden, which is surprising considering the otherwise enclosed and introspective character of these gardens intended for concentrated contemplation. The more attentive viewer will notice the persistence with which certain garden motifs appear in various periods and also that motifs of different origin - from Shinto, Daoism, Buddhism, or elsewhere - appear side by side. This shows the high degree of tolerance which enabled the survival of the old in Japan and its often fruitful symbiosis

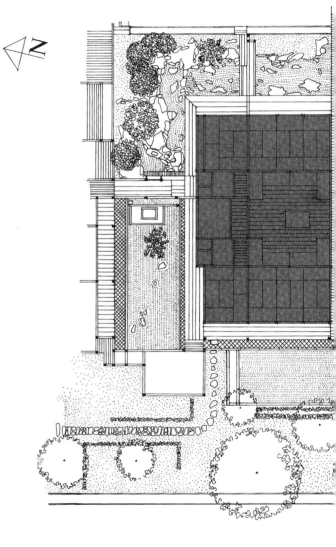

Daizen-in. The central temple is surrounded on all sides by elements of the dry garden, consisting of various sizes. The main motif, *kare-taki*, is attached to the left-hand (northern) corner, and ends in a large sand surface. The Sea of Nothingness is located in the southern section. The third major element is the Northern Garden, shown on the ground-plan beneath the *kare-taki*.

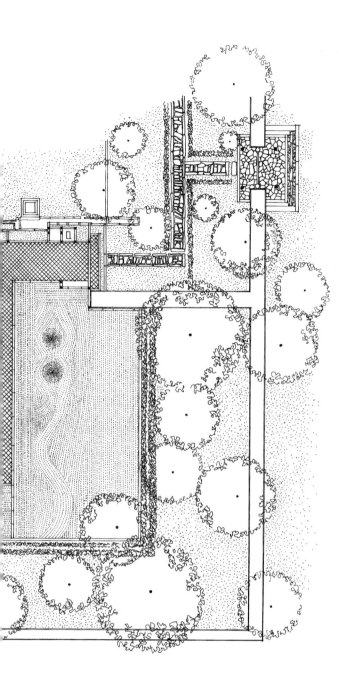

with the new. But another consequence of this tolerance is an interweaving of various motifs and periods which makes typological definition of the Japanese garden difficult. Therefore there are wide divergences of opinion among native specialists. Almost in each area one can find differing classifications which do not follow historical styles, as in Europe, but more often rely on structural characteristics (water garden, island garden, dry garden) or design (gardens for viewing from one point of rest, rotating gardens, and so on).

Materials

Rocks are by far the most important material used in all the varieties of Japanese garden. In a country of volcanic origin there are many different and interesting types of rock available in terms of shape, colour and texture. Most often used were rocks from mountains and shorelines which had been shaped by weather or water and thus given also a patina of age. The most highly valued were dark rocks with a solid appearance. White rocks and those with glittering surfaces were deemed unacceptable, as were sharp edges and grooves, which is a complete contrast to Chinese criteria, which demanded soft, white, calcareous stone, as perforated as possible. Even today, select samples of rock can reach a high price, as much as 10,000 dollars for a single piece.

In the dry garden, rocks are always accompanied by sand. It is usually prepared from granite into different sized granulations, depending on its intended purpose. When it forms the course taken by rapids or waterfalls, or when it accompanies larger rocks, a larger grain (10 to 12 mm) is used. For smaller motifs, grain size is correspondingly smaller (5 to 6 mm). Because its appearance is affected by the weather, it is renewed every year so as to maintain a fresh aspect.

Plants. It may be a surprise to some that moss holds a pre-eminent place in the Japanese garden. Its tiny, needle-grained texture forms an ideal contrast to rocks and paving stones. Without moss, in which stepping stones are set so that they appear as if they are floating on water, it would not be possible to imagine the picturesque pathways of the tea garden, which are like miniature landscapes. Moss demands a lot of moisture and partial shade, so it has to be watered during dry periods. It is a sign of hospitality if, before a visit, the host waters the moss so that it looks fresher.

The pine tree came to hold a special place in the garden not only because it was evergreen but also because it was valued for its gnarled picturesque growth and its needles. Other commonly used evergreens are: the camphor tree, katsura (*Cinnamomum camphora*), the conifers *Sciadopitys verticillata* and *Cryptomeria japonica*, camellias and various bamboos. Among flowering woody plants the following are especially valued: *sakura*, cherry trees (*Prunus serrulata* and *Prunus subhirtella*), crab-apple (*Malus zume*), azaleas, magnolias and maples, whose beautiful autumn colours draw masses of visitors to the garden, as do the flowering cherries in spring. Smaller plants such as chrysanthemum, peony and iris also play their part in Japanese garden culture.

Gardens today

Although traditional gardens can be found throughout Japan, they are mainly located in Kyoto and the surrounding area. This venerable city was the capital for almost a thousand years, from the end of the 8th century onwards. It lies at the foot of a charming range of hills, with a rich natural environment and a pleasant climate. It was built on a typical geometric grid pattern after the example of Chang'an, a Chinese capital in the Tang dynasty. In spite of wars, earthquakes and fires, many of its cultural riches were preserved, in addition to an exceptional number of gardens (almost 1,500 of them) mainly situated beside temples. If Suzhou forms the main treasury of Chinese garden art, this role is even better fulfilled by Kyoto in Japan.

Most gardens are open to the public, but entrance to some of those beside Buddhist temples are forbidden. Visits to the gardens of imperial villas and palaces are especially restricted. A written request has to be submitted a few days in advance in order to obtain a special permit. This is the only way to prevent a mass influx of visitors which would undoubtedly cause damage to these carefully maintained gardens.

The Byodo-in temple in Uji near Kyoto, which originated in 1053, deserves attention as one of the few remaining examples of the *shinden zukuri* style. In the centre of a small lake lies an island on which is built an Amida hall, called Hoodo (Phoenix Hall), in the architectural style of the Tang dynasty, with slightly arched roofs. From the central part, two open galleries run on each side and in front of it is a small sandy rectangle. The whole arrangement forms a garden in the paradise style, *jodoshiki*, in which the central element is a lotus lake.

The Joruri-ji temple near Kyoto, created around 1150. Like the previous example, it is executed in the *jodoshiki* style. In front of the hall of the Nine Amidas is a lake with a longitudinal island of which the northern arm is formed of gravel and rocks, like *suhama*. After thorough research, it was renovated after the last war by Osamu Mori.

Saiho-ji is one of the most famous and oldest gardens in the country. The name means Temple of the Western Fragrance. It is also known as Kokedera or the Temple of Moss, which describes the main feature of the garden whose ground is covered by several dozen kinds of moss. According to some accounts there was already a temple here in the 8th century and certainly by the 12th century, but today's layout was broadly outlined in 1339 by the greatest Japanese garden designer Muso Kokushi. The garden covers 1.8 hectares and is divided into two parts, separated by the Kokojan gate. In the upper part there is the oldest dry garden, *kare-sanzui*, in Japan. The whole rock arrangement is set on a slope and employs three motifs: a cascade, which roars its way through a mountain gorge (p. 220), a group of rocks, including Shumi-sen and a level meditation rock, *zazen-seki* and in the lower part is a tortoise island. The dry garden appeared here for the first time as an independent, self-contained composition. In the lower part of the garden lies the famous *ogonchi*, a lake taking the shape of the Chinese character for 'heart'. Beside it are paths that are not connected to the pavilion or the shore of the lake, which represents a movement on Muso's part away from Chinese models and a development towards the promenade garden. This type of lake is called *kiyu-shiki*, a lake garden for promenading. The rock arrangement and the design of the lake represent a great turning-point in garden design which made Saihoji into the most influential garden in the country. It served as a model for numerous other gardens and especially inspired the creators of the gardens beside the Golden and Silver Pavilions.

Tenryu-ji (the Temple of Heaven's Dragon). In terms of development this is a very important garden, though very small - covering less than half a hectare. It was renovated by Muso Kokushi in 1339. The centre of interest is a small (45 by 60 metres) lake in which a few interesting rock motifs can be seen, condensed into a very limited space. The three most impressive are a waterfall made from a few large rocks, a bridge

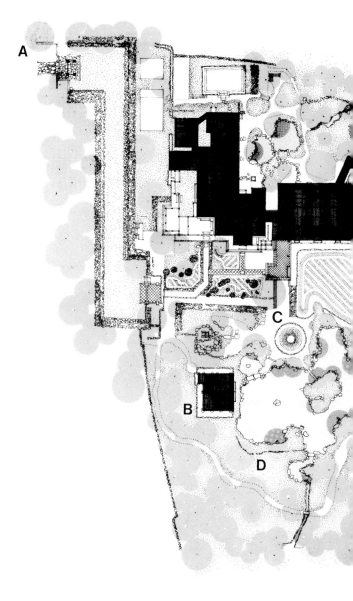

The garden of the Silver Pavilion presents itself as a richly articulated structure, within a variety of elements concentrated on a comparatively small area.
A - Entrance
B - Silver Pavilion
C - Sand Cone
D - Lower Garden
E - Sea of Silver Sand
F - Upper Garden
G - Fountain

206

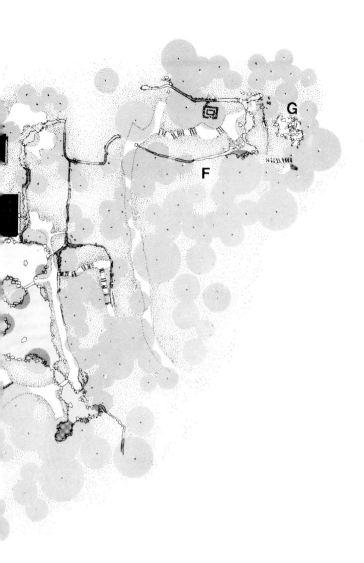

made of level, unshaped stones and, beside it in the water, an island. The latter is obviously intended to be an Isle of the Immortals and consists of vertically raised and horizontal stones in a balanced arrangement (p. 226). The difference between this vertical structure and the compact, rounded rocks of *kare-sanzui* in Saiho-ji is so great that it is undoubtedly based on two different aesthetic concepts. And moreover, the group in Saiho-ji is more naturalistic, considerably simpler, and more stylized. Kokushi's mastery of both design techniques proves his exceptional creative power and imagination. Numerous rock-islands and especially the narrow rocky peninsula, *deshima*, bring strong movement into the design.

Kinkaku-ji (The Temple of the Golden Pavilion) bears the name of the famous pavilion which is covered with gold leaf and planned on the model of the three-storeyed pavilion Shariden, in Saiho-ji. Its plan was probably drawn up by the shogun Yoshimitsu himself, who built a residence here at the time (around 1394) when Kyoto once more became the capital and the country once again lived in peace and prosperity. Renewed contacts with China are shown in a new wave of cultural influence which is visible in Kinkaku-ji, not only in the stylistic characteristics of the pavilion but also in the form of the small lake which lies in front of it and is the main attraction of this 23 hectare site.

Yoshimitsu was a great admirer of Chinese art and he said that the lake, with its numerous rocky arrangements, represented the nine mountains and eight seas of the Buddhist myth of creation. The influence of the art of the Chinese dynasty Song can be seen in the rock arrangements. Numerous rocks, *uki-ishi* or floating rocks, and a tortoise island break the surface of the water and are arranged so that the lake seems larger when viewed from the pavilion (p. 229). This impression is assisted by the fact that the water surface in the rear part of the lake is unbroken. So the lake is divided into two distinct parts and thus gives an impression of extension. This site got the name *Rokuon-ji* after the death of the shogun Joshimitsu, when it became a temple. Other buildings in this complex were destroyed during the centuries but the Golden Pavilion successfully survived numerous wars and storms. In 1954 it burnt down, but was rebuilt according to its original design so that today, together with the garden, it is one of the most attractive sites in Kyoto.

Ginkaku-ji (The Temple of the Silver Pavilion), the name comes from the central building which was, according to tradition, covered with silver. It is also known as *Jisho-ji* (The Temple of Bright Mercy). It was built during the years 1482-90 on the orders of the highly educated shogun Yoshimasa. He was probably also responsible for the design of the garden, in collaboration with the famous designer Zenami. It has been frequently renovated, most thoroughly in 1651 and most recently, mainly according to the original plan, in 1961. The Silver Pavilion is the centre of the garden and beside it is a small lake with an articulated shoreline and islands. The inspiration for the lake's design obviously came from Saihoji, which is in fact a model for the whole layout.

Besides the lake and the Silver Pavilion, most attention is attracted by the unusual sand shape, *sunamori*, in front of the pavilion. From quite a distance one can see the white, truncated cone whose shape recalls that of Fuji mountain. It is known as *kogetsudai* (moon-facing platform). In front of it lies the wavy *ginsadan*, "Sea of Silver Sand", (p. 217). This probably dates from the renovation which took place in 1615. Ginkaku-ji is more modest in scale than the Golden Pavilion and also more limited in its elements. In this one can see, among other things, a reflection of Zen thought. In terms of structure and character Ginkakuji is actually a paradise garden, *jodoshiki*, with some incorporated Zen elements.

Ryoan-ji (The Temple of the Peaceful Dragon). Undoubtedly the most famous garden in the country and perhaps the best known beyond its frontiers too. The garden's date of origin and the name of its creator are unknown, nor can we be sure how close the garden is to its original form. Presumably it was created at the end of the 15th century, at the same time as the temple was built. According to some authors the garden had originally been planted with trees and only later took on its present "dry" form. Theories about the arrangement of the rocks and their meaning differ (interpretations such as: mountains above a sea of fog, islands in the sea, tigers crossing the river, and so on) and even mathematical, geometrical interpretations have been attempted. Today, it is certainly a perfect example of the dry garden, *kare-sanzui*, derived from the aesthetics of Zen Buddhism. The atmosphere of concentration and contemplation at the rear of the garden is intensified by a wall and a screen of trees. On the 256 square metre sanded rectangle float rhythmically arranged groups of rocks of different sizes in horizontal or vertical positions and well thought-out reciprocal relations. The 15 rocks are arranged according to the *shichigosan* pattern 7-5-3, in groups 5-2/3-2/3. In this pure and abstract composition the rocks are so masterfully arranged that on this small surface (24 by 10 metres) an impression of considerable depth and extension is evoked (p. 221).

Daizen-in (The Great Temple of the Immortals) in the Daitoku-ji complex is also a famous dry garden. Whilst Ryoan-ji is a pure and simple abstract composition, Daizen-in is composed of a sequence of symbolic motifs. On scarcely 100 square metres we find mountain scenery, mythological islands, sea, rock-ships, practically the whole symbolic range of the dry garden. It dates from the Muromachi period (probably from the beginning of the 16th century) and is most likely the work of the founder of the temple, the abbot Kogaku Sotan. It was renovated after the last war and today presents quite a genuine impression, with the exception of the south garden, which was added during the last renovation. The *kare-taki* composition begins with vertical rocks representing high mountains from which a river falls steeply through a narrow gorge (p. 218). When it reaches the valley it divides, its western arm flowing across a sandy plain and the other flowing rapidly towards the south. There it opens into a large sandy Sea of Nothingness from which arise Shinto cones of purity, made of sand (p. 222).

On the western side of the central mountain motif there is a tortoise island, *kameshima*, and on the opposite side a crane island, *tsurushima*. The *jinko ishi* rock, whose top is level with the verandah, thus connecting it with the garden, and *takarabune* (the treasure ship), one of the most famous rocks in Japanese gardens, also have an important position. The northern part of the garden is rich in motifs which consist of over a hundred rocks and just a few symbolically employed evergreens (camellia and pine). This multi-faceted part of the garden is in structural opposition to those dominated by only a sandy plane. This opposition of static and dynamic clearly underlines the leading role of rocks composition.

Taizo-in, in the grounds of the Myoshinji temple. A dry garden whose mountain motif is similar to Daizen-in except that it is more static and has fewer vertical structures. Here, too, the river makes its way through rocks and a canyon below a bridge in order to flow to the lower level. The motif increases in depth as it develops from the left to right. The design is ascribed to the painter Kano Motonobu (1476-1559).

In the case of garden structures the design usually looks different in the ground-plan than when viewed from eye level. This does not apply to the Rioanji, where the garden structure is almost equally "readable" from both viewpoints and impresses by its unsurpassably pure design language. It clearly reveals the canons of Zen art, such as asymetry (fukinsei), simplicity (kanso), profundity (jugen), etc., as well as the formal principle of 7-5-3 arrangement of the elements (top).
By its simplicity of composition, the Shodenji resembles the Ryoanji; here, too, the principle of *shichigosan* (7-5-3) is applied (bottom)

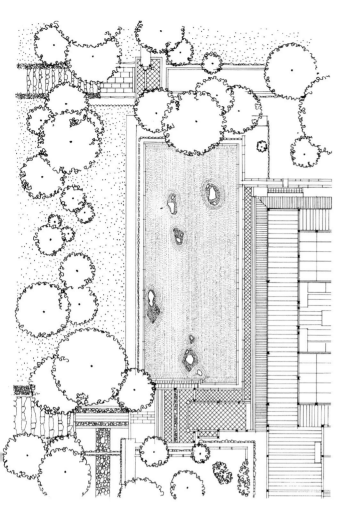

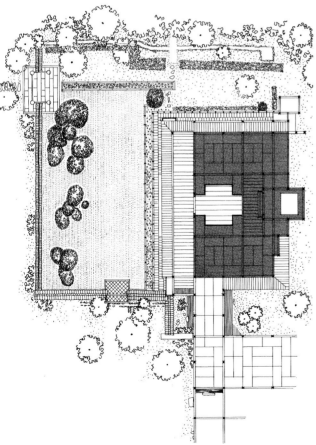

Zuiho-tei. The temple Zuiho-in was built in 1535. It was neglected until its renovation in 1961, when it was recreated by Mirei Shigemori in the shumi-sen style. The south garden (p. 213) is called Zuiho-tei (Zuiho, sacred peak) and also Dokuza-tei (solitary garden). It lies in front of the abbot's hall and is a very dynamic composition which intensifies through rocks and a moss-covered slope to a climactic, upwards-pointing central rock.

Ryogen-in. Like Zuiho-in, Ryogen-in belongs to the large monastic complex of Daitokuji, which consists of 22 temples. There are a number of very interesting gardens within it, such as *Totekiko* which is pristine *tsubo-niwa* (i.e. a very small garden, surrounded by buildings or walls) covering scarcely 9 square metres (p. 215). Both in its symbolism and in its design this is a typical Zen garden, dating from the 15th century, and was probably planned by the priest Tokei.

In a longitudinal sandy plane circular patterns are drawn, similar to those caused by a stone falling in water. This is probably a plastic interpretation of Zen teaching. One possible explanation for this creation is that Buddhism is like a sea into which one has to dive to reach enlightenment. There is a similar motif of sand and rock, called *Koda-tei* (p. 214), in the immediate vicinity.

The next point of interest near the Ryogen-in temple is the very pure garden design of *sanzon ishigumi*, a triple rock composition. The primary element is the central stone, which dominates with its size and unusual shape - slanting, with a level top (p. 226).

Shoden-ji (The Temple of Correct Tradition), Kyoto. The garden is small, measuring only 20 by 10 metres. It dates from the first half of the 17th century and was renovated by Mirei Shigemori in 1953. In its design it is a real dry garden and shows a surprising similarity to Ryoan-ji, except that here stones have been supplanted by pruned camellia and azalea shrubs. These are rhythmically arranged in groups on a 3-5-7 pattern, on a smooth sandy base, thus creating an interesting contrast. This is intensified by the contrast between the shrubs and the white wall which surrounds the garden. Shoden-ji is famous also for its adoption of *shakkei*, as Hieisan, a mountain in the background, is drawn into its visual scenery.

Shizen-do is one of the most unusual gardens in Kyoto. It was arranged by the samurai Ishikawa Jozan (1583-1672) beside his house after he left his military post. After his death it was abandoned until its renovation in the 19th century, when a few changes were made. It consists of three parts, the most interesting of which is the inner garden. The visitor enters it through a building, experiencing a dramatic transition from closed (an overgrown entrance path and a house) to open space. In front of a wooden verandah extends an exceptional scene with various stylistic components (p. 223). First, a sandy surface typical of Zen gardens, a little further on *o-karikomi*, and finally free nature. The arrangement of elements too is obviously significant. In the foreground is the precisely and geometrically defined human world of straight, rectangular forms. Deep in the background is infinite, unrestrained nature. Between these two oppositional worlds stand the rounded forms of pruned azalea shrubs which, as plants, belong to nature but by their regular clipped form, belong to the human world. These *o-karikomi*, robbed of their natural appearance as plants, remain elements of nature whilst emphasizing human design. Thus Shizen-do provides an exceptional definition of great mystery, the relationship between man and nature, which consists of three components:

The human world - *the pavilion.*

Nature beside man - *o-karikomi and the levelled sand.*

Nature itself - *the forest.*

Konchi-in is on the site of the Nanzen-ji temple in Kyoto. It dates from the beginning of the 17th century when Suden moved in as abbot and keeper of the temples in Kyoto. From the time of his war service he had been a friend of Kobori Enshu, who probably collaborated with him in the design of the garden. Konchi-in is the best preserved garden employing the mythological symbolism of the tortoise and the crane, and is very unusual in its arrangement. Viewed from the temple at the end of the sandy courtyard, a slope rises, covered with large, pruned shrubs. At the foot of the slope is a row of paradise islands. On the left is a tortoise island (p. 225) which imitates the shape of the animal in a picturesque but quite true-to-life way. Opposite, is a crane island consisting of vertical stones. Between these two are placed four other islands of paradise. In front of the whole arrangement, in the centre, lies a large rectangular slab of rock (1.5 by 4 metres) on which the abbot Suden performed rituals. The garden is quite well preserved and makes a strong impression with its island symbolism and its imaginative juxtaposition of a sanded surface and overgrown slope which is dramatically intensified by large, oval pruned shrubs. On the borderline between the plain and the slope is an imaginative arrangement of islands - the whole design showing the strong creative personality of Kobori Enshu.

Nanzen-ji. The garden in front of the abbot's hall, *hojo*, dates from around the end of the 17th century. The courtyard is covered mainly with sand and in its corner section are single standing rocks and partly-pruned evergreen shrubs. In contrast to the nearby Konchi-in, there is no distinct plan and because of this it is assumed that it is not the work of Kobori Enshu, but was created later.

Katsura. In Kyoto, there are a number of imperial villas among which Katsura, with its garden, is the most famous. The garden covers roughly six hectares and consists of a number of originally arranged and varied elements, which are placed alongside the pathways, as is essential to the style of the promenade or rotating garden. The garden was begun in the first decade of the 17th century and finished in 1659. It was intended as a residence for the Imperial Prince Toshihito. Its arrangement was continued by his son Noritada and completed by Prince Toshitada.

The garden was created alongside the main buildings, the old and new *shoin*, and the new palace, which together form a chain of low pavilions. All the buildings are designed and arranged in a pure geometric order whose rectangular shape is echoed in the façade. In contrast, the garden itself displays a free, organic design which also includes tea pavilions and other buildings. Paths which run alongside the lake connect the villa with the garden pavilions. Views of the lake and smaller, individual garden scenes appear in accordance with a carefully arranged scheme as one moves along the paths.

A formal perfection can be found here, brought to the attention chiefly by motifs in the lake and beside it, which is understandable as Katsura is, above all, a lake garden. In the northern part, a narrow piece of land known as *Ama no Hashidate* (heaven bridge) runs from the mainland into the lake, imitating very successfully one of the three most famous natural scenes in Japan - a peninsula with the same name in the bay of Myazu near Kyoto. Together with the Shokin-tei pavilion which stands opposite, it forms one of Katsura's most picturesque motifs (p. 231). On the lake there are two other islands, one of which is called the Isle of the Immortals.

There are, of course, many elements of the tea garden in Katsura which are visible not only in tea pavilions but in the design of the pathways and the arrangements alongside them. Paths lead through thick woods which open in places to provide interesting

The ground-plan of Katsura. The lake, with its numerous indentations, is the central motif of the garden. All the main subsidiary motifs are orientated towards it or situated on the water itself, e.g. several islands and peninsulas. All the major pavilions are arranged at prominent points around the lake. Because of this highly developed structure, Katsura gives the impression of large dimensions, though it is, as gardens go, small rather than big.
A - Shoin
B - Entrance section
C - Shokintei
D - Ama no Hashidate
E - Shoiken

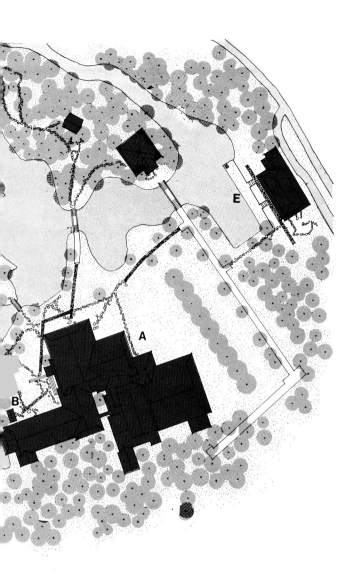

views, so that surprises come one after the other. The design approach *mie-gakure* ('seen and hidden'), is successfully followed here. The pathways are very varied, being covered either with gravel or with paving stones of natural and regular shape, or taking the form of stepping stones set in moss (p. 232).

The wealth of motifs in Katsura and their formal perfection bear witness to the peace and prosperity of the Momoyama period, and also to the work of many creators with a high level of cultural achievement. The designers of Katsura are not known, but the central personality was probably the highly cultivated prince Toshihito, and Kobori Enshu is thought to have collaborated. In view of its great intrinsic interest and value it is not surprising that so many works have been published about Katsura, also by such famous experts as Walter Gropius and Kenzo Tange. The garden can be visited only with written permission from the administration for imperial property in Kyoto.

Nijo-jo. Beside the Emperor's castle is a fortified citadel whose outer edge is surrounded by two concentric moats. Above the inner moat rises a high defensive wall, built in a picturesque composition of large trapezoid rocks (p. 227). Each rock was modelled according to a special formula in order to protect the walls from earthquakes. The castle was begun in 1602 and after it the garden, the most interesting part of which lies in front of the string of buildings which forms the palace Ninomaru. This is a lake garden, *chitei*, with a mythological *horai*-island and other rock elements (p. 226). The original plan, which was probably drawn up by Kobori Enshu, was later extended and modified by different arrangements.

Shugaku-in. This imperial villa with gardens, near Kyoto, was created between 1625 and 1655 for the Emperor Gomizunoo-teno after he gave up the throne. It is a large site, comprising three gardens separated by paddy fields. Gomizunoo was the nephew of Prince Toshihito, the first creator of Katsura, from whom he obviously received a lot of stimulus and inspiration. The similarity of the two gardens can be seen especially in the upper garden, which also shows characteristics of the lake garden, *chitei*. But certain differences are obvious: the scale of Shugaku-in is greater and the garden is open to the outside, whereas Katsura is turned inwards and is on a smaller scale. Shugaku-in is famous also for its "borrowed landscape", *shakkei*, and is one of the most celebrated examples of this technique in the country (p. 233). In the south part, on the slope above the lake called the "Dragon's Bath", *Jokuriuchi*, spreads a uniquely extensive motif of pruned shrubs, *o-karikomi*. The central and lower gardens lie beside interesting tea pavilions and partly reveal features of the tea garden, *roji*, especially along the paved pathways.

Kyoto boasts of other valuable gardens such as *Sambo-in, Sento Gosho* (a garden beside the Emperor's palace), *Entsu-ji, Sanzen-in, Shinju-an*, and others. The gardens beside the famous tea schools *Ura-senke* and *Omote-senke* are of unique value. There are other gardens of importance in Nara (*Jiko-in, Enjo-ji, Heijo-kyo* - an archeological site), as well as *Eiho-ji* in Taijimi, *Suisen-ji* in Kumamoto, *Ritsurin* in Takamatsu, *Tsuki Katsura* in Hofushi, *Koraku-en* and *Meiji* in Tokyo.

The Japanese garden was permeated by man's desire to spiritualize the world which surrounded him, to find in it a higher sense, so that this world, made better and more noble, would help him to develop spiritually and to leave his lasting mark on the environment. The achievements in this direction are unique. It could be said that the nature and spirit of the nation was reflected as nowhere else in *kare-sanzui* and in the tea garden, and that the Japanese garden shows a uniqueness and a degree of national identity that is present in almost no other area of Japanese art.

p.213
Zuiho-tei, Kyoto. A dry garden, arranged in the *shumi-sen* style. The rhythmically undulating composition rises from the lively patterned sandy ground, and over a number of rocks reaches its climax on the mountain top. The massive volume of a large-trimmed bush, *o-karikomi*, in the background supports the idea of the layout.

p.214
Koda-tei, from Ryogen-in Temple. Characteristic example of a Zen garden, with a circular sand motif and insular position of a rock at the centre.

p.215
Ryogen-in, Kyoto. One of the smallest *tsubo-niwas* in the country, designed in the Zen spirit.

p.216
The dry garden at Taizo-in represents a mountain scene comprising a stream, a bridge, a plain, the sea and islands.

p.217
Ginkaku-ji (Silver Pavilion). In the foreground, the Sea of Silver Sand, *ginsadan*, a striped sand formation that is a stylized imitation of the structure of the agitated sea. Adjoining the pavilion, a truncated sand cone, *kogetsudai*, represents a mountain of volcanic origin, such as the Fujiyama (top). Nanzen-ji, Kyoto. Dry garden in front of the abbot's hall, from the late 17th century (bottom).

p.218
Daizen-in, Kyoto. A magnificent mountain setting: the standing stones in the background, *tate-ishi*, represent mountains (top); a rivulet rushes down a number of cascades, runs under a bridge, forms the Crane Island (motif at right, under the pine tree) and continues southwards past the Ship of Treasures, *takarabune* (bottom), to end up in the vast Sea of Nothingness (see p. 222).

p.219
Rock triad in the northern garden of the Daizen-in.

p.220–221
Ryoan-ji, as viewed from the temple verandah. The first *kare-sanzui* in which the subject of the composition is no longer an imitation of some natural scene or the representation of symbolic motifs, but a pure abstract design (top).
As a most mature form of the dry garden, Ryoan-ji stands at the end of an evolution, started by Muso Soseki in Saiho-ji towards the middle of the 14th century (bottom). This composition represents a mountain waterfall, *kare-taki*. Typical of the concept is the use of predominantly rounded rocks, whose compact bodies create dramatic scenery.

p.222
Daizen-in, the Sea of Nothingness, with two Shinto cones of Purity.

p.223
Shizen-do, Kyoto. Inner Garden, representing a composition of three possible models of the world. In the foreground is the human world, made of geometrical, regular forms, well-ordered and open to the surroundings. In the extreme background is the endless, self-existing world of nature, represented by a forest. Set between these two worlds is the garden proper, a creation of man which is reflected in the abstractly levelled sand and the artificially shaped azalea bushes; composed of natural material, this intermediate world simultaneously manifests its adherence to nature. A symbolic image of the world, prefectly formed and philosophically suggestive.

p.224–225
Konchi-in, Nanzen-ji Temple, Kyoto. The most famous preserved representations of the Tortoise and Crane Islands. The left picture shows the Crane Island. The right one, the Tortoise Island, is more narrative. In the centre, a large, rounded stone stands for the shell, and the smaller stones around it represent the head and feet. A dry, crooked pine trunk rises from the tortoise's back. The foreground of the scene, against the verandah of the abbot's hall, is marked with lively sand

patterns, *samon*. In both arrangements *o-karikomi*, large trimmed bushes form a symbolic background to the scene.

p.226
Top left: Tenryu-ji, Kyoto. Lake featuring one of Japan's oldest rock arrangements. In the background of the picture the dominating feature is a cascade of upright rocks precipitously falling downhill in front of which a bridge and an island can be seen. At the right edge, a part of a peninsula, *deshima*, projects into the lake. Top right: a part of the lake garden, *chitei*, with numerous rock motifs, at the Ninomaru Palace, a part of Nijo-jo Castle, Kyoto.
Bottom left: Ryogen-in, Kyoto. A rock triad, *sanzon ishigumi*, with the characteristically truncated top and the slanting postition of the central stone. Bottom right: rocks with sand patterns in the traditional Zen style; a 20th century design at Mioshin-ji Temple, Kyoto.

p.227
An unusual rock structure in the wall of Nijo-jo Citadel, Kyoto, which is powerfully suggestive of a fortified building. The special arrangement of rocks prevents damage by earthquakes.

p.228
Among the lake gardens originating from the Heian period is the Daishu-in, at Ryoan-ji Temple, which has survived in a considerably altered form (top). Saiho-ji, Kyoto. A part of the lower lakeside garden, near two islands, The Island of the Morning Sun and the Island of Evening Sun. The characteristic "green" atmosphere of the garden is to a large extent due to the moss carpet (bottom).

p.229
Kinkaku-ji, Kyoto. The so-called Mirror Lake in front of the Golden Pavilion. The arrangements of rocks, single or in groups, representing, among other things, nine mountains and eight seas.

p.230
Katsura. Top left: lake bridge. Top right: pavement at the entrance gate, with its unusual rectangular and diagonal pattern of slabs. Bottom left: a fence of plaited bamboo, against the green backdrop of bamboo bushes. Bottom right: Shoiken. The rustic, unfinished wooden supports and the natural stones create an atmosphere of simplicity; the inclusion of rocks in the area beneath the projecting roofs of the building contributes towards the close links between house and garden.

p.231
Katsura, Kyoto. A motif from the garden of the Imperial Palace, at the Shokin-tei tea-house (Pavilion of Soughing Pines). In the foreground, a part of the Ama no Hashidate scenery, which imitates one of the famous seascapes of Japan.

p.232
Two characteristic examples of a *roji* (path in a tea garden), from Katsura. At left, the version using *tobi-ishi*, stepping stones set in a moss surface. Right: *nobedan*, solidly paved pathway. In both cases the green, thick, dusky atmosphere of a tea garden, suggests a wilderness.

p.233
Shugaku-in, Kyoto. View of the garden of the Imperial Villa, with Lake Yokuriuchi (Dragon's Bath) and the magnificent panorama of the surroundings, which enter the visual field of the garden according to the principle of *shakkei* (borrowed landscape).

p.234–235
The wall of a Japanese house, with large sliding screens, can be easily opened, and thus allowing very close contact between the garden and the interior of the house: Daitoku-ji on the left and Zuiho-tei on the right.

p.236
The garden culture of Japan not only boasts a long tradition, but is also exceptionally popular. Its outward expressions are, among others, the festivals of garden plants, flowering cherries, chrysanthemums, sword-lilies. Top: throng of visitors in the garden of Meiji Temple, Tokyo, during the flowering of the *hanashobu*, Japanese sword-lily (*Iris kaempferi*). Bottom: *hanashobu* in blossom.

234

Islam
Gardens of four rivers

Four rivers, four gardens
The Earthly Paradise
From Persia to Hindustan
Gardens today
Humayun - Sikandara
Itimad-ud-Daula - Taj Mahal
Agra Fort - Red Fort, Delhi
Shalamar Bagh - Nishat Bagh
Chasma Shahi

The roots of what is today regarded as Islamic garden art reach far into the past. They must be looked for in pre-Islamic styles formed since the dawn of history in ancient Persia. They can be traced back to the times of the Achemenid dynasty, in particular, the ages of Cyrus the Great, Darius I and their successors, whose Persepolis palaces were set in magnificent gardens as early as the 6th century B.C. This tradition inspired Alexander the Great, to whom the Greeks and the Hellenistic period owed their freer, leisure-orientated garden culture, which was later to influence the gardens of classical Rome.

Four Rivers, Four Gardens

The guiding principle of Islamic gardens is their evident four-sectioned composition, which is not merely a spiritual concept but also defines the basic physical structure. Almost all the preserved examples of Islamic gardening tradition show this layout, first appearing on Persian territory. The oldest testimony of this motif is a 4,000-year-old vase, which features the picture of two crossing canals, with trees and birds arranged in the four corners. This points forward to the motif of the four rivers, *chahar sur*, mentioned already in the ancient Indian Vedas, and reappearing in the Bible (Genesis 2:10-14). When Persia was conquered by the Arabs and became dominated by Islam in the 7th century, the concept was taken over by the new ideology and culture. In fact the Koran abounds with passages alluding to river-fringed gardens; Surah 18:32 mentions the gardens of Paradise laid out above the rivers, and Surah 47:15 describes, in even more detail, the four rivers of Paradise overflowing with clear water, milk, wine and honey. According to Sufist comprehension, the four gardens stand for the four esoteric states, and are called Garden of the Soul, Garden of the Heart, Garden of the Mind, and Garden of the Essence. Though these are internal, spiritual attitudes, the Garden of the Soul features, for instance, a fountain, running water, and a fruit tree, i.e. the main elements of an Islamic garden.

This Paradise symbolism finds its physical expression chiefly in closed gardens and patios laid out in the four gardens, *chahar bagh*, pattern. The central point of the pattern is marked by a garden pavilion, mausoleum or fountain, around which the four canals and four fields are symmetrically arranged. This gives a mandala-like image, where the central movement is towards the water, which is the symbolic centrepiece of the system, is balanced by the centrifugal trend, directed outwards into the garden, the emblem of Paradise. The *chahar bagh* formula is the fundamental aesthetic basis of Islamic landscape architecture. It was the indispensable guideline directing the layout of gardens throughout the wide world of Islam, proclaiming the universal character of Islamic art and culture. It is this consequent quadripartite composition that gives Islamic gardening tradition its unique features and unmistakable identity, preserved in geographically vastly distant regions. This underlines the fixed ideological and symbolical meaning of the *chahar bagh* pattern, and its primacy over local conditions. No other art can boast a similar universally valid formula.

The Earthly Paradise

Not only the four-sectioned design, but even the notion of the garden as an idealized spatial structure is derived from the Koran. Like Christianity, Islam believes in heavenly Paradise; but unlike Christianity, it dares to match the Koranic descriptions of Paradise on earth. This is, no doubt, a reflection of the mentality of the hardy desert population of the Middle East, to whom the rare fertile, green, well-watered oases

Most frequently the *chahar bagh* motif reappears in Indian sepulchral layouts. As a rule the mausoleum is placed in the centre. The oldest, completely surviving structure of the kind is the Humayun mausoleum in Delhi (top).
The memorial complex of the Sikandara is later, yet it shows a simpler, classical fourpart *chahar bagh* structure (centre).
Characteristic detail of Mogul garden design: the *anguri bagh*, grape garden, in the Red Fort at Agra; besides one at Amber the only surviving piece of the kind. In spite of its name, it was probably never used for the cultivation of vine. Its composite pattern enlivened the ladies' section, *zenana*, in the fortress (bottom).

The Chahar Bagh Avenue in Isfahan (previous page).

238

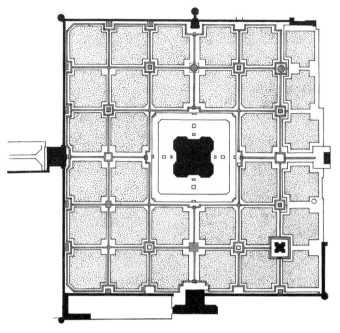

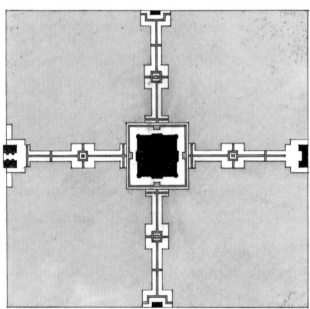

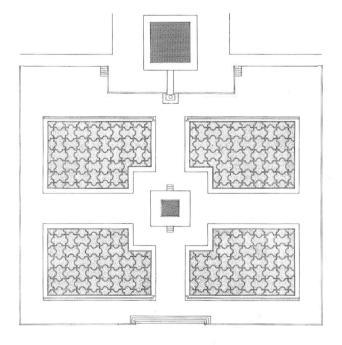

stand for life, while the surrounding endless tracts of desert mean the Enemy, the absence of life, and death.

In such a setting, water and the vegetation depending on it are the pre-condition of life, and therefore identified with life. Therefore the elements of an oasis, i.e. water, fertile soil and plants, are inevitably elevated to the level of symbolic components of a formal garden, the transformed, idealized counterpart of an oasis. Separated by walls from the profane desert, the garden features a network of canals and a tangle of luxurious vegetation. Water interpenetrates the entire garden structure, to the point of soaking every nook and cranny. The uses of water are infinite: optical, acoustic, climatic, irrigational, ritualistic, and even symbolic. Sometimes foaming white, sometimes undulating, sometimes a mirror surface, it appears in endless variations, such as fountains, or (an original feature of Islamic garden design) as *chadar*, an inclined stone slab with a grooved surface, down which the water trickles in curious patterns.

In addition, the water acoustically dominates the space, refreshes the air, allows ritual washings, and waters the garden plants. While the rivulets and other manifestations of water are strictly geometrically defined, the arrangement of vegetation is, on principle, free. This accounts for the pronounced sensual character of an Islamic garden, particularly the garden plants, with their colourful blossoms, intense fragrance, or luscious fruits. The relaxed world of pulsating, sensuous, prolific vegetation is therefore in sharp contrast to the ascetic, strict, Koran-based geometry underlying the basic ground-plan of the garden. The plants also tend to convey symbolic messages, for example in an alley of alternating cypresses and fruit trees, the evergreen cypress represents eternity and death, while the flowering or crop-bearing fruit-tree symbolizes the revival of life, and fertility.

From Persia to Hindustan

The Golden Age of Islamic gardening started with the Timurid dynasty, founded by the world-conquering and art-loving Tamerlane in the 14th century. Contemporary descriptions, some of them by European diplomats, praise the numerous luxurious gardens of Samarkand, developed by the illiterate tyrant into a glamorous garden city. After a century of eclipse, another, even more glorious bloom was ushered in by the cultivated Timurid ruler Babur, whose hobbies included literature, music and garden design. The most famous of his gardens was the *Bagh-i-wata*, Garden of Faithfulness, in Kabul. Babur, conqueror of India, also introduced Islamic garden art to the Indian subcontinent. The remains of his *Ram-bagh* are still traceable at Agra, on the bank of the Jumna river.

Babur's invasion of India marked a new period of architecture and gardening. He was followed by a number of successors who commissioned - or even designed - new palaces and gardens. The most remarkable of these Mogul rulers were Jahangir (1569-1627) and the unsurpassed Shah Jahan (1592-1658). The former immortalized himself by his Kashmiri gardens, where the abundant water supply and mild climate resulted in a peculiar variety of Mogul garden design, characterized by its extension along a longitudinal axis and its subdivision into a sequence of terraces. Shah Jahan, builder of the Taj Mahal, brought to perfection the mausoleum-type garden, whose prototype was the Humayun complex in Delhi. This is, as a whole, the most magnificent monument of Islamic garden art, strictly based on the *chahar bagh* as design pattern.

Simultaneously with Mogul creativity in India, Persian culture reached its heyday under the Safavid dynasty, in the 16th century. Its mightiest patron of arts was Shah Abbas, who transferred the capital to Isfahan, rebuilding it into a city of glamorous palaces, wide avenues and a profusion of lush gardens living up to the saying: Isfahan is half of the world, *Isfahan, nisf-i-jahan*. The most representative creations arose along Chahar Bagh Avenue, almost 2 kilometres-long by 60 metres-wide, marked by eight parallel alleys skirted by paved runnels. All along this celebrated promenade, there were gardens with pavilions: the Nightingale Pavilion, the Throne Pavilion, the Octagonal Pavilion, etc. To the north it extended into the famous *Chehel Sutun Garden*, continued by the *Hasht Bihesht Garden*, both with a complex ground-plan and outstanding for their water motifs, whose basic outlines are still distinguishable today. The splendour of Persian gardening art found its echoes far beyond the country's frontiers, in particular in the gardens of India.

Gardens Today

The Islamic gardening heritage is not preserved in all countries. It has survived intact chiefly at the two extremities of the one-time Islamic world, on the Indian and Iberian peninsulas (the latter will be discussed in a separate chapter). The Islamic gardening concept depends on water. Where this element is absent, the structure disappears, and the spirit fades beyond recognition.

It is for this reason that the Islamic gardens on the Indian peninsula show such an impoverished image which in many places is no more than a slight trace of a former splendour. The same refers to once renowned gardens of Persia. They all were designed as an earthly depiction of the Paradise where water and plants carry important symbolic values. As soon as they were deprived of water, the plant diversity was reduced and the large-scale framework, made of high vegetation, disappeared. The deterioration of those gardens in which water with cascades, sprinklers, fountains and mirroring surfaces used to contribute a significant component of their structure has been no less marked.

Gardens of India

The star role is played by the mausoleum gardens, where the building and its setting are fused in an integral design. They all strictly follow the *chahar bagh* pattern.

Humayun Mausoleum, Delhi. This is the most Persian-inspired of all Mogul layouts. It was created in 1566-1573. The building forms the centrepiece, and the four converging paths divide the garden in four sections, each subdivided into a number of smaller squares by the network of canals. Square-shaped basins of rather modest extent mark the crossings of the canals. The ground slopes gently towards the south, to allow the water to rush downhill over a number of small sloping stone blocks. The water is fed from the main tank, located in the building, into the irrigation canals. The ground-plan is fairly complex, but easy to survey (p. 239).

Sikandara, near Agra, is quite unlike the Humayun complex. It was established in 1605-1612. The design follows the simplest version of the *chahar bagh* pattern, the divisions marked by four wide, massive, elevated causeways, each featuring a large basin and a river down the centre. These rivers link the four basins on the causeways with the four open-air tanks fronting the mausoleum on each side (p. 246).

Itimad-ud-Daula, near Agra, is the mausoleum of the parents of Queen Nur Jahan. It stands out among Mogul constructions with its elegant lines, delicate choice of

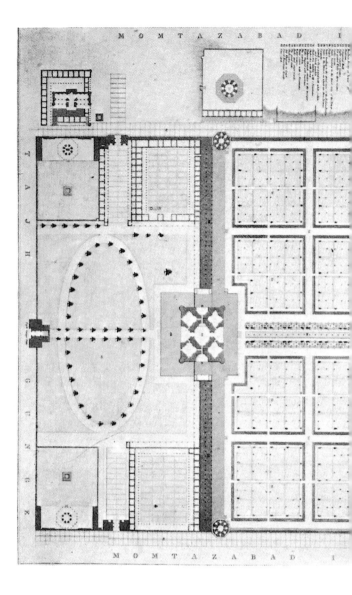

The ground-plan of the Taj Mahal, as drawn by Colonel Hodgson of the Indian Land Survey in 1828. The plan clearly shows a *chahar bagh* design, inserted between the two composition poles of the layout: the entrance pavilion to the south, and the mausoleum to the north. From the square pool in the centre run four axes - canals which further articulate the grounds into quadrangular compartments. The regular arrangement of trees, as seen in the ground-plan, does not appear in the present state of the garden; it has been largely replaced by informal planting.

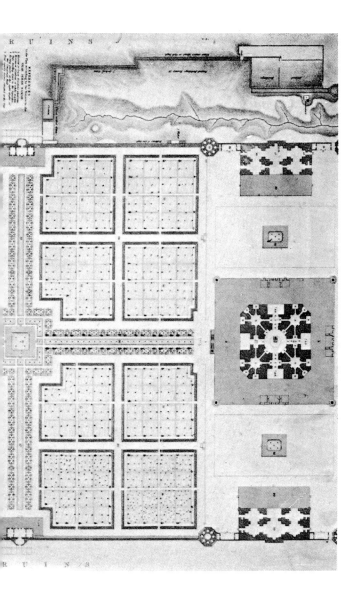

materials, and refined techniques of wall decoration. Both the inside and outside walls are covered with semi-precious stones, and the windows with a tracery of hewn stone. The building is set on a raised platform in the centre of a simple four-sectioned design. The divisions are marked by four symmetrical paths of access, leading up to the corresponding basins on the platform (p. 247).

Taj Mahal, Crown of the Palace, Agra. This is the memorial erected by Shah Jahan to his wife Mumtaz Mahal. With its magnificence and its perfect design it is, in its way, unique. It represents the climax of Mogul garden art and is remarkable for its original use of the *chahar bagh* formula.

The building is here, unusually, not placed in the centre of the layout, but on its fringe, overlooking the Jumna river. The mausoleum and the entrance pavilion hem in the quadripartite ground-plan of the garden formed by the cross-shaped pattern of the four canals. The crossing of the axes is marked by the elevated Lotus Tank, which is the focal point of the design. The canal linking the entrance pavilion with the mausoleum is distinguished by a number of fountains, which emphasize its special role within the composition, as compared to the otherwise similar transversal axis. The main south-north axis is further underscored by a cypress allée. The view from the entrance towards the mausoleum is a unique experience. With its glittering white façades and its hovering dome flanked by the two subordinate towers, it seems to rise out of the green-and-brown setting like a mirage (p. 249). The impression is heightened by the inventive solution of the access from the garden to the mausoleum platform. The two flights of stairs leading up to the mausoleum are located on the two sides, hidden to the visitor approaching along the main axis, so the building looks even more remote and unapproachable, especially in moonlight or veiled by morning mists.

Though the parterres of the Taj have been altered since, the details along the water axes are original. Their star-shaped patterns bear witness to a high level of decorative design (p. 248). The irrigation system of the complex combines formal and technical mastery, and is a masterpiece of Mogul hydraulic engineering. Originally, a complex system of pumping points fed the water from the Jumna river but today the work is done by electric pumps. The Taj was created by a whole team of designers and technicians, Persian, native, and even European. Yet the main features of the design seem to have been laid down by Shah Jahan himself, in 1631-1648. It is recorded that he intended to erect a mausoleum of black stone for himself on the opposite bank of the river but this plan was thwarted by his son Aurangzeb who usurped him.

Gardens of the Agra Fort. The citadel of Agra was erected by the Mogul emperor Akbar in the second half of the 16th century. It contains a number of splendid gardens. The most interesting of them, *Anguri Bagh,* Grape Garden, is preserved. The elevated central basin, or water tank, is the starting point for its quadripartite design, overlaid by a network pattern of sandstone borders. Together with the gardens at Amber in Jaipur, this is the only surviving instance of such an arrangement, a kind of Islamic parterre.

Gardens of the Red Fort, Delhi. The complex, also called *Shah-Jahanabad*, after its founder, is enclosed on three sides by high walls, and opens on the fourth side onto the Jumna river. Because of the abundance of water, the courtyards of the citadel once contained many gardens. Today there is no more water, and the original gardens are mostly overgrown with grass. The numerous canals allow us to imagine the layout and extent of the gardens. Some of the canals run through low pavilions, where the water cooled the atmosphere in the stifling Hindustani summers. This arrangement is

241

particularly impressive in front of the Shah-Burj Pavilion, where the remains of canals point to a proper *parterre d'eau*. Tolerably well preserved, though only in part, is the *Hayat Haksh Bagh*, Source-of-Life Garden, a fragmentary *chahar bagh* pattern.

Gardens of Kashmir

The best preserved gardens are situated near Srinagar, along the coasts of Lake Dal. They were laid out there because of the mild climate and the impressive panoramic views of the lake. The Mogul rulers used to retire to the Kashmir Valley to escape the scorching summers in their capital. In the 17th century the valley contained no less than 700 gardens, later mostly abandoned due to lack of water, a continuing scourge of the region. Therefore the atmosphere and character of the few surviving gardens can be best enjoyed in spring, when water supply is assured.

Shalamar Bagh, Abode-of-Love (p. 253). This was first laid out by Jahangir, and later expanded by his son Shah Jahan. The ground-plan is longitudinal, extending downwards towards the lake, and divided into three terraced sections. The original access, by boat from the lake, is today unfortunately blocked by the road. The three terraces are linked by a central canal, 6 metres wide, marking the axis of the garden. It is fed by a stream, but only in spring. In summer the water is diverted to the surrounding rice paddies. The first section was open to the public. Here the Mogul rulers held their official receptions in the Divan-i-Am pavilion. The second section was the emperor's private garden, and the third section was reserved for his harem. While the Divan-i-Kas pavilion that used to dominate the second terrace has vanished, the third terrace, added by Shah Jahan, is still centred around the Baradari pavilion, a structure of black marble opening out in four directions. It rises in the middle of a basin like a stony island surrounded by billowing water and spouting fountains. Behind the pavilion there is a two-stepped cascade, serving both to cool the air and to supply water pressure for the fountains lower down the hill. Shalamar Garden produces a cloistered, intimate effect as it is enclosed by a wall and fringed by huge plantains. Its charm is largely due to its water, glittering mirror surfaces and veils of mist rising from the numerous fountains. The most ingenious of these water effects makes use of pigeon holes, *chini-kana*, niches gaping in the walls behind the cascades. The lamps or candles placed in these niches illumine the translucent drapery of falling water, creating magical optical effects.

Nishat Bagh, Garden of Delight, is, like Shalamar, orientated towards the lake. But there is a vast difference between the two. Nishat Garden is more daringly graded, the breaks between the terraces are more pronounced, and the view of the lake is finer (p. 254–255), although it was not built as a royal garden. Originally it was laid out in 12 terraces, each devoted to a sign of the zodiac. Like Shalamar, it features a central canal, descending from terrace to terrace by a sequence of sloping stone blocks, or *chadars*. On their surfaces the falling water creates multiple patterns, to the accompaniment of a soft murmuring. The cascades are usually topped by a wide stone bench, called *chabutra*. The garden is perfectly harmonized with its natural backdrop of mountains, on one side, and lake on the other side, unfortunately now spoiled by the road.

Chasma Shahi, Shah's Well, is closest to Srinagar, and is named after a mighty spring, which guided the layout of the garden, created in 1632. The water from the spring runs through a smaller upper pavilion, and then descends to the lower terrace by a remarkable 5 metre-high, but narrow *chadar*. With its terraced structure and its use of running water, the garden is strangely reminiscent of Italian designs.

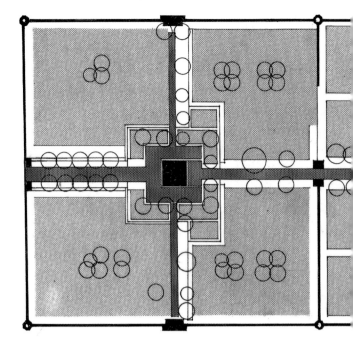

The ground-plan of Shalamar Bagh shows a longitudinal development of the scheme typical of Mogul gardens of Kashmir. This is probably due to its orientation towards the Dal Lake and the terraced structure. Close to the entrance are located facilities for public audience and, further up the intimate area, terminating by the *zenana*, women's apartments.

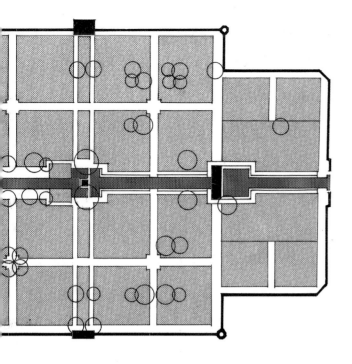

Two more Mogul gardens can be reached in about an hour from Srinagar. *Achibal* is arranged in terraces, with a profusion of water in its canals, basins and numerous fountains. Its most attractive features are a giant cascade and a long *chadar* carrying a whirlpool of foaming water. Nearby *Vernagh* is also based on an abundant spring. It was a favourite haunt of the Mogul rulers, but only a few remains survive, such as an octagonal tank and a 300 metre canal.

Related in spirit to the gardens of Kashmir, but rather closer to the Taj Mahal in layout is *Shalamar Bagh*, in the city of Lahore, Pakistan. It was commissioned by Shah Jahan about 1633, and consists of three terraces, of which the first and the third follow the *chahar bagh* pattern. The complex is, in fact, an extensive irrigated garden with marble pavilions, a royal throne charmingly placed opposite a picturesque *chadar* and more than a hundred preserved fountains. *Lahore Citadel* encloses a rectangular garden, laid out by Jahangir. It has an attractive *parterre d'eau* set off by fountains. Another feature of the same complex is *Paien Bagh,* a harem garden with a curious brick pavement. *Shahdara*, just outside Lahore, is the mausoleum built by Nur Jahan for her husband Jahangir. It stands in a garden of the *chahar bagh* pattern.

Gardens of Persia

Because of the recent political developments in Iran, travel restrictions have been imposed, and the current state of the country's famed gardens cannot be ascertained. Therefore the present book can not do justice to Persian gardening art. Though ravaged by time, the gardens of Isfahan, Shiraz, Tabriz, Kashan and the Caspian coast are an important contribution to the world heritage of gardening.

Gardens of Turkey

Throughout the centuries of Ottoman rule, numerous gardens were laid out in Turkey, but little is known of them. Only a few cloister gardens adjoining religious complexes have been preserved, such as the garden of *Suleymaniye Mosque*, Istanbul, a four-sectioned layout with a central fountain (p. 256). Interesting remains of gardens can also be found in the grounds of *Topkapi Palace*.

p.245
The *chahar bagh* pattern appears most clearly in the royal tomb complexes of India. The mausoleum is regularly placed in the centre. The axes proceeding from it divide the garden into four or more sections. The oldest integrally preserved layout of this type is the Humayun Mausoleum: a view from the building into the garden.

p.246
Sikandara, view of Akbar's mausoleum along one of the four axes (top). The Humayun mausoleum with one of the numerous small pools in the foreground (bottom).

p.247
Itimad-ud-Daula, mausoleum of the parents of Queen Nur Jahan. The garden that surrounds it is divided on the same simple quadripartite scheme as the Sikandara (top). Alifakovac, Sarajevo: high above the city is situated this garden of the dead, one of the most impressive Moslem cemeteries in the world. It has been heavily damaged during the Serbian siege of the city (bottom).

p.248
Taj Mahal: A view from the mausoleum along the main axis, towards the entrance pavilion in the east (top). One of the rich pavements in the garden, patterned as an intarsia of red and white stone (bottom, left). A part of the parterre along the main canal (bottom, right).

p.249
The Taj Mahal and its garden represent a very strong, complex axial composition, reinforced by numerous converging, longitudinal and vertical lines.

p.250
The stone lattice is among the highest achievements of Islamic environmental design. Carved screens, *jali*, used as windows or as a wall, provide for shelter from sun, ensure good circulation of air for cooling, create special optical effects and establish a visual contact between the interior and outdoors. A particularly intricate structure of this kind is the screen of carved marble that separates the Diwan-i-Kas and the Audience Hall, in the Red Fort in Delhi. The channel in the floor used to be supplied with running water for a cooling effect (top, left). The lattice-work in the roof pavilion of Itimad-ud-Daula in Agra (top, right). A window behind the sarcophagus in the Humayun mausoleum in Delhi (bottom).

p.251
A view through a large sophisticated lattice in the garden of the Red Fort in Delhi.

p.252
The stony citadel of Fatehpur Sikhri lacked water and the freshness of vegetation. Therefore water features, such as are frequent in Mogul gardens, were all the more welcome. A platform used for sitting in the open air is set in the centre of a pool and is only accessible by stone footbridges (top). Water courtyard with the centrally placed marble fountain in the complex of the Topkapi Saray in Istanbul (bottom).

p.253
Shalamar Bagh, a view along the central canal towards the south. In spring, before it is needed to irrigate the rice paddies, water is also available for the gardens. Then the canal comes optically alive and contributes mirror surfaces and mists rising from bubbling fountains. Unfortunately, the image is spoilt by the numerous recently added reflectors, supposed to increase the tourist appeal of the garden in the evening hours.

p.254
View of Dal Lake from the pavilion at the bottom end of Nishat-Bagh. The photograph on the next page was taken from the same spot but in the opposite direction. Such a placement of residential buildings reveals the inventiveness of the Islamic builders, who knew how to make maximum use of the visual potential of the scene.

p.255
Nishat Bagh. The garden rises in pronounced terraces from the lake towards the mountains in the background. The task of linking the terraces is entrusted to the central canal, which is at the same time the symbolic axis of the composition. Nishat Bagh is also famous for its mighty *chenars*, or Asian plane-trees *(Platanus orientalis)*.

p.256
A small courtyard within the large complex of the Suleymaniye Mosque in Istanbul.

Iberia
The meeting of Islam and the European tradition

Islam in Spain
Alhambra - Generalife
The courtyard of Oranges, Seville
Alcazar

Spanish Gardens after the Reconquista
Aranjuez - La Granja
Escorial

Portugal
Quinta da Bacalhoa
Fronteira Palace
Queluz

The garden art of the Iberian peninsula finds its richest expression outside the legacy of Moorish culture. The latter, being an exceptional phenomenon in Europe, is very well known but it gives only a one-sided picture of the heritage which developed here from the Moorish beginnings onwards. It is also particularly inadequate, since it represents only Spain, while saying nothing about the interesting country of Portugal, which remained outside the richer influence of Islamic garden art. In each of these countries the heritage came into being with its own features, and for this reason it is sensible to deal with them separately.

Islam in Spain

The map of Islamic culture shows how exceptionally widespread it was. In the east it reached to the Indian subcontinent, in the extreme west it covered the southern and central area of the Iberian peninsula; in between lay North Africa, the Near East and Central Asia. As regards the garden art heritage of this region, a surprising fact is noticeable today: in the central, classical countries, Syria, Iran and Iraq, where Islamic garden art was born and once flourished, its traces can now hardly be found. Yet in the peripheral countries of India, Kashmir and Pakistan on the one hand, and in Spain on the other, the gardens preserve this culture not only in the greatest number but also in more or less original form.

When the Moors at the beginning of the 8th century conquered almost the whole Iberian peninsula, they brought with them, besides other things, their architectural skill and highly developed garden culture. As a desert people, they were accustomed to adapting to hot and dry conditions, such as predominate in Granada and Andalusia. Furthermore, in the new country they discovered abundant water, whether from high mountains or lowland rivers, which they knew how to make full use of. In the 8th century the Omayyad dynasty, fleeing from Syria, established itself immediately after the occupation at the head of the Cordoba administration, and Cordoba became not only its seat but also one of the most flourishing centres of science and culture of that time. In the 10th century it grew into a large city with numerous gardens, and in its surroundings Abd ar-Rahman III had an extensive complex built - the Medina al–Zahra palace on the bank of the river Guadalquivir.

The palace with its extensive gardens today only has a few architectural remains. However, the well-known great Mosque, La Mezquita, in Cordoba has been well preserved. Abd ar-Rahman I started to build it in 786. Later it was extended several times, while in the 10th century a great courtyard of orange-trees, *Patio de los naranjos*, was built. The name derives from around 100 orange-trees growing within a triple-divided rectangle. It represents a typical Islamic arrangement enclosed with walls and buildings, symbolically marked by a fountain for ritual ablution and irrigation canals and a plantation of trees. The regular spacing of the trees is a conspicuous feature since this is quite unusual for an Islamic garden, where plants are generally set at random and without human control. A similar example can also be found in the courtyard beside the former mosque in Seville (p.265), now the site of the cathedral. The explanation for such an exceptionally regular arrangement probably lies in its dependence on the irrigation system where, in order to use water economically, the trees need to be equally spaced out. This phenomenon came about even in ancient Egypt and represents a formal stylization of the economic structure.

Alhambra, (from the Arabic *Al-Hamra*), the Red Fortress, Granada, is considered one of the outstanding monuments of Islamic architectural and garden art. Its first

La Mezquita, the great mosque of Cordoba, with the Patio of the Orange-Trees at the bottom of the drawing. The patio - in fact, a stylized fruit plantation - is paved with brick; the straight canals are constructed of pebbles and irrigate the circular pits around the trees. The fountain in the lower section of the garden served for ritual washing, and is still used today (top).
The Generalife, Granada. Ground-plan of the garden in its present-day extent. The original Moorish layout is restricted to the Patio of the Long Pool in the bottom section of the plan. Everything else was added later, as can be gathered from the disparate design: the simple elongated shape of the Moorish sector contrasts with the articulated parterres on the European pattern elsewhere in the garden. The exception is the most recent part, which tries to revive the spirit of Moorish design (bottom).

A pavement pattern in the Patio de la Reja in Alhambra (previous page).

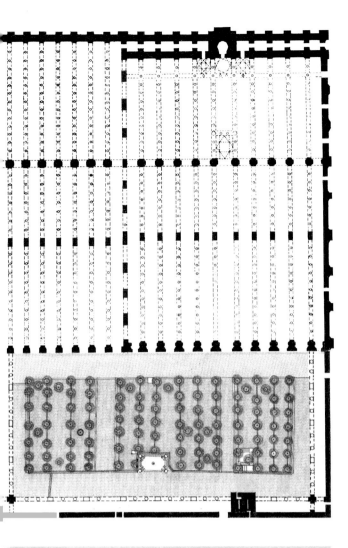

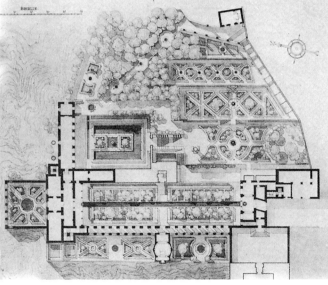

builder was Ibn Alhamar, founder of the Nasrid dynasty, and the beginnings of construction go back to the first half of the 13th century. Later it was added to so that today this fortress palace is 740 metres long and up to 200 metres wide. Inside are several interesting courtyard gardens, which are just as famous as its buildings. Its formation is based on the logic of Islamic spatial design, according to which built and open space, voids and solids, alternate.

It would be difficult to find anywhere in Islamic architecture a more appropriate illustration of this compositional principle than in the Alhambra where dark halls or corridors alternately follow bright courtyards containing water motifs, interesting pavements or vegetation. If we were to compare this construction with the Chinese layout where garden and building areas flow into each other, we would recognize a significant difference alongside the considerable similarity. In the Chinese layout the house is in the garden: here the garden is inside the house. This is overwhelmingly true of the Alhambra. Naturally, fine views of the surroundings are possible from some of its halls or other areas.

The most interesting open spaces are the Courtyard of Myrtles and the Courtyard of Lions. Both were built in the 14th century in the time of Yusef I (1333-1354) and Mohammed V (1354-1359, 1362-1391). The Courtyard of Myrtles, *Patio de los Arraynes*, or *Patio de Comares,* is the first one by the entrance into the area of the citadel. The courtyard measures 36 by 23 metres, and the pool inside it 34 by 7 metres. The main point of interest is the longitudinal pool, which with its reflecting surface dominates and at the same time gives calm to the area (p.269). At both ends of the axis the patio ends in colonnades but it is specially impressive on the northern side with *Torre de Comares*, beneath which it runs into the Hall of Ambassadors.

The Courtyard of Lions, *Patio de los leones,* is smaller but richer in design and measures 28 by 15 metres. It is built on the well-known *chahar bagh* pattern, on a cruciform base. In the centre is the famous fountain with 12 sculptured lions from which a perpendicular column of water rises and falls in spray like a constantly moving optical emphasis. Until some years ago the courtyard was covered with gravel to the level of the paved paths. Excavations, however, have revealed that originally the courtyard, with the exception of the fountain and the paths, was considerably lower and covered with 80 cm deep beds planted with flowers. The tops of the plants presumably reached the level of the pavement and thus created the impression of carpets of flowers. Unfortunately the recent planting, carried out according to these findings, does not in its concept or in its execution approach the spirit of such a design, as is evident from the photograph on page 268.

The courtyard is surrounded on all sides by a colonnade with the pillars closer together at each end of the longer axis, where it looks especially effective. It runs into various interesting halls and rooms, in particular the small *Mirador de la Daraxa* pavilion on the northern side, which provides a lovely view of the garden of the same name sited at a lower level.

The *Patio de la Daraxa* or *Lindaraja* (p. 270) with its irregular trapezoid shape and small size, approximately 16 by 16 metres is one of two interesting patios in the Alhambra which to a large extent demonstrate Moorish features although they came into being later, in the 16th century. The central fountain is surrounded by flowerbeds and a circle of cypresses. Part of its charm lies in the fact that it is situated one storey below the level of the palace and so it is possible to look down on it from there. Somewhat to one side is the *Patio de la Reja* (the name comes from the enclosing trellis), an even smaller courtyard with a fountain and four trees, and paved in an interesting pattern. Both courtyards are surrounded by high walls and the trees cast additional shade, which makes them very pleasant during the summer heat, the water from the fountains adding its own contribution.

Generalife (a corrupted form of *Jennat al-Arif,* which can be interpreted as the most precious of all gardens), Granada. According to the date of its foundation it is probably older than the Alhambra, being partly built as far back as 1319. Many of the gardens in their present state represent later arrangements, which nevertheless have maintained the Moorish spirit. The Generalife is also built on a slope with fine views of Granada and its surroundings from the terraces, balconies and miradors. It consists of a number of smaller, intimately enclosed gardens with water motifs and rich plantations. Among them the most alluring is the Courtyard of the Long Pool, *Patio de la Acequia* (p. 267), longitudinal in form with a central canal and jets of water and fringed with luxuriant plantations. In spite of re-arrangement, the original *chahar bagh* design has been preserved but not the level, for in Moorish times the patio was half a metre lower.

The **Patio of the Orange Trees** beside the former Great Mosque, Seville (p. 265). After the Reconquest the mosque was destroyed and the cathedral built in its place. There remained the minaret, which was altered into a bell-tower, *La Giralda,* and the courtyard of the mosque. Originating from the 10th century, it represents, like the one at Cordoba, a strictly geometrical layout; regularly placed orange trees grow in a brick pavement alongside which runs a picturesquely patterned network of irrigation canals. In the centre of the courtyard stands a fountain for ritual ablution.

Alcazar, Seville (from the Arabic *al-kasr,* palace, fortress). Originally it was a Moorish citadel, which the Spanish destroyed in 1248 in the Reconquest, when they reoccupied Andalusia. A hundred years later Peter the Cruel had it restored on a smaller scale but by craftsmen working in the Moorish tradition, the *mudejar* style, which characterizes numerous buildings in Spain up to the 16th century. The extensive park contains many Islamic features, but actually is more of Italian design. Within the palace are several interesting courtyards with a central fountain and colonnades. Fully in the spirit of Islam, some halls open into a garden with doorways or latticed windows. The park is divided into several more or less independent rectangular units, linked in Moorish fashion by paved pathways and refreshed by fountains and luxuriant, evergreen vegetation, among which the garden of Maria Padilla is the most outstanding.

In Seville, Moorish culture left behind it an influence that is still obvious in the arrangement of an enclosed courtyard beside the house - the patio. Contrasting with Moslem custom, however, the patio is not completely enclosed, often it opens onto the street by means of a latticed door or window (p. 266). In general the Moorish residential culture enriched the house-garden in Andalusia in that, among other things, the outer walls, too, were covered with coloured tiles, and pavements were executed in a greater variety of more elaborate patterns.

Spanish Gardens after the Reconquista

A picture of the Spanish landscape-architectural heritage can be rounded off with some gardens preserved from the 17th and 18th centuries, which bear the marks of the garden-design styles influential at that time. Among these the royal residences close to Madrid figure prominently.

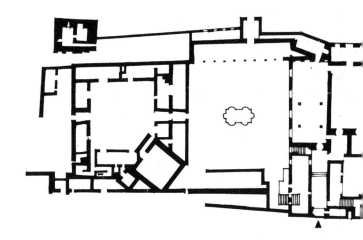

Both in its structure and its character, the Alhambra seems closely related to the large-scale villas and palaces of the Roman emperors, such as Hadrian's villa at Tivoli, Piazza Armerina in Sicily, or Diocletian's Palace at Split. It must be pointed out that the Alhambra owes its present-day dimensions also to constructions added after the expulsion of the Moors from Spain.
A - Patio of Myrtles
B - Patio of Lions
C - Patio de la Daraxa
D - Patio de la Reya

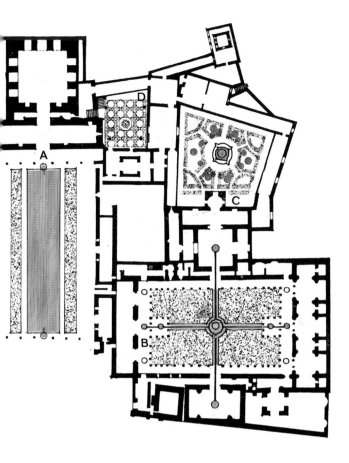

Escorial, commissioned by Philip II in the second half of the 16th century. It was built under his direct guidance for he introduced precisely his own views in designing it. This can be seen in the palace as well as the garden in the obviously non-decorative style, *estilo desornamentado*. In the spirit of its design the big courtyard garden is like a cloistered, monastery garden, as is also partly indicated by the name *Patio de los Evangelistas*. In 1717 a somewhat more articulate parterre of clipped box-trees was laid out. In the centre of the garden stands a rather small, octagonal temple surrounded by four fountains, and these in turn are surrounded by the rectangular sections of the parterre. The layout of the garden reveals an interesting combination of religious and secular aspects.

Aranjuez, lies 50 kilometres south of Madrid on an island between the Tagus and Jarama rivers, hence its name *Jardin de l'Isla*. The main element of the park layout was contributed by the Florentine Cosimo Lotti in the first half of the 17th century. He constructed many fountains and a number of amusing trick devices, which shower water on the unsuspecting visitor. The design is somewhat reminiscent of Isolotto in the Florentine Boboli Gardens. A smaller parterre on the east side of the palace is the work of the landscape architect Esteban Boutelou, who also laid out La Granja. The most striking motif was originally composed of four fountains with groups of sculptures by the Frenchman Dumandré but now only two nymphs and the Hercules fountain of 1661 remain. Further away, beyond a hanging bridge, is the Prince's Garden, *Jardin del Principe*, with many appendages fashionable at the time, a Chinese garden, an English garden, classical pavilions and fountains, and *Casita del Labrador*, the Labourer's house, a kind of Spanish Petit Trianon.

La Granja is another royal residence in Segovia to the north (p. 272). In its layout it bears the typical character of a ruler's residence and its design shows the strivings inherent in other courtly parks in Europe during that period. It was built in 1720-1740 on the western slopes of the Sierra de Guadarrama at an altitude of 1,200 metres. In spite of the park's size (it covers an area of 80 hectares) its mountain situation prevented the Baroque design from being executed on the necessary grand scale and with the true perspectives. The most outstanding feature of the park is the stepped marble cascade, *La Gran Cascada*, which drops down towards the palace. The park boasts also an exceptional collection of sculptures and especially fountains, 26 altogether, attributed to the sculptors Fremin and Thierry, while René Carlier and Esteban Boutelou designed the park.

Portugal

Despite the fact that Portugal was also under Moorish occupation from the 8th to the 11th centuries, no real obvious Islamic influence is observable in the country's garden culture. Its historical tradition followed European lines, influenced by the Italian Renaissance in the 16th century, and later by the Baroque, in the 18th century. So enclosed gardens of the Hispano-Arabic type are not to be found in Portugal. The only feature inherited directly from Islamic design was the abundant use of ceramic tiles (p. 274). These make an indelible impression, as they are strikingly placed not only on façades and the interior walls of the buildings, but on practically all the more important examples of garden architecture.

Although few in number, the Portuguese gardens represent a significant contribution to the European treasury of garden art and are unjustly overshadowed by the Islamic gardens of Spain. For in their originality and design characteristics they reveal many unique features. It is particularly interesting that at Conimbriga in the north there are well-preserved remains of Antique garden culture which can be found nowhere else, outside Italy. Moreover, Portugal can pride itself on marvellous examples of monastery gardens (see the chapter on the medieval gardens) in Batalha and Lisbon dating from the period when a mature Gothic style had developed there. It materialized architecturally in the characteristic Manueline style, which, however, did not find its way into garden design. This retained its medieval cloister patterns with a simple parterre. In the 16th century, which also saw the flowering of the state and its economy, larger gardens were established under the influence of the Italian Renaissance. These constitute the finest and most original examples of Portuguese landscape architecture.

Quinta da Bacalhoa, lies about 30 kilometres south of Lisbon on the Setubal highway, not far from Villa Fresca (p. 276). It is a country mansion with an extensive garden altogether measuring 300 by 150 metres, most of which is planted with fruit trees and vines. It was built in 1554 by Admiral Braz de Albuquerque following his visit to Italy where he developed a passion for the Renaissance style of building. The villa stands in the southeastern corner, its L-shaped ground-plan embracing a parterre, 28 by 26 metres, of basically Renaissance geometrical layout which is reminiscent of the Italian *giardino segreto*. Its patterns consist of clipped box-trees on a gravel foundation and radiate out from the centre, where stands a small fountain. From here a path runs alongside a high wall to another point of interest in the garden, a fairly large pool and pavilion beside it. The wall surrounding the garden has many niches and beside them benches of ceramic tiles, generally white, green or blue. The path from the villa to the pavilion by the water, and from there to a smaller pavilion in the opposite corner of the upper terrace, offers attractive views, all the way, of the lower terrace and the villa. With such an arrangement - a country villa, an alluring garden, abundance of water, extensive orchard and vineyard, an effective combination of the useful and the pleasant for both the spirit and the eye - Bacalhoa approximates to the ideal of the Antique *villa rustica* better than any other garden in the European Renaissance heritage. Bacalhoa was abandoned and remained in a state of decay until 1936 when an American, Orlena Zabriskie Scoville, bought and restored the villa and the garden. Both are now in very good condition and the garden, which is maintained in exemplary fashion, is open to the public.

Garden of the Fronteira Palace at Benfica, near Lisbon. As a whole, Fronteira ranks among the most original gardens in Europe. The mansion and its garden were built by the Marquis Fronteira in 1660-1670. The mansion was extended in the 18th century but the garden preserved its original layout. Fortunately both remained untouched by the great earthquake that devastated Lisbon in 1755. The garden is articulated with terraces in a typical Renaissance style. A high wall begins immediately beside the palace bearing allegorical images of music, poetry and arithmetic, rendered in ceramic tiles. A little further on, the parterre is bordered by a terrace with a marvellous gallery of busts of Portuguese kings. Below, a pool with four statues extends the length of the terrace, and mosaic portraits of knights, again in ceramic tiles, are built into the wall above the water. The great stretch of water beneath the massive stairway, and the stone terrace with its sculptures, dramatically underlines the articulation of the design and acts as a neutral element between the upper terrace and the lower garden parterre (p. 273). The latter is 65 metres by 65 metres, symmetrically divided into four parts, each of which is composed of four smaller square units. The parterre is divided by two axes, one running from the palace, the

La Granja was designed on a grand scale, with the clear intention of imitating Versailles. But the Baroque design is clearer in the ground-plan than in the actual layout, since it could only with difficulty be carried out in practice, owing to the steep slopes.

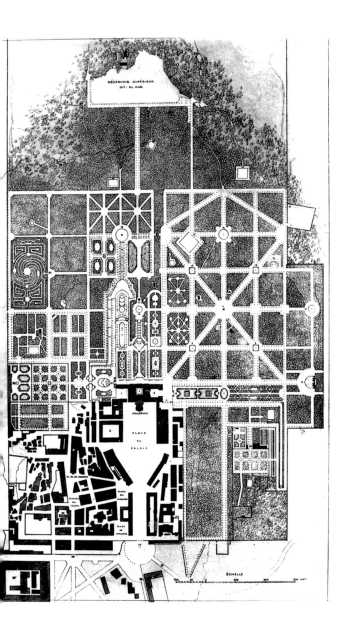

other cutting it at right angles and linking with the terrace. A fountain stands in the centre of each square, while statues, which are one of the most conspicuous features of Fronteira, occupy the corners. The parterre is traditionally geometrical, containing simple, pure forms with straight lines and presents a very compact appearance.

A special feature of Fronteira is the sculptural decoration. In addition to the numerous statues, a striking impression is made by the many large pictures composed of tiles, *azulejos,* predominantly in the famous Delft blue, they were made to order in the Netherlands. Especially renowned is the Hall of Battles in the palace, where the struggles for Portugal's independence are depicted in tiles with considerable historical veracity. Owing to their vulnerability and great value as art treasures, Fronteira is open to the public, with restrictions.

Both these gardens display every striking use of ceramic tiles for different purposes and indeed it would be impossible to imagine Portuguese gardens without them. They came to Portugal via Andalusia through the Moors and at the same time from the Netherlands as well. At first bright colours and simple, geometrical, especially chess-board motifs predominated. Later, firstly under Chinese and then under Dutch influence, the blue and white colour combination was mostly favoured, while the technique began to be introduced of arranging tiles into larger pictorial motifs. The most outstanding example of picture-making is the Fronteira Palace, but the finest example of the use of tiles is *Quinta dos Azulejos* in Lumiar, where the garden walls, benches and pools as a whole are covered in *azulejos.*

Queluz, the park at the royal court near Lisbon. The palace was built in the 1750s partly according to the plans of the French architect Jean Baptist Robillon, which Dutch gardeners executed under Gerard van den Kolk (p. 275). The main part of the park lies alongside the Rococo Palace on the upper terrace. In formal terms the design is determined by the central and side wings of the palace, the axes of which are indicated by the two main paths. At the end of the main axis is a rich motif of pool and statues. In general the whole lightly playful Baroque parterre is full of sculptured forms made of marble, lead or stone. Along the transverse axis, directly beside the palace, there is a smaller garden in Renaissance style, reminiscent of the Italian *giardino segreto*, while the lower part of the park is richly planted with trees. Here, among a variety of water motifs, the so-called Dutch canal attracts attention. Inlaid with ceramic tiles depicting ships, in May the level of the water rises up to the ships and creates the impression that they are sailing along, one of Robillon's playful, illusionist ideas. The restrained scale, the light touch of the design and the carefully balanced relationships between the park elements give Queluz less the character of a powerful ruler's residence and more the atmosphere of a peaceful, charming summer abode.

In Portugal interesting gardens or design elements in the open space have also been created alongside religious buildings, such as the garden of the palace in *Castelo Branco* or the famous monumental stairways in front of the church at *Braga, Lamego,* and *Bussaco.*

p.265
The Patio of the Orange-Trees in Seville beside the former mosque, with its regularly spaced tree plantation and picturesque geometrical network of irrigation canals running through a brick pavement. Like the courtyard of the Great Mosque in Cordoba, it was intended for ritual ablution. The layout is best seen from the former minaret of the mosque, which became a church tower after the Reconquest and was named La Giralda.

p.266
The patio has a multifaceted appeal. It provides privacy, creates a pleasant environment, affords protection from the heat and offers alluring views through variously patterned trellises or doorways and across luxuriant vegetation (left: one of the patios in the Alcazar, Seville; right: the patio in Seville).

p.267
The Courtyard of the Long Pool, or, of Many Fountains, is the most alluring motif at Generalife. It embodies the typical Islamic inventive scale for such an enclosed area, to which the intermingling spray from jets of water above the longitudinal canal gives simultaneously the optical effect of movement and the impression of considerable spaciousness, especially in contrast to the mass of abundant planting.

p.268
Having open and built spaces flow one into another is characteristic of Islamic design. It is often expressed, too, in the contrast of light and shade. Rarely has this been executed anywhere in such an accomplished and inventive manner as in the Alhambra. The Patio of the Lions fairly sparkles with the play of light and shadow along the colonnades, the central fountain with lions also contributing its share. Recently efforts were made to restore the original state of the patio by removing the gravel areas and replacing them by plant cover. Unfortunately, this attempt was unsuccessful, the Patio of the Lions fails to give the impression of a unified carpet of flowers that was found in historical research.

p.269
The neighbouring Patio of the Myrtles is apparently dominated by the mirror surface of the pool, above which rises the contrasting *Torre de Comares*, with its concave and convex, dark-light façade.

p.270
The *Mirador de la Daraxa*, overlooks the small patio of the same name, situated beneath (top, left). Two intimate, small patios at the Alhambra, the *Patio de la Daraxa* (bottom, left) and the *Patio de la Reja* (bottom, right). The optical world of Islamic enclosed courtyards is efficiently enhanced by rich tile decorations seen in this detail from one of the walls in the Alhambra (top, right).

p.271
A small courtyard of the synagogue in Cordoba also displays typical Andalusian features, such as the contrast between dark and light, open and closed, intimate scale and the pronounced pattern of the pavement.

p.272
La Granja, the purest surviving Baroque layout in Spain. A particularly interesting feature is the symmetrically designed and abundantly ornamented stepped cascade (top). The Italian Garden at La Granja adorned with numerous sculptures, urns and fountains (bottom).

p.273
The garden of Fronteira Palace at Benfica, near Lisbon. This unique 17th-century garden shows several unusual features, one of them being the long pool beneath the Gallery of the Kings. The wall above the pool is decorated with figures of horsemen executed in coloured tiles, *azulejos*.

p.274
Ceramic tiles, *azulejos*, are very popular in Portugal and used for many purposes as these pictures testify: a walkway with tiled wall and benches at Quinta da Bacalhoa (top); a tiled niche, also at Bacalhoa (centre); a courtyard at Tomar (bottom).

p.275
Queluz: the parterre in front of the rose-coloured Robillon wing of the royal summer palace laid out in the second half of the 19th century (top). The Palace is flanked by a formal garden, reminiscent of the Italian Renaissance style (bottom).

p.276
The intimate, enclosed parterre at Quinta da Bacalhoa is an Italian - inspired layout, well harmonizing with the villa in the background.

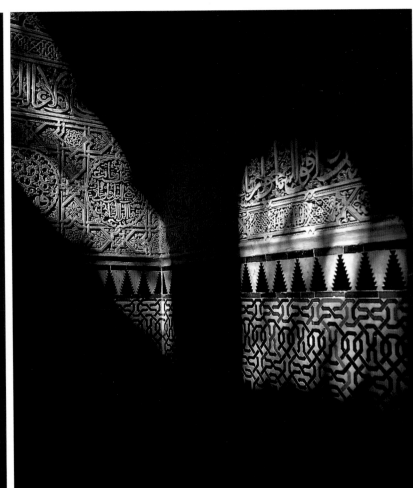

273

The German lands
Between nature and geometry

Renaissance and the Thirty Years War
Gardens of magnificence
Vienna gloriosa
The decline of Baroque
and the rise of the naturalistic style
The great trio: Sckell - Pückler-Muskau - Lenné
Gardens today
Belvedere - Hellbrunn
Laxenburg - Mirabell
Schönbrunn
Branitz - Brühl
Charlottenburg - Englischer Garten
Eremitage - Gross Sedlitz
Herrenhausen - Hortus Palatinus
Klein Glienicke - Kromlau
Muskau - Nymphenburg
Pomeranzengarten - Sanspareil
Sanssouci - Schleissheim
Schwetzingen - Veitshöchheim
Wilhelmshöhe - Wörlitz
Zwinger

The garden art of the German-speaking countries has, in spite of their political division, developed under more or less common influences and shows a number of related features. Therefore the heritage of garden art in the territories covered by Austria and Germany is best discussed under a common heading. Five centuries of development have left here an extraordinary legacy distinguished not only by the great number of historical gardens, but also by their variety of styles unmatched anywhere else in Europe. This variety can be ascribed to Germany's central position, which enabled her to absorb cultural trends and achievements from various neighbours, chiefly Italy, France, the Low Countries and England. The great number of representative gardens is due to the country's division into politically independent units. Each of them boasted its own court, with its inevitable paraphernalia of showy places and gardens - at first laid out in the regular styles, Renaissance and Baroque, and later swayed by the passion for landscape parks.

The growth of German cities in the Middle Ages laid good foundations for the appearance of gardens with a more pronounced and complex design at the turn of the 15th and 16th centuries. The boom of trade and handicraft assured a stable economy and the resulting wealth was favourable to artistic activities. The cities of Southern Germany, which established links to both Italy and the North, were the pioneers of this development. The influences followed the same route, northwards from culturally advanced Renaissance Italy. The merchant class was the most influential factor of this boom, therefore the establishment of magnificent, often famous gardens adjoining middle-class homes is in no way surprising.

These early gardens of the rich merchant class basically still followed medieval models. They were shut off from the outside world by high walls, and their relation towards the house was rather undefined. But their dimensions were fairly generous, and their layout increasingly sophisticated and varied. They were characterized by a regular division into usually rectangular flowerbeds, often raised above the level of the paths. The awakened interest in natural sciences showed in the collection and cultivation of exotic plants, such as orange trees and other Mediterranean species, that had to be removed indoors in winter. The showpieces of these gardens were grottoes, fountains and even capricious waterworks. A famous garden of this type was owned by Christoph Peller, of Nuremberg, only surpassed by the Fugger garden in Augsburg, also dating from the mid 16th century. The latter, in particular, was laid out with considerable sophistication and modelled on Italian prototypes, with fountains, classical statues and rare plant specimens, some of them gathered by the botanist Clusius.

Renaissance and the Thirty Years War

The nobility, too, devoted considerable attention to garden arrangements. The "grand tour" was just becoming fashionable and helped to infiltrate Renaissance ideals. In 1535, Ferdinand I established a garden that stunned the entire nation. It was completed in the second half of the century, and its terraced layout on a steep slope was a harbinger of Renaissance concepts. The garden adjoining the castle of Ambras, in the Tyrol, was created in 1564 on a similar sharp incline. It displays features that are clearly imitated from Italian fashion, such as two open pavilions decorated with murals, several grottoes, bird cages, and a private garden, *giardino segreto*. But the predominant layout of the period favoured level ground. There are several instances of this arrangement, for example Neugebäude near Vienna, a villa with a magnificent garden, Stuttgart's Lustgarten, Munich's Hofgarten or Hellbrunn near Salzburg, a rustic villa with an Italianate garden (1613-1619). The highly elaborate design of this last-named complex closely follows the

The Hortus Palatinus at Heidelberg is situated in a dominating position above the Neckar river. Rather than by its size, it surprises by its regular layout on the steep slope, which required not only bold creative foresight, but also exceptional constructional knowledge and efforts. Merian's print dates from 1645 (top).

An illustration from Pückler-Muskau's book Andeutungen über Landschaftsgärtnerei *from 1834 (previous page).*

278

taste of nearby Italy, in particular in its extensive *parterre d'eau*, its playful waterworks, its profusion of grottoes and statues and its considerable formal unity.

The high-water mark of this development was the Palatine Garden, *Hortus Palatinus*, in Heidelberg, one of the glories of German garden art. Hardly anywhere else had a representative garden been laid out on a slope as precipitous and demanding as this, rising above the Neckar river towards the castle, constructed by Frederick V. One cannot help being amazed by the dimensions of the long, straight terraces, and even more by the geometry of this large-scale layout, hardly believable on these steep slopes. Yet the giant terraces, in their perfect rectangular arrangement, produced the effect of almost self-evident orderliness. Each of the terraces stood out by its more or less individual programme, and the only links between them were fairly simple flights of steps. But they offered practically all the elements known to the landscape architects of the time, and some of these items assume exceptional dimensions. The Palatine Garden was, indeed, the crowning achievement of German Renaissance gardening and at the same time, by its magnificence, pointed forward to the succeeding Baroque age.

The progress was curtailed by the Thirty Years War, which broke out in 1620 and caused a long period of stagnation, as the religious and ideological conflict engulfed the country and brought about an endless succession of ravages. Surprisingly enough, new gardens continued to arise during the early stages of the war, such as the two Wallenstein gardens in Prague and Gotčin, both unabashedly Italianate (p. 349). Even a garden of international renown was established in the period, at Gottorf Castle, Silesia, with a rich repertory of recognized Renaissance features.

An outstanding figure in this age of suspended architectural activities was Joseph Furttenbach, master architect of Ulm. He published a number of books on building engineering, of which the most famous is entitled *Architectura Civilis* (1628), while a later work, *Architectura Recreationis* (1640), includes a number of garden designs. They all share a rigorous geometric design. The parterre is usually cross-sectioned, often with an emphatic axial plan. His prototype gardens were never carried out in practice but their flawless geometric pattern was one of the major stages leading towards the age of Baroque.

Gardens of Magnificence

While Germany was gradually recovering from the disastrous war, French Baroque burgeoned into maturity in the glamorous creations of the Mollets and, above all, André Le Nôtre in the 1660s. By their ostentatious regularity of structure, unprecedented scale and grand monarchical symbolism these gardens set a new standard for the courtly residences springing up throughout Europe.

The peace treaty of Westphalia, which ended the great war, established a number of more or less independent states, each with a court of its own. As centres of political and economic power, these courts also became the focal points of cultural life. They were certainly called upon to play the star role in the arts that helped to emphasize the social prominence of their rulers. One of these arts was landscape architecture, which brought about, between the late 17th and the mid 18th century, one of the most essential contributions to the European heritage of garden art. Almost overnight the demand for experts resulted in garden designers being called in from abroad, mostly France but Italian masters were also in great demand. This in itself implied the possibility of variety, a trend further stimulated by the widely differing personal inclinations of their employers, who favoured links to one or other neighbouring country. Therefore it is not surprising to find in the gardens of this glorious period French, Dutch and Italian features combined with highly original native ones.

The most engaging example is Hanover's Herrenhausen, the prototype, and probably the unsurpassed masterpiece, of German Baroque gardening. Its salient features were laid down by the Frenchman Martin Charbonnier, invited in 1682 by Duchess Sophia, wife of Ernst Augustus, ruler of Hanover. She was the prime mover behind the garden arrangements, for which she could find inspiration in her own youth, since her parents had been the founders of the Palatine Garden in Heidelberg. What is more, she spent a part of her life in the Netherlands, and later, when she was a duchess, visited Versailles, where Louis XIV himself showed her through the gardens. Her life history is the key to the structural variety characterizing Hanover's Great Garden. The basic concept is certainly French, with a pronounced main axis, a profusion of mythological sculptures, and a wide repertory of water motifs. Dutch influences can be seen in the flat parterre, unusual in Germany, in the rather limited development along the axis, and last but not least, in the canals surrounding the garden on three sides. This may lead to the frequently debated question of how much credit the employer should take in the creation of a garden (or architectural) design. Their contribution was often a creative and decisive one, occasionally documented by preserved plans or sketches (p.287).

Roughly at the same time, the Elector of Bavaria, Max Emanuel, began to create the first Baroque garden in his own domains: Schleissheim near Munich. He, too, was a personality of European outlook. He had a thorough knowledge of the Low Countries, where he had served as *stadhouder* for a number of years. Accordingly, this was the country where he sent his court architect, Enrico Zuccalli, for his first instructive tour. The experiences of this tour are evident in the concept of the garden, marked off by canals along the fringes, as well as in the circular motif that sets off the Pleasure Palace. In the war of the Spanish Succession, the Elector took the French side and had to take refuge in France when the Habsburg armies overran his territories in 1704. Only ten years later could he return to his capital and proceed with the embellishment of Schleissheim, this time aided by French masters. As early as 1701, Charles Carbonet had proposed a large-scale design of alleys, but the actual Baroque layout was contributed by Dominique Girard, who was emerging as the most important landscape architect of the French school working in Germany.

Thus the vagaries of politics played an important part in the development of both Herrenhausen and Schleissheim. The same happened at Nymphenburg, near Munich, whose original features were laid down by Zuccalli and Carbonet. They were superseded, after 1715, by Girard, and later by Effner and Dietz. This accounts for the predominantly French spirit of Nymphenburg, illustrated in particular in the magnificent entrance, with its semicircular court of honour, and in the garden itself, in the profusion of waterworks, fountains and similar motifs.

In another part of Germany, in Brühl near Cologne, the design was guided by a spirit similar to that of Nymphenburg. Here the initiator was Max Emanuel's son Clemens Augustus, Prince Bishop (and later Elector) of Cologne. The garden is mainly Girard's creation and is unrelated to the axis of the building, or rather linked to the side wing of the palace. This is a remarkable instance of divergence from the French Baroque pattern, and a phenomenon that was fairly frequent in Germany. However, at the same time, Brühl is perhaps the closest approach to the inventiveness of Le Nôtre's creations in its perfect proportions, its refined graduation of the height of parterres, and its lively axial development, running out into infinity in the accepted French fashion.

Hellbrunn near Salzburg. The principal features are practically independent of the castle. The layout is determined above all by large water parterres (top).
Schickhardt's original design for the garden at Pomeranzengarten, Leonberg. The parterre of flowerbeds is composed of two quadripartite halves, with a fountain in the centre (centre).
The rectangular fountains were never built; they were replaced by an octagonal fountain, as seen on the plan drawn for restoration by the landscape architect A. Elfgang (bottom).

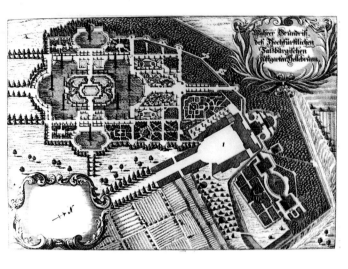

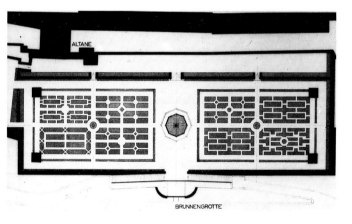

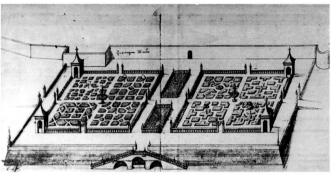

Nothing can illustrate the variety of German garden art of the time better than Wilhelmshöhe, near Kassel. Its creator, Count Karl of Hessen, unlike his contemporaries in Bavaria and elsewhere in Germany, was a lover of Italy and sought inspiration in her masterpieces, chiefly in the gardens of Frascati. Not only the arrangement on a steep slope but also the spirit of the garden shows the Italian influence. The mighty cascade, the occasional grotesque masses of volcanic tufa and the symbolic mythological sculptures emphasize this character. Certainly, the grand scale of Wilhelmshöhe far outreaches its model, the Aldobrandini villa, and this betrays the spirit of the age, which called for glorification of authority.

Saxony, then ruled by Augustus the Strong, could perhaps boast the most original, and certainly the most frantic, ambitions of the period. He was not merely a strong ruler, but also a cultured man, familiar with European achievements, and a magnificent patron of the arts. Guided by his ideas, quite a number of native architects and garden designers (Pöppelmann, Longuelune, Karcher, Meister etc.) conceived a complex of castles and palaces, surrounded by gardens. Each of these buildings was intended for a special purpose - a mark of grandiosity, matched only by the king of France. Indeed, Augustus cherished the ambition to equal, and possibly outshine, the splendour of the French court. The result was a number of buildings, each in its own garden setting: the Zwinger, in his capital, Dresden, conceived as an orangery and art collection; the Dutch Palace, with its Grand Garden for festivities; Pillnitz, a pleasure seat; Gross-Sedlitz, a countryside villa with an Italianate garden; and Moritzburg, a hunting park. It is no wonder that Augustus's Dresden court attracted artists from all parts of the country.

Vienna Gloriosa

As soon as Vienna had recovered from the wars with Turkey, building activities registered a new boom and the arts prospered. The coronation of Joseph I with the crown of the Holy Roman Empire gave a boost to grandiose designs befitting the dignity of a universal ruler. These, in turn, led to achievements unmatched anywhere else, destined to become the wonder and envy of Europe. In a comparatively short time, Vienna turned into a city of glamorous palaces and gardens. The crowning touch was to be the new imperial residence of Schönbrunn, for which the designs were prepared by Johann Bernhard Fischer von Erlach. As often in this period, his original concept proved to be utopian. It would have outstripped the size of Versailles but at the same time emptied the imperial treasury, another confirmation of the role of residences as symbols of a monarch's power and importance. Therefore Fischer von Erlach was asked to prepare a new design on a slightly more modest scale, so the erection of the palace could begin in 1696. A year earlier the layout of the gardens had begun under the guidance of the French tapestry and garden designer Jean Trehet, by that time an established personality in Vienna. The design of the Schönbrunn garden is outstanding because of the highly original termination of the vista, a triumphal arch added later (p. 295). This is another typical feature of German Baroque. As in France, the composition sets out from the palace but, instead of running out into open nature, it is shut off by an architectural element, as exemplified in the gardens of Schleissheim, Wilhelmshöhe and Vienna's Schönbrunn and Belvedere.

The Belvedere, a creation of Johann Lukas von Hildebrandt and Dominique Girard, is Vienna's second outstanding masterpiece of architecture and garden art of the period. The garden is inventively articulated and the composition carefully graduated, to rise from the lower, residential section towards the upper, representative section - a feature evidently inspired by the best designs of Le Nôtre.

Throughout Germany, Baroque creations proliferated: the gardens of Charlottenburg Palace in Berlin, Ludwigsburg near Stuttgart, Favorite near Mainz, Bruchsal, Karlsruhe, etc. This illustrates both the staggering number and the fairly even spread of gardens throughout the country. The most interesting among them was Karlsruhe, with its radial design, which sets off the castle as the focal point of the arrangement, the most perfect transposition into spatial terms of the spirit of absolute monarchy.

The Decline of Baroque and the Rise of the Naturalistic Style

Simultaneously with the mature Baroque style, the mid 18th century also saw the development of certain elements which were leading away from rigid Baroque geometry. The first harbingers of the change were Sanssouci - Frederick the Great's Potsdam fancy - Schwetzingen, the Bayreuth Eremitage and Veitshöchheim. Both the thematic orientation and the formal qualities of these creations define the age of German Rococo. The underlying carelessness and back-to-solitude moods found their expression in new spatial concepts, the flirting with irregular, quasi-natural structures gradually led into a new era - that of the landscape style.

The second half of the 18th century was marked by the awakening of German nationalism, which inevitably was reflected in the arts, especially in literature, championed by Klopstock, Goethe, Herder and Schiller. A concomitant trait of this movement was the revival of the past, of Germanic mythology and folk traditions, in which elements, such as the native landscape and pristine nature, played a considerable role. The landscape style suited all these tendencies. Moreover, a part of the cultured public regarded it, just as in England, as a symbol of political freedom. At the same time, however, the new style was also taken up by ambitious rulers, to whom the new gardens in the landscape style offered a possibility of identifying themselves with progress and popular ideas. Therefore the breakthrough of the landscape style in Germany was for a whole number of complex reasons and cannot be simply explained as a reaction to rigidly geometrical Baroque.

The first important garden in the new style was Wörlitz, commissioned by Prince Leopold after his return from a trip to England in the company of his court gardener Eyserbeck and his architect Erdmansdorf. The extensive garden is a reflection of the prince's cultured mind and predilection for classical antiquity. It features a Rousseau Islet and Arch, a Herder Arch, a number of classical temples, an array of grottoes, a "gothic" house and even a few freemason elements. The Goethe Garden in Weimar was laid out in a similar fashion and found an enthusiastic echo throughout the country. It is interesting to note that Goethe at a later time - especially after his return from Italy - frowned upon the landscape style, in which he missed order and regularity.

The Great Trio: Sckell - Pückler-Muskau - Lenné

The flowering of the landscape style is connected with the name of Friedrich Ludwig von Sckell (1750-1823), who started his career as a court gardener in Schwetzingen and completed his education in his native country, in Paris and in England. He accomplished a number of important creations, chiefly commissioned by his protector, Prince Carl Theodor. One of his earliest works was Schönbusch near Aschaffenburg, the first garden in the new fashion. Here Sckell gave up architectural elements, used as stage sets, and designed predominantly with landscape elements. In 1777 he began creating in Schwetzingen, on the fringe of the Baroque garden, a landscape park with clearings, a

The parterre of Schönbrunn, as painted by Canaletto, probably in the second half of the 18th century (top).
The Grand Cascade of the Belvedere, Vienna (centre).
Wilhelmshöhe: Guerniero's etching presents the entire arrangement along the two-kilometre-long axis, from the castle to the top of the Karlsberg, later renamed Wilhelmshöhe. With respect to the central role of the stepped cascade, with its grottoes and abundance of water, there is a clear influence of Italian gardening, especially from the Roman region. Of the ambitious design, only the upper section has been carried out (bottom).

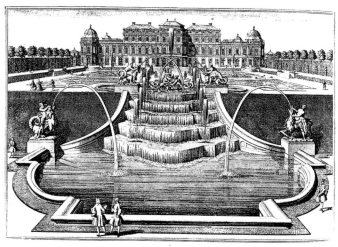

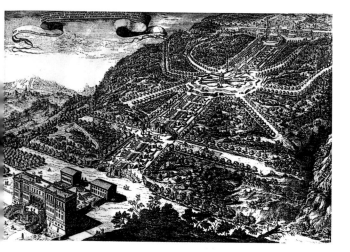

lake, ruins and exotic buildings (p.307). In the same spirit he redesigned a part of the Nymphenburg garden. He preserved the central Baroque design, but radically changed the nature of the bosquets along the diagonal auxiliary axes. Here he opened up large, oblong clearings with lakes, and developed certain original stylistic traits, such as his peculiarly shaped edges. His unique masterpiece is the English Garden in Munich, a large-scale landscape composition, located in the heart of the city. It is an efficient solution of the formal problems, posed by a sizeable object intended for the broad public. This first public park on the European continent is his epoch-making contribution to landscape and town planning.

The second original and remarkable figure of the period was Hermann von Pückler-Muskau, who also dabbled in poetry and travel writing. His two great accomplishments are the gardens of Muskau and Branitz. Both are shaped exclusively with landscape elements, and achieve picturesque effects by the juxtaposition of wide clearings with masses or clumps of trees.

Peter Joseph Lenné (1789-1866) was the third great personality of the German landscape movement. His numerous productions (well over 300) marked the first half of the 19th century. He developed a repertory ranging from smaller gardens to large-scale parks, from town plans to a wider regional level. This variety of scope was matched by his diversity of forms. He used both the landscape style and geometric designs. His prolific versatility pointed beyond his own age and set the pattern for the landscape architects of our own days. His best-known creations are his works for the Potsdam court, which include a number of regular designs in the Italian manner, as requested by the King. His other outstanding large-scale designs are Potsdam Island, Charlottenhof at Sanssouci and the Berlin Tiergarten. Lenné's name is also linked to the Beautiful Countryside movement (*Landesverschönerung*), which spread throughout the country, advocating the preservation of the rural landscape and introduction of greenery in the cities.

Gardens today - Austria

Belvedere, Vienna. The residence was built for Prince Eugen of Savoy, the victorious general against the Turks. The arrangement of the terraces had begun in 1693, under the guidance of the architect Johann Lukas von Hildebrandt (1668-1745) and was completed in 1702. The original garden was laid out in 1706. The first of the two palaces to be erected was the Lower Belvedere (1716). In 1717, Dominique Girard was invited to design, aided by the native Anton Zinner, the garden surrounding the Upper Belvedere, constructed in 1721-1732. The result is an extraordinary complex, ascending from the day-to-day residence of a feudal magnate to the heights dominated by the palace, intended for festivities and ceremonial use (p.294).

The garden is an axial design in the purest Baroque fashion but includes several Italianate elements. An example is the access from the Upper Palace to the garden, through a ground-floor hall. From there the first section of the slightly sunken *parterre de broderie*, sets out, flanking the large walk that marks the axis. At the end of the first parterre the pathway splits in two, leading down two lateral flights of stairs to a second, even more sunken, section of the parterre. Its beginning is marked by the stepped main cascade, with a semicircular basin on each side. The central walk is suddenly blocked by a terrace wall with a fountain, and divides once again into two strands, each leading down a lateral ramp of steps to the last level. The Belvedere is a masterly sequence of delicately staggered elevation effects, almost without comparison in Baroque garden art. At the same time, the interruptions of the central axis force the beholder to shift both the level and direction of his view, which means a considerable extension of the range of visual experience. The uphill vista is particularly overwhelming. This is also the direction in which the iconography of the garden sculptures must be read. Its purpose is the glorification of Prince Eugen as a conqueror and is achieved by subjects from classical antiquity, mainly Greek gods and heroes. The lower section presents Neptune and Thetis, the mother of Achilles, the central level shows Hercules and Apollo in victorious poses, while the upper terrace displays another version of Hercules and Apollo with Mount Parnassus.

Hellbrunn, near Salzburg. The residence and the garden were established by Marcus Sittikus von Hohenems, archbishop of Salzburg, in 1613-1619, from a design by Santino Solari. It is, emphatically, a Renaissance creation, which won wide acclaim north of the Alps. The garden is composed of two main sections. The first is represented by the water parterre, extending to the east of the castle in the guise of three symmetrically arranged basins. This longitudinal arrangement is concluded by a semicircular theatre, symbolizing the victory of Rome over the barbarians. The abundance of water motifs, the iconographical programme, the surprise waterworks, *giochi d'aqua*, and the ingenious use of local springs all point to Italian influences (p.293).

The second, larger section of the garden, to the west, is also perfectly preserved. Here, too, water motifs set the tone. The wall leading from the castle is flanked by a sequence of waterworks, grottoes, fountains and statues. The most endearing features of Hellbrunn are the grottoes of the castle, especially the Neptune Grotto, opening in the northern façade, towards the garden. It is fronted, along the axis of the building, by the Altemps Fountain and a star-shaped basin capriciously mirroring the façade of the palace. Hellbrunn is the oldest integrally preserved historical garden of the German-speaking countries.

Laxenburg, 17 kilometres south of Vienna (p.296). From the 14th century onwards this was a hunting lodge. In the reign of Maria Theresa both the castle and the garden were expanded. A more radical transformation, leading up to the present-day appearance of the complex, was carried out in the time of Joseph II, who had fallen under the spell of Ermenonville during his visit to France. Under this influence he had the Laxenburg park redesigned in 1782-1783 in the landscape style. Franz I (1792-1835) lavished even greater attention on the park. It was in his reign that Laxenburg was given its present character as Austria's largest landscape garden. At that time it was enlarged to its definite size of 220 hectares, and embellished with several ponds, artificial waterfalls, a rockery named Sophia Hill, with a grotto, and an artificial valley.

Mirabell, Salzburg (p.296). The castle was begun by the Salzburg archbishop von Raitenau, and completed by another archbishop, Markus Sittikus. The architects Fischer von Erlach and Hildebrandt were succeeded by the court gardeners Drestel and Darenreiter. The garden displays certain Italianate traits, but its design is orientated to the castle. The various sections of the garden are separated lengthwise by walls or low fences. In later times the parterre was given its embroidered patterns. The present-day flower-and-lawn parterre is stylistically incongruous, and seems calculated to impress the tourist. An original feature of the parterre is the basin, surrounded by statues created by Ottavio Mosto. The garden also preserves an open-air theatre formed by clipped hedges.

Schönbrunn, Vienna. Until the end of the 17th century this was a hunting lodge, destroyed several times, last of all by the Turks during the siege of Vienna in 1683. In 1690 Joseph I was crowned Roman emperor, which required a residence corresponding to his rank. The original plans, prepared by the court architect Johann Bernhard Fischer von Erlach (1656-1723), foresaw a complex on a scale far exceeding that of Louis XIV's Versailles. The over-ambitious design was soon dropped, and the complex erected

Herrenhausen in Hanover is strongly reminiscent of the spacious and flat Dutch layouts. In any case, it lacks the close link between palace and garden, so characteristic of Nymphenburg and other Baroque creations (top). Nymphenburg, a miniature by Gero. The most striking feature is the layout in front of the palace, surpassing even the French examples by its dimensions and structure. A second prominent characteristic is the continuous development of the design along the main axis. Both features place Nymphenburg among the best achievements of German Baroque gardening (centre). The most prominent feature of Schleissheim is its façade, which occupies the whole width of the park. The symmetric building both enhances the regular design of the park and defines the dimension of width (bottom).

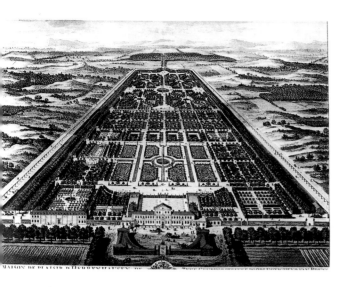

according to a modified, somewhat less ostentatious plan. This located the palace in its present position, rather than the original design which favoured a hilltop palace on the site of the later Gloriette (p. 295). The construction started in 1696. The Frenchman Jean Trehet began laying out the gardens a year earlier. The first stage was a long, axially orientated parterre. It was framed by the walls of the bosquets and the maze. In the early 18th century work was interrupted because of the War of the Spanish Succession. It was continued by Maria Theresa in 1744. The garden underwent some modifications, of which the most important was the Gloriette, a classicist building erected on the hilltop that looms on the horizon behind the castle and makes a most impressive view. At the same time the parterre was given an eye-catching termination with the huge Neptune fountain, positioned on the main axis. In the vicinity, some artificial Roman ruins were set up, and numerous obelisks and statues dispersed throughout the garden.

Gardens today - Germany

Branitz, near Cottbus. This is Prince Pückler-Muskau's last great design. He tackled it when he had run out of money at Muskau, which he was forced to sell in 1845. Until his death in 1871 he devoted himself to transforming a new tract of waste land into a landscape garden. It covers an area of some 100 hectares, extending from west to east. It is skirted by a belt of trees, fairly large in places, while the central part is made up of wide, open lawns. This impression of bright, open surfaces is further increased by artificial lakes. The excavated earth was shaped into hills and two pyramids. On the extensive clearings the masses of trees are fancifully arranged, to subdivide and shape the spaces, build up deep vistas, and offer surprising experiences of shifting scenery to the walker. The most original features are the tumulus and the pyramid; the latter is rising from the lake and contains the tombs of Pückler and his wife Lucie (p. 315). Along the castle there is a garden of regular design, to which the architect G. Semper added the well-known pergola.

Brühl, between Bonn and Cologne (p. 298). This summer residence, also called Augustusburg, was erected by Clemens Augustus, Prince Bishop of Cologne, on the foundations of a ruined castle. The garden was designed by D. Girard, from 1728 onwards. It is rather curiously orientated on the auxiliary south façade, where a raised observation terrace serves as a link between the parterre and the building. The *parterre de broderie*, somewhat sunken, is framed in by box-shaped clipped lime-trees, providing a well-ordered setting. Beyond the parterre, at an even lower level, there is a larger basin. On the threshold of the bosquet the optical axis finds its termination in a narrow column of water, behind which the view ranges, over the park outside the bosquet. The layout of Augustusburg garden shows a high degree of sophistication. The space is plastically articulated, subtly nuanced and dynamically developed along the axis, in a descending sequence castle - terrace - parterre - basin - bosquets - park. At the same time the balance of the various elements testifies to a delicate sense of scale. The garden was restored in 1933-1937, and again after the Second World War.

Charlottenburg, Berlin. This Baroque garden was designed by Simon Godeau, a disciple of Le Nôtre. It was created at the turn of the 18th century. Its salient feature is the 8-sectioned parterre, divided down the centre by an oblong strip of lawn flanked by two parallel walks. The focal point of the parterre was originally marked by an octagonal basin, adorned with a fountain. In the 19th century Peter Joseph Lenné reshaped the garden in landscape style. During World War II the castle and the park were gutted. After the war both the palace and the 52 hectare garden were restored to the original Baroque design (p. 298). The works were concluded in 1967-1968.

Englischer Garten, English Garden, Munich. Both by its central location and by its interesting structure it ranks, even today, after a century and a half, first among the city's parks. Its image was defined by L. von Sckell, assisted by an American, Benjamin Thompson, from 1804 onwards. The almost 7 kilometres-long grove along the Isar river is an authentic creation of the landscape school, with an important new touch, unique in its period, as it was designed as a public park, to serve all social classes. The extensive clearings run lengthwise, in a north-south direction, broken up by occasional transverse clusters of trees. In addition to the numerous brooks, the landscape is enlivened by a large lake in the upper section of the park. Sckell's vocabulary of forms is made up exclusively of landscape elements. The only exception is the Monopteros, a picturesque classical temple, impressively positioned on an elevation (p. 304), visible from various parts of this popular park.

Eremitage, Bayreuth. Development of the site began in 1715 when the Altes Schloss was built as a retreat in a monastic spirit. From 1736 on the talented Margravine Wilhelmine added the Neues Schloss (originally an orangery and bird-house), a building with a semircircular ground-plan, fronted by a large basin, and other features in the garden. The overall scheme shows a mixture of regular and informal features. In the lower part there stand out a remarkable grotto with a basin containing a group of nymphs and an open-air theatre built as a ruin (p. 310).

Gross Sedlitz, near Dresden. When August the Strong, king of Saxony, acquired the estate, he conceived an ambitious plan for a large residence set off by gardens. The garden is mainly the work of the Frenchman Zacharias Longuelune, who no doubt acted in collaboration with Mathias Pöppelman who was responsible for the total design. Even the ground-plan is remarkable, for it is centred on several diverging axes, and important sections of the garden develop transversally to the present-day main axis. This is partly due to the irregular terrain, and partly to the fact that the original concept has never been fully carried out. The bulk of the garden is based on two parallel axes. The first runs from the so-called Upper Orangery, crosses the parterre, and ends on the opposite slope in a cascade, today overgrown and waterless. The second proceeds from the Lower Orangery, descends into an almost square-shaped parterre, and ends in a highly interesting flight of steps. These stairs, axially underscored by two narrow canals dominating the sunken parterre, are shaped with considerable refinement, forming a typical Baroque *point de vue* (p. 299). They have been nicknamed Silent Music, *Stille Musik,* after the music-making putti on the balustrade. Gross Sedlitz is one of the rare examples of German Baroque gardens on sloping ground, and stands out because of its purposeful use of step motifs, pointing to an Italian influence.

Herrenhausen, Hanover. Originally, since 1638, a manor with a simple small garden, from 1666 onwards it was transformed into the summer residence of the dukes of Hanover. Its glamorous period began in the reign of Ernst Augustus, whose wife Sophia was, after 1680, the moving force behind the improvements. She invited, in 1682, the Frenchman Martin Charbonnier, who had carried out, by 1714, Germany's first masterpiece of Baroque garden art (p. 303).

The garden is of rectangular shape, skirted on three sides by a canal distinguished by a curved extension in the termination of the axis, a design reminiscent of Charleval, France. The palace, destroyed in World War II, faces a *parterre de broderie* with a central fountain, whose jets of water form a picturesque bell-shaped curtain. The next compositional element along the axis is made up of four square-shaped basins, framed in by walls of clipped shrubbery. Further parterre sections along the main axis form a

The playful Rococo parterre of the Dresden Zwinger, shown in the plan, did not survive. The present-day version has lost the arabesque motifs (top).
The garden at Gross Sedlitz near Dresden. It is surprising to observe the lack of development of the horizontal axis proceeding from the palace. The two parallel transversal axes, on the other hand, are clearly emphasized, though broken by terraces (second row). The original terraced garden of Sanssouci at Potsdam (third row).
The concept of palace and garden was laid down by Frederick the Great himself, as this sketch drawn by his own hand testifies (bottom).

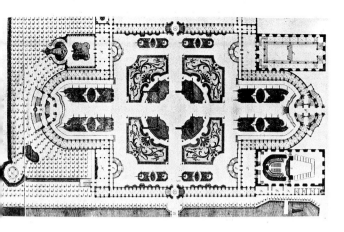

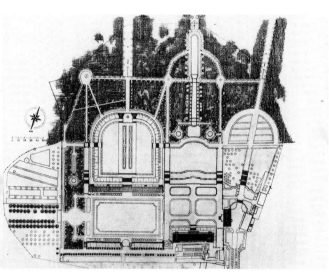

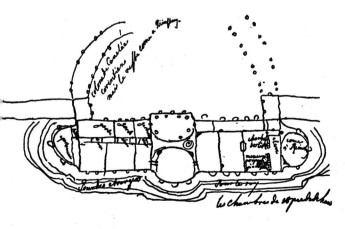

transition to the extensive bosquets. These cover more than half of the 50 hectare garden. They are divided, with perfect regularity, into four squares, each with a star-shaped pattern of paths. An octagonal basin marks the centre of each square, where the radial alleys converge. To link the four bosquet squares, a round basin with an impressive fountain is placed in their midst, along the main axis. Among the features very remarkable is one of Europe's most magnificent and best preserved open-air theatres, dating from 1689-1693, which can accommodate up to 800 spectators. A highlight of the garden is its complex waterworks system, perfected over a long period by ingenious experts, such as the mathematician Leibnitz and others. After the improvements of 1856 the Great Fountain boasted a jet of 67 metres as compared to the original 35 metres of 1720, and the 82 metres of today.

Compositionally, Herrenhausen clearly demonstrates a tectonic division. The upper half is dominated by open, richly articulated planes, while the lower section is less patterned, and mainly filled out with the arboreous masses of the bosquets. This means that the development along the axis is fairly restrained, a feature that indicates Dutch influences, which may be ascribed to Duchess Sophia's links with the Dutch court.

The garden was, like the castle, badly damaged during the last war. It was restored in time for the celebration of its 300th anniversary in 1966, and is splendidly maintained, which is certainly no easy feat, in view of the vast parterres, abundant water features, and 21 kilometres of clipped hedges and alleys, which all require a huge amount of upkeep.

Hortus Palatinus, Palatine Garden, Heidelberg. It was laid out in 1616-1619 for the Palatine Elector Frederick V, from a design by Salomon de Caus, and is certainly Europe's most daringly placed garden, consisting of deep parallel terraces cut in a slope high above the Neckar river. The garden was badly neglected and allowed to grow wild in the 17th and 18th centuries. The well-preserved terraces each displayed their own arrangement of parterres, fountains, pergolas, grottoes and sculptures (p. 297). What is most amazing about these terraces is their strictly geometric, rectangular layout on the abrupt incline, as well as their calculated staggered positioning, offering views of the lower terraces from the higher ones. Preparations for a partial restoration of the garden are in hand at the moment, and some preservation measures have already been carried out. This unique Late Renaissance garden certainly deserves them.

Klein-Glienicke, Berlin. This was originally a small garden created by P. J. Lenné for Prince Hardenberg at the outset of his career, in 1816. When it was acquired by Charles of Prussia, Lenné was commissioned to enlarge the grounds, and Karl Friedrich Schinkel erected, in 1826, the present-day castle, followed by a number of smaller buildings and pavilions, chiefly designed to house the king's art collections. The slightly undulating ground is further enlivened by trees, singly or in clumps, mostly consisting of native species (p. 314). The 116 hectare estate is today a well-frequented public park.

Kromlau, near Bad Muskau. The 110 hectare garden was laid out about 1850. Gradually it has developed into a rich collection of garden trees and shrubs, particularly distinguished for its extensive rhododendron and azalea plantations. From the formal viewpoint it is interesting for its late Romantic features. These are mostly concentrated around the lake, which is surrounded by a thick wall of trees. The atmosphere is heightened by an arched bridge and by numerous stalagmite groups sculptured from basaltic rocks (p. 316).

Muskau. This is a great creation of Prince Pückler-Muskau, and probably Germany's most famous garden in the landscape style. The artist spent no less than thirty years, from 1815 onwards, reshaping the 500 hectare ground along the Neisse river. He skilfully

287

exploited the natural configuration, the gently undulating terrain, the abundance of water and the existing stands of trees. The section on the western bank, closer to the city, is more deliberately formed, especially in connection with the mansion (p. 314). Here the ground slightly slopes towards the valley, a trait Pückler inventively emphasized by a sequence of long open lawns running downward and skirted or dissected by masses of vegetation. He also developed a rich repertory of water motifs, either standing or moving, and delicate, unobtrusive paths, which follow the natural features of the terrain. In spite of his dedication to the natural, he laid out three regular flower gardens in the vicinity of the mansion.

In the last war, the mansion was gutted and the garden allowed to run wild. Gradual restoration of the grounds is in progress, and a reconstruction of the palace is planned. The large section of the garden beyond the Neisse river, today on Polish territory, is also in need of restoration.

Nymphenburg, Munich. This grandiose Baroque design developed out of a hunting lodge erected for Princess Adelaide in 1662. On his return from the Netherlands, Max Emanuel commissioned an extension of the palace, carried out by Zuccalli and Viscardi from 1701 onwards. The architects also added two lateral pavilions connected by gallery wings allowing free passage. This original solution is a more fluent design, linking the front garden with the bulk of the grounds. About at the same time the modest original garden was replaced by a new layout contributed mostly by the Frenchman Carbonet and partly by Zuccalli. It is an extensive Baroque arrangement marked off by canals. Because of the War of the Spanish Succession the works were suspended, to be continued in 1715, when the celebrated fountain master D. Girard was called in. He finished the canals and basins and constructed a vast waterworks system comprising, in addition to the technical installations, some 600 playful water motifs.

The Baroque design of Nymphenburg was gradually perfected in the second half of the 18th century. The result is a mature creation of high formal qualities. The access from the city leads along a canal flanked by a double alley, ending in a large semicircular court surrounded by an array of pavilions and other auxiliary buildings. Together with the extensive water surface marking the main axis, it creates an overwhelming impression, both by its size and its complex structure, in no way inferior to its French models. On the garden side the palace is skirted by a small park composed of a parterre curiously flanked by canals, lateral bosquets and other features, such as a maze, an open-air theatre and a game court. The third division of the complex is based on a long central canal leading up to a giant cascade conceived by Effner and finished by Girard (p. 305). Roughly halfway, the canal is intersected by the transversal axis linking the small pavilions of Pagodenburg and Badeburg.

The fashion for the landscape style did not bypass Nymphenburg, but on the whole the Baroque character of the complex is preserved intact, thanks to Ludwig von Sckell, who introduced landscape concepts, such as the wide clearings with lakes on both sides of the canal, with care. So the 200 hectare garden is a showpiece of German garden art of two stylistic trends.

Pomeranzengarten, Leonberg, 20 kilometres from Stuttgart. The garden was created when the castle was redesigned for Duchess Sybilla, wife of Frederick of Württemberg, in 1609. It was laid out by Heinrich Schickhardt in the Italian manner, as a terraced garden on a slope, with a fine view of the city and its surroundings. The chief component was a two-sectioned parterre composed of simple flowerbeds. The centre was marked by an octagonal fountain enclosed by a colonnade. After 1742, the garden was neglected and

Petri's ground-plan of the Schwetzingen garden. Standing out from the layout is a single circular parterre. The longitudinal axis is indicated by a double alley, which extends the space in depth (top).
Wörlitz Park stands at the very beginning of development of the landscape style in Germany. As usual in the case of such arrangements, the chief role in the total structure is played by the water (bottom).

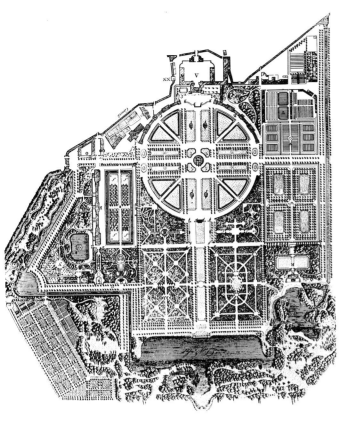

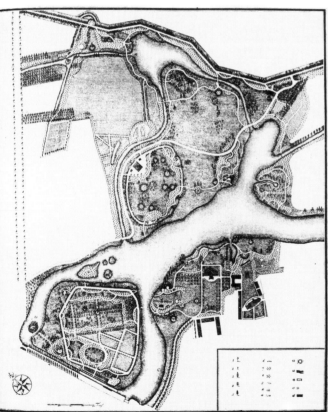

allowed to run to seed, but the original design was not affected by any later alterations. Restoration works, based on careful study of historical sources and archaeological excavations, were carried out in 1974-1980. Today this Orange Garden is an exemplary reconstruction of a historical garden, and a major asset of German landscape-architectural heritage (p. 297).

Sanspareil, near Bayreuth, is another work of Markgravine Wilhelmine, in character even more peculiar than the Eremitage. The core of this "Felsengarten", or rock garden, consists of a large rock grove which is one of the earliest arrangements of the kind on the eve of the coming landscape style on the continent. The garden was first laid out in 1774 and takes its inspiration from the mythological theme of Telemaque's search for his father Odysseus.

Sanssouci, Potsdam. This is a creation of the art-loving king Frederick the Great. He was not inclined to courtly luxury, and the plan of residence is of unusually modest character and proportions. The detailed design and its execution was carried out by the architect Wenzeslaus von Knobelsdorff. In 1745-1747 a garden was laid out on a slope, in the guise of a sequence of six glassed-in fruit-growing terraces (p. 312). The practical, horticultural aspect of this unique complex was mitigated by the showy flights of stairs along the axis of access to the castle and by the eye-catching pyramids of trimmed yew-trees. A symmetrical four-part parterre was arranged in front of the castle. Beneath it a long transversal axis developed in west-east direction is interrupted by roundels and basins and set off by alleys. This axis found its termination in the Neues Palais, built in 1764-1769.

A second important period followed in the 19th century, when Charlottenhof Palace, designed by Schinkel, was built in the southwestern corner of the grounds. Around it P. J. Lenné laid out a garden in the landscape style, with large clearings and deep vistas (p. 311). The most engaging features of this creation are the *Marly Garden*, of a landscape character, and the *Sicilian Garden*, where Lenné fell back onto a rigid geometrical plan.

Schleissheim, Munich (p. 302). The 82 hectare garden adjoining the residence of Max Emanuel, Elector of Bavaria, was given its basic features when the court architect Enrico Zuccalli constructed a garden casino, *Lustheim,* to the east of the old palace in 1684. At the end of the century the garden was surrounded by a moat, which runs out in a semicircle behind the casino. The erection of the new palace, also designed by Zuccalli, reorientated the complex. The building, with its side wings and lateral pavilions, filled the entire space between the bordering canals at the western end. The monumental palace required a suitable parterre which was created by Dominique Girard after 1715. The sunken parterre is of the *boulingrin* type, the French version of the English bowling green. It is framed by alleys, from which the walker glimpses splendid views of the flower patterns and basins. On the threshold between the parterre and Zuccalli's bosquets Girard set up a giant cascade, with an acoustically and visually interesting arch-shaped waterfall. The cascade is fed by the central canal, dug in 1781 and replacing the original alley walk. The canal emphasizes the main axis between the castle and the casino, which is the focal point of the vista. Along a 700-metre section the canal is accompanied by square-shaped bosquets, intersected by paths in eight different directions.

Schleissheim is an unusual Baroque structure. Dominance of flat surfaces and the important role played by canals places it closer to contemporary Dutch models than to French prototypes. What is unique about the design is the extent of the palace, cutting across the entire garden, defining its width, and giving a convincing unity to the whole. The garden was neglected for some time and partly restored in 1825-1848, under the guidance of C. Effner. A more radical and adequate reconstruction was carried out after World War II.

Schwetzingen. This High Baroque creation was commissioned by the Palatine Elector Carl Theodor (p. 306). The arrangement of the garden was started in 1753, from a design by Johann Ludwig Petri and Nikolaus Pigage. The core of the design is a circular parterre hemmed in at the upper end by the two curving buildings, and at the lower end by a bower and a grille with a promenade. To overcome the rigidity of the circular plan, the artists introduced a main and a transverse alley. At the intersection of the two alleys they placed a large circular basin with an Arion Fountain, but this only accentuated the concentric design. The composition was given a dimension of depth when Pigage added an extension running out in a large rectangular basin. To mark the termination of the axis, two river gods were placed on the fringe of the basin together with a group of sculptured stags placed on the periphery of the circle.

At the same time a varied repertory of elements was introduced, such as the open-air theatre, with a Temple of Apollo (Pigage, 1761-1776), the bath and, along its axis, an elliptical trellis decorated with water-spouting birds. The young Ludwig von Sckell, as an exponent of landscape movement, introduced new, exotic or Romantic features, such as a Temple of Mercury, a mosque, a Roman aqueduct, and a Temple of Minerva. In the course of the last decade Schwetzingen has undergone an extensive restoration, exemplary for its faithfulness to the historical style.

Veitshöchheim, 6 kilometres north of Würzburg. This was the summer residence of the Prince Bishop of Würzburg. The castle, dating from the 17th century, was extended in the 18th century and is located in the northwestern corner of the grounds, in the centre of a square-shaped parterre. The main garden consists of a rectangle extending from north to south made up of three main sections running in the same direction. The eastern section, which covers one half of the area, culminates in the most impressive feature of the garden, a semicircular basin called the Great Lake (p. 309), with a Parnassus Group dominated by the figure of Pegasus. The iconography is inspired by one of the *Metamorphoses* by Ovid according to which, after the Deluge, the mythical mountain Parnassus will rise from the sea anticipating the return of the Golden Age. As the group was built around the 1763, this could be explained as a metaphor of the end of the Seven Years War.

From the Great Lake the transverse axis proceeds westwards, where the second section is centred on a circular motif. This is surrounded by limes and by trimmed hedges, whose niches house 32 statues and stone benches. The axis ends in a giant cascade. From the formal viewpoint the garden is characterized by its high clipped hedges which divide it into numerous independent compartments. Each of these is orchestrated by its own set of sculptures, which total 300, with themes ranging from Greek mythology to musicians, dancers and exotic figures. The design does not aim at Baroque grandeur, but rather stresses Rococo voluptuousness and playfulness.

Wilhelmshöhe, Kassel (p. 300–301). The initiative for this curious 250 hectare-large complex was given by the landgrave Charles of Hessen, inspired by his travel to Italy in 1699-1700. The plans were prepared by the Italian Giovanni Francesco Guerniero from 1701 onwards. The original concept was one of the most grandiose ever contemplated. The palace was to be linked with a hilltop, 2 kilometres away and 283 metres higher, by a magnificent cascade complemented by a varied programme of secondary features. Only the upper section, about a third of the original design, was carried out. But this, in itself, is one of the most staggering complexes of landscape architecture in existence. The

An illustration from Ludwig von Sckell's book *Beiträge zur bildenden Gartenkunst* from 1819 demonstrating his composition technique (top).
Pückler-Muskau explained his design technique in detail in his book *Andeutungen über die Landschaftsgärtnerei* (1834). The sketches in the book illustrate the design approaches that mark his personal style. The sketch explains the creation of three-dimensional composition by appropriately placed clumps of trees (bottom).

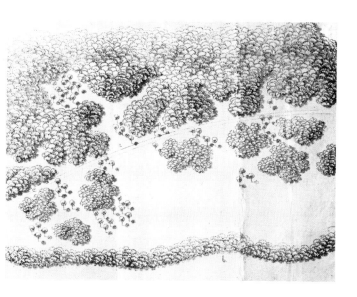

arrangement starts from the top of Karlsberg Hill, with the Octagon, a Colossus Castle, and continues downhill in a flight of stairs, 11 metres wide by almost 250 metres long, interrupted by transverse terraces and basins. The thematic guideline of the complex is the Gigantomachy, or Battle of the Giants, who stormed Mount Olympus, but were defeated by Hercules, whose 9 metre statue is placed on a 30 metre pyramidal pedestal above the Octagon. Beneath, on one of the terraces, the recumbent head of one of the defeated giants is wedged in a stone block, spouting a jet of water in impotent rage. Further mythological motifs follow all along the stairs, ending with the Neptune Grotto, across which the water cascades into the Neptune Basin. The basaltic tufa of Hessen, used in the construction, is rather sensitive to weathering. This was, together with the technical difficulties of construction on a precipitous grade, one of the reasons why the works were suspended in 1718. Only at the end of the 18th century were the operations resumed, when Wilhelm I had several elements in the new landscape style added to the complex. They include temples, a huge "ruined" aqueduct, a Chinese village, temples and a Devil's Bridge. Today the 250 hectare park offers an interesting juxtaposition of the creations of two contrasting epochs.

Wörlitz, near Dessau, is a 120 hectare-large area of a complex structure and mixed character. Parkland, woodland, extensive agricultural land and many waters, merge into the first landscape park in the country, arranged in the second part of the 19th century and admired by many visitors, especially by Goethe. It is a work by Prince of Anhalt-Dessau and his gardeners, mainly J. F. Eyserbeck. The grounds are subdivided into five individual sections with various features. These are organized around three lakes with attractive and sometimes far-reaching vistas of various motifs, such as the Gothic House, the Temple of Venus, the Pantheon, the classicist palace, the '*Stein*' (Rock) with the Villa Hamilton. Among several islands, the Isle of Rousseau stands out, almost identical with the original structure at Ermenonville (p. 313). The walks and sightseeing are made possible by numerous, sometimes originally designed bridges, among the most remarkable the Golden Bridge and the Chain Bridge.

Zwinger, Dresden. Within a large complex of palatial buildings, the Zwinger was conceived as an orangery, with several supplementary functions. In addition to the housing of King Augustus's beloved orange trees, it doubled as festival hall, theatre and baths. Matthäus Pöppelmann laid out a large gallery-enclosed court, featuring a garden parterre, several basins and a huge Nymphaeum (p. 308). The parterre was renovated in 1924-1936, and again after the last war, during which it had been razed together with the building. The reconstruction follows Pöppelmann's design.

The garden art of the German-speaking countries shows a balanced historical development unmatched elsewhere in Europe. Though the Renaissance was introduced later than in other European countries, this was more than made up for in the age of Baroque, Germany's most glamorous period in the development of the garden art. In the 18th and 19th centuries an original version of the landscape style was developed, pioneering projects for rural landscape preservation and for the introduction of public green into modern cities. A consequence of this development is the preserved legacy of garden art, mostly splendidly maintained.

p.293
Upper section of the water parterre at Hellbrunn near Salzburg. Behind the basins there is the Roman theatre, with the statue of a Roman emperor in the central niche and two vanquished barbarian chieftains in the side niches. Above the emperor is a figure of *Roma victrix* (Victorious Rome). Everything is mirrored in the clear water, whose quality and abundance certainly gave rise to the garden on this site.

p.294
Vienna's Belvedere, viewed from the terrace fronting the Upper Palace. In the background of the picture, the Lower Belvedere blocks the garden along its entire width. In the foreground is the upper, somewhat sunk parterre, which was originally composed of embroidery patterns (top). Sculptural iconography at Belvedere serves one single purpose - to glorify the victories of the owner, Prince Eugen of Savoy (bottom).

p.295
Characteristic of Schönbrunn are the vistas bordered by high trimmed walls, accentuated by single motifs, such as obelisks or sculptures (top). A long trellis flanks the palace Schönbrunn (centre). Parterre of the Schönbrunn Gardens, Vienna. The optical conclusion of the parterre is formed by the big Neptune Fountain, situated on the axis. Above it looms the silhouette of the Gloriette, which efficiently closes the total composition (bottom).

p.296
Laxenburg: the Diana Temple built by Empress Maria Theresa in 1755 (top, right) and the Concordia Temple, erected in 1795 (top, left). Garden parterre to Mirabell Palace in Salzburg is a present-day re-creation, not an adequate substitute for the original *parterre de broderie* (bottom).

p.297
A successful restoration of the Renaissance garden (Pomeranzengarten) at Leonberg near Stuttgart (top). Very little survives of the once magnificent Hortus Palatinus at Heidelberg: a fountain with the figure of Rhine (bottom).

p.298
Augustusburg at Brühl: a stylistically pure Baroque parterre (top). Parterre of Charlottenburg in Berlin (bottom).

p.299
Stille Musik (top) and the flat, modestly elaborated parterre at Gross Sedlitz, near Dresden (bottom).

p.300
Wilhelmshöhe. The Octagon, with the Pyramid, dominates the nearer and farther space of the garden (top, left). The figure of Hercules surmounting the Octagon, commands the whole area and is visible even from the long distance (bottom left). The Grand Cascade ends in the Neptune Basin (bottom, right). Later addition from the Romantic period, the Temple of Jussow (top, right).

p.301
Wilhelmshöhe. An entirely different, highly picturesque image is offered by the view from the Pyramid to the Cascade, with its basins and terraces. The monumental design is without peer in European garden art.

p.302
Schleissheim. View from the New Palace along the axis. In the foreground is a sunk parterre whose spatial conclusion is underlined by the palace, the side alleys and the frontal walls of the bosquets. Along the axis of the garden there is a broad canal flanked by strips of lawn replacing the double alley in this section. The termination of the vista and its climax is formed by the "Lustheim" in the background of the illustration (top). Old Palace with the parterre filling in the distance to the New Palace (bottom).

p.303
Statues and *palissade a l'italienne* of pleached limes are framing the parterre at Herrenhausen (top). The main parterre with the basin (bottom). The open-air theatre uses false perspective as a device to enhance the effect of depth (bottom).

p.304
Monopteros on Lake Badenburg in Sckell's picturesque part of Nymphenburg (bottom). Monopteros in the Englischer Garten, another work by Sckell, also in Munich (top).

p.305
The formal parterre at Nymphenburg (top). In continuation of the main axis, the canal terminates in the great cascade as a *point de vue*, with statues of river gods and various mythological figures (bottom).

p.306
Schwetzingen's most original motif is the elliptical trellis with singing birds. At the far end of the scene is seen a sunlit *trompe-l'oeil* landscape, the "End of the World" (top). A section of the unique circular berceaux surrounding the main parterre (bottom).

p.307
Three motifs from the picturesque part of Schwetzingen: the Turkish Mosque (top, left); the Temple of Apollo, placed above the grotto (centre); the lake with the Temple of Mercury (right). A part of the circular parterre, meticulously restored in 1974 to match the original Petri layout (bottom).

p.308
A large nymphaeum, surmounted by a terrace at the Zwinger, Dresden (top). The grass parterre of the Zwinger (bottom).

p.309
All over the garden, Veitshöchheim boasts Rococo statuary by the sculptor Ferdinand Tietz, like the Pegasus dominating the lake (top). A garden pavilion at Veitshöchheim (bottom).

p.310
A large basin fronts the semicircular New Palace at the Eremitage, Bayreuth (top). In the lower garden is situated an interesting grotto with numerous figures and water jets (bottom).

p.311
Schloss Charlottenhof, a work of Karl Friedrich Schinkel, in an impressive landscape setting, designed by P. J. Lenné (top). An intimate atmosphere around the pavilion at Sanspareil, near Bayreuth (bottom).

p.312
Terraced vineyards form a Royal Garden at Sanssouci, Potsdam (top). The Orangery belonging to Sanssouci (centre). An elegant wrought-iron trellis stands at the entrance to Sanssouci gardens (bottom).

p.313
The first great landscape garden in Germany, Wörlitz, features many interesting components. The Rousseau Island at the entrance, a replica of the one at Ermenonville (right). The garden façade of the Gothic House (top). The Golden Bridge, one of the peculiar structures of this kind at Wörlitz (middle). A view from the Hamilton Ruin (bottom).

p.314
Lenné's small work at Klein-Glienicke, Berlin (top). A scene from Muskau, one of the two landscape gardens made by Prince Hermann von Pückler-Muskau (bottom). It is an eloquent demonstration of his composition technique, shown in the sketch from his book on the page 291.

p.315
The swan-song of Pückler-Muskau was the park at Branitz, here he was buried together with his wife in the pyramid on the lake.

p.316
Neo-Romantic elements, the arch and stalagmite-shaped rocks, provide for an unusual mood in Kromlau.

314

The Low Countries and Scandinavia

Netherlands
Beeckestijn - Het Loo
Middachten - Rosendael
Twickel - Weldam
Zeist

Belgium
Annevoie - Beloeil
Freyr - Rubens's House

Sweden
Drottningholm - Haga

Denmark
Fredensborg - Frederiksberg
Frederiksborg

In spite of their geographic, social, political and cultural differences, the small countries stretching along the Northern Atlantic show certain common features in their garden art. They all have introduced the landscape style from England, sweeping away, especially in the Netherlands and Scandinavia, almost all the creations of Renaissance and Baroque.

Netherlands

In the Netherlands, as in the rest of Europe, both burghers and nobles have surrounded their residences with gardens since the Middle Ages. A detailed description is given by the Dutch humanist Erasmus of Rotterdam in his *Convivium Religiosum* (1518), which lists features like the flower garden, the garden fountain, the arboretum, the bower and the game court.

The 16th century was to a large extent preoccupied with the war against Spain. Therefore the influences of Italian Renaissance infiltrated the country with some delay. The progress can be followed in the copper etchings of Vredeman de Vries, whose famous collection *Hortorum Viridariorumque elegantes et multiplicis formae* (1583) depicts either existing or prototype gardens. They are still clearly middle-class, of smaller size, surrounded by green bowers or alleys and intersected by hedges or arbours.

Their features are comparatively modest, flowerbeds or a simple parterre, a central tree, a smaller pavilion or fountain. Even earlier portrayals, for example in Brueghel's paintings, illustrate the developed state of horticulture, or rather, the art of plant cultivation, which often outstrips formal design. This was probably the reason why Dutch gardeners were in such demand all over Europe. An indication of the general interest in plants is the foundation of the famous botanical garden of Leiden, one of Europe's first. The introduction of tulips and other bulbs has not just marked their dominance in the composition of gardens, but converted flower growing into a national passion. The resulting excesses of tulipomania led to financial speculations with sensational new varieties that often shook the national economy. The obsession was soon over, but the plants themselves and the art of flower growing survived, and have continued to exert a more or less decisive influence on garden design ever since.

When the Netherlands gained independence in 1648, there was a period of economic boom based on navigation and trade with the Far East. General welfare was the hallmark of Holland's Golden Age, when architecture and art rose to extraordinary heights. For a long time the country remained a republic, and because of the democratic tendencies prevailing on the cities and provinces the rulers never had the absolute power secured by the kings of France and other European monarchs. Yet the new-fledged world power still needed a suitable array of representative buildings and gardens. The initiator of this building flurry was the highly cultivated and educated *stadhouder* Frederik Hendrik. In 1633 he invited André Mollet to design the garden adjoining his Honselaersdijk Palace, where the country's first Baroque parterre was laid out. The statues for the garden were imported from France. Frederik Hendrik also established two other gardens, Nieuwburg and the celebrated Huis ten Bosch, near The Hague.

This development of Dutch garden art reached its high-water mark in the age of Willem III, later to become King William of England. The garden of his residence at Het Loo, created about 1690, already shows certain formal features first developed by Le Nôtre in France. The king's trusted ambassador to France was Bentinck, Duke of

Heemstede belongs among the great Dutch gardens of the late 17th century. In addition to the emphasized axial design and the detailed structure of the parterre, the most striking feature is the role played by the two side strips, with numerous beds of plants. Particularly characteristic is the perfect integration of the garden within the rectangular pattern of its wider surroundings (top).
One of the famous gardens on the Vecht river. Characteristically, they present their best aspects to the river, so they could be admired from the passing boats. They served at the same time as summer residences and as status symbols (bottom).
Het Loo, residence of Willem III of Orange, is a creation evidently modelled on the great examples of French Baroque (opposite page).

An engraving by Vredeman de Vries depicting a 16th-century Dutch garden of an impressively rich structure (from his Hortorum Viridariorumque elegantes et multiplicis formae, *1583).*

Portland, who established direct contact with Le Nôtre and probably influenced the design of this garden, otherwise ascribed to Daniel Marot. The castle and its surroundings form a harmonious whole, while the garden sports motifs such as basins with large statue groups, a profusion of single statues and vases. Marot presumably also collaborated in the layout of Heemstede garden near Utrecht, property of the statesman Van Veldhuysen. It was established after 1680 and shows a large-scale design, harmoniously set into the rectangular network of fields, plantations, canals and roads that typically make up the Dutch landscape.

A peculiar feature of the period are the country villas with gardens laid out by rich burghers or the lower nobility. They were called *buitenplaatsen* and were particularly famous along the Vecht, Amstel and Vliet rivers. They were lined up on the river banks, rather like the houses along the canals of Amsterdam, and displayed the wealth of the owners by opening towards the river, so the parterres, fountains and clipped figures could be admired by any traveller. While the Baroque appeared simultaneously with developments in France, the landscape movement only swept the Netherlands in the late 18th century, but then it ruthlessly overran all other traditions. The regular gardens of the earlier periods were either left to decay or more often reshaped in the modern English fashion. But there were no convincing achievements, in spite of the endeavours of J. G. Michael and J. D. Zocher, landscape designers of German origin, active in the second half of the 19th century.

Today's heritage of Dutch garden art is to a great extent marked by the initiatives in the late 19th century to restore the famous gardens of the 17th and 18th centuries. The outstanding figure of this movement was the landscape architect Hugo Poortman, who was trained in France, and more or less successfully recreated Middachten, Weldam and Zeist.

Beeckestijn, near Velsen. This 16th century estate was given a regular design in the 18th and 19th centuries, and sections in the early landscape style later added. Since the last war both the house and the garden have been restored. There are a number of interesting features such as the informal and geometrical sectors, as well as a herbal garden bordered by the characteristic serpentine wall (p. 328).

Het Loo, near Apeldoorn. The celebrated garden of the Dutch royal family was laid out for the *stadhouder* Willem III of Orange. On his accession to the English throne both palace and garden were considerably enlarged (1692 and later), probably from a design by D. Marot. The basic layout is axial, with several transverse axes. The most splendid feature was the so-called Lower Garden adjoining the palace and composed of eight parterres, four of them being *parterres de broiderie,* with three large basins. Along the parterres there were further sections with semicircular terminations. All these sections were more or less separated by alleys, hedges or walls, which reflect earlier Dutch traditions. In the second half of the 18th century both castle and garden were sadly neglected, and Louis Bonaparte had the garden covered with sand and rearranged in the landscape style. After several years of preliminary studies the Dutch government began restoring the castle and garden in 1978, on the basis of the surviving remains. It is one of the most comprehensive and most carefully studied reconstructions of a historical garden ever attempted (p. 330).

Middachten, near Dieren. In the first half of the 18th century a Baroque garden was laid out to set off the castle's picturesque waterside location. The longitudinal axis, with a single long parterre, was flanked by a number of sections consisting of rectangular tree plantations and by two large mazes. Later on the regular design was abandoned, to be partly restored in 1900, from a plan by H. Poortman.

Rosendael, in the city of Rozendaal. The garden was already in existence in the 14th century. At the end of the 17th century, features were introduced, such as rocaille grottoes, fountains and the well-known Tea Cupola. In the 19th century Zocher and Petzold reshaped the garden in the landscape style. In the 1970s the rocaille gallery and the Tea Cupola were restored.

Twickel, near Delden. The first residence was erected on this site in 1551. An engraving by Marot shows the regular arrangement of the gardens. In the 19th century Zocher, succeeded by Petzold, set out to redesign the park in the landscape style. In the heyday of the return to pre-Romanticism, at the turn of the century, Poortman reintroduced a regular plan, supposed to be truer to the traditional Dutch spirit (p. 325).

Weldam, near Goor. In the mid 18th century there was a regular garden in front of the castle. Today's arrangement, with parterres, a maze, a long arbour walk and other geometric elements, surrounds the moated castle on all four sides (p. 326). It has been laid out since 1886, from designs by Poortman and Weaterley, and represents an attempt to revive the native traditions of gardening.

Zeist. One of the large-scale gardens of the reign of Willem III, it was laid out in the late 17th century from a design by D. Marot. The garden was surrounded by a wide canal. Along the main axis centered on the castle there was a succession of parterres with semicircular terminations, and then a sequence of rectangular bosquets. Zeist shared the fate of Holland's other regular gardens and was "anglicized" in the 19th century, remaining in that state since.

Belgium

The complex ethnic and cultural structure of Belgium is also reflected in her garden art. In the Flemish region an ancient horticultural tradition survives, particularly in the surroundings of Ghent and Antwerp, rather along the same lines as in the gardening centres of neighbouring Holland. Indeed, the seafaring and merchant towns of Flanders, such as Antwerp, Bruges and Ghent, were the focal points of the Flemish Renaissance. Later development has, as in the Netherlands, modified the original Renaissance and Baroque designs. Therefore this region can today only boast a few reconstructed gardens from those periods, such as the garden of Rubens's house in Antwerp.

The southern region of the country, on the other hand, shows the overwhelming influence of French Baroque, represented in a number of notable garden designs. They were usually carried out on the estates of noble families, which has assured their continued survival to the present day. The Walloon part of the country has evidently, like France, remained faithful to the Baroque style as a matter of national principle. It is probably to this nationalist spirit that we owe the great number of gardens more or less preserved in the spirit of their original design, such as Beloeil, Annevoi and Freyr.

Annevoie, near Namen. The basic design of the garden was laid down by Charles-Alexis de Montpellier, whose family had owned the garden since the 16th century. The plan is symmetrical and pronouncedly longitudinal. The smaller parterre elements and the framework of clipped hedges are arranged along an axis that is not linked to the palace. The peculiar feature of Annevoi is its abundance of springs that feed (both in summer and winter) a great number of fountains, of which the most famous is the *Buffet d'eau*. The parterre and other parts of the garden are dotted with statues, some of them made of cast iron, examples of the local ironworks tradition.

Beloeil, south of Brussels. The 120 hectare estate of the princes of Ligne dates from the 12th century. The garden is first mentioned in 1519. The chief Baroque features

J.G. Michael's design of Beeckestijn. With its blend of rectilinear geometric elements and free-flowing wavy features, the layout recalls examples from the early period of the English landscape style, such as Pope's Twickenham or Lord Burlington's Chiswick.

were introduced in the mid 18th century by Prince Lamoral II, on the advice of the French architect Chevotet. After 1775 a small section in a landscape style, including an Island of Flora, was added south of the castle. The main garden is situated to the north of the palace to which it is symmetrically placed. The focal point is a large lake (440 by 130 metres), of rectangular shape, but with an oval extension emphasized by the Neptune group (p. 332). Along both sides of the lake the sections of the garden are arranged lengthwise, defined by clipped hedges, the Boulingrin, the Ladies Basin, the Cloister, the large Quincunx and the Mirror Canal. The most salient feature of Beloeil is its composition based on the central axis formed by the extensive *parterre d'eau*.

Freyr, near Waulsort. This 14th century estate passed into the hands of the dukes of Beaufort in 1410. A Renaissance garden is documented in the first half of the 18th century. It was enlarged and given its present Baroque character in 1760. It is situated along the bank of the Maas and shows a pronounced bipartite structure. The first part, parallel with the river, is defined by the axis passing through the *cour d'honneur*, bisecting the castle, continuing through the parterre, and ending in two orangeries. The parterre is divided into sections marked off by pools and trimmed rectangles (p. 331). The lower sector boasts a plantation of 300-year-old orange trees. The lateral axis, which runs at right angles to the river and bisects the parterre, is flanked with large trimmed bosquets shaped like the chief symbols of playing-cards.

Garden of Rubens's House, Antwerp. This is a fairly authentic reconstruction based on the famous painting *The Artist, Hélène Fourment and his son Nicholas walking in the Garden* (in the Alte Pinakothek, Munich), where the painter portrayed himself with his family. Both the house and the garden had been designed after Rubens's return from Italy at the beginning of the 17th century, and show traces of inspirations picked up during the grand tour. The garden is situated in the city centre, and is therefore of small size. The parterre is composed of four independent sections marked off by trimmed hedges (p. 331). Both the entrance and the exit are set off by low wooden gates. The scene is dominated by a smaller pavilion with statues of Hercules, Venus and Bacchus. An example of inventive reconstruction is the pergola made up of arch-shaped curved slats. Though the garden was faithfully reconstructed, the flower arrangements seem somewhat gaudy and obtrusive.

Sweden

In a comparatively short time Sweden caught up with European development trends, mainly owing to the influence of French masters. As early as 1637 Simon de la Vallée came from the Netherlands, where he had been employed by the court. He laid out a few regular arrangements, with alleys, canals and parterres, such as Ekolsund. An even more prominent figure was André Mollet, who worked in Stockholm from 1646. He transmitted French fashions in court garden design, and introduced elements like *parterre de broderie,* axial layout, and fusion of palace and garden, exemplified in the Royal Garden near St. James's Church, the Kungsträdgården, and Jakobsdahl. On the occasion of her coronation in 1650, Mollet dedicated to Queen Christina his famous book *Jardin de Plaisir,* which is a precious compendium of the landscape architecture of this period. As elsewhere in Europe, further development followed the fashions of the court, where the most successful designers were Nicodemus Tessin the Elder and his son. They created both the palace and the Baroque gardens of Drottningholm. The latter are chiefly attributed to Tessin the Younger, who had been educated in France. Towards the end of the century another important name emerged, that of Johan Hårleman, a royal gardener, who collaborated with the younger Tessin at Drottningholm.

The swing towards landscape style also set in fairly soon in Sweden. About 1746, Carl Hårleman, son of Johan, produced designs for the rearrangement of Ulriksdal, and the layout of a new park, Stola, in the landscape style. In 1753 the court architect Carl Frederik Adelkrantz constructed the Chinese Pavilion at Drottningholm, the harbinger of a new concept inspired by Chambers' Chinese elements in London's Kew Gardens. Adelcrantz's particular merit was his championship of Frederik Magnus Piper (1746-1824), who was granted a royal scholarship to study in Italy and England. Piper's legacy are two first-rate creations, the landscape section of Drottningholm, and Haga, as well as numerous studies and plans, which have earned him the first place among Scandinavian landscape architects.

Drottningholm, near Stockholm (p. 333). The garden sets off the palace built for Queen Hedvig Eleonora. The original design was produced by Nicodemus Tessin the Elder in 1662, but the design of 1680 is due to his son, and a further decisive stamp was contributed by Johan Hårleman in the 1690s. The castle is erected on a raised terrace reached by a magnificent staircase, whose axis extends into the parterre. The chief landmark of the parterre is the Hercules Fountain. This is followed by a sequence of 8 basins forming a kind of *parterre d'eau*. Drottningholm's second great age dawned in the late 18th century, when F. M. Piper, on the initiative of Queen Louise Ulrika, laid out a substantial sector of the park in the English style. He also proposed a design for the rearrangement of the Baroque parterres, but this proposal was vetoed by King Gustav, who had taken a fancy to classicism during his travels in Italy. In the western part of the garden, Piper was given a free hand to lay out a large-scale landscape with several lakes and (one of his most original ideas) an island first conceived as Diana's Isle. After the King's death, the architect converted it into a circular Memorial Hill surmounted by a monumental granite pedestal. The islet is the focal point for 36 radially arranged alleys combined into 4 strands (p. 13).

Haga, Stockholm. This is Piper's second masterpiece, and Scandinavia's foremost example of the landscape style. It was laid out for Gustav III from 1780 onwards. The central motif, still perfectly preserved, is the Great Clearing, a slightly undulating, oblong tract of lawn. It is fringed by architectural items like the Gustav III pavilion and a set of exotic copper tents. In the immediate vicinity Piper also included in his layout an extensive wilderness rockery, a tribute to the Romantic taste of the end of the 18th century. Its most original feature is the confrontation of pristine nature with artificial elements inspired by the restoration work since 1977.

Sweden also preserves a number of other interesting gardens whose original design is less perfectly preserved. They include *Sandemar*, a formal garden from the early 18th century, with extensive trimmed elements and whitewashed wooden sculptures emphasizing the main axis leading towards a lake; *Sturefors*, in Ostergotland, and two outstanding landscape gardens, *Stola*, in Västergotland, and *Forsmarks*, in Uppland.

Denmark

The rise of Danish garden art to European level is due to King Frederik IV (1671-1730), who had, as a prince, visited the countries of gardening fame, chiefly Italy and France. At first he devoted his attention to the royal garden of Frederiksberg, in Copenhagen, for which he had the first plans drawn by the younger Tessin. Later on Hans Scheel, a military engineer, produced a more complex and playful design.

In Sweden, too, the palaces were sometimes erected close to the shore, with an emphatic access through the garden, as exemplified by Sandemar in the late 17th century (top).

Frederiksborg is one of the most original Baroque solutions. Krieger faced the difficult task of creating a Baroque layout on a slope, linking it with the fortified Renaissance castle on the island, and bridging the intervening water surface. The link is well established: when looking from the castle towards the garden on the opposite shore, the dominating axis is marked first by a small parterre on the water, then by the fountain, finally by the terraced cascade. In the opposite direction, integration is achieved mainly by the high jet of the fountain (bottom).

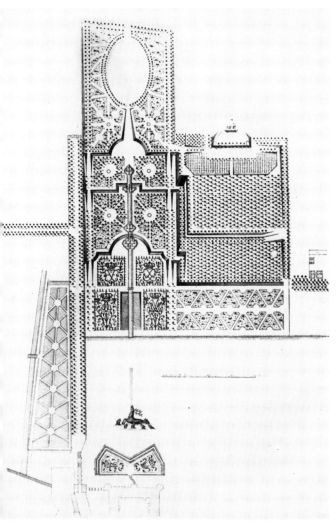

Finally Johan Cornelius Krieger (1683-1755), Denmark's foremost landscape architect, made his appearance. He gave the final touch to Frederiksberg by emphasizing the original layout by a bulky terrace structure fronting the castle. His next masterpiece was Fredensborg, designed to commemorate the peace between Sweden and Denmark, which was finished in 1720. The ultimate achievement of Krieger was Frederiksborg, where he orientated a Baroque garden design across a lake towards the Renaissance castle.

The breakthrough of the landscape movement, which swept the small northern countries with particular violence, was rather ruthless towards the products of the short bloom of Danish Baroque. It reshaped both Fredensborg and Frederiksborg. In the latter park the fashion for Chinese elements, such as pavilions, bridges and pagodas, very much in the spirit of William Chambers, was introduced in this period. An echo of Romantic trends is Liselund on the Island of Møn, established in the late 18th century, with a picturesque stream, lakes, waterfalls, and cottages in various national styles.

Fredensborg, near Copenhagen. This was originally a hunting park. About 1720 Krieger gave it a regular design with prominent alleys. The central alley extends, on the opposite side of the castle, into a large avenue accentuated by rows of statues on pedestals leading towards the lake (p. 334). In 1760 and later, N. H. Jardin introduced extensive changes, such as a Marble Garden with numerous sculptures.

Frederiksberg, Copenhagen. The original arrangement dates from the turn of the 17th and 18th centuries. The first project was prepared by Tessin the Younger, at the request of Frederik IV. Later designs were produced by Scheel and, finally, Krieger. It was Krieger who introduced the terrace layout centred on the castle which is still in evidence today, though overgrown with grass. In 1799 the park was redesigned in the landscape style, which meant the introduction of extensive clearings fringed with clumps of trees and interesting architectural objects. These included an Ionic Temple set against a backdrop of trees, a remarkable Chinese Bridge (p. 336) and a Chinese Tea Pavilion.

Frederiksborg, at Hillerød near Copenhagen. This is the most original production of Danish landscape architecture. Krieger laid out a daring Baroque scheme on a slope facing the castle, which is situated on an island. The lakeside castle and the garden are linked by an axis: the view ranges over a succession of cascades and rests on a large oval-shaped basin. The 400 by 100 metre rectangle is dissected into four terraces with parterres and bosquets. The composition is bordered lengthwise by mighty walls of trimmed lime trees emphasizing the terraced structure of the slope (p. 335). Viewed from the upper floors of the castle, the total effect of the arrangement is that of a sumptuous stage set.

p.325
Twickel, a characteristic Dutch moated castle. Access is, as usual, only possible from one side, originally protected by a drawbridge. The wide moat was an efficient means of defence. Later on, as fire-arms undermined the importance of walls and ditches, the water was retained merely as an interesting historical component of the garden composition.

p.326
Weldam is another attempt at a return to the native Dutch tradition of regular garden design. It was arranged in 1886, after a design by H. Poortman, who also restored Twickel and Middachten. In the foreground is seen a part of the maze of trimmed *arbor vitae*.

p.327
A part of Twickel Garden, restored at the end of the last century. The numerous trimmed shapes and potted plants recall the traditional gardening skill of the Dutch (left). A *buitenplaats*, "outside place", located in the countryside, used to be a popular form of *villa suburbana* in 17th-century Netherlands (right).

p.328
One of the few original features surviving in the Rosendael garden (top). A crinkle-crankle, or serpentine wall, delimits the herbal garden at Beeckestijn. It was originally intended to provide sheltered sites for growing less hardy fruit trees (bottom).

p.329
Large courtyard of the Frans Hals Museum, restored in the 17th-century style of the Dutch Renaissance.

p.330
The restoration of the Royal Gardens of Het Loo at Apeldoorn was carefully studied using the historical data and was then meticulously carried out. The Great Garden with the Royal Palace in the background (top). The Queen's Garden on the upper level is featured by box parterre, clipped trees and intricate wooden trellis (bottom).

p.331
The main axis of the garden at Freyr runs in the same direction as the river Meuse. In the background four quincunx formations surround the round basin, dating from the Renaissance period. Beyond, the roofs of the two orangeries can be seen (top). A detail from the garden to the House of Peter Paul Rubens in Antwerp: a section of the parterre with the garden pavilion in the background, dominated by the statue of Hercules. The restoration has chiefly followed the painter's own depictions of the garden, which was clearly inspired by his travels in Italy. However, the abundant and colourful planting in the parterre is alien to the historical nature of the garden (bottom).

p.332
Beloeil, Hainault, is the most brilliant creation of Baroque garden art in Belgium. It is distinguished by its varied repertory of formal components and its abundance of water. Its structure is unique, insofar as the axis is formed by a water parterre that covers almost 6 hectares and is skirted on both sides by regular clipped palisades of lime trees (top). The bottom illustration shows the Ladies' Basin, circled by a walk marked by skilfully clipped beech-trees imitating pillars and arches.

p.333
Parterre of the Baroque garden adjoining the royal palace of Drottningholm near Stockholm. In the centre of the illustration, the basins are combining into an eight-part water parterre (top). Fredrik Magnus Piper's extensions to the Drottningholm gardens in the picturesque style match the formal qualities of the Baroque layout. Also, they reveal his skilful manipulation of land and tree masses as well as an ability to deal with a large-scale layout (bottom).

p.334
Fredensborg was established as a memorial to the Dano-Swedish peace treaty of 1720. The illustration shows the remains of the one-time Baroque main alley, viewed towards the palace.

p.335
Among the triad of splendid gardens of Frederick IV, Frederiksborg at Hillerød is the most original, and at the same time the only one that has preserved its historical authenticity. The concept of axial structure is here realized under difficult conditions, on sloping terrain, with the garden and the palace separated by a lake. Yet Krieger has developed a sequence of highly interesting views, not only from the palace, but also in the opposite direction. Top illustration: view from the oval basin and, in the centre, from the lower terrace. The bottom illustration shows green walls of clipped lime-trees hemming in a terraced garden.

p.336
The Chinese Bridge, with a pagoda-like roof, leads to an island with another Chinese attraction, the Tea Pavilion, both at Frederiksberg, Copenhagen.

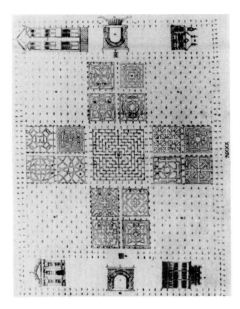

The Slav Countries
Diversity of cultures, unity of styles

Czechoslovakia
Hradčani, King's Garden
Wallenstein Garden - Vrtba Garden
Kroměříž - Buchlovice
Lednice - Milotice
Pruhonice

Croatia
Sorkočević Gardens - Maksimir

Slovenia
Dornava

Poland
Pieskowa Skała - Wilanów
Arkadia - Nieborów
Łazienki

Russia
Summer Garden - Petrodvorets
Oranienbaum -Tsarskoe Selo
Pavlovsk - Gatchina
Kuskovo - Arkhangelskoe

Ukraine
Alexandria - Sofievka
Trostyanetski Park

The social, political and cultural development of the Slav countries was far more prone to violent upheavals and shifting influences than that of the Romance or Germanic countries. But the trends of gardening art that held sway in Europe also influenced the Slavs, sometimes instantly, sometimes with a certain delay. Pronounced regional traits developed in some instances. But the stormy history of Eastern Europe, especially in recent times, has also devastated a great part of her gardening heritage. What is more, even the existing stock of historic gardens has not been sufficiently studied and appreciated, for there are practically no full-length treatises on the subject, and even fewer comprehensive surveys of the various national heritages. This is an urgent task that should no longer be delayed, since it is the precondition for efficient protection and restoration.

Czechoslovakia

Bohemia, wedged in between the Western countries, has since early times been susceptible to the cultural trends of Europe. The first links were established in the 9th century, and in the late 13th and early 14th centuries, during the reign of Charles IV, her Gothic architecture was the wonder of Europe. The first description of a garden goes back to 1130, and refers to a plot of ground donated by Prince Soběslav to the monks of Vyšegrad for meditation and recreation. The oldest, partly preserved garden is about a century younger. It adjoins the Bishop's Palace in the ancient suburb of Malá Strana, Prague, and dates from 1248.

In the 14th century a garden was laid out in Prague for King Charles IV. The King's Garden near Prague Castle achieved considerable fame in the 16th century, and survives to our own time, though in a rather changed condition. Its most celebrated detail was the singing fountain created by the Italian artist Francesco Terzio (p. 350). The Italianate fashion for terraced gardens suited the hilly terrain of Prague, and a number of Renaissance complexes grew around the city's noble palaces. Most of them were reshaped in the Baroque style after the Thirty Years War.

After Gothic, Baroque was the most glorious period of Bohemian art. At first Italian masters were preferred. Therefore the gardens of the 17th century retain certain Renaissance characteristics, especially the sectioned parterres. These are very much in evidence in the two best-known Baroque creations, the Wallenstein Garden and Kroměříž. The same applies to the Baroque gardens crowding around the splendid palaces of Prague's Hradčany and Malá Strana quarters. They were mostly residences of noble families such as Lobkovicz, Schönborn, Černin, Ledebour, Palfy, Fürstenberg, Kolovrat and Vrtba. Most of them preserve important details from the period, such as stairways, terraces and fountains, and partial reconstruction of the gardens might be feasible. Unfortunately, some of the finest palaces have been converted into embassies and are inaccessible to the general public. The most outstanding of Prague's Baroque gardens is Troja, laid out in 1650.

Surprisingly, the greatest number of large and well-preserved Baroque gardens can be found in Moravia. The crowning achievement is Kroměříž, setting off the magnificent castle built by Vienna's leading architect, Fischer von Erlach. In the 18th century numerous other Austrian architects were commissioned, such as Hildebrandt and Dientzenhofer, who also designed gardens to their buildings. Further famous Moravian gardens are at Buchlovice, Milotice, Slavkov and Lednice.

The Baroque fashion lingered on far into the second half of the 18th century in the two Czech-speaking provinces. The landscape style only made its appearance towards the end of the century, and found general acceptance in the 19th century. An outstanding creation is the garden of Kačina Castle, in Kutná Hora (1800-1820), with a lake and a temple, a profusion of other water surfaces and clearings. An even more distinctive example of the

The original appearance of the so-called Flower Garden at Kroměříž, Moravia. The dominant position of the central axis marks the layout as a mature Baroque; but several components of the parterre are still in Renaissance style, a frequent occurrence in the country (top).
In the 17th and 18th centuries, Prague's Malá Strana became a proper district of villas. Here the aristocracy laid out, adjacent to their palaces, gardens with a typical terraced structure, as exemplified by the Lobkovický complex, here shown on a print from the first half of the 18th century (bottom).

Garden of the Russian court at Ismailovo after a drawing from the 17th century. The smaller rectangles represent parterre units, mostly planted with various flowers. The larger ones sported fruit trees, included within the central square, which also served as a maze. The pavilions along the fringe were intended for amusement (previous page)

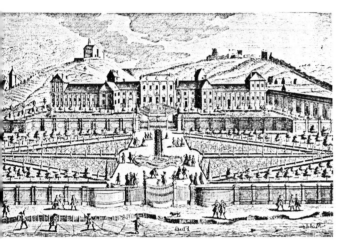

style is the Park at Lednice, which is in fact a wide tract of countryside with many architectural and landscape elements. A third interesting creation is the Kinský Garden, dating from 1820. Later gardens increasingly assumed a horticultural character, or faded into arboretums and botanical collections, a typical instance is Pruhonice, where aesthetics and botany are in a precarious balance.

King's Garden, Prague. This is the most famous garden of the Bohemian Renaissance, and the oldest fully preserved example of the country's gardening heritage. A small summer palace was erected on the site about 1535, from a design by Paolo della Stella. A terrace laid out beneath Hradčany Castle commands a fine view of the city - an example of Italian inspiration. The palace, one of the first Renaissance buildings of Central Europe, was called, naturally enough, Belvedere. In front of it, an Italian master named Francesco arranged a flower parterre in 1541. F. Terzio provided a double-basin singing fountain, which has fortunately survived (p.350). The present-day parterre is an attempt to reconstruct the original design which is not reliably documented.

Wallenstein* (**Valdštejn**) *Garden, Malá Strana, Prague. The complex was conceived by G. Pieroni, A. Stezza and B. del Bianco in 1620-1630 for General Albrecht Wallenstein. The main section of the Renaissance parterre directly merges into the three-arched loggia of the palace. Down the centre there are two rows of statues set on high pedestals and portraying battle, hunting or love scenes, or extolling courage (p.349). They were cast in lead by the Dutchman Adriaen de Vries. In the 17th century the occupying Swedish army removed the original statues to Drottningholm. Since 1938 they have been replaced by bronze copies. The symmetrical arrangement of the chief elements of the parterre foreshadows the Baroque manner but the general character of the parterre harks back to the Renaissance. These are also traceable in the grotto and in the aviary built of tufa blocks. The same material was used for the high wall linking the two elements, therefore this part of the garden has a grotesque, naturalistic spirit occasionally found in Italy.

Vrtba Garden, Malá Strana, Prague. Like most complexes in the Malá Strana quarter, the garden of the Vrtba family is arranged in terraces. The smaller garden fronting the loggia is a creation of F. M. Kaňka and dates from about 1720. Its central motif, a two-ramp stairway, emphasized by a balustrade, vases and statues, is preserved and well-restored (p. 350).

Kroměříž, South Moravia. The garden was designed in a Late Renaissance style by the Italian Filiberto Lucchese and built in 1665-1675 for the Bishop of Olomouc, Karel von Liechtenstein, on the outskirts of this small bishopric town. The main feature is a vast parterre, called the Flower Garden, containing numerous flower parterres, fountains and the centrally placed octagonal pavilion, summer-house, with rich sculptural decorations. The entire length of the parterre is flanked by a 223 m long gallery, the Colonnade, decorated with statues and topped by a roof terrace. The remaining three sides were originally enclosed with walls and are now shut off by tall clipped hedges. The garden is gradually being restored according to the original design. The bishop's palace in town is situated in a 64 hectare large park, prevailingly in a landscape style with an outstanding feature - an island with a Chinese Pavilion. Remains of former regular layouts survive only around the large edifice. In the 19th century an intimate Pompeian Colonnade was added to the garden.

Buchlovice in South Moravia is also the work of an Italian designer, Domenico Martinelli. The layout is quite unique: two symmetrically placed castle buildings with semi-circular courtyards enclose the central open space which is partly arranged as a regular garden. The original terraced layout is still preserved on the eastern side and is laid out along the central axis (p.351). In the 19th century a 50 hectare large landscape park was added to the grounds. The whole is perfectly maintained.

Lednice and *Valtice*, near Breclav in South Moravia. The original Baroque castle and gardens were remodeled in the 18th century in a neoclassical fashion. Later, the layout of gardens was radically altered by the introduction of features in the landscape style. Among these stands out a 34 hectare large lake with 15 islands. At the beginning of the 18th century several narrow vistas were cut through the park, leading the eye towards landmarks like the Minaret, Gloriette, the Temple of Apollo, and the Belvedere. The only surviving regular layout is a flower parterre, today adjoining the castle at Valtice, reshaped in a Neo-Gothic style in 1845. Since the end of World War I, the frontier between Austria and Czechoslovakia bisects the grounds.

Milotice, South Moravia. The Baroque layout in front of the castle was executed in the early 18th century. An outstanding staircase leads down to the garden which is developed along the central axis with fountains and parterres, once decorated with flower patterns which are missing today. In the northern part a large landscape park was added in the 19th century.

Pruhonice, south of Prague. The 200 hectare complex was created from 1885 onwards. It imitates a particular version of the landscape style championed by Count Pückler-Muskau. The creator of the garden was Count Silva-Tarouca, a prominent amateur dendrologist. He has skilfully used the rolling terrain with abundance of water to arrange several extensive clearings and three lakes. The informal plantings are largely composed of tree species from various parts of the world, so the garden is primarily an interesting arboretum.

Croatia

The first gardens arose around the ancient Roman villas along the Adriatic coast but of these, except for details unearthed by archaeological excavation, nothing remains of these activities. Unfortunately, no clues exist of the size and structure of the gardens adjoining the Emperor Diocletian's grandiose palace in present-day Split. The age of the Renaissance has left a remarkable gardening legacy, mostly dating from the 15th to the 17th centuries, in the territory of the city republic of Dubrovnik. Because of the social equality of her citizens, no grand-scale gardens arose that could be compared to some Italian creations. The designs followed simple geometrical patterns. The terraced structure was usually emphasized by pergolas lining the paths and alleys. Because of the Karstic terrain, water was sparingly used, but the irrigation network was often attractively designed. Seaside villas often sported a salt-water fishpond, serving both practical and aesthetic purposes. Dubrovnik's outstanding architectural monuments include also two cloisters from the 14th and 15th centuries, one of them with a well-preserved garden in a peculiar ground-plan (p. 42).

After the collapse of Turkish power at Vienna, a kind of construction boom began. At the turn of the 18th century the local nobility hastened to rebuild existing or establish new castles and gardens in the Baroque style fashionable at the Viennese court. Most of these gardens were of modest size, but showed the typical Baroque ambition of fusing the building and its setting into a single layout. Of this legacy only the park at Oroslavje partly survives with remains of the parterre, garden sculptures and the gate. While all these trends appeared more or less simultaneously with developments elsewhere in Europe, the landscape style emerged comparatively late, only in the course of the 19th century and only a modest number of gardens were laid out in the new style. The most remarkable, both for its design and its size is Maksimir, on the outskirts of Zagreb, commissioned by Bishop G. Havlik, and developed from the end of the 18th century onwards, with practical educational features blended with the usual elements of a landscape park.

The design of Zagreb's Maksimir Park was adapted to the views from the kiosk, situated on elevated ground. From here the eye ranges over extensive clearings and water surfaces, picturesquely bordered by masses of native oak (top).
Begunje near Radovljica, Slovenia (called Kazenstain under the Austro-Hungarian monarchy). The danger of Turkish raids dictated an enclosed garden and a compact architectural complex. Etching from the 17th century (second row).
Ground-plan of Pieskowa Skała Castle, with a parterre garden on a narrow longitudinal terrace (third row).
Wilanów: ground-plan of the garden in its 18th-century state. The axial design is apparent, yet not sufficiently developed in the Baroque sense, since the two terraces and their parterres extend in width rather than in depth. The same applies to the line of bosquets delimiting the parterre against the lake in the background (bottom).

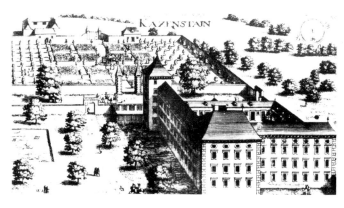

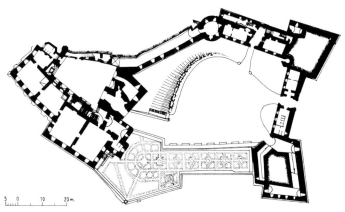

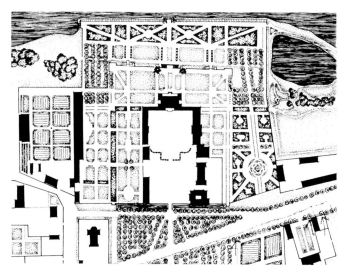

Sorkočević Garden at Lapad Peninsula, Dubrovnik (p.355). This 16th century work is the best preserved creation of the Dubrovnik Renaissance. The villa, in a transitional style between Gothic and Renaissance, opens onto the garden through a loggia. It is fronted by a rectangular fishpond directly connected to the sea, a suggestive inclusion of the vast natural expanses into the orderly world of man. The remaining part of the garden is laid out in terraces and connects with the upper floor of the villa. Another Sorkočević garden, with a remarkable staircase on the sea is only partly preserved and is located in nearby Rijeka Dubrovačka. A part of the garden was restored in the 1980s but seriously damaged during the hostilities in 1992.

Maksimir, Zagreb. The park was laid out from 1838 onwards under the guidance of Bishop G. Haulik. It was designed to provide education, relaxation and amusement to the local inhabitants, an example of public spirit unheard-of in its age. The focal point of the layout is a kiosk set on an elevated site (p.354). It is reached by a long straight alley, the only regular feature of the park. From the kiosk, deep vistas open up in all four directions over a scenery of clearings, valleys and lakes, as well as the surrounding countryside. The most attractive motifs, concentrated in the vicinity of the lakes, have been largely spoiled by the zoo, introduced in this century, and by some recent historically incorrect interventions. Nevertheless, Maksimir remains the country's largest and stylistically most distinguished creation in the landscape style and a most important urban park.

Slovenia

The country has been for centuries part of the Austro-Hungarian Monarchy which is manifest in their almost identical cultural developments. Some partly preserved remains togethet with some historical documents prove the existence of cloister gardens already in the Middle Ages. Gardens of the Renaissance period are amply illustrated in the topographic books of Janez Vajkard Valvasor (*Topographia Ducatis Carnioliae Moderna*, 1679) and Georg Matthäus Vischer (*Topographia Ducatus Stiriae*, 1681). With their comparatively simple layouts they are strongly reminiscent of medieval gardens. This is mainly due to frequent Turkish raids, since resources were used principally for defence and little was left for non-functional structures. After the Turks had been repulsed at the siege of Vienna, a more prosperous period followed with vivacious construction activity. New residences were built in the Baroque fashion with adjacent gardens. A well known garden from the transition period was Črnci, later fully remodelled. The only conspicuous and integrally preserved example of the Baroque legacy is Dornava near Ptuj. The clear-cut design is outstanding because of the exceptional length of the main axis, 1.8 kilometres. The Romantic period made its effect only in the 19th century, usually in the form of collections of exotic woody plants, the most distinguished among them being Dol near Ljubljana where a staircase, a tree avenue and a neoclassical pavilion remain to this day. From the latter period, a garden worth mentioning is the one at Štanjel, arranged in an Art Nouveau spirit.

Dornava, near Ptuj (p.355). The Baroque palace and garden were designed for Count Attems at the beginning of the 18th century. The salient feature of the ground-plan is the 1.8 kilometre main axis, starting from a sculpture marking the beginning of the alley of approach. Behind the building, on the garden side, the axis leads first through a courtyard embraced by the two side wings of the castle, then across a 90 metre-long parterre divided into four sections and centred on a circular basin, dominated by a Neptune figure. The basin is skirted first by a ring of dwarfs, then by a taller ring of ancient philosophers. Further down the axis, the formal character of the garden is gradually relaxed and the view ranges over a regularly designed orchard and a clearing, to find its termination in a memorial on the river bank.

Poland

In view of the great number of monasteries in medieval Poland, it is not surprising that the first recorded gardens are in their cloisters, for example Mogiła near Cracow (p.35), Oliwa and Koprzywnica. A number of descriptions and plans document the country's Renaissance gardens, some of simple, others of fairly complex design. An example of the former is Wisnicz, with its parterre composed of 3 by 5 regularly arranged and equally-sized squares. The more complex type is represented by Mogilany and by the Royal Palace Gardens at Lobzow near Cracow, whose size and sophistication almost compete with Italian models. The age of Baroque reached its climax in the reign of King Jan Sobieski. Gardening art was subservient to architecture, exemplified by the Italian Augusto Locci and the Dutchman Tylman van Gameren. The outstanding achievement of the period is the royal residence of Wilanów, where Baroque tendencies are tempered by touches of Italian Renaissance design. Other important gardens of the time are: Puławy, with its characteristic double-axis ground-plan, Białystok, with its sumptuous parterre crowded with garden sculpture, and the Royal Gardens of Augustus II, in Warsaw, with a garden theatre, a maze, and a fine formal arrangement in front of the palace.

The landscape style is abundantly represented in Poland. It prevailed in the second half of the 18th century, under French rather than English influence, owing to the close ties of Polish high society with France. Most of the gardens of this period show the romantic, or even sentimental, traits common to the landscape style of Central European countries. An early example of the fashion was the Aleksandria Garden in Siedlce. Later gardens include Powazki, the Polish Petit Trianon, Arkadia, Łazienki and Łańcut, whose pureness and unity of concept are hardly equalled anywhere else in Europe. Puławy deserves special mention as a Late Romantic garden designed in the early 19th century by Izabela Czartoryska, writer of a book on landscape design. It was a vast landscape complex, with a varied repertory of elements from earlier stylistic periods and numerous buildings of classic, romantic or exotic character. As in other European countries, the 19th century was a time of intense nationalism, therefore most gardens of this period were entrusted to native designers.

Pieskowa Skała, 20 kilometres north-west of Cracow, in a narrow valley, whose slopes are strewn with numerous picturesque boulders. A Renaissance castle was built on Gothic foundations in the late 16th century and the garden was presumably established at the same time. An 18th century restoration masked the Renaissance features. Since the last war the castle has regained its original appearance. At the same time a small parterre garden of clipped box has been re-established on a narrow terrace (p.357).

Wilanów, Warsaw. This royal residence of the *villa suburbana* type was built for King Jan Sobieski, from 1677 onwards. The garden was designed by Adolf Boy, a military engineer from Gdansk. It is symmetrically orientated on the axis of the palace, and consists of two terraces with parterres of clipped box (p.356). The gradiant between the terraces is bridged by a two-ramp stairway surmounting a grotto. The niches set in the wall separating the two terraces were once filled with statues and fountains. The terraced structure, at right angles to the axis, reveals Italian rather than Baroque concepts, probably under the influence of Augusto Locci, architect of the palace. In 1733 Wilanów passed into the hands of the Czartoryski family, succeeded by the Lubomirskis, who extended the formal garden and added an Anglo-Chinese garden in 1784-1791, from a design by Szymon Zug. After 1799 Wilanów was owned by the Potocki family, who introduced new elements in the landscape style in the early 19th century. At that time a large landscape garden was added to the north, complete with a Roman bridge, a classical and a pseudo-Gothic pavilion and a Chinese cottage. In the last war the garden was gutted, but has been restored since,

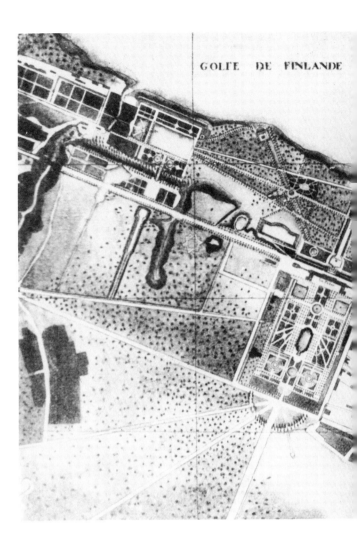

The ground-plan of Petrodvorets from 1775, when the garden was already complete. There is an interesting contrast between the dense articulation of the Upper Garden and the scattered arrangement in the Lower. Other prominent features are the dominating compositional role of the central axis and the linking effect of the long transversal walk, called Marly Alley.

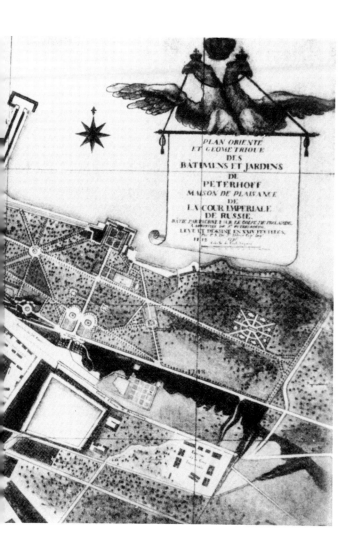

retaining the stylistic traits of its various periods of construction. Only the terrace wall needs restoration, to round off the image of Poland's most remarkable garden complex.

Nieborów, near Lowicz, is a historically important formal garden. Both the palace and the garden were designed by the Dutch architect Tylman van Gameren for Cardinal Radziejowski in the late 17th century. The formal garden, symmetrically orientated on the building and enclosed by walls of trimmed lime-trees with a *parterre de broderie*, was laid out at that time. In the 18th century Szymon Zug added a landscape section for the family of Radziwiłł who were the owners at that time. The garden has been restored by plans of Gerard Ciołek around 1950.

Arkadia, near Lowicz, is the creation of the romantic Princess Helena Radziwiłł, who devoted 40 years of her life, from 1778 onwards, to this garden. She engaged the help of Polish artists, such as S. Zug and H. Ittar. The thematic programme of the garden is the myth of Arcadia, as a symbol of happiness, love and death, represented by a number of features, for example a Temple of Diana (p.356), an old water-mill, a sarcophagus, several obelisks, a Sybilline Grotto, a Greek Arch, an aqueduct with a cascade, a chapel and an island of poplars. Everything is pervaded by an atmosphere of mystery and emotional tension, typical of the period of High Romanticism, which has here found its perfect expression in a dense programme of garden motifs. The garden is fairly well preserved.

Łazienki, Warsaw. Originally a formal garden, it was reshaped into a landscape park in the second half of the 18th century, during the reign of King Stanislaus Augustus. The salient features of the complex are an extensive water motif in front of the castle, a Roman bridge, an amphitheatre, fake ruins, and several Chinese themes. A considerable number of these details have survived.

Russia

The close ties of ancient Russia with Byzantium were reflected in her church architecture, accompanied by Byzantine-style gardens recorded in ancient documents. There is more detailed evidence of 16th century gardens, which were chiefly intended for fruit-growing. The consolidation of the country in the 17th century allowed the establishment of pleasure gardens in the Moscow area, chiefly along the Yausa and Moskva rivers. A typical example are the gardens of the Tsars' residence at Ismailovo (p.337), a simple rectangular design composed of a sequence of square-shaped parterres. They seem to imitate the parterre patterns fashionable in Western and Central Europe in the 15th and 16th centuries. An incredible boom of architecture and gardening followed Peter the Great's reforms, which westernized Russia. When he had secured Russia's frontiers by successful military campaigns and opened a corridor to the Baltic, he founded a new capital, St. Petersburg in European style. The accompanying Baroque-style gardens were not merely the inevitable settings of the new residences, but also symbols of the Tsar's autocratic power and the new age. This is proved by the personal attention paid by the Tsar to the projects and designs of the new buildings and gardens. He often had them altered, sometimes illustrating his suggestions by a drawing in his own hand. It is well known, for instance, that he reproached the French architect Le Blond for his lack of showy, grandiose-scale concepts. He attracted a whole team of renowned Western architects, who not only designed the buildings, but often also the garden arrangements, for example Le Blond, Rastrelli, Trezzini, Michette, Rinaldi. He also called in numerous foreign landscape architects and gardeners, chiefly from Holland and Germany, for example Roosen, Harnigfeldt, Fock, Schröder, Busch. They were aided by native assistants, such as Zemtsov, Borisov, Davidov and Surmin. In a few decades a number of palaces with Baroque gardens arose in and around St. Petersburg, beginning with the Summer Palace (1704). Their formal structure became increasingly complex, culminating in the middle of the century in Peterhof (now called Petrodvorets), the last, somewhat belated highlight of European Baroque gardening. After Peter the Great's death, a reaction against his modernization trends set in, causing a period of stagnation and confusion in building activity.

A new departure in gardening art began with Catherine II, a high-handed ruler who introduced the landscape style. She flirted with the Enlightenment and corresponded with, among others, Voltaire and Diderot. To catch up with the new fashion, she called in a number of renowned foreign architects and designers, who created, together with Russian experts, a number of truly splendid complexes. The most outstanding masters were Cameron, Quarenghi, Rossi and Gonzaga, active in the St. Petersburg area, and Gilardi, employed in the Moscow region, and their native counterparts were Neyelov father and son, Lvov and Voronikhin. Catherine's first constructions in the new style were Tsarskoe Selo, followed by Gatchina, Pavlovsk, Oranienbaum, and, in the Moscow area, Tsaritsino, Ostankino and Kuzminki. Innumerable other complexes have either disappeared or are still awaiting restoration.

Summer Garden (Letny Sad), St. Petersburg, laid out opposite the Summer Palace of Peter I. The designs go back to 1704, but have undergone several changes, under the guidance of a number of foreign and native masters, such as A. Le Blond, I. Matveyev, J. Roosen, M. Zemtsov and A. Schlütter. In its heyday, towards the middle of the 18th century, the garden was a rich collection of regular features and included a large grotto with a water organ, an aviary, lattice-work bowers, an orangery, a maze with fountains representing subjects from Aesop's fables, numerous other fountains (51 in total) and about 200 statues. The flood of 1777 ravaged the garden. Catherine II seized the occasion as a pretext to make large-scale changes. The regular structure of the garden was altered by tree plantations. Only the main alleys survive, complete with their original Italian 18th century sculpture (p.358). Today the 11 hectare garden only covers the areas of the so-called First and Second Summer Gardens. It is picturesquely located on the bank of the Neva river, from which it is separated by a classical grill of wrought iron, created by J. Velten.

The Third Summer Garden was laid out adjoining the palace of Catherine I, and is today called Mikhailovski Garden. Its original regular design was reshaped in 1815-1819, when C. I. Rossi built the Mikhailovski Palace. At that time an extensive clearing, hemmed in by compact tree plantations, was opened in front of the building. The garden opens on the Moika river, where a garden pavilion allows access to the water.

Petrodvorets (formerly Peterhof), 29 kilometres west of St. Petersburg. The magnificent summer residence of Peter the Great on the southern shore of the Gulf of Finland is the crowning achievement of landscape architecture in Eastern Europe, and bears comparison with the world's finest gardens. On an empty tract of coast chosen by the Tsar himself, a provisional wooden lodge was built first. From 1714 onwards the existing buildings arose. At the same time the extensive gardens, covering a total of some 1,000 hectares, were taken in hand.

The grounds are topographically delimited by a terrace ending at the Grand Palace. The length of the palace determines the size of the Upper Garden, which provides a formal approach to the complex. It is arranged along a main axis centred on the castle and emphasized by three basins with waterworks, and a huge Neptune Fountain (p.358). The axis is flanked by clipped lime trees, walks with lattice-work bowers, and parterres of trimmed shrubbery. From a wide platform to the north of the palace the view ranges over the Lower Garden, jointly created by the architects Braunstein, Le Blond, Michette,

Tsarskoe Selo (Pushkin). The oldest section is a geometrical layout fronting the palace, with the Hermitage on its axis. Above the palace, to the north, four square-shaped elements are arranged along the extension of the axis; they were conceived as a parterre, but never finished. The south-western section is a landscape arrangement by Neyelov, with numerous buildings, whose location is calculated in relation to their scenic effects within the waterscape (top). Oranienbaum (Lomonosov). The formal Lower Garden, with a lower parterre, is situated to the north of the Grand Palace (A). The southeastern sector is covered by Petrovski Park, with two lakes (B), between which stands the palace of Peter II (C). The Upper Park in the western sector is in its northern part dissected by an unusual geometrical grid of paths (D). To the south it terminates in an informal area around the Chinese Palace (E)(bottom).

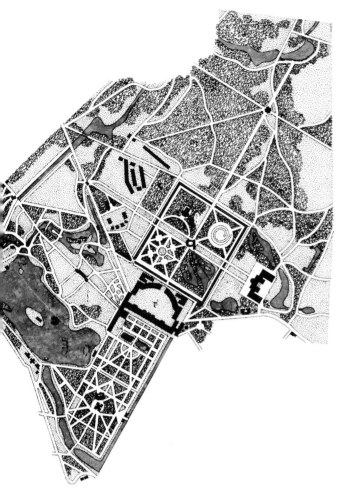

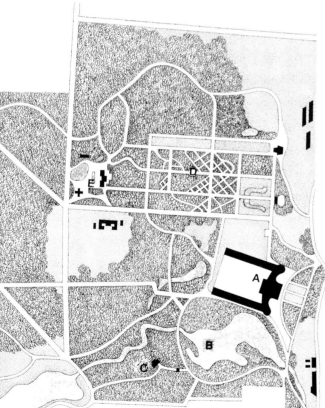

Zemtsov, Rastrelli, the garden designers Harnigfeldt, Borisov, Fock, the fountain masters Sualem, the Barattini brothers, Krylov and Ryliov, as well as a number of foreign and native sculptors.

The focal point of the design is the Great Cascade, a three-stage stepped construction, with a huge grotto at the centre and a profusion of decorative sculptures. At the bottom of the cascade there is a semicircular basin topped by a sculpture of Samson vanquishing a lion (p.359): an allusion to the battle of Poltava, won by Peter the Great over the Swedes. The iconographic programme in the vicinity of the cascade has a single purpose, the glorification of the Tsar, and chiefly presents subjects from classical mythology. Grand Canal continues the axis of the garden, running out into the Baltic. From the Grand Cascade, a diagonal alley leads eastward to Monplaisir, and a second one westward to the Hermitage. The former building is a smaller pleasure seat on the seaside, surrounded by several miniature gardens, which belong to the earliest Petrodvorets arrangements. From there a straight walk leads southwards, passing a monument to Peter I and two fine Roman Fountains, and ending at the four-step Dragon, or Chessboard Cascade, marking the brink of the terrace. The Chessboard Cascade is a symmetrically placed pendant to the Marly Cascade at the western end of the park. The main west-east communication is the Marly Alley, which sets out from a basin placed in front of Marly Castle, a copy of Louis XIV's Marly-le-Roi. To the south of the castle the outstanding landmark is the Marly Cascade, also called the Golden Hill. Like the Dragon Cascade, it is flanked by mythological figures, including Venus, Flora and Neptune. Both sections of the garden include a number of other features, a Pyramid Fountain, the Sun and Chinese Fountains.

Throughout, water motifs set the keynote of Petrodvorets. Since the Lower Garden, wedged in between the terrace and the shore, was too short to satisfy Peter's grandiose ambitions, the main development is not along the main axis, in depth, as required by Baroque compositional precepts, but rather in width. Petrodvorets was gutted in the last war, and has since been restored to a semblance of its former splendour.

Oranienbaum (since 1948 Lomonosov), 40 kilometres west of St. Petersburg. Originally the summer residence of A. Menshikov, centred on the Grand Palace, begun by G. M. Fontana and continued by J. G. Schadel in 1711-1727. In front of the building a regular garden with fountains, flower parterres and sculptures was arranged; it was linked with the palace by large-scale terraces and flights of stairs. This so-called Lower Garden was grassed over and haphazardly planted in the 19th century, to be restored to regularity in 1975-1976. When Oranienbaum passed into the hands of the future Tsar Peter III, A. Rinaldi added, from 1756 onwards, a further area called Petrovski Park. Its thematic highlight is the Rococo palace, while the valley of the Karost river was used as a landscape setting for two lakes with picturesque waterfalls. The lower lake served for boating and celebrations. The third and largest section of Oranienbaum is the Upper Park, whose focal point is the Chinese Palace erected by Catherine II, from a design by A. Rinaldi, in 1762-1768 (p.360). To the north of the building, behind a modest parterre, there is a rectangular pattern of extensive bosquets and wide alleys. On the northern fringe of the area Rinaldi built an original structure called Skating Hill and a smaller exhibition pavilion. To the south of the palace there is a little lake skirted by a stone pergola and enlivened by sculptures.

Tsarskoe Selo (Pushkin), 25 kilometres north of St. Petersburg. This is stylistically the most disparate creation of Russian landscape architecture, consisting of a number of independent sections. The oldest, situated in the southeastern part of the complex, is

Katarinski Park, whose original features, by Jan Roosen, date back to the turn of the 18th century. The axis of the regular geometric ground-plan is linked to the magnificent palace built by B. Rastrelli in the middle of the century (p.361). Below it, an interesting Hermitage, also by Rastrelli, is hidden among bosquets. Smaller, but more effectively located, is the Rastrelli Grotto, on the edge of the old garden, overlooking the Great Lake, providing one of the most picturesque motifs of Katarinski Park. The northwestern section of the complex, called Alexandrowski Park, was to include four square-shaped 200 by 200 metre bosquets fronting the palace. None of them was carried out according to the original plan, which was thwarted by Catherine II. Traces of a regular layout survive in the first of them, the third bosquet has disappeared, while the fourth one was revamped in the landscape style, with an artificial lake. Catherine II not only barred all further construction according to the original Baroque plan, but also enforced the new landscape style. From 1762 onwards a large-scale landscape sector, sprinkled with numerous buildings, arose in the southern part of the complex. The most prominent feature, a gallery erected by Charles Cameron, shuts off the area of the Old Gardens from the southern extension. Other attractive structures are: the Granite Terrace, the Chinese Village, a kitchen-cum-ruin conceived by G. Quarenghi and a Turkish Bath with a minaret. The arrangement, encircling the Great Lake, is probably due to V. J. Neyelov and his son, who had been sent to England to study the new style. A direct result of their tour is the Palladian Bridge on the lake, the only copy of the celebrated Wilton bridge outside England. Towards the end of the 18th century, the lake shores were decorated with mementos of the Russian victories over Turkey, such as the Chesma Column, rising from the lake itself, and the Kagul Obelisk. The formal patterns of Tsarskoe Selo largely disappeared after the 18th century, but they have been restored since the last war on the basis of documents.

Pavlovsk, 30 kilometres south of St. Petersburg. This is the country's largest (600 hectares) and most important park in the landscape style, designed for Tsar Paul I. Its basic outlines were laid down from 1777 onwards by the British architect Charles Cameron, who introduced a number of features unheard of in 18th century Russia. He is, above all, the creator of the structures skirting the lifeline of the complex, the valley of the Slavyanka river. The main building is the Grand Palace, an outsized Palladian villa set on an elevation (p.364) opposite the Apollo Colonnade and the Cold Baths. Further along the valley there is the Temple of Friendship, the first construction in the Doric style on Russian soil. Near the palace a private garden encloses Cameron's Pavilion of the Three Graces.

His successor, Vincenzo Brenna, created a regular flower parterre surrounded by a ring of sculptures. At some distance from this motif he conceived the elaborate Stony Stairway leading down to the river, a formal feature striking a jarring chord among the free-flowing, natural outlines of the environs. A third creative period, in the early 19th century, was dominated by the figure of the painter and decorator P. Gonzaga, who contributed a few more regular features, and at the same time made the most of the picturesqueness of the landscape composition, especially on the fringes of the park. To the left and right of the main waterway, the Slavyanka, the extensive groves and clearings are criss-crossed by paths converging on each bank in a star-shaped pattern centred on a Circular Pavilion and on Gonzaga's roundel motif, the White Birches. In spite of the considerable disparity of landscaped and architectural components, Pavlovsk somehow manages to preserve a certain formal unity, mainly owing to the vast dimensions of the garden and the dominant role of natural elements, which seem to absorb any discord.

Gatchina, 50 kilometres south of St. Petersburg. This large landscape-style garden was laid out after 1766, simultaneously with the construction of the palace, designed by

Ostankino: the original design was regular and symmetrical; at the end of the 18th century (when our map was drawn) a landscape arrangement, with interesting garden buildings, was added close to the palace. The palace is famous for its exceptionally rich interior (top).

Kuskovo near Moscow, as it looked in the 18th century. The garden lies between the palace and the orangery, which mark the beginning and the end of its axis. This axis continues across the geometrical lake, to run out in a canal lined with trees (bottom).

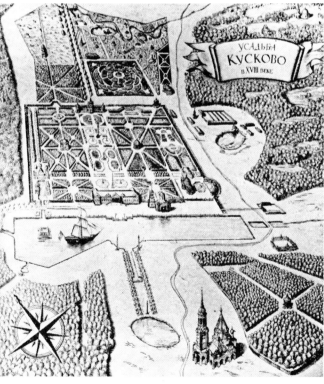

A. Rinaldi and V. Brenna. At the core of the complex are the White and Black Lakes, around which numerous architectural and sculptural features are arranged. A peculiar attraction are the islands interconnected with bridges, offering a number of alternative routes to visitors. The two regular gardens on each side of the palace, the lower in Dutch and the upper in Italian style, have been restored. Gatchina was seriously damaged in the last war. Reconstruction works are under way.

Kuskovo, 10 kilometres from Moscow. The estate belonged to the Sheremetev family. The garden, today covering an area of 31 hectares, was established in 1720 and given its definite shape by the 1780's. The classical house, situated on the lake, defines the width of the central section of the flower parterre extending northwards to the Orangery (p.362). On both flanks there are parallel bosquets with garden pavilions, where the alleys converge in a star-shaped pattern. There are some peculiar features, such as the Dutch Homestead, which once portrayed the folk customs of that country, complete with a small tulip-and-narcissus garden. Nearby there is a Hermitage, and at the eastern end of the complex, on the river bank, a grotto, both close copies of Rastrelli's St. Petersburg creations. The garden as recently undergone extensive restoration.

Arkhangelskoe, 23 kilometres from Moscow. The garden was several times remodelled in the 18th century, most radically in the 1780s, when the complex was given its dominant note, the two terraces in front of the house (p.362), probably contributed by the Italian architect G. Trombara. The edges and central stairways of the terraces are profusely decorated with sculptures, mostly alluding to classical mythology. From the terraces the view ranges over a lawn parterre to the valley of the Moskva river and the surrounding forests. To this regular design, a more up-to-date landscape section was added later.

The Ukraine

The Ukraine, with her checkered history, can look back on a highly varied legacy. As early as 1635, the Italian designer Del Aqua erected a palace for Hetman Konetspolski at Podgortsi, with a Renaissance-style garden including grottoes and fountains. A famous Baroque garden was owned by the Muishekov family at Murvanoye. Several large-scale landscape gardens were laid out in the 18th and 19th centuries, for example Sofievka, Alexandria, Trostyanetski Park, Sokirinski Park and Mayevski Park. They are distinguished by the inventive use of local natural resources (chiefly the abundance of water) and of typical native plant species, most frequently birches.

Several major gardens from the 18th and 19th centuries survive. The best-known is *Sofievka*, near Uman. It was designed in 1796 by a civil engineer, de Metzel, for the Polish owner, Count Potocki. The 129 hectare complex is outstanding for its abundance of lakes and streams, but also for a number of Romantic additions, such as a Temple of Flora, several grottoes, cascades and waterfalls. The more remarkable arrangements follow the same landscape pattern. *Alexandria*, at Belaya Tserkov, dates from 1797; it makes use of the valley of the Ros river as well as the native oak woods, interspersed with numerous pavilions, fake ruins, sculptures and water motifs. *Trostyanetski Park*, from 1834, covers an area of 204 hectares, and is distinguished by vast artificial lakes and hills, producing a spectacular effect in the otherwise flat countryside.

The heritage of the garden art of Slavonic countries has not been adequately explored so far and is insufficiently known, both at home and abroad. Intensified research and restoration might add further valuable examples to the European treasury of gardening art.

p.349
The Renaissance parterre of the Wallenstein Garden, Prague, is symmetrically arranged in front of a triple-arched loggia. The axis of the design is marked by sculptures by Adriaen de Vries, images of fighting, hunting, love and courage.

p.350
Among the numerous gardens of Hradčani Castle the oldest is the so-called King's Garden (Královská zahrada) from the mid 16th century. The centre of the restored parterre is marked by the fountain with its two basins, designed by Francesco Terzio (top). The Vrtba Garden at Malá Strana, Prague, is famous for its double flight of stairs, richly decorated with sculptures and vases (bottom).

p.351
The formal central garden on a terrace at Buchlovice is enclosed by two parts of the palace (top). The lower garden has an axial layout and is orientated towards the central part on the terrace (centre). Only a skeleton of the once Baroque layout survives at Milotice (bottom).

p.352
The small bishopric town Kroměříž boasts a rich garden heritage. The most celebrated are the Flower Garden with a rich parterre and the central Rotunda with an octagonal ground-plan: a view from the terraced colonnade (top). Another interesting structure adjoins the Bishop's Castle. In a remote corner of the picturesque part a Chinese Pavilion stands on the island (bottom).

p.353
The park of Lednice, near the Austrian border, has two distinct stylistic characters. Near the castle an arrangement from the 19th century is strictly regular (bottom). At the turn of the 18th century a large-scale romantic layout was introduced including various buildings, like a minaret, shown here (top).

p.354
Pruhonice near Prague, developed as an arboretum by Count Sylva-Tarouca and dendrologist Camillo Schneider. One of the wide clearings hemmed in by masses of native and exotic trees (top). The formal structure of Maksimir Park, Zagreb, is to a large extent based on the contrast between clearings extending into the depths of the garden, on the one hand, and the expansive masses of native oak-trees, on the other. This is most clearly evident in the view from one-time Dahlia Valley towards the kiosk (bottom).

p.355
Garden of the Sorkočević Villa at Lapad, Dubrovnik. In the foreground, in front of the villa and its loggia, there is a rectangular pond fed by sea water. The building on the right is an interesting feature of Dubrovnik gardens - the orsan, or boat-house, whose flat roof served as a terrace for the first floor of the villa (top). 18th-century Baroque layout at Dornava near Ptuj. View from the front garden; in the background, the access road, with alley, and the sculpture marking the beginning of the axis of the layout (bottom).

p.356
Wilanów, Warsaw: view from the lower terrace towards the palace. In the background runs the breast high wall with niches which once alternately housed statues and fountains (top). The photograph of the romantic Arkadia Garden shows a view of the lake with the Diana Temple (bottom).

p.357
Pieskowa Skała, a 16th-century Renaissance castle, is situated on a steep slope in the narrow Pradnik Valley. It was restored in 1948-63. On this occasion, the parterre of trimmed box on the lower terrace was renovated after a design by A. Majevski.

p.358
Petrodvorets: the Upper Garden, to the south of the palace, is arranged as a monumental approach. The central motif along the axis is a basin with the Neptune Fountain (top). The Grand Alley with an 18th-century sculpture in the Summer Garden. The luxuriant trees have almost completely blurred the original formal layout of the first imperial garden at St. Petersburg (bottom).

p.359
The Grand Canal is the carrier of axial design at Petrodvorets. In the foreground is the semicircular basin with the figure of Samson defeating the lion; it symbolically gathers the waters of the cascade and all the 60 fountains and waterworks along it. The symmetrically arranged colonnades by Voronikhin and the skirting fountains set in circular pools emphasize the central role of the Grand Canal.

p.360
A large lake with the Mosque in the royal park of Tsarskoe Selo (top). Oranienbaum (called until recently, Lomonosov): it is the Chinese Palace with its surroundings that perhaps best preserves the one-time picturesqueness (bottom).

p.361
Tsarskoe Selo: Baroque parterre in Catherine II's park fronts the Rastrelli's palace in a peculiar combination of Baroque and the local tradition. In the 18th century the garden boasted a great number of statues brought here from St. Petersburg.

p.362
Kuskovo: a view over the lake towards the panorama of garden and palace, behind which there is a geometrical parterre with bosquets. At the extreme right the dome of the grotto is seen (top). Arkhangelskoe near Moscow. View of the terraces with rich sculptural decoration and an emphatic central flight of stairs: the flanks were once covered by rectangular bosquets, subsequently overbuilt with pavilions typical of a later, Romantic period (bottom).

p.363
Charles Cameron inventively used the natural characteristics of the gently rolling, well-watered valley of the Slavyanka river when placing his buildings in the park of Pavlovsk near St. Petersburg: the Temple of Friendship accentuates the picturesqueness of the narrow valley (top). The Apollo Colonnade is situated on a slope so as to project itself better against the background (bottom).

p.364
The Palladian mansion at Pavlovsk in a setting reminiscent of similar arrangements from the Picturesque Movement in 18th-century England and elsewhere.

356

359

America and the 20th Century

America has made an original and important contribution to the world heritage of landscape architecture. Here, too, it is interesting to observe how social and economic conditions find their expression in the designed landscape.

Old Trends in the New World

Fledgling garden art grew out of the European traditions brought by the early settlers. None of the early gardens of New England or the Dutch settlements around New Amsterdam, today's New York, have survived. The agricultural prosperity of the Southern colonies, in particular tobacco-growing Virginia, allowed the establishment of larger plantations, with stylish houses and gardens, in the course of the 18th century. These colonial gardens were based on a regular design, reflecting the traditional styles of English and Dutch 17th-century residences. The most typical example is the garden of the Governor's Palace, Williamsburg (p. 376), along with a few other Virginian plantation gardens, such as Westover, Shirley, Gunston Hall and Mount Vernon. South Carolina, too, abounded in large-scale plantations, but there are very few preserved gardens. The same applies to French Louisiana, where only a few gardens and occasional attractive fragments, such as alleys of access, survive intact.

The outstanding figure in architecture of that time was Thomas Jefferson, third president of the U. S. A., a versatile man in the true Renaissance tradition. He was a successful farmer, diplomat, politician, architect and landscape designer. As a leading ideologist of the young liberal state he felt a kinship with the philosophical background of the landscape movement, which regarded classical architecture and landscape designed on natural patterns as spatial symbols of a democratic world. This probably accounts for his partiality for Palladian architecture, which he introduced to America with his house in Monticello, and, inevitably, the corresponding garden was laid out in the landscape style (p. 378). Jefferson's stylistic orientation was even more clearly demonstrated in the Charlottesville University campus. By that time the landscape style had also become popular in New England, where it was favoured by the rich middle classes. Large residences were being built, complemented - in the fashion of the age - with English-style gardens. The movement was pioneered by A. J. Downing, a highly authoritative and influential writer on the subject, but less important as a practising designer.

Parks for People

In the middle of the century, in 1851, the state of New York passed a law stipulating the establishment of a park on public ground for the requirements of the city population. The man destined to translate it into action was well prepared for the task, and had studied agriculture, horticulture and parks during his tour of Europe, as well as being thoroughly informed about America's social issues. Frederick Law Olmsted (1822-1903), was put in charge of the nascent New York Central Park, the first of its kind in the United States. A year later he and his partner C. Vaux won the first prize for their plan, and led the works, with some interruptions, until 1878 .

Central Park, like a few earlier British parks, represented a new orientation that strove to adapt the programme of features to the needs of a metropolitan population. The design of the park arose from Olmsted's belief that nature contains a moral power that could improve the city and offer a fuller life to its residents. This was the guideline for the layout of the garden, which recalls the rural landscape through a number of features, and only allows limited scope for regular and architectural elements. Later

Plan of Prospect Park, from 1901. The most prominent motif, in the upper section, is the Long Meadow, a large green plane. Its formal counterpart in the lower section is the lake. In between there is a sequence of programmatic elements. Alleys running all along the outer fringes both round off the park and separate it from the built-up area of the surrounding city (top).
One of Lebisch's designs, which includes typical Art Nouveau elements: chessboard pavement, pergola, flight of steps and formally trimmed vegetation. The spirit of the design is quite close to Olbrich's work at Darmstadt (bottom).

The Poet's Garden, designed by Ernst Cramer for the exhibition G59 in Zurich (1959), is an original attempt at a modern geometrical poetics in landscape architecture. The pyramids and cones, as spatial elements, form a tense contrast with the horizontal pavements and water surfaces (previous page).

on Olmsted designed a number of parks around the country with resounding success. His activity opened up a new chapter in the history of town planning, and defined the modern role of landscape architecture in spatial management. It is largely owing to his vital contribution that green spaces were successfully integrated within the development plans of American - and European - cities. His work set a tradition that is still very much in evidence in American landscape design today.

American Gardens Today

Williamsburg, Garden at the Governor's Palace. It has been reconstructed, together with the building, on the basis of archaeological excavations carried out in 1930-1931 and some documents; it is thought to represent it as it was in the mid 18th century. A new, more faithful restoration is contemplated. The layout is perfectly regular, and symmetrically arranged around the palace. The first section of the garden consists of a sequence of rectangles made up of clipped box, while the lower sector consists of parallel flower beds, paths and clipped hedges (p. 376). At the bottom the regular part of the garden is concluded with a fence and a ha-ha. Beyond it there is a maze planted with native holly, which is not the only indigenous species in the garden. Williamsburg also boasts several smaller houses with gardens reconstructed in 18th century colonial style.

Gunston Hall. The home of George Mason, author of Virginia's Declaration of Rights, is situated 30 kilometres south of Washington, on the Potomac river. Here, too, the garden has been restored to simulate the original design from the mid 18th century, with regular patterns of trimmed box (p.376).

Mount Vernon. Plantation of George Washington, first president of the United States, 25 kilometres south of Washington. The estate, with its large garden, spreads on the bank of the Potomac river, offering splendid views from the house. On the other side of the comparatively modest mansion, constructed of wood, there is a three-sectioned garden. In front of the house there is a wide, open lawn, framed by tall trees and flanked, left and right, by a number of restored smaller features, a kitchen garden, flower garden and botanical garden all in formal style.

Westover. This is a typical Virginian plantation. The brick mansion, in Georgian style, faces the James river. Adjoining the house, the outlines of the original formal garden are fairly well preserved. The strongest impression is produced by the location of the building in a riverside landscape, emphasized by a row of mighty tulip trees on the lawn.

Rosedown, Louisiana. A well restored plantation garden from the first half of the 19th century (p.377). The house is approached by an impressive allée of very large white oaks. To the left and right of the allée are situated formal gardens, a flower garden and a box parterre, with abundance of camellias, azaleas and other flowering and evergreen trees and shrubs.

Monticello, 10 kilometres from Charlottesville, Virginia; home of Thomas Jefferson and centre of a large plantation. Here Jefferson erected a Palladian-style mansion, the first ever on the American continent, between 1771 and 1809. The building is located on a hilltop and surrounded by a landscape garden, with clumps of trees gradually blending into the forest. The transition between interior and garden is solved in an original way, by two wide wooden verandahs that at the same time serve to shelter the basement (p. 378). The verandahs run out in two lateral pavilions, between which an oval-shaped lawn runs westward, fronted by a circular path and a flower border.

Terraces with further flowerbeds and orchards are cut in the southern slope. The restoration of the garden was tackled in 1939, on the basis of detailed archaeological excavations. The work is still in progress.

Campus of Virginia University, Charlottesville. Here, too, the Palladian inspiration prevails. The core of the design is a compact array of buildings centred on the rotunda-shaped library, from which side wings extend on both directions, housing the one-storied student dormitories and porticoed residences of the faculty, all linked by a continuous colonnade (p. 378). The intermediate open spaces are planted with grass and trees, while the actual gardens extend along the edges of the rectangular layout, enclosed by serpentine brick walls. Jefferson did not merely draw the plans, but also supervised the works in 1817-1826. He considered it one of his greatest achievements.

Central Park, New York. This is not only the most famous park in the United States, but also one of the major milestones in the history of landscape architecture. F. L. Olmsted here achieved the prototype of a public park featuring a social programme tailored to the needs of the city population, and it is destined to exert a long-term influence on the theory and practice of town-planning in the 19th and 20th centuries. The work started in 1858 and lasted for several years. The park covers an extensive area shaped as a narrow rectangle whose length four times exceeds its width. Because of this pronounced oblong shape Olmsted has arranged his programme in a longitudinal direction, alternating, on a large scale, wide-open clearings with artificial lakes and masses of vegetation. The design aims at maximum "naturalness", in a sense of the English picturesque style. But it also includes certain urban elements contributed by Olmsted's partner, the architect C. Vaux, for example a promenade, a terrace, an esplanade, and a music hall. Olmsted solved the problem of inevitable transverse roads by underpasses, so the spatial integrity of the park is fully preserved (p.375).

Prospect Park, Brooklyn, is Olmsted's next important design. Owing to more favourable conditions, it is formally even more attractive. It is made up of three distinct sections. On one side a well designed lawn, the Long Meadow (p. 375) runs the entire length of the park, the opposite side is covered by a long lake with islands and the intermediate space consists of stands of trees, interrupted by smaller clearings. With this park Olmsted produces an overwhelming impression reminding one of Capability Brown, and it probably ranks as his most perfect achievement.

Franklin Park, Boston, is Olmsted's third famous creation. The core of the composition is an unusually large extent of lawn, skirted by masses of vegetation, with a varied programme of games and amusement. The carefully graded lawn, cutting across the clumps of trees, creates a lively, plastic impression, and suggests boundless dimensions.

The 20th Century

After the boom of the formal and, somewhat later, the landscape style, the creative impetus waned in the 19th century. Though numerous gardens and parks sprung up in the cities of the Old and the New Worlds, no new style emerged. The new arrangements were based on the existing principles, and used a jumble of stylistic traits from all preceding periods. Therefore the bulk of the 19th century is marked by eclecticism, in the guise of neoclassicism or Neo-Romanticism. Flower ornaments often played a prominent part, masking the lack of original design by their gaudy patterns. This artificiality and lack of formal order provoked two contrasting doctrines. On the one hand, William F. Robinson (1839-1935) championed the return to simpler

Far more than in earlier periods the fine arts, especially painting, influenced the forms of 20th-century landscape architecture. Particularly active were the new currents of abstraction, such as Cubism, as can be clearly gathered from Braque's composition (top).

The new approach in artistic composition brought new impulses for landscape design, based on relations between the shapes, colours and tonal values of the various elements of the picture. Lines became almost autonomous, independent of reality, especially concentrating on the relationship between straight lines, lines broken in a certain angle, circular lines and winding lines. In particular the American school of landscape architecture experimented a great deal in this sense, as the plan of the garden at Sonoma, California, by Halprin and Church shows. The combination of straight and rectangular features with wavy elements in the landscape layout marks the tentative beginnings of the new 20th-century design. The creation stands out by the refined execution of the rounded lines of the pool, lawn and features of greenery (bottom).

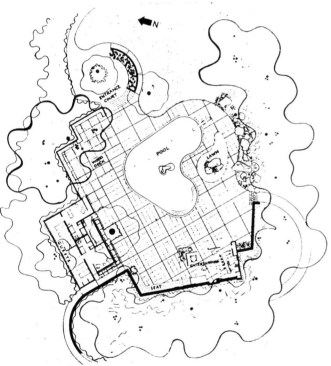

designs employing plants, especially flowering perennials, in a style closer to nature. His type of "English flower garden" was widely copied throughout the world. On the other hand, his no less authoritative adversary, Reginald Blomfield (1856-1942), advocated the revival of formal layouts. The two diametrically opposed trends both helped to accomplish something like an aesthetic "purge" over the last decades of the century. Their ideas were taken up towards the end of the century by the architect Edwin Lutyens (1869-1944) and the landscape designer Gertrude Jekyll (1843-1932). Their numerous joint creations clearly show a regular compositional framework of architectural elements or trimmed vegetation, complemented by informally shaped plant groups, chiefly composed of flowering shrubs and perennials (p. 138). This principle of double composition, contrasting formal and free forms, was perfected by the two partners to the point of virtuosity, and continues to influence the landscape design of our own days.

Art Nouveau, a radical reaction to 19th century historicism, was a welcome refreshment, reorientating European art at the turn of the century. It was particularly influential in the field of architecture, both by championing pure forms and new materials, such as concrete, and by introducing a new pattern of façade decoration based on geometric and vegetable motifs. On the other hand, the movement could never quite prevail in landscape architecture. It might be interesting to analyse the reasons for this unusual development. Only a small number of preserved gardens can be lumped under the heading of Art Nouveau. They feature a profusion of architectural elements based on geometric, usually rectangular, patterns: pergolas, flights of stairs, benches, balustrades and pavements. The Art Nouveau taste for emphatic ornamentation is well reflected in the chessboard pattern of pavements, never used in open-air arrangements by any of the earlier period styles. The vegetation is usually organized in regular designs, either trimmed in spherical or column-shaped motifs, or planted in trellis arrangements. The majority of these productions stem from the circle of Viennese Secession, the Austrian version of Art Nouveau.

The largest and probably best preserved complex is *Mathildenhöhe*, the grounds of the Darmstadt artists' colony, designed under the guidance of Joseph Maria Olbrich (p. 380). A creation that also attracted considerable attention at the time was the *Palais Stoclet*, Brussels, with its adjoining garden, both created by Joseph Hoffman in 1905. A remarkable figure of the movement was a Viennese designer Franz Lebisch, who carried out few designs in practice, but in his numerous projects most persuasively defined the concept of a Secessionist garden.

A member of the movement, proceeding largely from the same ideological background, was the Spanish architect Antonio Gaudi (1852-1926). His *Parque Guëll,* in Barcelona, is probably the only practical transposition of the wavy, rhythmically agitated line, which is the hallmark of Art Nouveau painting, into the language of landscape design in Europe. The entire design seems to be undulating: the fences, benches, walls, galleries and the rich mosaic decorations (p.379). It was intended to serve the residents of the Guëll Garden City, which was never accomplished. But the park remains, a treasured landmark of the city and unique monument of its age.

A New Visual World

In the meanwhile, the turnabout in artistic perception and expression that had started with Impressionism went on. The visual arts increasingly distanced themselves from the objective world and abandoned the portrayal of reality. They sought and created a new reality, by resorting to simpler forms and pure colours. In the course of a few decades, painting dissolved natural structures and shapes, replacing them by a visual formulation removed from reality and consisting of simplified means of expression. The tentative experiments of a multitude of creative minds resulted in an entirely new visual world, practically unlimited in its expressive possibilities. These developments inevitably found their echo in landscape design, even though they often reached this discipline by devious paths. Here, too, the new artistic sensibility allowed new paths to be trodden, expression through new design methods. Particularly encouraging in this context was the fact that Cubism disclosed the possibility of dissecting the natural world into a series of regular figures, a compositional procedure long since accepted in landscape architecture. The further development of abstraction, especially Mondrian's Neo-Plasticism and Malevich's Suprematism, asserted the independence of pure forms, whose interrelations, supported by tonal or chromatic values, could now create self-contained visual organisms.

Abstraction, in the sense of a greater or smaller deviation from the original natural structure, is inherent in landscape design. Therefore it was not difficult to assimilate certain discoveries of modern abstract art. Among them ranks the development of a coloured or textured plane, which has asserted itself as a significant means of artistic expression in the 20th century. One of the chief trends of abstraction in painting was to eliminate the three-dimensionality of objective reality and reduce it to flatness. In the same way, plants and other materials, when massed together, lose their natural individuality and visually operate only as a flat surface, by the colours of their blossoms, by the tonalities or grain of their leaves, sands, etc.

This is one of the major aspects which, within the framework of the new visual poetics, co-influenced the definition of the formal expression of 20th century landscape architecture; here, too, the principle of "less is more", proclaimed by modern architecture, prevailed. A further source of inspiration in the same direction was the trend in architecture and urban design that regarded functionalism as the point of departure towards form, according to the famous slogan "form follows function". Its chief ideologist was Le Corbusier, in whose visions of the new, modern city, greenery was accorded a major role. Though it might be true that his theories and initiatives have not led to satisfactory results, it is an irrefutable fact that his concepts were guided by a desire to humanize the city; for the first time in town-planning theory, the landscape was to contribute to the urban ambience.

To a considerable extent, the simplification of landscape design must be ascribed to the increasing claims of usefulness and cheap maintenance, especially of plant components. This accounts for the appearance of large tracts of lawn that can be machine-mown, the large-scale use of ground-cover plants and the abandonment of perennials or annual flowers requiring a great amount of care.

In spite of the described simplifications, landscape architecture has maintained its form-generating richness, since its field of application has spread considerably: from traditional arrangements around individual dwellings to parks, squares, city green spaces, the environment in residential settlements, school gardens, recreation areas, roadside arrangements as well as cemeteries and roof gardens. The variety of functions they serve would already be a sufficient demand for diversity in design, and is additionally intensified by cultural tradition and local environmental conditions. Thus, in this century creativity in landscape design demonstrates not only its own features,

During his activity in France (1921-1931), Gabriel Guévrékian created several pioneering designs, beginning with the gardens for the *Exposition des Arts Décoratifs* (1925), and the terrace garden to the Villa Heim (1927), both in Paris. However, his most influential work has been the garden at Hyères in the south of France, made for Vicomte de Noailles. The layout introduced an important novelty: spatial organization in gridded geometry as an overall concept (opposite page).

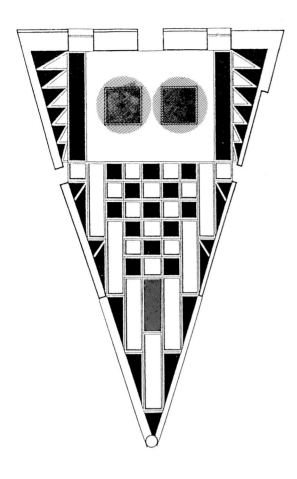

but also a great diversity. A major contribution in this direction can undoubtedly be attributed to the exceptional flourishing of the profession of landscape architecture and its numerous schools in various parts of the world.

Design characteristics and national schools

The legacy of landscape architecture of the 20th century is mainly characterized by an unusually rich diversity of form. It extends from works based on pure geometry to designs of an organic character in the tradition of the landscape style and that of William Robinson and Gertrude Jekyll, as well as transitional forms between both compositional styles. In contrast to classical, regular styles, the 20th century consistently avoids symmetry; the arrangement of geometric elements is always asymmetrical. The return to basic shapes such as the square, rectangle, circle and triangle, sometimes arranged into larger grid systems, is entirely in the spirit of the time (p. 384). A new design approach is the decomposition of basic forms, which was developed in particular by Scandinavian landscape architects. Another interesting novelty is the reductionist approach where only individual elements, for example a plane or a landform, are applied, whose design perfection allows them to function as a self-sufficient landscape structure (p. 386). A prominent characteristic is the diversified use of landscape material, often in emphatically contrasting combinations. New ideas were implemented through two concepts:

1. Constructivism, which is manifest in the use of simple, geometrical forms: square, rectangle, circle, ellipse, often organized as grid patterns in a repetitive rhythm.

2. Purism, displayed in a preference for simplified design vocabulary, especially large-scale planes, made of lawn, monochrome (usually geometrical) flowerbeds or homogeneous surfaces of ground-cover plants instead of mixed plantings. This would often take place in combination with regular water surfaces, thus strongly demonstrating the well pronounced purist approach in spatial organization. Never before has design syntax so much relied upon recombination of planar structural elements. Perhaps we could identify here the same underlying concept as in the façades of Adolf Loos, Le Corbusier and Mies van der Rohe's buildings, without referring to Mondrian and other exponents of such visual concepts, although the same common denominator could certainly be traced in the thinking behind them all.

Design in this century has lost its ability to include a wealth of meanings, even in landscapes, primarily as a result of design simplification and functionalistic endeavours. This is a serious loss, especially if today's creations are compared to the great creations of previous periods and their clearly recognizable and socially justified metaphors. However, some works created in recent times indicate the undeniable return of the metaphor to landscape design, and this is especially notable in the works of Lawrence Halprin in the U.S.

Despite the fact that all fields of artistic creativity throughout the world have been subjected to a high level of internationalization, individual national schools - the successors of various cultural traditions, natural and even social conditions - are still recognizable in landscape architecture. It is surprising that modern landscape design has its roots in France, where adherence to tradition is otherwise exceptionally strong. From the 1920s onward, the works created by P.-É. Legrain, Rob Mallet-Stevens and the brothers André and Paul Vera stand out with their pure geometrical designs, as well as the work of Gabriel Guévrékian in particular, who developed gridded designs in the Constructivist spirit. One of the pioneers of modern times is also Christopher Tunnard, who was initially active in England and later in the U.S.A. Important work in Great Britain has been contributed by Geoffrey Jellicoe.

A special position in landscape design is held by the Scandinavian school led by C.Th. Sørensen, a designer of extraordinary invention whose experimental searching has contributed greatly to the development of modern design. Characteristic of this school is a clear and simple design concept, as shown in the works of its distinguished contemporary representatives Sven Hansen, G. Brandt, Gunnar Martinsson and Sven-Ingvar Andersson. In Germany, a rich tradition and a high level of horticulture have promoted the development in this area with numerous creators in the pre-war and especially post-war periods. The most prominent among the older generation are Otto Valentin, Herman Mattern and Gerta Hammerbacher, followed by Hans Luz and several younger designers, in particular the brothers Hans-Jakob. Similar to the German is the Swiss school, whose outstanding representatives are the original designers Ernst Cramer and Willy Neukom.

The contribution of the United States is a chapter in itself. Already in the pre-war period there appeared a group of landscape architects who turned away from the prevailing tradition of Beaux Arts and began to tread new paths. Prominent among these are Thomas Church, Dan Kiley and Garrett Eckbo. After World War II, notable achievements were made by Tadeo Sasaki, Zion & Breen, and in particular Lawrence Halprin, and more recently by Peter Walker and Martha Schwarz. Worth mentioning among those from Latin America is undoubtedly the Mexican Luis Barragan with his unique designs based primarily on vertical and horizontal water planes or walls of penetrating colours. Roberto Burle Marx, residing in Venezuela, is famous for works in which he used plant materials in a design technique typical of modern painting.

Trends

The use of statues in gardens and parks is known since Roman times, and this tradition has been continued to this day. The sculpture was subordinated to a certain order of the whole (e.g. in the Renaissance and Baroque), or, as in the gardens of the landscape style, it had an individual message. As such, it was always tied to the spatial framework into which it had been placed. However, modern, non-figurative sculpture can enter into spatial relations with its environment more independently, whether in the open space of a city or in a landscape.

The more recent period has seen the flourishing of a trend in sculpture known as land art, or environmental sculpture, where the sculpture as a rule is no longer independent, but incorporated into the site. This enables new possibilities of expression, but also changes the nature of the work, as the sculpture no longer has the same degree of independence as it did previously. The more it takes root in the space, especially the ground, the more it is bound with it into a new whole, simultaneously losing its authenticity. A unique path in this respect was chosen by Isamu Noguchi, who successfully crossed the magical boundary line between sculpture and landscape design. In a number of his works, individual elements reveal a clear sculptural intention and treatment, and are at the same time incorporated into the spatial context to such an extent that they are no longer autonomous and are becoming constituent parts of a new structure. This can be clearly seen in his layout of the gardens alongside the UNESCO palace in Paris and especially of the Californian Scenario in Costa Mesa. The initial task in the arrangement of open space is always the solving of a certain problem which is not the case with the sculptural intervention in the environment. Although land art cannot

Superimposition is an important and promising innovation in the landscape design of the 20th century. It became widely known when Bernard Tschumi won, in 1983, the famous La Villette competition in Paris. His entry was submitted in a brilliant and convincing graphic presentation. However, it seems that the layout, when implemented, may not fully work in accordance to the expectations, because the spatial elements that carry the composition are too large and go far beyond the scale of perception. Three years before, in 1980, Peter Walker produced a noted design for Burnett Park in Fort Worth, Texas. It is built from several formal layers; these begin with a simple grid and proceed towards a more complex final layout, which is demonstrated in the sequence of drawings above. Here, a superimposition of several layers makes a coherent design, which works even better when put into practice (top).

Another effort to superimpose structural layers of the composition is illustrated by the competition entry for the small cemetery of Št. Jernej in Slovenia (bottom). The underlying concept is a rectangular scheme composed of cemetery compartments, individual graves, walls and clipped hedges organized in a regular arrangement that is as severe as death itself. Above this geometry of death, a wavy line of trees is floating as a metaphor of man's unceasing attempt to escape the inevitability of his passing (design: D. Ogrin).

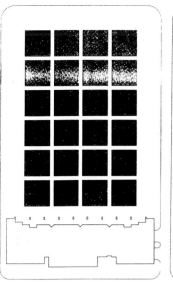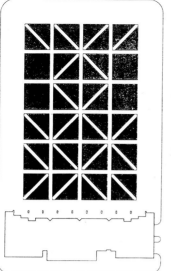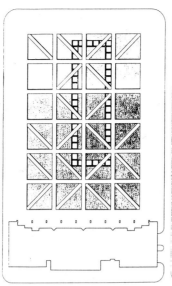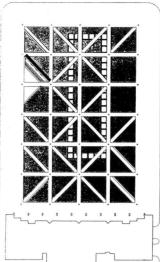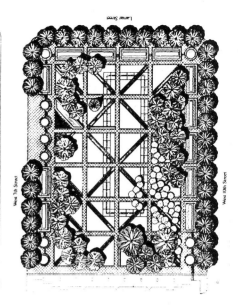

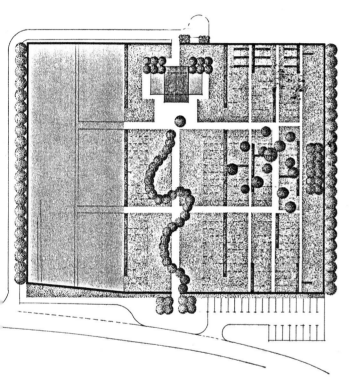

provide such solutions, it does generate numerous design incentives, interesting even for landscape design.

Recent years have brought some new views on the role of landscape in urban space. These range from complete negation on the one hand, as advocated by certain ideologists of urban design, most obviously by E. Aillaud, to extreme mystifications of genuine natural landscape on the other. The urban landscape is firmly rooted in the structure of the city; this is historically proven, confirmed by the present, and will undoubtedly play an even more important role in the future life of cities. In recent years, however, the question has been raised by some whether it would not be more reasonable to replace designed landscapes with entirely natural structures. This trend has been widely manifest in some West European countries.

In reply to this question, the needs of man must inevitably be borne in mind. Genuine nature represents a unique asset for a city, but it primarily needs to be considered in planning the future use of space, when it can be protected most efficiently. In this way it will also have the greatest ecological value. However, the case is completely different with new arrangements, which must fulfil a variety of social needs, as well as bear specific messages. These cannot be replaced by natural landscapes. Throughout the entire history of civilization, man has needed spatial symbols which he has used to mark his times and express the entire span of his existence - from painful hardships to the greatest exhilaration. This is the way it has been until now and there is no reason why it should be any different in the future. Consequently, the most promising endeavours in contemporary landscape design appear to be those searching for new forms of expression, even in symbolic presentations of landscape, as shown in the works of Halprin, Walker and some younger landscape architects.

In the future, the true wealth of man's environment will be expressed in its highly developed complexity, including genuine nature, which takes shape and evolves according to its own laws, and a number of imaginatively designed landscapes, which will be a response to man's varying needs. Thus, garden or landscape art will not only be an attractive component of historical heritage and a testimony of our past, but will remain - in its new, broader understanding - man's indispensable companion on the road to an exciting, unknown future.

373

p.375
Two great layouts by Frederick Law Olmsted. The Sheep Meadow in Central Park, an extremely popular and much used open space in the midst of the metropolis, under giant skyscrapers (top). Another equally popular and well-designed structure in New York is the Long Meadow in Prospect Park (bottom).

p.376
The garden of the Governor's Palace at Williamsburg, upper section of the parterre (top). Gunston Hall, Virginia, is an effort towards the revitalization of the garden in Colonial style (bottom).

p.377
A similar attempt was made in the city of Philadelphia through planting in the spirit of the middle of the 18th century (top). Rosedown, a typical traditional plantation in Louisiana with formal parterre of box and stately native white oak trees (bottom).

p.378
Central section of the campus of the University of Virginia, Charlottesville. The open space is defined by the side wings with the students' dormitories and the teachers' pavilions. This enclosed space creates an atmosphere of intimacy and introspection, suited to the world of learning (top). The link between house and garden, which Jefferson achieved at Monticello through two verandahs, is unique in Neo-Palladian architecture (bottom).

p.379
The main characteristics of Gaudi's design in Parque Güell in Barcelona from the beginning of the 20th century are: wavy lines, mosaic decorations and lively articulation expressed by stairs, terraces and galleries.

p.380
An artists' colony at Mathildenhöhe, Darmstadt, by Joseph M. Olbrich (from 1901 onwards): a part of the park below the House of Arts. In addition to the optically striking chessboard pavement, the simple cast-concrete pergola deserves a special mention. It weaves a formal link between the building and its surrounding; at the same time it helps to conceal the difference in height. In the background at right is placed the grid-like arrangement of plane-trees, in the style of the ancient Roman quincunx (top). A typical Art Nouveau design, with the heavy pillars strongly contrasting with the smooth surface of the pool, also at Mathildenhöhe (bottom).

p.381
One of the few genuine Art Nouveau layouts (by Max Läuger) survives in Baden Baden; it is characterized by large tectonic clipped cubes, a form favoured also in some Art Nouveau architecture (top). Palais Stocklet by Josef Hoffmann in Brussels with interesting elements in the garden surrounding the house (bottom).

p.382
Use of the horizontal or vertical plane as a main composition device in three examples from various parts of the world: a park at the hospital in Copenhagen by Sven Hansen (top, left); an interesting dialogue between the lawn as a ground plane and richly articulated plane of the façade of the university library in Bonn (top, right); and a vertical sheet of water as a main design feature in Paley Park, the smallest, yet perhaps the most visited park in the world, near Fifth Avenue in New York (bottom).

p.383
A conspicuous example of landscape design consistently carried out in rectangular forms: a roof garden on the top of the garage of the insurance company in Karlsruhe by Gunnar Martinsson (top). A simple outdoor environment in cubic forms in the well-known housing area of Kingohusene at Helsingor, Denmark (bottom).

p.384
Gridded designs have been very popular during the Modern Movement, mostly executed with quadrangular or hexagonal basic units: rose garden in Vondel Park in Amsterdam (top, left); a part of the Mariebjerg Cemetery in Copenhagen, one of G. N. Brand's most original works (top, right); the bank courtyard of the Sverige Riksbanken in Stockholm by C. Th. Sørensen (bottom, right); a detail from the city park in Stuttgart (bottom, left).

p.385
Although the circle, an archetypal form, has been amply used in almost any known cultural period, the Modern Movement has made use of it again and again in a number of ingenious applications. The Park on the Rhine in Bonn during the horticultural exhibition in 1979; the scheme is based on circular forms and was developed by the brothers Hans-Jakob (top). Allotment gardens do not normally score aesthetically; this does happen in a design by C. Th. Sørenssen at Naerum from 1949 (bottom).

p.386
An inventively shaped topography, without any extraneous element, becomes a final and complete achievement of landscape design in the residential area of Schlieren, Zurich, by Willy Neukom (top). A plaza fronting the Town Hall of Erlangen, Bavaria, with an original attempt at using new forms to develop an irregular formality (bottom).

p.387
Tivoli in Copenhagen is a peculiar, fanciful landscape for entertainment, defined by playful, sometimes exotic forms (top, right). Keukenhof in Holland is arranged to provide an exciting panorama of colourful bulbs, displayed in large masses (top, left). Modern botanic gardens often comprise well-designed and at the same time instructive sections, as in Berggarten, Hanover, where ericaceous plants make an attractive spring scenery (bottom).

p.388
Tanner's Fountain by Peter Walker, built in 1984 in the precincts of Harvard University, represents a most successful combination of archaic inspiration and contemporary design treatment (top, left); the composition emanates even more mystery when during the winter time sprinkling water is replaced by excess steam from the central heating (top, right). A hard landscape in the renovated area of Oslo harbour with symbolic use of maritime forms (bottom).

p.389
Lawrence Halprin's water plazas are milestones in modern landscape architecture. They are the outcome of an innovative design that has produced extremely meaningful works in an entirely novel language of forms. Their historical merit is also that they have brought back a lost metaphor in landscape design. The Ira Keller Fountain (1970) stands at the beginning of a rich open-space sequence in downtown Portland, Oregon (bottom, right). In Freeway Park, Seattle, Washington (1976), Halprin has created a series of most imaginative abstract transfigurations of a rugged mountain landscape (bottom, left). Levi's Plaza in San Francisco (1978) is executed in a familiar idiom; it is notable as an attempt to adapt the open space design to the formal character of the buildings flanking the plaza (top).

p.390
A combined effort of two artists, a painter and the landscape architect Hans Luz, called simply The Image. Any attempt beyond this statement, aiming at fusion with the landscape, would endanger the integrity of the artistic work (top). "Artificial Trees", an innovative contribution by Hans Luz in the design of a small courtyard (a joint project with Max Bächer) in Stuttgart (bottom).

p.391
Two sculptural works almost ideally fitting the designed landscape: Donell Garden at Sonoma (1948) by Halprin and Church, sculpture by Adaline Kent (top). Floating Sculpture by Marta Pan (1961), made for the sculpture garden of the Kröller-Müller Museum, designed by Jan Bijhouwer (bottom). Both statues were commissioned for the site.

p.392
Sculpture in various environmental contexts. Concetto spaziale naturale (1960) by Lucio Fontana; the sculpture is placed on the ground and not anchored in the site (bottom, right). That it can be removed is obvious from the fact that an identical group is on display also in the Hirshorn Museum in Washington. A sculpture, built into the ground and thus inseparable from its physical environment: Bruikleen (1979) by P.A.M. Siegers (bottom, left). Dubuffet's Jardin d'Email, Enamel Garden, (1974) is an abstract representation of the garden (top, right). These three works can be seen in the Kröller-Müller Museum near Arnhem. Top, left: an environmental sculpture in the grounds of the Horticultural Exhibition in Vienna 1974.

p.393
Isamu Noguchi's exceptional achievements successfully combine the technique of sculpture and landscape composition: Landscape of Time (1975) in front of the Federal Building in Seattle, Washington (top). A detail from another Noguchi work, California Scenario, Costa Mesa, California (bottom).

p.394
The garden to the UNESCO Palace in Paris demonstrates Noguchi's skilful sculptural approach when handling landscape material.

Bibliography

GENERAL

Chaunu, P.
Civilisation de l'Europe classique.
Paris 1966

Clark, Sir K.
Landscape into Art. London 1961

Clifford, D.
A History of Garden Design.
London 1962

Cottrel, L.
Lost Worlds. New York. 1962

Cowell, F. R.
Garden as a Fine Art. London 1978

Enge, T.O., Schröer, C.F.
Gartenkunst in Europa. Cologne 1990

Frazer, J.G.
The New Golden Bough.
New York. 1959

Giedeon, S.
The Eternal Present: the Beginnings of
Architecture. Princeton 1964

Gotthein, M.-L.
Geschichte der Gartenkunst I-II.
Jena 1914

Grimal, P.
Mythologies des steppes, des forêts et des
îles. Paris 1963

Gromort, G.
L'Art des Jardins I-II. Paris 1953

Hauser, A.
Sozialgeschichte der Kunst und Literatur.
Munich 1967

Hansmann, W.
Gartenkunst der Renaissance und des Barock.
Cologne 1983

Hennebo, D., Ev.
Gartendenkmalpflege. Stuttgart 1985

Jellicoe, G.&S., Goode, P., Lancaster, M.
The Oxford Companion to Gardens.
Oxford 1986

Jellicoe, G. and S.
The Landscape of Man. London 1975

Laird, M.
The Formal Garden. London 1992

Majdecki, L.
Historia ogrodów. Warsaw 1972

Matthaeus Merian
Die schönsten Schlösser, Burgen und Gärten.
Hamburg 1965

Moore, C.W., Mitchell, W.J., Turnbull, W.
The Poetics of Gardens. Cambridge 1988

Moser, M., Teyssot, G.
The History of Garden Design.
London 1991

Nieuwenhuis, H.
De Ordentlyke Tuyn. Zutphen 1980

Sørensen, C. Th.
Europas Havekunst. Copenhagen 1959

Sørensen, C.Th.
The Origin of Garden Art.
Copenhagen 1963

Thacker, C.
The History of Gardens. London 1979

Toynbee, A.
A Study of History. London 1976

THE ANTIQUE WORLD

Cernival, J. L. de
Egypte. Epoque pharaonique.
Fribourg 1964

Davies, N. M., Gardiner, A. H.
Ancient Egyptian Painting I - III.
Chicago 1936

Hennebo, D.
Betrachtungen zur altägyptischen
Gartenkunst. Archiv für Gartenbau
III (1953) 3:175-218

Hirmer, M., Lange, K.
Egypt. London 1956

Michailowski, K.
Art of Ancient Egypt. New York 1977

Rosselini, J.
I Monumenti dell'Egitto e della Nubia II.
Pisa 1834

Vandersleyen, C.
Das Alte Ägypten. Propyläen
Kunstgeschichte. Berlin 1975

Boethius, A.
Das Römische Weltreich. Propyläen
Kunstgeschichte. Berlin 1967

Boethius, A., Ward-Perkins, J.B.
Etruscan and Roman Architecture.
London 1970

Grimal, P.
Les Jardins Romains. Paris 1943

Jashemski, W.
The Gardens of Pompei.
New York 1979

Longus
Daphnis and Chloe

Martin, R., Stierlin, H., Bill, M.
Griechenland. Fribourg 1966

Ovid. Metamorphoses.

Vitruvius
The Ten Books on Architecture

MIDDLE AGE

Bazin, G.
Paläste des Glaubens I-III. Cologne

Bogler, P. Th.
Maria Laach. Munich 1978

Braunfels, W.
Monasteries of Western Europe.
London 1972

Crisp, F.
Medieval Gardens. London 1924

Durliat, M.
L'Art roman. Paris 1982

Fillitz, H.
Das Mittelalter I. Propyläenkunstgeschichte 5.
Berlin 1969

Simson, O. von
Das Mittelalter II. Das Hohe Mittelalter.
Propyläenkunstgeschichte 6. Berlin 1972

Harvey, J.
Mediaeval Gardens. London 1981

ITALY

Ackerman, J.S.
The Villa. Form and Ideology of Country
Houses. Princeton 1990

Alberti, L.B.
De Re Aedificatoria. Florence 1485,
London 1985

Berenson, B.
The Italian Painters of the Renaissance.
London 1967

Burckhardt, J.
The Civilizattion of the Renaissance in Italy.
London 1955

Coffin, D.R.
The Italian Garden. Dumbarton Oaks 1972

Coffin, D.R.
The Villa in the Life of Renaissance Rome.
Princeton 1979

Colonna, F.
Hypnerotomachia Poliphili. 1499

Dami, L.
Il Giardino Italiano. Turin 1924

Fagiolo, M.
La Città Effimera e l'Universo Artificiale del
Giardino. Rome 1980

Falda ,G.B.
Li Giardini di Roma.
Rome 1683, 1980

Heydenreich, L. H.
Eclosion de la Renaissance. Universe des
Formes. Paris 1972

Hunt, J.D.
Garden and Grove: The Italian Renaissance
Garden in the English Imagination
1600-1759. Princeton 1986

Jestaz, B.
L'Art de la Renaissance.
Paris 1984

Lazzaro, C.
The Italian Renaissance Garden.
London 1990

Masson, G.
The Italian Garden.
London 1961

Mignani, D.
Le ville Medicee di Giusto Utens.
Florence 1980

Murray, P.
Renaissance Architecture. London 1971

Panofsky, E.
Renaissance and Renascences in Western Art.
New York 1972

Puppi, L.
Andrea Palladio. Milan 1977

Shepherd, J. C., Jellicoe, G. A.
Italian Gardens of the Renaissance.
London 1953

Wittkower, R.
Architectural Principles in the Age
of Humanism.
London and New York 1971

FRANCE

Adams, W. H.
The French Garden 1500 - 1800.
London 1979

Chavigny, J.
Le Château de Menars. 1954

Ganay, E. de
André le Nostre. Paris 1962

Hazlehurst, F. H.
Gardens of Illusion. The Genius of André
le Nostre. Nashville 1980

Hazlehurst, F.H.
Jacques Boyceau and the French Formal
Garden. Athens 1966

Louis XIV
Manière de montrer les Jardins de Versailles.
Paris 1982

Marie, A.
Jardins Français Classiques des XVIIe et
XVIIIe Siècles. Paris 1949

Marie, A.
Jardins Français créés à la Renaissance.
Paris 1955

Mollet, A.
Le Jardin de plaisir. Stockholm 1651, 1981

Norberg - Schultz, C.
Baroque Architecture.
New York 1971

Wiebenson, D.
The Picturesque Garden in France.
Princeton 1978

Woodbridge, K.
Princely Gardens.
London and New York 1986

ENGLAND

Batey, M., Lambert, D.
The English Garden Tour.
London 1990

Bermingham, A.
Landscape and Ideology.
Los Angeles 1986

Brown, J.
Gardens of a Golden Afternoon.
Harmondsworth 1985

Brownell, M.R.
Alexander Pope and the Arts of Georgian
England. Oxford 1978

Buttlar, A. v.
Der englische Landsitz 1715-1760.
Mittenwald 1982

Buttlar, A. v.
Der Landschaftsgarten.
Munich 1980

Clark, H.F.
The English Landscape Garden.
Gloucester 1980

Claude Lorrain 1600-1682.
Washington 1982

Hadfield, M.
The English Landscape Garden.
London 1989

Hewlings, R.
Chiswick House and Gardens.
London 1989

Hunt, J.D.
Gardens and the Picturesque.
Cambridge 1992

Hunt, J.D., Willis, P.
The Genius of the Place. London 1979

Hussey, C.
English Gardens & Landscapes 1700-1750
London 1967

Hussey, C.
The Picturesque. London 1967

Jacques, D.
Georgian Gardens: The Reign of Nature.
London 1983

Jarrett, D.
The English Landscape Garden.
London 1978

Jourdain, M.
The Work of William Kent.
New York 1948

Pevsner, N.
The Picturesque Garden and its Influence
Outside the British Isles.
Dumbarton Oaks 1974

Streatfield, D.C., Duckworth, A.M.
Landscape in the Gardens and the Literature
of Eighteenth-Century England.
Los Angeles 1981

Strong, R.
The Renaissance Garden in England.
London 1979

Stroud, D.
Capability Brown. London 1975

Stroud, D.
Humphry Repton. London 1962

Tavernor, R.
Palladio and Palladianism.
London 1991

Turner, R.
Capability Brown and the Eighteenth-century
English Landscape.
New York 1985

Wittkower, R.
Palladio and English Paladianism.
London 1974

CHINA

The Analects of Confucius.
New York 1938

Boyd, A.
Chinese Architecture and Town Planning
1500 BC - 1911. London 1961

Bussagli, M.
Architettura orientale. Venice 1977

Cahill, J.
Chinesische Malerei. Geneva 1960

Chuin Tung
Gardens in Eastern China. 1963

Chuin Tung et al.
Gardens of Suzhou. Beijing 1978

Danby, H.
The Garden of Perfect Brightness.
London 1950

Dye, D.S.
Chinese Lattice Designs.
New York 1974

Erdberg, E. von
Chinese Influence on European Garden
Structures. Cambridge, Mass. 1936

Fontein, J., Hempel, R.
Propyläen Kunstgeschichte. Bd. China,
Korea, Japan. Berlin 1968

Fung Yu-lan
A Short History of Chinese Philosophy.
London 1948

Graham, D.
Chinese Gardens.
London 1938

Ih Tiao Chang, A.
The Tao of Architecture.
Princeton 1981

Inn, H., Shao Chang Lu
Chinese Houses and Gardens.
Honolulu 1940

Keswick, M.
The Chinese Garden. London 1978

Lao Tzu
Tao Te Ching

Legeza, L.
Tao Magic. London 1975

Lin Yutang
Imperial Peking. Seven Centuries of China.
London 1974

Mai-Mai Sze
The Mustard Seed Garden.
Shanghai 1978

Pirazzoli-t'Serstevens, M., Bouvier, N.
China. Munich 1970

Pirazzoli -t' Sestervens, M.
China. Weltkultur und Baukunst.
Munich 1970

Rawson, P., Legeza, L.
TAO. The Chinese Philosophy of Time and
Change. London 1973

Schafer, E. H.
China. Das Reich der Mitte.
Reinbeck - Hamburg 1976

Schafer, E.H.
Tu Wan's Stone Catalogue of Cloudy Forest.
Berkeley 1961

Sickman, L., Soper, A.
The Art and Architecture of China.
Harmondsworth 1958

Siren, O.
China and the Gardens of Europe of the
Eighteenth Century. New York 1950

Siren, O.
Gardens of China. New York 1948

Siren, O.
Histoire des arts anciens de la
Chine. I-IV. Paris 1930

Summer Palace. Peking 1981

Thilo, N.
Klassiche chinesische Baukunst.
Leipzig 1977

Willets, W.
The Foundations of Chinese Art.
London 1974

Watson, W.
L'art de l'ancienne Chine. Paris 1979

Wu, N.
Chinese and Indian Architecture
Harmondsworth 1956

JAPAN

Biusson, D.
Temples et Sanctuaires au Japon.
Paris 1981

Bring, M., Wayembergh, J.
Japanese Gardens. New York 1981

Conder, J.
Landscape Gardening in Japan.
New York 1964

Drexler, A.
The Architecture of Japan. New York 1955

Elisseeff, D. et V.
L'Art de l'ancien Japon. Paris 1980

Fukuda, K.
Japanese Stone Gardens.
Rutland - Vermont - Tokyo 1970

Gropius, W. Tange, K., Ishimoto, Y.
Katsura. New Haven 1960

Hayakawa, M.
The Garden Art of Japan. Tokyo 1973

Inoue, M.
Space in Japanese Architecture. Tokyo 1985

Itoh, J. - Iwamiya, T.
Imperial Gardens of Japan.
Sento gosho - Katsura - Shugakuin.
New York 1978

Ito, J., Iwamiya,T., Kamekura, Y.
The Japanese Garden. London 1972

Itoh, T.
The Gardens of Japan. New York 1986

Itoh, T.
Space and Illusion in the Japanese Garden.
NewYork 1973

Kokusai Bunka Shinkokai
Tradition of the Japanese Garden.
Tokyo 1962

Kuck, L.
The World of the Japanese Garden.
New York - Tokyo 1968

Nitschke, G.
Gartenarchitektur in Japan.
Cologne 1991

Okakura, K.
Le livre du thé. Lyon 1964

Okamoto, T., Takakuwa, G.
The Zen Gardens. Tokyo 1962

Paine, R.T., Soper, A.
The Art and Architecture of Japan.
Harmondsworth 1974

Schaarschmidt-Richter, J.
Der Japanische Garten. Fribourg 1979

Shikiba, M.
The Tale of Genji. New York 1976

Tachibana-no-Tashitsuna
Sakutei-ki. Reprint 1976

ISLAM

Ardalan, N., Bakhtiar, L.
The Sense of Unity. The Sufi Tradition in
Persian Architecture. Chicago 1973

Bakhtiar, L.
Sufi. Expressions of the mystic quest.
London 1976

Barucand, M., Bednorz, A.
Maurische Architektur in Andalusien.
Cologne 1992

Critchlow, K.
Islamic Patterns. An Analytical and
Cosmological Approach. London 1976

Crowe, S., Haywood, S.
The Gardens of Mughul India.
London 1972

The Encyclopedia of Islam I-IV.
Leiden - London 1960-78

Ettinghausen, R., Grabar, O.
The Art and Architecture of Islam 650-1250.
Harmondsworth 1987

Firdusi, A. Q.
Sháhnáme - Book of Kings.
Zagreb 1989

Godard, A.
L'Art de l'Iran. Paris 1964

Hoag, J.D.
Islamic Architecture.
New York 1977

Die Kunst des Islam.
Propyläenkunstgeschichte 4.
Berlin 1973

Lehrman, J.
Earthly Paradise. London 1980

MacDougal, E., Ettinghausen, R.
The Islamic Garden.
Dumbarton Oaks 1976

Michell, G.
Architecture of the Islamic World.
London and New York 1978

Moynihan, E.B.
Paradise as a Garden. New York 1979

Papadopoulo, A.
L'Islam et l'art musulman. Paris 1976

Pickthall, M.M.
The Meaning of the Glorious Koran.
New York 1959

Volwahsen, A.
Islamisches Indien. Munich 1969

Welch, S.C.
Royal Persian Manuscripts.
London 1976

Wilber, D.N.
Persian Gardens and Garden Pavilions.
Tokyo 1962

Würfel, K.
Isfahan. Zürich 1974

IBERIA

Barrucand, M., Bednorz, A.
Maurische Architektur in Andalusien.
Cologne 1992

Bowe, P., Sapieha, N.
Gardens of Portugal. New York 1989

Carita, H., Cardosa, H.
Portuguese Gardens. 1990

Dickie, J.
The Hispano-Arab Garden, its philosophy and
function. Bull. School of Orient. and Afric.
Stud. 31 (1968)237-248. London

Grabar, O.
The Alhambra. London 1978

Gromort, G.
Jardins d'Espagne. Paris 1926

Guart, A.O.
Real Sitio de Aranjuez. Madrid 1975

Lozoya, M. de
Palacios Reales de La Granja de San
Ildefonso, Riofrio y Museo de Caza.
Madrid 1976

Pieto-Moreno, F.
Los Jardines de Granada.
Madrid 1973

Serrano, M.L.
El Escorial. Madrid 1972

Soustiel, J.
La céramique islamique.
Fribourg 1985

Villiers - Stuart, C.M.
Spanish Gardens. London 1929

THE GERMAN LANDS

Der Englische Garten zu Wörlitz.
Berlin 1987, after orig. ed. 1798

Günther, H.
Peter Joseph Lenné. Stuttgart 1985
Hennebo, D., Ed.
Gartendenkmalpflege. Stuttgart 1985

Hennebo, D., Hoffmann, A.
Geschichte der Deutschen Gartenkunst.
I. Gärten des Mittelalters.
II. Der architektonische Garten.
III. Der Landschaftsgarten. Hamburg 1962

Herrenhausen 1666 - 1966.
Hanover 1966

Hirsch, E.
Aufklärung und Frühklassik.
Leipzig 1985

Hirschfeld, C.C.L.
Theorie der Gartenkunst I-V.
Leipzig 1779-1785, 1973

Hojer, G., Schmidt, E.D.
Nymphenburg. Munich 1979

Hojer, G.
Schleissheim. Munich 1976

Kurland, K.H.
Der Muskauer Park. Bad Muskau 1982

Pückler-Muskau, H. v.
Andeutungen über Landschaftsgärtnerei.
Stuttgart 1834, 1977

Rippl, H.
Branitzer Park. Cottbus 1977

Schmid, E.D.
Englischer Garten München.
Munich 1983

Sckell, F.L. v.
Beiträge zur Bildenden Gartenkunst.
Munich 1825

Wimmer, A.
Parks und Gärten in Berlin und Potsdam.
Berlin 1985

Zenkner, O.
Schloßgartenführer Schwetzingen.
Schwetzingen 1979

Zykan, J.
Laxenburg. Vienna 1969

LOW COUNTRIES.
SCANDINAVIA

Beeckestijn. ANWB n.d.

Bienfait, A.G.
Hollandsche Tuinen. The Hague 1943

Blunt, W.
Tulipomania. Harmondsworth 1950

Harris, W.
Een Beschrijving van 's Konings Paleis en
Tuinen van Het Loo. The Hague 1985

Fredrik Magnus Piper and the Landscape
Garden. Stockholm 1981

Lund, H.
De kongelige Lysthaver. Gyldendal 1977

Parken, Tuinen en Landschappen van
Nederland. Amsterdam 1979

Pechère, R.
Parcs et·Jardins de Belgique.
Brussels 1976

Sypesteyn, C.H.C.A. Van
Oud-Nederlandsche Tuinkunst.
The Hague 1910

Taine, H.
La peinture dans le Pays-Bas. Paris 1909

SLAV COUNTRIES

Baniukiewicz, E., Wisniowska, Z.
Zamek w Lancucie. Warsaw 1980

Bašeová, O.
Pražské zahrady. Prague 1991

Beletskaya, E.A., Pokrovskaya, E.K.
Gilliardi, D.I. Moscow 1980

Dubyago, T. B.
Russkie regularnye sady.
Leningrad 1963

Enciklopedija likovnih umjetnosti III.
Zagreb 1964

Enciklopedija Slovenije 5. Ljubljana 1991

Fijalkowski, W.
Wilanów. Warsaw 1972

Gurevich, I.
The Fountains of Petrodvorets.
Moscow 1980

Kiuchariants, D.A.
Antonio Rinaldi.
Leningrad 1984

Krivoručko, D. M.
Oleksandrija. Kiev 1979

Kuchumov, A.M
Pavlovsk. Leningrad 1980

Parki – umetnost oblikovanja prostora.
Ljubljana 1992

Piljavski, I. V.
Giacomo Quarengi. Leningrad 1981

Rapoport, V. L. et al.
Kuskovo, Ostankino, Arkhangelskoe.
Moscow 1981

Raskin, A.
Petrodvorets. Leningrad 1978

Šišić, B.
Dubrovački renesansni vrt.
Dubrovnik 1991

Uspenski, L., Gubanov, G., Bakhtin, V.
Leningrad. Leningrad 1977

V okrestnostyah Moskvy. Country Estates
around Moscow. Summary in Engl., French
and Germ. Moscow 1979

Zinkow, J.
Ojcow - Pieskowa Skała. Cracow 1976

AMERICA. 20th CENTURY

Ambasz, E.
The Architecture of Luis Barragan.
New York 1982

Benjamin III, L.W.
The Art of Designed Environments in The
Netherlands. Amsterdam 1983

Burle Marx, R.
The Unnatural Art of the Garden.
New York 1991

Le Corbusier et Pierre Jeanneret
Oeuvre Complete I-VIII. Zürich 1965
Contemporary Landscapes in the World.
Tokyo 1990

Fein, A.
Frederick Law Olmsted and the American
Environmental Tadition. New York 1972

Fein, A.
Landscape into Cityscape: Frederick Law
Olmsted's Plans for a Greater New York City.
Ithaca 1967

Foerster, K.
Vom Blütengarten der Zukunft. Berlin1922

Garrett Eckbo
Philosophy of Landscape. Process:
architecture 90. Tokyo 1990

Herman Mattern 1902-1971.
Berlin 1982

Hunter, S.
Isamu Noguchi. New York, n.d.

Lawrence Halprin: Changing Places.
San Francisco 1986

Lawrence Halprin. Process:
architecture 4. Tokyo 1978

L'Invention du parc. Parc de la Villette. Paris,
concours international. Paris 1984

Lippard, L.
Overlay. New York 1983

Marrast, J.
Jardins. Paris 1925

Shepheard, P..
Modern Gardens. London 1958

Sonfist, A., Ed.
Art in the Land. N. Y. 1983

Sørensen, C.Th.
Haver. Copenhagen 1975

Tunnard, C.
Gardens in the Modern Landscape.
London 1950

Vera, A. Les Jardins. Paris 1919

Vitou, É. et al.
Gabriel Guévrékian 1900-1970. Une autre
architecture moderne. Paris 1987

Walker, P. Landscape as Art.
Process: architecture 85. Tokyo 1989

Index

Page numbers in bold
refer to illustrations